Stephen A. Douglas and Antebellum Democracy

This thematic biography demonstrates how Stephen A. Douglas's path from a conflicted youth in Vermont to dim prospects in New York to overnight stardom in Illinois led to his identification with the Democratic Party and his belief that the federal government should respect the diversity of states and territories. His relationships with his mother, sister, teachers, brothers-in-law, other men, and two wives are explored in depth. When he conducted the first cross-country campaign by a presidential candidate in American history, few among the hundreds of thousands who saw him in 1860 knew that his wife and he had just lost their infant daughter or that Douglas controlled a large Mississippi slave plantation. His story illuminates the gap between democracy then and today. The book draws on a variety of previously unexamined sources.

Martin H. Quitt is Professor Emeritus of History at the University of Massachusetts, Boston, where he has served as Dean of Graduate Studies and Vice Provost for Research. He has published books on the history of the family and the colonial Virginia legislature, as well as essays in social and political history. His article on English–Indian relations at Jamestown received the Lester J. Cappon Award in the *William and Mary Quarterly*.

Stephen A. Douglas and Antebellum Democracy

MARTIN H. QUITT

University of Massachusetts, Boston

To Rich,

Thanks for
interviewing + your
questions.

Martin

CAMBRIDGE
UNIVERSITY PRESS

CAMBRIDGE UNIVERSITY PRESS
Cambridge, New York, Melbourne, Madrid, Cape Town,
Singapore, São Paulo, Delhi, Mexico City

Cambridge University Press
32 Avenue of the Americas, New York, NY 10013-2473, USA

www.cambridge.org
Information on this title: www.cambridge.org/9781107639010

First published 2012

Printed in the United States of America

A catalog record for this publication is available from the British Library.

Library of Congress Cataloging in Publication data
Quitt, Martin H.
  Stephen A. Douglas and Antebellum democracy / Martin H. Quitt.
    p.   cm.
  Includes bibliographical references and index.
  ISBN 978-1-107-02478-6 (hardback)
    1. Douglas, Stephen A. (Stephen Arnold), 1813–1861.   2. Legislators – United
  States – Biography.   3. United States. Congress. Senate – Biography.   4. United
  States – Politics and government – 1845–1861.   5. Legislators – Illinois – Biography.
  I. Title.
  E415.9.D73Q58   2012
  328.73′092–dc23
  [B]   2012012497

ISBN 978-1-107-02478-6 Hardback
ISBN 978-1-107-63901-0 Paperback

Contents

Acknowledgments

This project began as an article that was never completed, not even as a book chapter. While reading, in 2005, Robert Johannsen's great 1971 biography of Douglas, I had a flash – Douglas was the "towering genius" that Lincoln had in mind during his well-known 1838 speech at the Young Men's Lyceum in Springfield. This speech, given two weeks before Lincoln's twenty-ninth birthday, warned of an ominous figure who would some day tear down the great national edifice created by the founding fathers. Scholars with a psychological bent had turned an analysis of the speech into a mini–academic industry regarding Lincoln's motives. Most believed that Lincoln was really speaking about himself. I was certain that he was warning about Douglas. I reviewed the literature *that I knew* about the topic and was satisfied that no one had identified Douglas as Lincoln's bête noir. I then did my own research in published sources concerning the circumstances of the speech. In September 2005 I drove from my home in Massachusetts to Illinois to do firsthand research at the University of Illinois Library in Urbana and to examine the Lincoln and Douglas papers at the Abraham Lincoln Presidential Library (ALPL) in Springfield.

I had arranged to meet Tom Schwartz, Illinois State Historian, at the end of my visit to the ALPL. After three days of work at the library, I met Tom and told him generally of my interest in the relationship between Douglas and Lincoln and my particular interest in the Lyceum speech, without sharing my insight. Almost in passing, Tom said that I might want to look at the appendix of Michael Burlingame's psychological study of Lincoln, in which he makes the case that Douglas was the "towering genius." I was stunned. I was familiar with the 1994 book, but not the appendix. When I drove back to Massachusetts, I could not find my own copy. I raced to a library and read the four-page appendix. Alas, not only did Burlingame identify Douglas as a "Target" of Lincoln's address, he relied on the same sources and circumstantial evidence that I had drawn on independently. What to do? After financing the trip to Illinois myself, I would be embarrassed to abandon my Douglas project.

Fortunately I had taken extensive notes on a manuscript that I had found at the ALPL – Douglas's copybook from his year at the Brandon Academy, when he was sixteen and seventeen. (Tom Schwartz had arranged for its accession in 1989.) I am most grateful to Cheryl Schnirring, Manuscripts Curator at the ALPL, for her assistance while I was there and in response to a later request. I decided to build on the copybook by driving to Brandon, Vermont. Fortuitously, on my first day at the Town Office I met Blaine Cliver, a retired architectural historian who lived nearby and was doing research on Douglas's birthplace and his Vermont family. A modest man, Blaine did not mention that his interest and expertise were more than a hobby. At the time he was president of UNESCO's International Centre for the Study of the Preservation and Restoration of Cultural Property. During the next few years, as I researched and wrote the first three chapters of this book, Blaine's own research and photos, usually emailed, provided indispensable help to me. His guided tour of the birthplace before it was renovated demonstrated what a gifted interpreter of material culture could reveal. He also arranged for me to visit the Brandon home where Douglas grew up, as well as the site of the district school he attended. Blaine and Mary Cliver were also generous hosts with whom I could discuss our common interests in Douglas, the Boston area, and the Red Sox.

On that first research trip to Vermont in October 2005, I stopped at the Middlebury College Library. I am grateful to Andy Wentinck, Director of Special Collections, and his staff for making available records of the origins and early history of the college. Like others, I wanted to ascertain whether Douglas's father attended, as the family claimed. At the Vermont Historical Society in Barre, Paul Carnahan, curator, was extremely helpful in locating relevant newspapers and manuscripts. The record book of the district school Douglas attended adds to our understanding of Douglas's early education and of New England common schools at the time. At this point I was confident that I had enough new materials to undertake a reassessment of Douglas's childhood and development.

I made three trips to Illinois. On the first I met John Hoffman, Illinois History and Lincoln Collections Librarian and Manuscript Curator at the University of Illinois at Urbana. He found and copied sources, then and more recently. He also arranged for Greg Olson, a reporter with the *Journal-Courier* in Jacksonville, to show me around the town where Douglas opened his law office at the age of twenty.

On the second trip I spent a week with the Douglas Papers at the Special Collections Research Center of the University of Chicago Library, which made my stay in 2007 invaluable; in addition, the center has provided follow-up support by photocopying or scanning documents I have requested. I am especially beholden to Associate Archivist Daniel Meyer for obtaining permission from Douglas descendants for me to access newly discovered letters to Adele Cutts Douglas before their donation was formalized. I am grateful to Eileen Ielmini, Director of Archive Processing and Digital Access, and Christine Colburn, Reader Services Manager, for scanning and transmitting the documents and for identifying one of the letter writers. David Pavelich arranged for the copying and transmission of documents earlier. I learned about the new cache of Douglas papers in the March 2011 issue of the newsletter of the Stephen A. Douglas Association.

The purpose of my third trip was to air my early ideas on Douglas's constitutionalism before the annual meeting of the Society for Historians of the Early American Republic in Springfield in July 2009. The meeting was held there for Lincoln's bicentennial birthday. At the opening session, after listening to four distinguished panelists discuss Lincoln and wholly ignore Douglas, I exclaimed, "No Douglas, no Lincoln." While the point was acknowledged, I do not imagine that Douglas will ever come out from under Lincoln's giant shadow. Nevertheless, he deserves more attention than he usually receives. I am grateful to Graham Peck, who commented on my paper at the meeting and sent me a copy of his astute criticism. My colleague Jonathan Chu, a legal scholar, heard my paper and shared his thoughts on our return trip to Boston.

I am grateful to the executive director, Ed Varno, and staff of the Ontario County Historical Society in Canandaigua, New York, for searching for marriage records after I visited and providing illustrations. Wilma Townshend, the curator, was delightful and helpful in a long phone conversation. Staffs at public offices in Vermont – the Rutland County Probate Court in Rutland, the Brandon Town Office, and the Public Records Division in Middlesex – were unfailingly courteous and helpful when I researched there.

I am grateful to William R. Ellis, Jr., Archivist, Federal Judicial Records, at the National Archives, who found, copied, and transmitted the agreement that Douglas redrafted in 1859 for his partnership in a Mississippi plantation.

The American Antiquarian Society in Worcester occupies a lush urban setting to which one can drive and park for free. The staff is tireless and gracious in bringing oversized volumes of nineteenth-century newspapers to visitors. The complete run of the *Rutland Herald*, which had not yet been digitized when I researched it, is an extraordinary resource. Vincent Golden, Curator of Newspapers and Periodicals, has reason to be pleased with its acquisition. Philip Lampi, head of the AAS First Democracy Project, shared his unique knowledge of early American election practices with me in person and by email.

Even in the day of digital access from a home computer, living near the libraries and archives in the Boston area is a researcher's good fortune. Peter Drummey, Massachusetts Historical Society Librarian, provided his normally cheerful assistance as I used the Edward Everett Papers. The holdings of the Harvard libraries are incomparable, although admission for unaffiliated scholars is not without limits. At Langdell Hall the young law library staff could not have been more gracious or helpful to me in my work with the microfiche collection of state laws. No other law library in the area possessed the complete set. Visiting scholars may easily use the O'Neill and Law Libraries of Boston College. I made extensive use of an alumnus's borrowing privileges at Brandeis University's Goldfarb Library, for which I am especially grateful. Whittemore

Library at Framingham State University provided a microfilm reader and paper for me to print countless pages from newspaper reels.

My Boston Public Library card provides online access to its U.S. Serial Set, which contains reports of congressional committees on which Douglas served. Membership in the New England Historic Genealogical Society enabled me to connect from home to two newspaper databases, *19th Century U.S. Newspapers* and *Early American Newspapers*, Series I, *1690–1876*. Few ante-bellum Southern newspapers, however, have been digitized. In order to trace Douglas's 1860 campaign in the South, I required borrowed microfilm from several states. Most helpful was Patricia Wilson, Senior Archivist, Alabama Department of Archives and History, who located and sent microfilm of six newspapers from 1860. I also needed to read some Northern newspapers that had not been digitized. In one case, a local librarian went beyond the normal call of duty. Michael May, Adult Services Librarian, Carnegie-Stout Public Library, Dubuque, Iowa, searched for, scanned, and sent me electronically several issues of the *Dubuque Herald*. Martha Reid, Vermont State Librarian, and Paul Donovan at the Vermont State Library tracked down and copied for me a rare issue of the *Northern Visitor*.

My greatest institutional debt is to the University of Massachusetts, Boston, my home for the past three decades. Its Healey Library has become an indispensable resource for serious scholarship. Its expanding databases, remarkably good book holdings, and terrific interlibrary loan operation under the supervision of Janet Stewart have enabled me to complete this project. Provost Winston Langley has made certain that the scholarly activities of retired faculty members are supported and recognized.

For more than a decade Peggy Tippit has been the Apple specialist at the UMass Boston Information Technology Help Desk. She has been my lifesaver numerous times. Her responsiveness, patience, and expertise always surprise me, and she invariably solves my problems.

I am most thankful to busy scholars who fulfilled promises to critique what I sent them. Gerald Leonard agreed to read early versions of my two chapters on constitutionalism, and his comments were extremely helpful. His essay on the literature of the *Dred Scott* decision, moreover, pointed me to a body of work I needed to assimilate. Rosemarie Zagarri read an early version of Chapter 4 and offered her encouragement and suggestions in a long telephone conversation. John Wallis responded to a comment regarding the Constitution and internal improvements and shared two papers bearing on the topic. Roxanne Marcus spurred me with a postmodernist perspective on portions of Chapter 4. Burt Kaufman read and commented on a previously published portion of Chapter 5. The anonymous readers for Cambridge University Press were thorough and made invaluable suggestions. I am grateful to the University of Pennsylvania Press and the Society for Historians of the Early American Republic for permission to reprint a few pages from my article "Congressional (Partisan) Constitutionalism: The Apportionment Act Debates of 1842 and 1844," *Journal of the Early Republic*, 28:4 (Winter 2008), 627–651.

The idea for doing something on Douglas came while I was giving a lecture on Lincoln at an assisted-living facility in 2005, part of a series on American presidents I presented at the prodding of Nancy Baer. The series originated in a short course I had taught the preceding year at the request of Wichian Rojanawon, Director of the Osher Institute for Lifelong Learning (OLLI) at UMass Boston. Vivian Fox, with whom I collaborated on a family history book more than thirty years ago, and I reexamined our study on the basis of recent work in a course we taught for OLLI in 2006, an experience that stood me in good stead when I wrote Chapters 1 and 3. I also tested my approach to Douglas's constitutionalism and 1860 campaign in different courses and talks at OLLI. UMass Boston has always been hospitable to older learners. OLLI members, now more than one thousand, are knowledgeable, engaged, and demanding.

The Boston Biographers Group (BBG) has been a continuing source of intellectual exchange, information, warmth, and encouragement as publishing changes from day to day. We interact as a group and individually. Ray Shepard and I have met at lunch to discuss Douglas, slavery, and his book-to-be on the Emancipation Proclamation. All BBG members owe debts to Nigel Hamilton, a truly generous scholar; to Elizabeth Harris, whose minutes are a boon to the occasional absentee; and to Phyllis Steele, who arranges our meetings and updates our roster. The group prodded me to include illustrations, but after considerable thought I decided to be true to my faith in language and am glad that Lewis Bateman and Anne Lovering Rounds at Cambridge University Press agreed to restrict artwork to the cover. I introduced myself in a long email to Lew because I drew much on two books he had recently edited. He invited me to submit my manuscript for consideration. I will always be grateful to him. He, Anne, Mark Fox, and the Newgen staff have been close partners in converting the manuscript into a book.

When I was at college, history professors usually downgraded "speculative" or "hypothetical" paragraphs. Then came John Murrin, my mentor in graduate school, who demonstrated the value of counterfactual propositions. My brief rumination in Chapter 8 on how Douglas, had he lived, would have reacted to Lincoln's policies during the Civil War is offered only because of the respectability that John has given to such exercises. I am indebted, indeed, to the rich scholarship of American history from the Revolution to the Civil War, reflected only partially in quoted authors, who are indexed. The full range of my use of this literature is made clear in my notes.

Friends and family have listened with a lot of forbearance, a bit of amusement, and, most important, encouragement as I have compulsively spoken about Douglas over the past several years. Jack Jagher, who trained as a biologist but preferred history, lent an ear whenever I deviated from our discussion of the Red Sox. His wife, Sandy, devours novel after novel but assured me she would read this biography. Richard Forman, with whom I spoke about history and politics on the beach and at dinner summer after summer before his untimely death, would have loved to have read the book. I have shared each part of the odyssey with my longtime colleague and friend Ron Polito, a historian of photography. He advised me on searching for images and securing permissions before I decided to rely exclusively on my prose. Ken Berk, a gifted photographer, gave me his panoramic view of Fenway Park for respites from my writing. Vivian Fox was a friend, collaborator, and booster for forty years. Sadly she died while the manuscript was in press. Sandy Shapiro listened and pressed questions as we drove to the opera, and so too did Jane Schneider whenever we spoke, at dinner, in the car, or on the phone. Andy Davis, who unboxed, set up, and taught me how to use my first Mac twenty-five years ago, and Gayle Davis invariably drew me out while only occasionally rolling their eyes. Mark and Arlene Lowenstein worked in Rutland, still love Brandon, and have embraced this project since they learned about it. Jordan and Jean Krasnow listened, smiled, and listened again. Lou Esposito and I discussed the project during our dinners at restaurants in Lexington. Musician Bill Slocum had me update my progress and thinking every summer at Bank Street beach. I met musicologist Ralph Locke on Cape Cod after my manuscript was being read by Cambridge. Coincidentally Ralph was working on his second book for the Press. His emails provided helpful advice regarding the publishing scene. Charlie McMillan, a history major once upon a time, urged me to put my manuscript online in order to share it freely with the world. He refuses to believe that Northerners went to war in 1861 for a purpose other than ending slavery. I hope to change his mind regarding both propositions.

Two friendships go back longer than Douglas lived. Both date from our days at Brandeis when the three of us majored in history. Burt Kaufman and I were roommates. He became a prolific historian, who wrote his book on the retirements of American presidents while I did this one. We have shared perspectives on American history for a long time. Howard Marcus earned his doctorate in Latin American history but became a criminal lawyer in Toronto. He provided an ear and wonderful wit whenever I became too serious about my project. A third friendship dates from graduate school at Washington University, where Harry Fritz was a roommate. A resident and historian of Montana, he embodies the popular imagination of a Western man. Six feet five inches tall, with a natural ease and fluid mind, he has impersonated Abraham Lincoln in talks on Mississippi riverboats and other venues. We could stand in physically for Lincoln and Douglas respectively, but I'd be no match for him in a debate.

One always wonders about friends who are accomplished scientists, engineers, or social scientists when they hear how engaged a humanist is with his subject. But Dick Fey, Steve Finn, and Charles Schulman respect serious research in all fields, Stan Klein has a son who is a philosopher, and Russ Harter's wife, Marilyn, is an English professor. Murray Frank does public policy and remains a social activist but values research that is not applied. Michael Schneider loved to read biographies of great men, to which he invariably brought fresh perspectives. He died before this project began, yet I still ponder what his critical mind would have thought about various issues.

Mark Watson, a gifted handyman, astute conservative (and therefore exasperating) thinker, and descendant of Massachusetts men who fought in the Civil War, continues by emails to make me sharpen my argumentative skills. Terry Mortimer and Fuad Safwat, colleagues at UMass Boston and lunch companions for many years, and Ruth Bennett have listened to and encouraged me. So too has Paul Wright, who knows the history of the book in America and academic publishing today. To Baheej Khleif, sociologist, poet, playwright, and novelist, writing is like breathing and he does it in English, Hebrew, and Arabic. Returning to writing full time, I feel more connected to my old friend than I had been as an administrator.

My mother, Ida, valued the life of the mind. I spoke to her of Douglas's sister and mother, comparing their relationship to the one between her, my sister Elaine, and me. Sadly she died before the manuscript was finished, but at ninety-seven she would have read the book.

My emphasis on the unpredictability of the past in no small way has been influenced greatly by my own children. Our son, Adam, a scholar-athlete in college, became a U.S. Marine, firefighter, competitive boxer, mixed martial arts fighter, wrestler, coach, and personal trainer. Adam and Tara produced our three grandchildren, Nora, Andrew, and Raina, all while I worked on this book, providing us much joy. Our daughter, Alisha, a sociology major with a concentration in race relations, has surprised us by finding satisfaction in the business world. No one has boosted my spirits more than she. She has been with Parag since I began this project, and their relationship has been a source of pleasure to Deborah and me.

Debbie, who taught social studies at The High School (a.k.a. Brookline High School), for thirty-eight years, vetted every page of every version of this manuscript. She reads novels while I read academic stuff, but she has an extraordinary grasp of American history that always astonishes me. A friend says she likes our company because the continuous laughter gives her an endorphin rush. In fact my state of well-being since I met Debbie in 1970 has been due in no small part to her humor, which, among her other qualities, keeps me grounded whenever my prose becomes too fanciful or florid.

My greatest intellectual debt is to the subject of this book. I tried to understand Douglas while I was in awe of him. At the same time I tried not be so admiring as to be unaware of his inconsistencies and self-delusions. The awe derived from his precocious rise to prominence, his remarkable energy and staying power, his exceptional intelligence, his emotional connection to the people, and his genuine faith in local majorities. Personal comparison fueled my reaction: he became a political star before the age at which I graduated from college, and he was all done at forty-eight, an age at which much of my career was still ahead of me. The criticism of him derives in part from the sensibility of our times. Racism and slavery are so condemnable it is hard to approach Douglas without an edge, particularly after stitching together his steady involvement with the institution during the last quarter of his life.

Abbreviations

CG	*Congressional Globe*
CG, APP	*Congressional Globe*, Appendix
CWAL	Roy P. Basler et al., eds., *The Collected Works of Abraham Lincoln*, 9 vols. (New Brunswick, NJ, 1953)
EAN	*Early American Newspapers*, Series I, *1690–1876*
Johannsen, *SAD*	Robert W. Johannsen, *Stephen A. Douglas* (New York, 1973)
L-DD	Rodney O. Davis and Douglas L. Wilson, eds., *The Lincoln–Douglas Debates* (Urbana, IL, 2008)
Letters of SAD	*The Letters of Stephen A. Douglas*, ed. Robert W. Johannsen (Urbana, IL, 1961)
SAD Papers	Stephen A. Douglas Papers, Special Collections, University of Chicago Library
USN	*19th Century U.S. Newspapers*

Introduction

Why did Stephen Douglas become a Democrat, not a Whig? We ought to know, because he was an architect of the antebellum party system; he forged an uncommon bond with voters; and he embraced and reformulated the principles of the Democratic Party.[1] After his arrival in Illinois at the age of twenty,

[1] Historians differ in periodizing and labeling the evolution of political parties before the Civil War. Whether or not they recognize political divisions before 1820 as constituting a party system, they agree that a new two-party alignment arose in the middle to late 1830s. For an overview of the historiography on party development in the United States before 1860, see John L. Brooke, "To Be 'Read by the Whole People'; Press, Party, and Public Sphere in the United States, 1789–1840," *Proceedings of the American Antiquarian Society*, 110:1 (2000), 41–118, esp. 49–50, 87–89. See also his "Print and Politics," in *An Extensive Republic: Print, Culture, and Society in the New Nation, 1790–1840*, ed. Robert A. Gross and Mary Kelley (Chapel Hill, NC, 2010), 179–190, esp. 186; Donald B. Cole, *Vindicating Andrew Jackson: The 1828 Election and the Rise of the Two-Party System* (Lawrence, KS, 2009), esp. 157–178, on party organization; John Ashworth, *Slavery, Capitalism, and Politics in the Antebellum Republic*, vol. 1: *Commerce and Compromise, 1820–1850* (New York, 1995), 369–381; Joel H. Silbey, *The American Political Nation, 1838–1893* (Stanford, CA, 1991), esp. 7, table; Paul Kleppner, ed., *The Evolution of American Electoral Systems* (Westport, CT, 1981), esp. essays by Ronald P. Formisano, William G. Shade, and Paul Kleppner.

   On the emergence of the party as a central political institution in Illinois during the 1830s and the prominence of Douglas, whom he calls a "rabid partyist," see Gerald Leonard, *The Invention of Party Politics: Federalism, Popular Sovereignty, and Constitutional Development in Jacksonian Illinois* (Chapel Hill, NC, 2002), esp. 138–140.

   Recently historians of antebellum America have taken a broader view of politics than of parties and governmental institutions, both enclaves of white men, by conceptualizing and investigating a more inclusive "civil society." See John L. Brooke, "Consent, Civil Society, and the Public Sphere in the Age of Revolution and the Early American Republic," in *Beyond the Founders: New Approaches to the Political History of the Early American Republic*, ed. Jeffrey L. Pasley, Andrew W. Robertson, and David Waldstreicher (Chapel Hill, NC, 2004), 209–250. Glenn C. Altschuler and Stuart M. Blumin, *The Rude Republic: Americans and Their Politics in the Nineteenth Century* (Princeton, NJ, 2000), find a gulf between antebellum party cliques and the people, who turned to nonpartisan ways of political participation. Understanding Douglas's rise to power in Illinois during the 1830s, in fact, requires us to look at the world beyond parties, and Chapter 4 draws on the insights of scholars of gender and the family. Nevertheless, as Joel H. Sibley argues, the role of party loyalty in preserving the social order in the 1830s and 1840s should not be

he became an essential builder of the Democratic Party in the 1830s, an influential voice for it the party in Congress during the 1840s and 1850s, and its standard bearer in 1860, when, accompanied by his wife, he was the first presidential candidate in American history to campaign across the country. While his three presidential rivals complied with the code against campaigning, he openly explained and defended the Democratic platform that he had shaped. Historians often focus less on his ideas than on his motives, but both merit attention, because the principles his party stood for mattered greatly to him.

Douglas believed that his political allegiance was "fixed" forever at the age of fifteen, during the presidential contest of 1828, when he and fellow apprentices supported Andrew Jackson against his employer's preference, John Quincy Adams.[2] Yet the full story of his adolescence makes it difficult to imagine his ever joining the Whigs, whom he associated with the discredited Federalists.[3] His crisis-laden journey from youth in Vermont to manhood in Illinois bent him toward the Democrats' vision of the Republic as an expanding union comprising disparate but equal states and territories.[4] Following his trials with family,

underappreciated. "Comment on Sean Wilentz's *The Rise of American Democracy*," *Journal of the Historical Society*, 6:4 (Dec. 2006), 521–525. Douglas became a consummate party politician, whose connection to the people, as depicted here, diverges from Altschuler's and Blumin's overall thesis. If popular interest in politics was "the most striking feature of Illinois life in the 1850's," as Don E. Fehrenbacher wrote, Douglas contributed mightily to making it such. *Prelude to Greatness: Lincoln in the 1850's* (Stanford, CA, 1962), 14.

[2] "Autobiographical Sketch," *Letters of SAD*, 58.

[3] Douglas was a staunch political secularist put off by Whig moralistic rhetoric. He and Illinois Democrats referred to Whigs as "Federalists" because of their elitism, nativism, central economic planning, opposition to territorial expansion, constitutionalism, and morality. Mark A. Noll suggests that the Whigs added "morality to the earlier confidence of the Federalists in the use of central governmental authority." *God and Race in American Politics: A Short History* (Princeton, NJ, 2008), 22. On evangelical morality and the Whigs, see also Daniel W. Howe, "Religion and Politics in the Antebellum North," in *Religion and American Politics: From the Colonial Period to the Present*, ed. Mark A. Noll and Luke E. Harlow, 2nd ed. (New York, 2007), 123–125, 130–131. On the Democrats regularly tarnishing Whigs as "Federalists," see Michael F. Holt, *The Rise and Fall of the American Whig Party* (New York, 1999), 2. Daniel W. Howe, *The Political Culture of the American Whigs* (Chicago, 1978), 90–91, contrasts Whigs and Federalists.

  Scholars do not agree as to why Lincoln became or stayed a Whig; see Chapter 4, note 108. William L. Miller, *Lincoln's Virtues: An Ethical Biography* (New York, 2002), 108, suggests, admittedly "by superficial criteria," that "Lincoln and Douglas each by original identity belonged in the other's party." This suggestion owes more to Miller's discomfort with Lincoln as a Whig than with Douglas's background, which Miller describes in inflated terms.

[4] For a comparison of Democratic and Whig visions, see Daniel W. Howe, *What Hath God Wrought: The Transformation of America, 1815–1848* (New York, 2007), 582–585. On the religious followers of each party see Richard Cawardine, "Methodists, Politics, and the Coming of the American Civil War," in *Religion and American Politics*, ed. Noll and Harlow, 169–202. There were major divergences within each party that are explored, respectively, by Sean Wilentz, *The Rise of American Democracy: Jefferson to Lincoln* (New York, 2005), 483–507, which charts a "revolution in American conservatism" led by "New-School Whigs," and Yonatan Eyal, *The Young America Movement and the Transformation of the Democratic Party, 1828–1861* (New York, 2007), which depicts a younger generation of "forward-looking Democrats" featuring Douglas. For the influence of classical liberalism on the Van Burenites in the Democratic Party, see James A. Henretta, "The Rise of American Liberalism: New York, 1820–1860," in

romance, school, and illness between his fourteenth and twenty-first birthdays enables us to understand why he believed that every place did not suit every individual, that America should be large and diverse enough to enable every person to find the particular locale in which he or she could thrive. The emotionally intense years of his adolescence, which he revisited consciously time and again as an adult, provided the psychological foundation for his lifelong political disposition.[5]

This is not to suggest that his youthful development necessarily foreclosed later political turns. Douglas had an uncommon mind: he could assimilate a staggering amount of information, store it in a capacious memory, and draw on it at will to construct a telling argument. His effectiveness in legislative debates, party meetings, and on the stump came from a quick tongue, a charismatic personality, recall, and preparation. He usually did his homework and thought through his positions before he went public. He fortified himself with the history of American independence, constitution making, and congressional legislation. In short, he had the intellectual firepower to reverse or modify his viewpoints with credibility. Yet there was a striking consistency to Douglas's beliefs in national expansion, national unity, and local self-government. These pillars of his political faith had lasting emotional and empirical truth for him.[6]

Republicanism and Liberalism in America and the German States, 1750–1850, ed. Jürgen Heideking and James A. Henretta (Cambridge, 2002), 165–185.

[5] In a review essay on a biography of Lincoln, Adam I. P. Smith writes, "It is a conceit of the post-Freudian age … that the ultimate motivation for public behavior can be reduced to an individual's psychological make-up." "The Challenge of Biography: What Do They Know of Lincoln Who Only Lincoln Know?" *Journal of the Abraham Lincoln Association*, 31:2 (Summer 2010), 71. If "reduced" were replaced by "related," Smith's statement could apply also to my biography of Douglas. My "conceit" is that one cannot fully understand political behavior without connecting it to underlying psychological inclinations, uncovered by empirical research that is guided but not determined by theory. Indeed, recognizing the relationship between Douglas's adolescence and later political behavior requires no knowledge of psychological theory, only a measure of openness to emotional issues.

Social scientists have examined two major paths toward party affiliation: childhood socialization and policy preferences. Investigators of the former find that people are predisposed to follow the political attachment of their parents. The policy preference school stresses the correspondence between party platforms and individual attitudes. Douglas's case points to a variation of each approach. First, he believed that his lifelong affiliation began in opposition to a parental surrogate's presidential choice. His was a case of negative identification in which the significant influence was not a biological parent. Second, there was a fit between his transition to manhood and the central tenets of the Democratic Party. This suggests how the connection between a platform and a partisan can be grounded in one's earlier psychological development. For a succinct overview of the two approaches to party affiliation, see Jon A. Krosnick, Penny S. Visser, and Joshua Harder, "The Psychological Underpinnings of Political Behavior," in *The Handbook of Social Psychology*, ed. Susan T. Fiske, Daniel T. Gilbert, and Gardner Lindzey, 5th ed., 2 vols. (Hoboken, NJ, 2010), 2: 1288–1342, esp. 1311–1313.

[6] This consistency enabled him to become a leader of the progressive "Young America" group in his party without forfeiting his position among Democratic conservatives. On the group's emergence, see Eyal, *Young America Movement*, which broadens our perspective of Douglas and his party beyond the issue of slavery in the territories and states' rights in the late 1840s and early 1850s.

This consistency reinforced his sense of confidence in what he had to say. He displayed this attitude most dramatically in breaking the code against presidential campaigning. The fear of misspeaking kept his three opponents on the sidelines in 1860. In contrast, he traveled to more than 150 towns in twenty-three states in every section, except the Far West. And he spoke at stop after stop, from a few minutes to three hours, depending on his voice and the size of the crowd. Opposition newspapers waited to report his contradictions, especially between what he might say in the North and the South. The grueling campaign would surely reveal any doubts he himself harbored about his message, and the press was there to expose him. Yet Douglas never stopped talking. He evinced a seemingly guileless trust in the straightforwardness, clarity, and logic of what he spoke.

Douglas's confidence in what he said was strengthened by how he was received. His connection to the people in section after section, state after state, town after town was similar to what it had always been in Illinois – he made them feel good about their local institutions, and they reciprocated by cheering even if they did not vote for him. This mutual admiration and affection was at the core of his populism. He did not fake it and they knew it.

Although he and the white crowds he addressed shared a presumption of superiority over blacks, in one conspicuous way Douglas set himself apart from the American people in 1860: he took no stand on the morality or desirability of slavery. Without the benefit of polling, we can infer that while most white Americans were racist, they had divergent opinions about slavery, and few were indifferent to it.[7] Abraham Lincoln represented the position of most of the 1.8 million men who voted for him: he believed that blacks were inferior to whites but that slavery was abominable and ought not to be permitted to expand. Outside the South, many of the 1.3 million Douglas voters, unlike their candidate, also were antislavery.[8] Whatever their moral scruples about slavery, however, they supported Douglas's plea to push it aside from federal policymaking in the hope of dampening Southern ardor for secession.

Douglas's neutrality on slavery is the most off-putting facet of his career. It is difficult to approach someone who claimed to care not whether the institution was voted up or down, only that the decision be left to local majorities. How could Douglas not really care about slavery? In 1853 Frederick Douglass thanked Douglas publicly for sending him a copy of his speeches and expressed hope that the senator would live to "see not only that his course was morally,

---

[7] In its *Dred Scott* decision, the Supreme Court exemplified the racism of antebellum America. As two legal scholars put it, "To whom does America belong? Who are 'We the People' in whose name the Constitution is ordained? For Taney (and, equally important, for a majority of the Court), the answer was that America was a country of white persons who migrated to this continent from Europe." Jack M. Balkin and Sanford Levinson, "Thirteen Ways of Looking at Dred Scott," *Chicago-Kent Law Review*, 82 (2007), 54.

[8] On antislavery "as an abstract feeling" throughout the North, see Eric Foner, *Free Soil, Free Labor, Free Men: The Ideology of the Republican Party before the Civil War* (New York, 1970), 308.

a crime, but that it is, politically, a mistake."[9] Even if Douglas was not expressing his personal sentiments but only his preferred national policy, Abraham Lincoln pressed him to acknowledge that slavery was wrong and that people did not have the right to choose wrong. "That is the real issue.... It is the eternal struggle between these two principles – right and wrong – throughout the world."[10] Douglas did not relent. "[Lincoln] tells you that I will not argue the question whether slavery is right or wrong. I tell you why I will not do it. I hold that under the Constitution of the United States, each State of the Union has a right to do as it pleases on the subject of slavery."[11]

Which was the greater sin, secession or slavery? To Douglas the answer was clear. He denounced the proposition to dissolve the American Union as "moral treason."[12] For more than a decade he foresaw civil war if the question of slavery in the territories was controlled by ultras on either side. He wanted to remove the issue from Washington politics because it endangered national coherence. He believed that the overriding purpose of the Constitution had been to achieve the Union; therefore, its preservation was the highest constitutional value.[13] He saw himself in the tradition of the founders, who were willing to compromise on slavery.[14] As Eric Foner and Olivia Mahoney have written, "Douglas was the last great political leader to build a career on sectional compromise."[15] On the question of perpetuating the Union, however, he was uncompromising.

---

[9] USN, *Frederick Douglass' Paper* (Rochester, NY), May 6, 1853. Douglas was known for sending his speeches to constituents and to correspondents who asked for them. USN, *Daily Register* (Raleigh, NC), May 25, 1853. Douglass became much more critical of Douglas after his debates with Lincoln. John Stauffer, *Giants: The Parallel Lives of Frederick Douglass and Abraham Lincoln* (New York, 2008), 374–375.

[10] CWAL, 3: 315; L-DD, 285. On Lincoln's criticism of Douglas for ignoring the immorality of slavery, see Nicole Etcheson, " 'A living, creeping lie': Abraham Lincoln on Popular Sovereignty," *Journal of the Abraham Lincoln Association*, 29:2 (Summer 2008), 1–26.

[11] CWAL, 3: 266; L-DD, 233.

[12] CG, 31st Cong., 1st sess. (Feb. 8, 1850), 319.

[13] Nicole Etcheson suggests that "majority rule and self-government were the highest moral principles for Douglas and the Democrats." "The Great Principle of Self-Government: Popular Sovereignty and Bleeding Kansas," *Kansas History*, 27 (Spring–Summer 2004), 26. See also David Zarefsky, *Lincoln Douglas and Slavery in the Crucible of Public Debate* (Chicago, 1990, 1993), 166–197, which considers Douglas's commitment to local self-government to have been a moral stand, not an apology for slavery. Although he does not consider Douglas, George W. Van Cleve provides a context for examining him when he writes of "two utterly irreconcilable visions of the moral foundations of America and its constitution" resulting from the Missouri controversy of 1819–1821. One anchored the Constitution in higher law, with a mandate to expand freedom and end slavery; the other ignored slavery and rested freedom on the expansion of popular sovereignty. *A Slaveholders' Union: Slavery, Politics, and the Constitution in the Early Republic* (Chicago, 2010), 226.

[14] David Waldstreicher writes, "[W]hile the notion of compromise may explain the Constitutional Convention, it does not tell the whole story, for if the framers' compromise intended to keep slavery out of national politics, it failed miserably." *Slavery's Constitution* (New York, 2009), 17.

[15] Eric Foner and Olivia Mahoney, *A House Divided: America in the Age of Lincoln* (New York, 1990), 77.

Opponents blamed outsize ambition for his position on slavery and his professed constitutional principles, which they dismissed as opportunistic and disingenuous. Some historians also have considered Douglas to be so driven by self-aggrandizement that he pushed principles aside in order to achieve personal gain. Even a sympathetic biographer has noted that he wanted to affect an arm's-length distance from slave owning while he received income from managing a Mississippi plantation that his sons inherited from their maternal grandfather.[16] His relationship to slavery there was in fact more complicit than he admitted even to himself, let alone the public. It merits special examination.[17] Nevertheless, it is necessary to bear in mind that his neutrality toward slavery long preceded his direct involvement with the institution. He is also accused of repealing the long-standing federal ban on slavery in territory covered by the Kansas–Nebraska Act in order to pave the way for a transcontinental railroad that purportedly would enhance the value of land he owned. His critics, however, have not given sufficient weight to a steadiness in his core beliefs. From early in his congressional career, he leaned toward granting territories a large measure of self-rule and urged colleagues to leave the slavery question to local resolution. "Nonintervention" and "popular sovereignty" became catchwords for principles he had long held.[18]

"Popular sovereignty" was for him less a product of political calculation than a reflex conditioned by an intimate relationship that he enjoyed with voters. The candidate who mingled with people from Massachusetts to Iowa and from Wisconsin to Alabama in 1860 had reveled in the crowd's embrace since he first stood up to speak in Illinois at the age of twenty. Unlike his rivals, he thrived on physicality with white men: he rose on their shoulders, sat on their laps, and clasped their hands.[19]

His physical ease with crowds flowed from his comfort with their choices. His own overnight prominence in Illinois had been due to the reception of a speech. The people who had carried him on their shoulders in Jacksonville instantaneously transformed him into a Morgan County celebrity, motivating him to settle there. This popular acclaim came unexpectedly and left him permanently grateful. When he urged yielding to local majorities, he had a personal

---

[16] Johannsen, *SAD*, 208–209, 211.

[17] See Chapter 9.

[18] Michael Morrison, *Slavery and the American West: The Eclipse of Manifest Destiny and the Coming of the Civil War* (Chapel Hill, NC, 1997), 142–147, offers a balanced analysis of the influences behind Douglas's territorial policies. He does not dismiss financial or partisan gain as motives, but places them alongside genuinely held principles. David H. Fischer, *Liberty and Freedom* (New York, 2005), 303–304, notes the criticism of Douglas on moral grounds but counters that he was guided by "strong ethical principles" his entire life.

[19] Douglas's racism targeted all nonwhite people. He specifically named Africans, Native Americans, Fijians, and Malays as inferior to whites. David R. Roediger, "The Pursuit of Whiteness: Property, Terror, and Expansion, 1790–1860," *Journal of the Early Republic*, 19:4 (1999), 592. His racism, however, was not the Anglo-Saxonism of New England intellectuals. See Nell I. Painter, "Ralph Waldo Emerson's Saxons," *Journal of American History*, 95:4 (Mar. 2009), 977–985. Douglas's physicality with men is explored in Chapter 4. His racism is placed in a broader context in Chapter 6.

framework. His insistence that geographical diversity was essential to American freedom was neither abstract nor dispassionate: he felt strongly that white men like himself needed to be able to find a place where they could bring their own baggage. And he knew a fundamental truth about his contemporaries: "In the nineteenth-century," Nicole Etcheson concludes, "few whites cared about the suffering of slaves, but they did care about their own political rights."[20]

From the moment he was appointed to the Illinois Supreme Court in 1841 until his death twenty years later, Douglas preferred to be called "Judge." Everyone who knew him, including family members, used that designation. In Congress the title had a double meaning. It conveyed respect for his previous service and an expectation for his manner as a legislator. His first assignment as a freshman congressman was to judge the legality of the election of four delegations. He wrote the majority report for his committee, laying out the Democratic Party's interpretation of the Constitution. As a legislator he balanced unevenly his primary responsibility as a policymaker with the obligation to determine what was constitutional. Like his congressional colleagues, Douglas was capable of invoking the Constitution to support or oppose bills. Yet, like many of them, he also took seriously the need to understand constitutional meaning. He did not use the document cynically as a weapon in debate. Although politicians did not follow the same rules as jurists in ferreting out the intention of constitutional text, Douglas approached the task with the earnestness of a judge.[21] The inherent tension between those roles occasionally produced strained arguments that weakened his credibility.[22]

---

[20] Nicole Etcheson, *Bleeding Kansas: Contested Liberty in the Civil War Era* (Lawrence, KS, 2004), 3.

[21] Legal scholars have given considerable attention to the extrajudicial understanding of the Constitution. Collectively their work elevates the historical importance of presidential, congressional, agency, and partisan constitutionalism. My thinking here has been influenced by Keith Whittington, *Constitutional Construction: Divided Powers and Constitutional Meaning* (Cambridge, MA, 1999); Whittington, *Political Foundations of Judicial Supremacy: The Presidency, the Supreme Court, and Constitutional Leadership in U.S. History* (Princeton, NJ, 2007); Mark A. Graber, *Dred Scott and the Problem of Constitutional Evil* (New York, 2006); Graber, "Constitutional Law and American Politics," in *The Oxford Handbook of Law and Politics*, ed. Keith Whittington, R. Daniel Kelemen, and Gregory A. Caldeira (New York, 2008), 300–320; Larry D. Kramer, *The People Themselves: Popular Constitutionalism and Judicial Review* (New York, 2004); William N. Eskridge, Jr., and John Ferejohn, *A Republic of Statutes: The New American Constitution* (New Haven, CT, 2010); Gerald Leonard, "Party as a 'Political Safeguard of Federalism': Martin Van Buren and the Constitutional Theory of Party Politics," *Rutgers Law Review*, 54 (Fall 2001), 221–281; Leonard, "Law and Politics Reconsidered: A New Constitutional History of Dred Scott," *Law and Social Inquiry*, 34 (Summer 2009), 747–785; and David P. Currie, *The Constitution in Congress, 1789–1861*, 5 vols. (Chicago, 1994–2005).

Nevertheless, legal scholars do not always credit the sincerity of Douglas's constitutionalism. For example, Louise Weinberg reduces his motives in the Kansas–Nebraska Act to seeking a Northern railroad route through Illinois and giving "a sop to the South for this blow to its ambitions for a Southern route." "Dred Scott and the Crisis of 1860," *Chicago-Kent Law Review*, 97 (2007), 113.

[22] This was particularly the case with his forced treatment of the Northwest Ordinance. See Chapter 6.

For Democratic lawmakers, representing constituents and respecting the Constitution were not principles that could be easily reconciled. If Douglas's early life explains his partisan allegiance and constitutional predisposition, his career illustrates the complex interplay between policymaking, partisan advocacy, and constitutional adherence experienced by congressional leaders. Douglas took his own constitutional principles seriously enough to weight them heavily before formulating various policy proposals.

His interpretation of the Constitution was rejected in 1860 and ultimately supplanted by the Republican vision enshrined in the Thirteenth, Fourteenth, and Fifteenth Amendments, but he spoke for an understanding of American government that was widely shared before the Civil War. Indeed, although circumvention of the Supreme Court's decision in the *Dred Scott* case became a centerpiece of Douglas's last two campaigns, his constitutionalism was largely consistent with the jurisprudence of the Taney Court.[23] Had he won the presidency he would have pressed his view on territorial rights into a new constitutional construction.[24]

---

[23] On the Civil War amendments, see Michael J. Sandel, *Democracy's Discontent: America in Search of a Public Philosophy* (Cambridge, MA, 1996), 39. A major theme of Austin Allen, *Origins of the Dred Scott Case: Jacksonian Jurisprudence and the Supreme Court, 1837–1857* (Athens, GA, 2006), is that the Taney Court, composed of a Democratic majority, "developed an antielitist, fundamentally amoral conception of judicial authority that took deference to popular will as its foundation" (14). In the authority it accorded state legislatures as embodiments of popular sovereignty (13–35) and in its "acquiescence to slavery, whatever a justice's personal view regarding the institution" (79), Taney's Court, as described by Allen, shared the major principles of Democratic constitutionalism that Douglas absorbed and developed. Mark A. Graber suggests that "Stephen Douglas understood the constitutional order better than Abraham Lincoln" and associates Douglas's constitutionalism with Taney's. *Dred Scott and the Problem of Constitutional Evil*, 1. In his "John Brown, Abraham Lincoln, *Dred Scott*, and the Problem of Constitutional Evil," in *The Dred Scott Case: Historical and Contemporary Perspectives on Race and Law*, ed. David T. Konig, Paul Finkelman, and Christopher A. Bracey (Athens, GA, 2010), 49–67, Graber refers to the constitutionalism of "Roger Taney / Stephen Douglas" (51). This identification, however, should not obscure Douglas's differences with Taney's decision in *Dred Scott*, which, as Paul Finkelman notes, placed Douglas "in an awkward position" because of his commitment to popular sovereignty. "The Strange Career of Dred Scott: From Fort Armstrong to Guanidnamo Bay," in *The Dred Scott Case*, ed. Konig, Finkelman, and Bracey, 231. Earl M. Maltz, *Slavery and the Supreme Court, 1825–1861* (Lawrence, KS, 2009), 148, finds that until 1856 Taney Court justices were Jacksonians "committed to the maintenance of sectional harmony." This was a core value for Douglas as well.

An otherwise excellent essay tracing the transformation of Roger Taney from antislavery lawyer to proslavery justice concludes that he reflected the way the Democratic Party shifted the discussion of slavery "from the nation's founding principles" to "protecting the property rights of southern slaveholders." Timothy S. Huebner, "Roger B. Taney and the Slavery Issue: Looking Beyond – and Before –Dred Scott," *Journal of American History*, 97:1 (2010), 37. Douglas's career, however, illustrates how "founding principles" remained a steady, powerful force for him and his party.

[24] On "construction," see Whittington, *Constitutional Construction*, 210–211. Lincoln's outrage at the *Dred Scott* decision reaffirmed his skepticism regarding claims to judicial supremacy and his belief in departmental constitutionalism, which he acted upon as president. Kramer, *The People Themselves*, 212–213. See also Daniel Farber, *Lincoln's Constitution* (Chicago, 2003), 177–188, which is more favorable to judicial supremacy.

Douglas's commitment to popular sovereignty came into conflict in 1857 with his even older commitment to party loyalty when President Buchanan, whom he helped elect, submitted the proslavery Lecompton constitution to accompany the admission of Kansas to statehood. The process by which the Lecompton document was produced was notoriously unrepresentative of the antislavery majority in the territory. If Douglas had backed it, he would have strengthened his ties to the administration and the Southern wing of his party and would have ensured his nomination at the next Democratic national convention. Lecompton, however, made a mockery of popular sovereignty, and Douglas never hesitated. His opposition to it cost him more politically than he gained; but it also involved a conflict of competing principles.[25] He had come of age in Illinois as an organizer of the new Democratic Party and now was one of its transcendent figures nationally. To split with the titular leader of his party was not an easy decision for him, no matter how deeply he felt about popular sovereignty. Yet he did so, winning praise from Republicans, some of whom wanted him to become their candidate for the Senate from Illinois in 1858, and historians, who applaud his stand against Buchanan as courageous.[26] His action, albeit principled and gutsy, contributed to what he certainly did not envision or want – the breakup of the Democratic Party, which imperiled the Union, the overriding value of his constitutionalism and politics. As brilliant as he was, Douglas could not anticipate, let alone control, the full consequences of his policy decisions.[27] His life and career exemplify the one certainty of history – its unpredictability.

Just as unexpected popular acclaim in Illinois propelled his transition into manhood, the unexpected greeting he received in Vermont during his presidential campaign tour closed the circle of his personal story, and the reception he met in all sections strengthened his resolve to preserve his beloved Union. His wife's contribution to his last campaign deserves recognition. Adele Douglas, unlike his first wife, was his soul mate and political partner. Despite the death of the couple's only child in June, she became the first wife to tour with a presidential candidate.[28] Assuming a role similar to that of her great-aunt Dolly

[25] His most recent biographers examine the tension between his principles and his political interests in his decision to oppose Lecompton: James L. Huston, *Stephen A. Douglas and the Dilemmas of Democratic Equality* (Lanham, MD, 2007), 135–137; Johannsen, *SAD*, 582–583; Damon Wells, *Stephen Douglas: The Last Years, 1857–1861* (Austin, TX, 1971), 42–47.

[26] On Republican wooing, see David M. Potter, *The Impending Crisis, 1848–1861*, completed and ed. Don E. Fehrenbacher (New York, 1976), 321; and Allen C. Guelzo, *Lincoln and Douglas: The Debates That Defined America* (New York, 2008), 24–25. His stand against Buchanan elicits admiration from Jean H. Baker, *James Buchanan* (New York, 2004), 104–106; Wilentz, *Rise of American Democracy*, 718; and Richard H. Sewell, *A House Divided: Sectionalism and Civil War, 1848–1865* (Baltimore, 1988), 65.

[27] In 1854 Douglas knew that his revocation of the Missouri Compromise in the Kansas–Nebraska Act would "raise a hell of a storm," but he could not anticipate the full impact on the party system. James M. McPherson, "Out of War, a New Nation," *Prologue Magazine*, 42:1 (Spring 2010), 6–13.

[28] A premature child had died after only a few hours in February 1858. Johannsen, *SAD*, 605.

Madison, she hosted levees, charmed politicians and reporters, stunned crowds with her beauty and grace, and encouraged her husband to go on without her after she sustained a serious injury in Alabama.[29] Most of the hundreds of thousands who saw them had no idea of their private grief because, while his presidential rivals stayed home and stayed silent, he stayed the course, pleading with Southerners to remain in the Union should Lincoln win.

After Lincoln won, Douglas did not ease up on either his need to remain a player or his desire to preserve the Union. From a dogged but futile effort to work out a compromise in Congress to a conspicuous attempt at courting and co-opting the new president, he tried to prevent national dissolution. It was not his finest hour, however, for he contradicted principles he had long stood for and tried to present himself in a more influential role than he actually had. Once the Confederacy attacked Fort Sumter, he accepted the irreconcilability of the conflict and spoke eloquently in defense of the president's call to arms. In his last major speech, two weeks before the onset of his final illness, he noted the credibility that he brought to a message of patriotism: "I believe I may with confidence appeal to the people of every section of the country to bear testimony that I have been as thoroughly national in my political opinions and actions as any man that has lived in my day."[30] It was a fitting reflection on what his overall career represented. He was in fact a man for every section.[31]

Although it encompasses all aspects of Douglas's personal and professional life, this is a thematic biography that does not unfold in strict linear progression.[32]

---

[29] For Dolly Madison as Washington wife, see Catherine Allgor, *Parlor Politics: In Which the Ladies of Washington Help Build a City and a Government* (Charlottesville, VA, 2000), 48–101. Her book deals astutely with the role of political wives in the early Republic. See also her "Political Parties: First Ladies and Social Events in the Formation of the Federal Government," in *The Presidential Companion: Readings on the First Ladies*, ed. Robert P. Watson and Anthony J. Eksterowicz (Columbia, SC, 2003), 35–53; and Shawn J. Parry-Giles and Diane M. Blair, "The Rise of the Rhetorical First Lady: Politics, Gender Ideology, and Women's Voice, 1789–2002," *Rhetoric & Public Affairs*, 5:4 (2002), 565–600, esp. 567–572. Rosemarie Zagarri, *Revolutionary Backlash: Women and Politics in the Early American Republic* (Philadelphia, 2007), covers the range of early female political activism, from that of an "operative" like Dolly Madison (133) to women who adorned their hats or dresses with partisan symbols (85–86).

[30] *Chicago Tribune*, June 6, 1861. Following Douglas's death, the paper printed his speech of April 25 before the Illinois legislature in its entirety for the first time.

[31] Even before the emergence of the Republicans as a sectional party, Democratic Party leaders portrayed themselves as truly national. In 1852 Franklin Pierce asked his campaign biographer to depict him "as a man for the whole country." Quoted in Jean H. Baker, *Affairs of Party: The Political Culture of Northern Democrats in the Mid-Nineteenth-Century* (Ithaca, NY, 1983), 323.

[32] Several narrative biographies have guided my way. The one to which I owe the greatest debt is Robert W. Johannsen, *Stephen A. Douglas* (New York, 1973). Johannsen made his notes available to scholars at the Illinois History and Lincoln Collections in the University of Illinois Library. James L. Huston's *Stephen A. Douglas and the Dilemmas of Democratic Equality* is a narrative biography that effectively pursues its titular theme. Gerald M. Capers's *Stephen A. Douglas: Defender of the Union* (Boston, 1959) is elegantly written, typical of the volumes in the once famous Library of American Biography series edited by Oscar Handlin. George M.

Accordingly the chapters vary in length. Douglas's adolescent crisis, family relations, and education are covered separately in chronologically overlapping chapters. Chapter 4, on his rise in Illinois, focuses on the 1830s. Each of the next two chapters, on his constitutionalism, is organized around topics rather than timelines. Chapter 7, on his campaign of 1860, offers a summary of presidential canvassing from Washington to Lincoln in order to place Douglas's trailblazing travels in historical context. Chapter 8 examines his need to find a place for himself in the post-election shadow of Lincoln. Chapter 9 reassesses Douglas's involvement with slavery in Mississippi and its relationship to his politics. This is the shortest chapter but provides some details of what happened to his sons and second wife after he died.

Sources unknown, unexamined, or unused by previous biographers have influenced the treatment of themes in this book. New genealogical and property data about Douglas's household in Vermont deepen our understanding of his conflicted feelings about his native state and require a reconsideration of his adolescent crisis there. Two manuscripts – the record book of his common school and his copybook at Brandon Academy – increase our knowledge of his schooling and of rural learning in New England during the 1820s. Moreover, a vetting of the educational claims of his mother and sister raises doubts about the U.S. Census as a source for estimating literacy.

Unpublished letters, including a batch only recently discovered, add emotional color to Douglas's family relationships, but scholarship in family history also impels a reassessment of this topic in Chapter 3. Why Douglas became a Democrat is answered most directly in Chapter 4, where his relationship to other young men is central. His newly revealed expression of love for a boy at the Brandon Academy and his practice of sitting on men's laps in court and on the hustings are integrated into an analysis of his connection to the male political community. The two chapters on Douglas's constitutionalism owe much to online databases, especially the American Memory website of the Library of Congress, which literally places congressional debates, journals, bills, and statutes at one's fingertips. I could not have systematically traced Douglas's thinking on noncitizen voting, apportionment, internal improvements, and slavery in the territories without this federal resource. These chapters on constitutionalism, moreover, owe much to the encouragement I take from recent legal scholars who seriously consider the constitutional thought of politicians.[33]

Coverage of Douglas's presidential campaign of 1860 draws on newspaper databases that have enabled me to track his travels more comprehensively than anyone could before. The principal angle of the chapter, however, is the disjuncture of the continuing taboo against personal campaigning in a nation that

Milton, *Stephen A. Douglas and the Needless War* (New York, 1969; reprint of 1934 edition), draws on some sources that are no longer available.

[33] See note 21.

experienced "relentless democratization" after 1800.[34] The appendix to this volume details his campaign itinerary from his nomination to Election Day. The last chapter draws on previously unexamined materials in an integrated treatment of Douglas's relationship to slaves. Chronological biographies have described it in only a segmented fashion.

I have not modernized the spelling or grammar of direct quotes from manuscripts or printed sources.

---

[34] The quoted phrase is from Gordon Wood, *Empire of Liberty: A History of the Early Republic, 1789–1815* (New York, 2009), 312.

I

Adolescence in Vermont

My mother would prefer to let her stories stand and her workings of the past remain definitive.... It is no wonder that people prefer memory to history.

Richard White[1]

Central to Stephen A. Douglas's sense of self were his experiences in three states: Vermont, New York, and Illinois. His time in each coincided with a decisive phase of his growing up. He considered each state through the prism of his own development. He spent his childhood and early adolescence in Vermont, his late youth in New York, and transitioned into young adulthood almost overnight in Illinois. He loved Illinois, respected New York, and was ambivalent about Vermont. His belief that locality mattered in the lives of people was grounded in his personal story.

During his senatorial debates with Lincoln in 1858, Douglas amused his Illinois audience by recalling that when he received an honorary doctorate from Middlebury College seven years earlier, he had been asked to give a speech, in which he had said: "My friends, Vermont is the most glorious spot on the face of this globe for a man to be born in, *provided* he emigrates when he is very young."[2] Although contemporary reports of the commencement did not reference the provocative remark, and some, including one by his adult son, later tried to put a benign spin on it, a Middlebury graduate remembered that it did create a "decided sensation."[3] Douglas was reminded of his insult and forced to address it when he campaigned in Vermont in 1860. That Douglas would claim to have insulted his native state at the moment that it honored him indicates how conflicted his own memory and understanding were about his adolescence there.

[1] Richard White, *Remembering Ahanagran: A History of Stories* (Seattle, 2004; reprint of 1998 ed.), 5.
[2] CWAL, 3: 141; L-DD, 123.
[3] Edward S. Marsh, comp. and ed., *Stephen A. Douglas: A Memorial* (Brandon, VT, 1914), 37–40; "Illustrious Vermonters," *Vermonter*, 2:6 (1897), 93–94.

Douglas never forgot his Vermont upbringing and tried to shape what the public knew about it. The dramatic moment in the story that he told was the face-off he had with his uncle and mother when he was "about fifteen" and left home for the first time. The story of his youthful crisis was essential both to his sense of selfhood and to the image he wanted to project. There are three versions of what happened, and he was responsible for two of them. The first appeared in his autobiographical sketch of 1838, written when he was twenty-five but not published during his lifetime.[4] The second was the story he shaped for Henry Wheeler, who narrated it in his *History of Congress* in 1848.[5] This version would influence campaign biographies. The third came from his sister, with his mother's approval, when Douglas ran for president in 1860. It was reported in several newspapers and no doubt embarrassed him.[6]

That there were three narratives suggests how much importance he and his family attached to the event through the remainder of his life. His self-image would always be tied up with how he remembered his initial departure from home. He could talk about it because the antagonist in both his stories was his uncle, not his parent. Douglas cast himself as a gutsy youth who had not heeded his uncle's wishes but had instead persuaded his mother to let him leave home to make his own way in the world. In his earliest account he did so for his own benefit; in the later redaction he did so to ease the financial pressures on his family as well as to pursue his own ambitions. In his two versions,

---

[4] "Autobiographical Sketch," *Letters of SAD*, 56–68. There is no title page or title in Douglas's hand on the manuscript. SAD Papers, 2nd series, box 41, file 17. Although the autobiography was closest in time to the events of his youth, it is memory, not history, and requires careful vetting. Several works have informed my understanding of autobiography as a genre: Stephen C. Arch, *After Franklin: The Emergence of Autobiography in Post-Revolutionary America, 1780–1830* (Hanover, NH, 2001), 6, 10–11, 47–53, suggests that by 1830 American autobiography emerged distinct from earlier forms of "self-life writing" to become a narrative emphasizing the development of a person as "an independent, often original, agent." Lawrence Buell, "Autobiography in the American Renaissance," in *American Autobiography: Retrospect and Prospect*, ed. Paul J. Eakin (Madison, WI, 1991), 48–50, finds that earlier forms of self-writing focused more on circumstances than on the self. Leigh Gilmore, "Policing Truth: Confession, Gender, and Autobiographical Authority," in *Autobiography & Postmodernism*, ed. Kathleen Ashley, Leigh Gilmore, and Gerald Peters (Amherst, MA, 1994), 69, shows how a twentieth-century autobiographer fills in the gaps in history and memory with fictions that "fit so neatly in her narrative that they attain the status of remembered fact." Jeremy D. Popkin, *History, Historians, & Autobiography* (Chicago, 2005), 11–32, discusses the "distrust" that historians traditionally have had regarding first-person accounts and, as I read him, invites us to enter into the subjective understanding of the autobiographer while retaining our discipline's respect for empiricism. A biographer who vets the "autobiography" of his subject according to historical rules of evidence, similar to what I do here with Douglas's "autobiographical sketch," is Robert E. McGlone, *John Brown's War Against Slavery* (New York, 2009), 53–54, 59–62.

[5] Henry G. Wheeler, *History of Congress – Biographical and Political: Comprising Memoirs of Members of the Congress of the United States, Drawn from Authentic Sources* (New York, 1848), 60–63.

[6] Her interview was datelined July 6, 1860, and was published initially in the *Troy Whig*. USN, "A Visit to the Mother of Stephen A. Douglas," *New York Herald* (New York), July 14, 1860; *Vermont Patriot* (Montpelier), July 21, 1860.

leaving home at fifteen had been a bold, courageous action that reflected well on his character. The story told by his sister, however, cut his youth down to size. He left because he balked at continuing to attend school, as his mother wanted, but she yielded with the expectation that he would return home and to school. In his sister's account, then, the youthful Douglas benefited less from his own inclinations than from the wisdom of his mother.

In light of the three conflicting accounts (his earliest, Wheeler's, and his sister's) and new genealogical data, it is necessary to sketch a fourth narrative of Douglas's adolescence. What follows is a reconstruction of his Vermont household that incorporates both new information and recent scholarship about women and childrearing in the early Republic. It also sorts through the three conflicting versions in order to infer what "truths" can be relied upon.[7]

The following facts are consistent with all accounts: Stephen was born in Brandon on April 23, 1813, to Dr. Stephen Arnold Douglass and his wife, Sarah "Sally" Fisk Douglass.[8] They had married there in January 1811 and rented a small house in the center of town that was ideal for receiving patients.[9] Their first child, daughter Sarah, was born in Brandon on October 29, 1811. When Stephen was two months old, his thirty-one-year-old father died suddenly, while sitting on a chair "holding his infant child."[10] Deprived of her source of income, the twenty-four-year-old widow moved with her children three miles north of the center to live with her brother Edward, who was to manage the farm while she was to "keep house for him."[11] In fact, a single house that dates from the 1820s survives on the property and appears to be the home in which Stephen Douglas spent most of his first seventeen years.[12]

---

[7] Johannsen, *SAD*, 7, 877n, dismisses Wheeler's version and claims to rely on both the autobiography and the sister's account. In fact, he relies entirely on the autobiography because it was closest in time to the event. His approach is reasonable but overlooks how place (geographic and developmental) can influence memory as much as chronological proximity. A classic examination of the link between personal memory, an event, and place is Alfred F. Young, *The Shoemaker and the Tea Party: Memory and the American Revolution* (Boston, 1999). The relationship between geographic place and memory has been explored generally for groups or localities. See, for examples, Ian Tyrrel, "Public at the Creation: Place, Memory, and Historical Practice in the Mississippi Valley Historical Association, 1907–1950," *Journal of American History*, 94:1 (2007), 19–46; Jeffrey P. Shepherd, "At the Crossroads of Hualapai History, Memory, and American Colonization: Contesting Space and Place," *American Indian Quarterly*, 32:1 (2008), 16–42; David Glassberg, *Sense of History: The Place of the Past in American Life* (Amherst, MA, 2001).

[8] For Stephen's dropping of the second "s" from his surname, see Chapter 3.

[9] The house survives and has been renovated as the Brandon Museum at the Stephen A. Douglas birthplace. Architectural historian Blaine Cliver has traced the ownership of the Douglas birthplace from c. 1800 to the present. From 1812 to 1815 John Richardson owned the property. I am grateful to Blaine for making his research available to me and for a tour of the house in June 2007, before it was remodeled.

[10] *Rutland Herald*, July 7, 1813. The newspaper placed him at age twenty-nine, but his tombstone in the Brandon cemetery indicates he was in his thirty-second year.

[11] "Autobiographical Sketch" (Sept. 1, 1838), *Letters of SAD*, 58.

[12] For her birth on March 24, 1789, Brandon Land Records, 4: 263. Architectural historian Blaine Cliver dates the home to the 1820s. I am grateful to him and the current owner for a tour in June 2007.

There is a dissonance, however, between the story told by surviving deeds and that told by Douglas and his biographers. According to his accounts, his mother and uncle inherited adjacent farms; therefore, it was practical for the bachelor and the widow to live together. Douglas never wavered from the claim that the siblings shared "their patrimonial estate."[13] Nathaniel Fisk, Douglas's maternal grandfather, however, sold half of his "home farm" to one son in 1798 and conveyed the other half to Edward shortly after he reached his majority.[14] Edward was one of three brothers who received land from his father in 1809, probably in lieu of his making a will in anticipation of dying.[15] Nathaniel never transferred real estate to his daughter. He certainly was deceased by 1813, when Edward's brother sold his half of the Brandon farm to a nonsibling.[16] Had Nathaniel left an estate but no will, it would have been divided equally among all of his children under Vermont law.[17] In the absence of a recorded court division of his estate and of any deed transfer involving Sarah "Sally" Douglass, the claim that she and her brother were equal heirs is questionable. We conclude, then, that Stephen's mother believed she was entitled to half-ownership of the farm and conveyed her understanding to her son, who internalized it with a measure of his mother's resentment.

Edward Fisk was two years older than his sister and unmarried. The home they jointly set up exemplified the differences between a household and a family. Although Edward Fisk was listed under "Heads of Families" in the U.S. Census, enumerators were expected to name the heads of "households," which could contain multiple families.[18] From the perspective of the growing children, however, there was little doubt that Sally was the head of their family. That is clear from all three narratives. Douglas had to secure her approval, not his uncle's, to leave home.

---

[13] The phrase is from James W. Sheahan, *The Life of Stephen A. Douglas* (New York, 1860), 3. Douglas revised the manuscript as Sheahan submitted sections to him. *Letters of SAD*, 442n.

[14] Nathaniel Fisk to Rufus Fisk, Feb. 13, 1798, Brandon Land Records, 3: 66; Nathaniel Fisk to Edward Fisk, Feb. 21, 1809, Brandon Land Records, 6: 482.

[15] Nathaniel Fisk to Rufus Fisk, Feb. 21, 1809, Brandon Land Records, 6: 491; Nathaniel Fisk to Nathaniel Fisk, Jr., Feb. 21, 1809, Brandon Land Records, 6: 501.

[16] Rufus Fisk to Nathan Parmenter, Sept. 23, 1813, Brandon Land Records, 8: 174. Nathaniel Fisk's death is noted in the deed.

[17] Equal division of property among sons and daughters was the intestate rule after the Revolution. Marylynn Salmon, *Women and the Law of Property in Early America* (Chapel Hill, NC, 1986), 142. See, for example, the intestate division of Edward Fisk's brother Nathaniel in July 1831. Estate of Nathaniel Fisk of Brandon, Vermont, Rutland, file 849, Rutland Probate Court. Each of his four sons and three daughters inherited one-seventh of his whole estate.

[18] *U.S. Statutes at Large*, 1st Cong., 2nd sess., 1790, 101; Daniel Scott Smith, "The Meanings of Family and Household: Change and Continuity in the Mirror of the American Census," *Population and Development Review*, 18:3 (Sept. 1992), 421. Despite the growth of women's power, writes Carole Shammas, "the household could not have two heads. Only the man could represent the family to the outside world." *A History of Household Government in America* (Charlottesville, VA, 2002), 12–13.

In his autobiography, written only ten years after the crisis, Douglas referred to his uncle as a "hard master" who was unwilling to release his nephew from farm work in order to attend school more than three months a year. At twenty-five Douglas, having absorbed his mother's spin regarding the property, recalled chafing at the fact that his uncle could benefit from his mother's farm and his labor without providing more than his food and clothing. At "about fifteen" he decided to leave home to become an apprentice to a cabinetmaker. After much resistance, his mother yielded to his departure. He left for Middlebury, where he undertook an apprenticeship with "one Nahum Parker," a cabinetmaker. He loved the trade and stayed for almost a year, until Parker and his wife demanded that he perform "some menial services in the house." He demurred and returned home, but so missed "the life of a mechanic" that he apprenticed himself to a cabinetmaker in Brandon. He stayed with him for "about a year," until the winter of 1829–1830, when sickness forced him to return home. A physician advised him to choose another occupation because he was "too feeble" to be a cabinetmaker. Accordingly, he entered the Brandon Academy, where he studied until December 1830, when he left with his mother, who married a man living in Canandaigua, New York.

In his earliest account, then, Douglas was eager for additional schooling, was thwarted by a hardhearted uncle, and left home, after extracting the consent of his mother, in order to prepare for a career as a cabinetmaker. By 1848 Douglas had modified the story he told Wheeler, who depicted the fifteen-year-old as wanting to build on his "good common-school education" by preparing himself for college, "according to the understanding which was well known to exist in the family." With the advice of his mother he approached his uncle, who acted surprised, professed his love for Stephen, but cited his own new family obligations and urged him "to abandon the foolish idea of going to college." Suddenly realizing that his mother could not afford to send him to school on her own and that she had hardly "enough to support her and her daughter," Douglas decided "to leave his uncle … and to rely upon his own exertions." With the "almost extorted consent of his mother," he went to Middlebury and became an apprentice to Nahum Parker. Although he often said that "his happiest days had been spent in the workshop," he left after six or eight months because he objected to doing "menial" duties that Parker insisted were usually required of the youngest apprentice. He gave Parker notice and returned home, but remained committed to the trade "which he had selected as the business of his life" and apprenticed himself to a local cabinetmaker. Ill health forced him to take a leave from the shop. When his physical condition did not improve, he and the Brandon cabinetmaker agreed that he should not come back. At this point Douglas "determined to revive his original plan of securing an education, and devoting himself to a profession." He then entered Brandon Academy.

In this second version, Douglas was eager for additional schooling, was blocked by a well-meaning uncle, who recently had started a family of his own, and realized that his mother was hard-pressed just to support herself and his sister. He, therefore, left home in order to lessen the economic burden on his mother and tried to become a cabinetmaker, until his health forced him to prepare for another career. This became the public narrative until newspapers reported his sister's interview when he ran for president.

In 1860, two weeks after Douglas secured the presidential nomination of his party, his sister, Sarah, inverted the long-standing explanation of his departure for Middlebury at fifteen. She denied their "mother was so very poor" that he "had been obliged to work at cabinet-making." Sally Douglas had "both the means and the inclination to give her son a thorough education and to that end kept him at school. The boy tired of this" and begged her to allow him to learn a trade. His ambition at that age was to work, not to study. She "refused repeatedly" but consented at last "with the thought that the way to cure the boy's liking for a trade – for which he was physically unfit, being weak and puny – was to put him to it." Her strategy was vindicated, according to her daughter, by Douglas's return home, after only three months, with a commitment to resume school and stay as long as his mother wanted. "This he did," and when his mother remarried and moved to Ontario County, New York, he was enrolled as a boarding student at Canandaigua Academy.

In his sister's narrative, then, Douglas grew weary of school, was eager to take up a trade, begged his mother to let him leave home, and, after she shrewdly permitted him to find out for himself how ill-suited he was for cabinetmaking, refocused on educating himself for a professional career.

The major discrepancies in the three versions have to do with the respective roles of his mother and uncle, as well as his youthful attitude toward school and cabinetmaking. Contemporaries were especially interested in whether Wheeler's story that Douglas had become an apprenticed cabinetmaker to help his mother and sister financially was true. His sister's version caused a stir in the middle of his presidential campaign. Her interview with an enterprising correspondent for the *Troy Whig* was datelined July 6, 1860. In August a new campaign biography by Robert B. Warden, a former justice of the Ohio Supreme Court, reacted to the latest story with dismay and resistance. He acknowledged the satisfaction that Douglas supporters had long drawn from the belief that he had been a mechanic "not as a diversion but as a necessity."[19]

What should Douglas supporters now believe? "Are we to have our hero elevated into youthful comfort and exalted into a gentlemanly joiner, where we knew him as a common 'prentice hand?'" Did Douglas take up cabinetmaking merely because he "loved to whittle" and his affluent mother thought it would be a learning experience for her somewhat recalcitrant schoolboy? Or did he seriously consider it as a career because he loved the craft and needed to relieve his poor mother of having to feed him? Warden suggested that neither scenario was fully on the mark and that it was misguided to try to bolster one or the other.[20]

[19] Robert B. Warden, *A Voter's Version of the Life and Character of Stephen Arnold Douglas* (Columbus, SC, 1860), 30. The book was first advertised in August. USN, *Boston Daily Advertiser*, Aug. 22, 1860.

[20] Warden, *A Voter's Version*, 30–31.

Nevertheless, Douglas had nurtured for so long the image of himself as a poor boy who valiantly tried to become a craftsman that he himself may well have believed it to be true. Certainly the cabinetmakers who organized Douglas clubs during the summer of 1860 to support "their old craftsman," someone who had "once worked at the bench himself," wanted to believe the older narrative.[21]

Douglas's two versions of his initial apprenticeship after leaving home were essentially the same. He traveled to Middlebury, where he entered the shop of Nahum Parker, a cabinetmaker, and "was delighted with the change in home and employment." What he did not note even in his private autobiography was that his engagement with Parker was prearranged. Parker's wife was the stepdaughter of Stephen's paternal grandfather, Benajah Douglass. This made Nahum and Sarah Parker Stephen's step-uncle and step-aunt. This relationship suggests that Stephen's departure at fifteen was not quite as brave as he continued to characterize it.[22] The plausibility of his sister's rendition of 1860 is strengthened, for we can imagine Stephen's mother reluctantly agreeing to his taking up a trade as long as he was going to be placed with relatives.

Douglas was consistent in explaining why he left the Parkers. He did enjoy cabinetmaking, to the point that he could claim as a politician, according to Wheeler, that "his happiest days had been spent in the workshop, and the bitterest hour of his life was that in which the loss of health compelled him to leave it."[23] It is evident that his labor for Parker was not as taxing as a subsequent apprenticeship would be. Indeed, his step-uncle may have been so avuncular that Douglas was able to last there for six to eight months, until a "misunderstanding" arose between them. He balked at doing some menial chores around the house that he thought were more suitable for a domestic servant. In light of his acknowledged physical limitations, we can infer that the Parkers may have made the new demands to compensate for Douglas's lighter load in the workshop. Douglas would have none of it, however, and made the fourteen-mile return to Brandon.[24]

Douglas was able to leave Parker because he was not indentured to him. In the 1820s apprenticeship was most often an informal arrangement between master and teenager, with the understanding that either party could terminate the arrangement if it did not work out. The best possible situation for the learner was to apprentice himself to a distant kin, who could be expected to

[21] EAN, *Wisconsin Daily Patriot* (Madison), Aug. 1, 1860, 2.

[22] The marriage of Nahum and Sarah (Harris) Parker took place in Middlebury on January 1, 1821. Marriage Records, Town Office, Middlebury, Vermont, book I, 50. For Benajah's marriage to Sarah Harris, see their nuptial agreement, Jan. 26, 1819, Brandon Record Books, 13: 51–52. The son of Nahum and Sarah asked Douglas to explain to the Pensions Department "that Widow Harris and Widow Douglass is one and the same person." Nathaniel Harris to Stephen A. Douglas, Apr, 3, 1857; SAD Papers, series I, 5:6.

[23] Wheeler, *History of Congress*, 62.

[24] In 1860, when Douglas came to Vermont as a candidate for president, he noted that Parker "and his woman" came to the depot at Middlebury to see him. ProQuest, *New York Times*, Aug. 2, 1860.

provide a more benign environment, which is what the Parkers provided.[25] Upon his return home near the end of 1828, Douglas did not do what his sister in 1860 remembered. He did not "resume the school," but instead resumed his trade. He spent "about a year" in the shop of a Brandon cabinetmaker, Caleb Knowlton. Here he would have remained, according to both of his versions, had it not been for his health. During the fall of 1829, he was put to "making French bedsteads of curled maple, a very hard labor, which proved too severe for his delicate constitution." All three accounts agree that physically he could not handle the work. His sister remembered his apprenticeship as totaling only three months in one shop, but she was invested in vindicating their mother's "foresight" in believing that Douglas's physical unfitness for the work would bring him back to school. She conflated his two consecutive apprenticeships into a single shortened one with Parker. His journal recollection and Wheeler's version name both masters. Altogether he spent at least a year and a half, from the spring of 1828, when he was fifteen, until the fall of 1829, in apprenticeship.[26] In his autobiography he said that his physician informed him that he was "too feeble" to continue in cabinetry and that he should find another occupation. Wheeler's version varies: While Douglas was recuperating, with the expectation that upon recovery he would return to Knowlton's shop, he enrolled at Brandon Academy. Finding his health only somewhat improved, Knowlton agreed that he should not return to the shop, that he should pursue another occupation, "and, upon the advice of friends, he determined to revive his original plan of securing an education, and devoting himself to a profession."

What are we to make of all this? Did Douglas want to continue his schooling, feel frustrated by the unavailability of family resources, leave home to learn cabinetmaking, love it but find himself not strong enough to make it in that trade, and go back to school "upon the advice of friends?" Or did he yearn to become a craftsman, much to the consternation of his mother, who permitted him to leave with the expectation that he would eventually discover he was better suited to rely on his brains than his hands for a living?

What we can extrapolate with certainty from the three accounts is that he enjoyed most of the work he performed in the shops of Parker and Knowlton and seriously considered a career as a cabinetmaker. He was more than a "whittler." He spent the better part of his fifteenth and sixteenth years in cabinetmaking when apprenticeship was viewed as a preparation for a career, and terms were loose in order to enable the uninterested or ill-suited to leave. It was a long time to spend had he not been serious about his prospects as a

[25] W. J. Rorabaugh, *The Craft Apprentice: From Franklin to the Machine Age in America* (New York, 1986), 55; John E. Murray and Ruth W. Herndon, "Markets for Children in Early America: A Political Economy of Pauper Apprenticeship," *Journal of Economic History*, 62:2 (2002), 356–382, fig. 358.

[26] [Henry M. Flint,] *Life of Stephen A. Douglas, United States Senator from Illinois, with His Most Important Speeches and Reports, by a Member of the Western Bar* (New York, 1860), 17, correctly stated that Douglas "worked at this trade for eighteen months."

"mechanic." All three stories agree that it was his physical limitations that pushed him away from this career. Had it not been for his infirmities, he might have remained in a workshop. This was not mere political posturing to curry favor with mechanics.

Douglas's youthful yearning to become a mechanic clashed with his uncle's desire for him to do more work on the farm and with his mother's expectations that he would continue his schooling. His relationships with his uncle, mother, and sister carried mixed emotions that persisted until his death. His sister's willingness to risk undermining his presidential candidacy in 1860 by so dramatically revising the story he had told for decades itself testifies to the strains in their relationship and to the family's fixation on their time in Vermont. Moreover, it is now clear that Douglas tried to suppress or embellish features of the Brandon household that come to light when the genealogical and literary sources are vetted anew.

In his autobiography Douglas referred to his uncle as an "old bachelor" at the time he set up house with Sally and her children. Here Douglas made no mention of his uncle's marriage or issue, leaving the reader to believe that Fisk was still unmarried when his nephew departed at "about fifteen." Yet Douglas told Henry Wheeler, his biographer of 1848, that "about fourteen years" after setting up house with his sister, Edward Fisk visited "some relatives in the western part of New York" and returned with a "young and beautiful wife" who, "in the fourth quarter of the ensuing year," bore a son. This indicates that Fisk married in 1827 and had a son in 1828.

The evidence, however, points to an earlier start to Fisk's family. In September 1852 the Rutland County Probate Court named Fisk's heirs to be a daughter and two sons – Ermina M. Ford, Julius Granger Fisk, and Edward E. Fisk, "a minor."[27] Their birth dates can be extrapolated from the U.S. Census of 1860, where Ermina Ford's age is thirty-five and Julius Fisk's is thirty-three.[28] Their respective dates of birth, then, were late 1824 or 1825 and late 1826 or 1827, which would mean that their parents should have married by 1824, some four years before Douglas turned fifteen.

While Douglas ignored Ermina's presence, he supplied Wheeler with numerous temporal details regarding Fisk's trip to New York, his marriage, and the birth of his son: (1) Fisk visited New York after fourteen years of living as a bachelor with his sister. (2) He went there to visit relatives he had not seen "for nearly a quarter of a century." (3) "In a few months" he returned to Brandon with a new wife. (4) "Time rolled on, and in the fourth quarter of the ensuing year" the wife bore a son. These references obscure the actual chronology by pushing the whole time frame forward and omitting the birth of Ermina. The inclusion of the four temporal minutiae and the omission altogether of his female cousin are disproportionate.

[27] Brandon, Vermont Land Records, Grantee to Grantor, bk. 22, pp. 44–45.
[28] The 1860 Census for Vermont lists Ermina Ford in Brandon, Rutland County, and Julius Fisk in Isle la Motte, Grand Isle County. Ages were given as of June 1, 1860.

Compounding the problem of balance is the exclusion of his aunt's name. Both the autobiographical sketch of 1838 and Wheeler's account give the names of the cabinetmakers with whom young Douglas apprenticed in Middlebury and Brandon. Both documents record the names of his teachers at academies in Brandon and Canandaigua, as well as the names of the father and son that his mother and sister respectively married in 1830. Yet not only is Edward's daughter, Ermina, never acknowledged, his wife's name is not given. She was, according to genealogists, Emily Granger, daughter of the same Gehazi that Douglas's mother married in December 1830. Although the claim for the union of Edward Fisk and Emily Granger has not been verified with a marriage record or newspaper notice in Vermont or New York, their son's full name, Julius Granger Fisk, testifies to Emily's surname and lends support to the genealogists.[29]

Why is Ermina never part of Douglas's story about the Fisk household? Wheeler and later biographers implied that the birth of Fisk's son darkened the prospects of both Stephen and his sister because Julius was now heir to his father's estate. In fact, this was not the case. Ermina also became an heir, when her father died intestate. By not drafting a will, Edward Fisk, like his brother Nathaniel, left equal shares of his estate to his sons and daughter.[30] The omission of Ermina, then, cannot be explained by her being a lesser rival for Edward's resources. When Edward told Douglas that he could not afford to pay for his schooling because he now had a family of his own, he certainly included Ermina in his rationale.

The most plausible answer to why Douglas wholly eliminated his uncle's marriage and children in his autobiography and why he omitted the presence of Ermina in information he gave Wheeler is that the circumstances of her birth invited gossip. As an attorney and a judge, Douglas knew how seriously people of Illinois viewed bastardy, which was one of the most frequently prosecuted sexual crimes in the state because of its economic consequences.[31] Newspapers across the country regularly reported convictions for bastardy, often juxtaposed to prostitution.[32] He did not want to be tainted by such behavior, especially when people were reading about "illegitimate families."[33]

---

[29] James N. Granger, *Launcelot Granger of Newbury, Mass., and Suffield, Conn.: A Genealogical History* (Hartford, CT, 1893), 294; Ancestry of Adelaide Granger Archer, file 6012 Archer, Ontario County Historical Society. No marriage records for the period survive either at the office of the Brandon Town Clerk or at the Public Records Division, Middlesex, Vermont. No notice can be found in the *Rutland Herald*, for which a complete run is available at the American Antiquarian Society. A search of the records at the Ontario County Historical Society by the executive director revealed no marriage date. Ancestry.com dated the marriage to 1818, but telephone and email communications indicate that the researcher credited with providing the data has now disclaimed responsibility for it. Emails between Martin Quitt and Scott Barker at Lineages.com, Dec. 10, 2007, Jan. 3 and Jan. 8, 2008.

[30] For the division of Edward Fisk's estate, see note 27. For the division of Nathaniel Fisk, Jr.,'s estate, see note 16.

[31] *Lincoln Legal Briefs: Quarterly Newsletter of the Lincoln Legal Papers*, no. 41 (Jan.–Mar. 1997).

[32] USN, *New-York Spectator*, Oct. 1, 1838; USN, *Daily National Intelligencer* (Washington, DC), Oct. 1, 1838; USN, *North American and Daily Advertiser* (Philadelphia), June 2, 1840.

[33] USN, *Boston Courier*, Dec. 5, 1839.

If Edward Fisk married Gehazi Granger's daughter Emily, as genealogists assert, Douglas may also have worried about ridicule sparked by the complicated relationships that the three marriages produced. The marital sequence involved, first, his uncle and Gehazi's daughter; second, his sister and Gehazi's son; and third, his mother and Gehazi. Emily Granger Fisk, therefore, would have been both the stepdaughter and sister-in-law of his mother and the aunt and sister-in-law of both Douglas and his sister, Sarah. Worse, his uncle would have been not only his mother's brother but also her stepson. The early nineteenth century labeled as incest marriages that broke traditional barriers, for which there was a good deal of confusion. The crisscross of affinal relationships that the Fisks and Grangers created was better left out of Douglas's story, even though they did not transgress a particular taboo.[34]

Once Douglas moved with his mother to Gehazi's home in Clifton Springs, New York, the absence of surviving correspondence with the Fisks suggests that his ties with them attenuated.[35] In her interview with the reporter in 1860, Sarah did not mention their uncle's role in Douglas's adolescent crisis. Nevertheless, their mother made summer visits to Brandon before her brother died.[36] After Edward's death, Ermina, with her husband and daughter, visited the Grangers in 1850, as reported by Douglas's niece.[37] There was no direct contact between Douglas and the Fisks of Brandon after 1830. Douglas did not return to Vermont until after his uncle died, when he received his honorary degree at Middlebury.

Despite his own estrangement from Fisk, Douglas appears to have softened his feelings about his uncle over time. His recollection of him for Wheeler's 1848 biography replaced the hard-nosed taskmaster of his autobiography with an affectionate, well-meaning man who was now constrained by responsibilities to "a family of his own." The difference in characterizations tells us as much about how Douglas remembered his youth as it does about Fisk.

"The place from which a memory is recalled shapes the content of that memory," says historian Michael Berenbaum.[38] Douglas began his autobiography on September 1, 1838, when he believed he was about to learn of his election to Congress, capping a meteoric rise in Illinois politics.[39] His recollection

---

[34] For views of incest and marriage formation in the late eighteenth and nineteenth centuries and the attending confusion, see Brian J. Connolly, "Domestic Intercourse: Incest, Family and Sexuality in the United States, 1780–1870," Ph.D. diss. (Rutgers University, 2007), 107–166. "Affinal" refers to a close, nonconsanguineous relationship created by marriage, most particularly, as Connolly shows, union with a deceased brother's wife. See also his " 'Every Man Become a School of Abominable Impurity': Incest and Theology in the Early Republic," *Journal of the Early Republic,* 30:3 (Fall 2010), 413–442.

[35] This conclusion is based on an examination of the indexed correspondence to Douglas at the Regenstein Library, University of Chicago, and *Letters of SAD.*

[36] Stephen A. Douglas to Adelaide Granger, May 30 and July 28, 1849, *Letters of SAD,* 170–171.

[37] Adelaide Granger (Manchester, NY) to Stephen A. Douglas, Sept. 18, 1850, SAD Papers, series II, 41:11.

[38] Michael Berenbaum, "When Memory Triumphs," *Oral History Review,* 22:2 (1995), 95.

[39] His rise is the subject of Chapter 4.

of his adolescent crisis was colored by a strong sense of vindication about his own inclinations and choices. His presumption of victory in 1838 reinforced his sense of rectitude regarding his youthful behavior. He recalled himself as drawing a line in the soil regarding his uncle. He had been the strong-willed agent in his departure from home as assuredly as his own determination had carried him to the threshold of Congress. In the context of his expected election, it is understandable that he would educe his own will as having been decisive ten years earlier. Also understandable is his considering it appropriate that his motive at fifteen had been how best to advance himself, without concern for the welfare of the household. The twenty-five-year-old luminary was focused exclusively on how his uncle had thwarted his path to achievement, not on the competing pressures that might have operated on Fisk. This single-mindedness regarding his own ambition rendered his uncle's own family an extraneous matter.

By 1848 Douglas was much more sympathetic to his uncle than he had been when he was a decade younger. Like Fisk, Douglas remained a bachelor longer than most men.[40] Married in April 1847 for the first time, he was more sensitive to the marriage of his uncle than he had been earlier. The thirty-five-year-old Douglas viewed the confrontation through the lens of someone who was developing an understanding of the burdens of married men. His wife was expecting their first child. His place in 1848 was different from what it had been in 1838.

There was also a public relations consideration for the Wheeler version. In his twenties Douglas relished notoriety. In his thirties he was more cautious about his reputation. The self-interested fifteen-year-old who appeared in his autobiographical sketch of 1838 would not do as much for his image as would a youth who yearned for more schooling but who left home to take up a trade in order to ease the burden on his widowed mother. Wheeler's account was entirely for public consumption. The depiction of the youthful Douglas as a dutiful son and brother served his image well.[41] At the same time that he was portraying his uncle more benignly to Wheeler, Douglas was suppressing details that might embarrass him, especially now that he was prominent on a national stage.

One other source of anguish in the memory of his Vermont adolescence could be traced to the Brandon Academy, which he entered in the fall of 1829, while he was trying to decide whether he would be able to resume his work

---

[40] Men normally married in their mid-twenties. See Michael R. Haines, "Long-Term Marriage Patterns in the United States from Colonial Times to the Present," *History of the Family*, 1:1 (1996), 15–39.

[41] Wheeler's *History of Congress* contained biographical sketches of twenty-four representatives and only one senator, Stephen Douglas. The flattering account of Douglas took up 112 pages, or fully 20% of the book. A year later, when Wheeler needed to line up endorsements for a proposed book on the Wilmot Proviso, he turned to Douglas, whom he no doubt deemed grateful and likely to do him the favor. Henry G. Wheeler to Stephen A. Douglas, July 25, 1849, SAD Papers, series I, 1:10. The letter is indexed as unintelligible, but Wheeler's signature and some of the words are decipherable. In a Senate speech in 1850, Douglas would read a passage from Wheeler's book to document his position regarding slavery in the Mexican cession. CG, APP, 31st Cong., 1st sess. (Mar. 14, 1850), 372.

in cabinetmaking. He wrote in his copybook, "Prey tom if you love me say so." He wrote it three times lengthwise in the margin so that the boy sitting to his left could read the sentiment at a glance. He wrote other names of both boys and girls but none with an expression of feeling.[42] His infatuation with "Tom" appears not to have been reciprocated. There is no extant correspondence between them, and Douglas never alluded to the relationship in either of his narratives or any letter.[43]

His last year in Brandon had to have been very stressful for the sixteen- and seventeen-year-old. He had to relinquish his dream of becoming a mechanic because of his physical weakness. He pined for a schoolboy who did not requite his feelings. His family also was breaking up. His grandfather, Benajah Douglass, died in 1829, and in early 1830 his sister married and moved to upstate New York. His mother missed her to the point of marrying her father-in-law and following her to the Grangers' place at the end of the year. Uncle Edward was too busy with his own family and, perhaps, too disappointed in Stephen's disinterest in farming to give the youth positive attention. And his deceased grandfather's debts were blazoned in the local newspaper for weeks.[44] No wonder that Douglas did not return to Vermont for more than twenty years and, when he did, could not repress the pain he still carried within.

The real story of Douglas's Vermont youth, then, goes something like this. After his father died, his mother moved in with her unmarried brother. She conveyed to her children her belief that she was an equal partner in the farm, but in fact her father had not conferred a share on her. Her brother Edward expected Stephen to do farmwork as most boys did. Stephen's resentment at this labor intensified in his early teens when his uncle married and had two children of his own, making it clear that the nephew would have no claim to the uncle's resources. Stephen's female cousin, moreover, may have been born out of wedlock, and he repressed her very existence. Stephen enjoyed working with his hands but not in the fields. He was not physically strong but wanted to make furniture. He pressed to leave the farm to prepare for a mechanical career, and his reluctant mother permitted him to go to Middlebury when he was fifteen, knowing that he would be under the watch of his grandfather's stepdaughter and her husband, a cabinetmaker. Stephen, however, balked at the household chores demanded of him by the Parkers and after several months returned home to take up cabinetmaking in Brandon. His size and strength forced him to give up this career and return to school, this time at a new academy, where his feelings for a boy were unrequited. His grandfather died, leaving an estate burdened by debts. When Stephen's sister and mother respectively married a son and father from upstate New York in 1830, only two years after Stephen had first left Brandon on his own, he was relieved to join them and leave Vermont behind for good.

[42] Copybook of Stephen A. Douglas, SAD Papers, Abraham Lincoln Library, SC 415, folder 1.
[43] This episode is discussed within the broader context of his relationship to men in Chapter 4.
[44] *Vermont Telegraph*, Dec. 15, 22, and 29, 1829.

2

Schooling, Learning, and Passing the Bar

> Bishop was our first teacher – a poor creature who didn't know what else to do, so he kept school. I worked all summer, and went to school in winter, and learned my letters out of Dilworth.
>
> Lyman Beecher (b. 1775)[1]

Although Douglas described his common-school education in Brandon in positive terms, it is hard not to view his experience as the triumph of an intellectually gifted boy over an inadequate system. The Arnold Hollow District School that he attended had all of the features that reformers in Vermont attacked. It was crowded, it grouped children of disparate ages together, it hired teachers on the cheap, and it offered a stunted curriculum. It was not the kind of school designed to motivate youths to advance their formal education. That Stephen, brilliant as he was, ended his time there wanting to take up a trade suggests how stultifying the district school could be.

The school was about a mile down the road from the Fisk farm.[2] In the year Douglas was born the school introduced a summer session for girls, called a "woman's school" because of the teacher's gender.[3] The practice of women teaching very young children and older girls during summer sessions dated in New England at least to the 1760s.[4] It was generally assumed that women could more

---

[1] Barbara M. Cross, ed., *The Autobiography of Lyman Beecher*, 2 vols. (Cambridge, MA, 1961), 1: 18. Despite all of the talk in the early Republic about the importance of education, Douglas's early schooling in Brandon was not much different from Beecher's in Connecticut four decades earlier, except that Noah Webster's *American Spelling Book* probably replaced Thomas Dilworth's *New Guide to the English Tongue*. Charles Monaghan and Jennifer E. Monaghan, "Schoolbooks," in *An Extensive Republic: Print, Culture, and Society in the New Nation, 1790–1840*, ed. Robert A. Gross and Mary Kelley (Chapel Hill, NC, 2010), 305, 308.

[2] Theodore W. H. Johnson, "Did Stephen Douglas Attend the Arnold District School?" *Vermont Quarterly*, n.s. 20 (1952), 306–307. I have driven and measured the distance.

[3] Brandon, Vermont School District No. 1, Record Book, 1811–1849, ms. 974.31 B734, Vermont Historical Society, 5; Carl Kaestle and Maris A. Vinovskis, *Education and Social Change in Nineteenth-Century Massachusetts* (Cambridge, MA, 1980), 26.

[4] Nancy Cott, *The Bonds of Womanhood: Woman's Sphere in New England, 1780–1835* (New Haven, CT, 1977), 30.

easily control girls and younger boys who attended summer sessions, when the older boys worked the fields.[5] The winter term initially was called a "mans [*sic*] school" because of the teacher.[6] By the time Douglas became a teenager, these labels were dropped, both boys and girls attended each session, and the committee "equally divided" public money between the winter and summer schools.[7] In common schools young boys were able to go to summer sessions until they were old enough to labor on the farm.[8] In 1820 the Brandon District Summer School session was extended to five months.[9] The winter term of Vermont common schools usually did not exceed ten to twelve weeks.[10] The Brandon district school annually contained from sixty-three to eighty-four scholars between four and eighteen years old.[11] Population growth put pressure on the school between 1820 and 1830, when Brandon experienced a 30 percent increase that made it the fastest-growing town and fourth largest in Rutland County.[12]

Praise of common schools was a feature of republican cant. They were hailed as "nurseries of intelligent freemen – the life and soul of a republic."[13] Educational reformers knew better. One condemned the "parsimony of parents" in Vermont for refusing to divide their crowded districts. "When 70 or 80 children, most of whom are under 12, are in school," he complained, "no one can teach them." Brandon hired one teacher a term. The reformer asserted that in such packed schoolrooms, "no single teacher can accomplish half of what should be taught in a day."[14]

In the 1820s the Vermont legislature twice increased the poll and property tax to support schools, altogether tripling the amount of funding required of the towns.[15] The mandated funding was not expected to be sufficient, and towns were empowered to raise additional money "by subscription, or otherwise."[16]

---

[5] Carl Kaestle, *Pillars of the Republic: Common Schools and American Society, 1780–1860* (New York, 1983), 19.

[6] Brandon School District No. 1, Record Book, 1.

[7] Ibid., 39, 48, 62, 65.

[8] In Wilton, New Hampshire, from 1804 to 1818, Warren Burton stopped attending summer school at ten in order to do farmwork. *The District School as It Was [1833], Scenery-Showing, and Other Writings* (Boston, 1852), 40.

[9] Brandon School District No. 1, Record Book, 39.

[10] USN, *Vermont Watchman and State Gazette* (Montpelier), Oct. 26, 1830.

[11] Brandon School District No. 1, Record Book, 3, 4, 12, 17, 28, 31, 38. Local variation was the norm in the size and quality of common schools. Some might have only a handful of students. William J. Reese, *America's Public Schools: From the Common Schools to "No Child Left Behind"* (Baltimore, 2005), 29.

[12] Only two villages with thirty-two and thirty-four inhabitants respectively in 1820 had a greater increase. Calculations are from census tables in Leonard Deming, *Catalogue of the Principal Officers of Vermont ... 1778 to 1851* (Middlebury, VT, 1851) and *Rutland Herald*, Dec. 7, 1830.

[13] *Rutland Herald*, Sept. 1, 1829.

[14] *Rutland Herald*, Jan. 12, 1830.

[15] Vermont Session Laws, 1824, 10; 1826, 22.

[16] In New York before 1838 more than half the cost of schooling was covered by parents and private sources. Sun Go and Peter Lindert, "The Uneven Rise of American Public Schools," *Journal of Economic History*, 70:1 (Mar. 2010), 5–6.

In 1827 the first comprehensive act dealing with schools in the state prescribed how each town should organize its common-school system, established a statewide board of commissioners, and introduced a requirement that teachers be examined and certified by a superintending committee annually elected by each town meeting. Teachers had to be qualified "for the instruction of youth in orthography, reading, writing, English grammar, geography, arithmetic, history of the United States, and good behavior."[17]

Nevertheless, some families still refused to send their children to school, and towns remained tightfisted in their support.[18] In 1829 the new Brandon newspaper published an article complaining that common schools too often hired teachers "whose important qualification is cheapness of service."[19] None of Douglas's teachers at the district school made enough of an impression to be named in his journal. And he wholly ignored the association between his uncle and the school. Edward Fisk served on the school committee twice in the 1820s.[20] In fact, Stephen made no mention of his time there other than to say that he "enjoyed the benefits of a common school education three months each year." Vermont's attempt to oversee the quality of common schools came too late to benefit Stephen. In 1828 the new Board of Commissioners provided a list of books recommended, not mandated, for the common schools in the state. The list extended over subjects that the board expected to be taught: spelling, reading, geography, grammar, history, and arithmetic.[21] Stephen had just finished with the Brandon district school. Although he left before state-urged improvements were made, for all its limitations his common-school experience was most likely better than it would have been in other parts of the country.[22]

The absence of particular recollections about the district school is noteworthy because Douglas attended it for many more years than he would spend later at academies in Brandon and Canandaigua, New York. He probably began his education at the district school when he was not much older than four or five, and stayed until he was about fifteen.[23] Like most rural boys, Stephen was put

---

[17] Vermont Session Laws, 1827, 19–28, esp. 19.
[18] Randolph A. Roth, *The Democratic Dilemma: Religion, Reform, and the Social Order in the Connecticut River Valley of Vermont, 1791–1850* (Cambridge, MA, 1987), 112.
[19] *Vermont Telegraph*, Dec. 15, 1829.
[20] Brandon School District 1, Record Book, 40, 43.
[21] *Rutland Herald*, July 8, 1828.
[22] As measured by the proportion of children in school and the ratio of teachers to school-age children, "the rural North stood out among regions in the same way that the United States stood out among countries." Go and Lindert, "Uneven Rise of American Public Schools," 5. Studying the period 1790–1840, Nancy Beadie notes the "very high levels of mass school attendance and funding" in the northern United States prior to state support. "Education, Social Capital and State Formation in Comparative Historical Perspective: Preliminary Investigations," *Paedagogica Historica*, 46:1–2 (Feb.–Apr. 2010), 15–32, quote on 15. Gerald F. Moran and Maris A. Vinovskis concur that New England "led the rest of the nation in school attendance." "Schools," in *An Extensive Republic*, ed. Gross and Kelley, 290.
[23] This was the norm in rural areas. Kaestle, *Pillars of the Republic*, 15. The Brandon district school stipulated that pupils had to be older than four and younger than eighteen "to receive any

to work on the farm as soon as he was old enough, probably not until at least the age of ten. Some boys were able to do farm labor younger, but Stephen was much smaller and weaker than his peers.[24] We can only speculate about his relationship to other children. We know that Stephen was "weak and puny," in his sister's words, and that boys who could not handle themselves physically were commonly tyrannized by bigger, tougher peers. Older boys picked on younger ones, especially when they were packed into the same room. Even if a boy was not the target of bullying, he would have his identity contested in snowball fights and wrestling matches. A contemporary remembered his school days in rural New Hampshire when boys were "combatants" and "warriors" engaged in "battles" wherein "the game is to put each other down, down, to the bottom of the hill. There is pulling, pushing, pitching, and whirling, every species of manual attack, except the pugilistic thump and knock-down."[25]

Achieving manhood is problematic in any setting. In a schoolyard the physical appearance of a youth counts much more than it does inside the schoolhouse. Adolescents most readily associate muscularity, height, and athleticism with manliness. The absence of these traits can challenge a youth's sense of identity, especially when the culture encourages boys "to develop aggressive qualities."[26] Stephen lacked size and strength. These deficits were powerful enough to have short-circuited his potential career as a cabinetmaker. They inexorably affected his intercourse with his schoolmates. He might have overcome his shortcomings with guile or courage. However he managed it, he did learn how to get along with other boys.

On the basis of his oratorical skills at twenty, we can surmise that Stephen's tongue was an instrument of survival with schoolmates when he was younger. Note that the comprehensive act of 1827 did not prescribe declamation or recitation for the common schools. It is unlikely that there was any speech training.[27] What Douglas learned in the schoolyard was how to be facile, to handle verbally ruffians whom he could not otherwise fend off. He did not shy away from the world of roughhousing boys. He was scrappy. His most effective weapon, however, was his mouth, which he first learned to use with his mother. If we can extrapolate from his exchange with her when he was fifteen, her style was one of prescribing but relenting. She tried to influence her son's behavior while permitting him to express and act on his own will. She neither

---

benefit of public money." Brandon School District, Record Book No. 1, 28, 45. In his "authorized" campaign biography, H. M. Flint claimed that Douglas attended the "common schools of the neighborhood" from the age of ten to fifteen. *Life of Stephen A. Douglas* (Philadelphia, 1863), 16. There was only one school in Arnold Hollow. Neither in his autobiography nor in Wheeler's sketch did Douglas indicate at what age he entered the common school.

24 Burton, *District School as It Was*, 40.

25 Ibid., 110–113. For a succinct, excellent description of rural boyhood culture, see Steven Mintz, *A History of American Childhood* (Cambridge, MA, 2004), 83.

26 Brian J. Connolly, "Domestic Intercourse: Incest, Family and Sexuality in the United States," Ph.D. diss. (Rutgers University, 2007), 11.

27 See "Oratory in the Public Schools," *New England Conservatory Quarterly*, 3:3 (May 1897).

indulged nor crushed his spirit, but nurtured a high degree of self-confidence. She clearly did not second-guess him. Even at his most introspective and retrospective, Douglas never regretted what he had done; he never felt guilt. He was always willing to explain his decisions, but only to show why he had been right. He grew up without self-censoriousness. What came out of his mouth worked well for him; he did not worry about saying the wrong thing.

His mother emphasized the importance of education, although neither she nor her daughter appears to have been schooled enough to write more than her name.[28] Stephen grew up with the expectation that he would go to college like his father, who was depicted as a "graduate of Middlebury College."[29] Did his father attend Middlebury College? Stephen described his physician father as a Middlebury graduate in his journal. Wheeler repeated the information in his 1848 sketch, as did James Sheahan in his campaign biography of 1860.[30] Yet there is no report that he cited his father's graduation when Stephen received an honorary degree from Middlebury in 1851.[31] His father's name is not in a compilation of degree recipients preserved by Middlebury trustees. Nor is he on undergraduate class lists of 1804, 1806, or 1807.[32] After a search of the records, the president of Middlebury sadly concluded in 1913 that there was no basis for the claim.[33] It is possible, however, that the father attended the Addison County Grammar School, chartered in 1797, that was housed in the same building as the college until 1805.[34] When a catalog of Middlebury College graduates was published two years after Douglas received his honorary degree, the omission of his father became public information.[35]

How did Dr. Douglass train to become a physician? He came to Brandon with his family in 1795 when he was thirteen. He may have been sent to the Addison County Grammar School. Even if he had attended Middlebury, he would not have received any medical instruction there. The nearest available institutional medical education was offered at Dartmouth College, which

---

[28] For an assessment of their literacy, see Chapter 3.

[29] "Autobiographical Sketch," *Letters of SAD*, 57. Frederick C. Waite, *The Story of a Country Medical College: A History of the Clinical School of Medicine and the Vermont Medical College, Woodstock, Vermont, 1827–1856* (Montpelier, VT, 1945), 21–22, finds that in the early nineteenth century it was common for a man who attended only a single session of a medical college to describe himself as a "graduate."

[30] Henry G. Wheeler, *History of Congress – Biographical and Political: Comprising Memoirs of Members of the Congress of the United States, Drawn from Authentic Sources* (New York, 1848), 60; James W. Sheahan, *The Life of Stephen A. Douglas* (New York, 1860), 2.

[31] Contemporary newspaper reports are excerpted in Edward S. Marsh, ed., *Stephen A. Douglas: A Memorial* (Brandon, VT, 1914), 37–39. The original newspaper issues have not been located.

[32] Records of the Trustees of Middlebury College, vol. 1, 1800–1839, in Middlebury College Library, Special Collections. For annual class lists, see annual catalogs at Special Collections.

[33] Marsh, ed., *Stephen A. Douglas*, 40.

[34] Vermont Session Laws, 1797, 36–38; Duane L. Robinson, comp., *General Catalogue of Middlebury College* (Middlebury, VT, 1950), xii–xiii.

[35] Thomas S. Pearson, [ed.], *Catalogue of the Graduates of Middlebury College, Embracing a Biographical Register and Directory* (Windsor, VT, 1853).

appointed a medical professor in 1797.³⁶ Men prepared for a career in medicine in a variety of ways, taking courses at a medical school, visiting hospital wards, acquiring experience in the military, or, most commonly, apprenticing themselves to a practitioner.³⁷ The first medical society in Vermont was organized in Rutland County. In 1802 it laid down requirements before a candidate for membership could be examined. He needed to spend three years "in the study of Physic and Surgery, with a regular Practitioner, unless [he] had a liberal education; in such case two years only shall be required."³⁸ A physician, to be sure, could enhance his prestige if he claimed to be a college graduate, and Dr. Douglass doubtlessly did so, probably by conflating the grammar school with the college.³⁹ Stephen obviously took pride in describing his father as a Middlebury graduate. More important, his mother brought him up with the expectation that he would attend college himself.

During Douglas's last three years in Vermont, his mother's desire for him to go to school was reinforced by a continuing drumbeat in the press for the importance of education. Newspapers extolled the value of good schools, on the one hand, while celebrating famous autodidacts, on the other. Henry Clay was the *Rutland Herald*'s favorite example of a self-taught man who owed little to "early tuition in the schools." His father had died when he was very young, leaving his mother unable to pay for her children's education. But Clay "embraced every opportunity" to make up for the lack of schooling by studying on his own.⁴⁰ By his own account, Douglas's education outside of school took a great leap forward while he was an apprentice in Middlebury during the presidential campaign of 1828. Douglas remembered becoming a supporter of Jackson mainly because Nahum Parker, his employer, was a Whig. He and his fellow apprentices spent evenings and Sundays reading about and discussing politics. Critics claimed that common schools taught reading "in the worst possible manner" by stressing pronunciation rather than understanding.⁴¹ Not until he left the Brandon district school did Douglas develop his "taste for reading, particularly political works." He embodied the ideal republican youth by recognizing the essential nexus between education and citizenship. His engagement with the presidential campaign fired his interest in reading. The fifteen-year-old mechanic-in-training could have been an advertisement for what the founders had envisioned.⁴²

³⁶ Waite, *Story of a Country Medical College*, 15;
³⁷ Marcia S. Blaine, "'Mere Trade' or 'Learned Profession'? Medical Practice in Dover, 1780–1850," *Historical New Hampshire* 64:1 (Summer 2010), 2–26; Thomas N. Bonner, *Becoming a Physician: Medical Education in Britain, France, Germany, and the United States, 1750–1945* (Oxford, 1995), 49–50.
³⁸ EAN, *Vermont Mercury* (Woodstock, VT), Aug. 2, 1802, 2.
³⁹ Waite, *Story of a Country Medical College*, 21.
⁴⁰ *Rutland Herald*, May 6, 1828.
⁴¹ *Rutland Herald*, Nov. 2, 1830.
⁴² On the importance of education to founders of the Republic, see Jeffrey A. Smith, *Franklin and Bache: Envisioning the Enlightened Republic* (New York, 1990); David W. Robson, *Educating Republicans: The College in the Era of the American Revolution, 1750–1800* (Westport, CT,

However inadequate the quality of instruction may have been at the district school, Douglas had mastered reading, penmanship, spelling, and grammar. He preferred becoming a cabinetmaker but, as we have seen, could not hack it because of his physique and wound up returning to school. Fortuitously, in October 1829 a revived academy opened in a new brick schoolhouse at Brandon center.[43] Unlike its predecessor, this academy would admit boys and girls.[44] Stephen was sixteen when he matriculated. When the school began on October 26, Stephen was probably seated, for he kept a copybook in which one of the few dates he recorded was a day in 1829.[45]

There was no standardized curriculum for academies in the 1820s.[46] Incorporation authorized trustees to appoint officers, hire and fire instructors, receive donations, and build schools, but did not touch upon curriculum. The Brandon Academy received statutory incorporation in 1806.[47] This did not guarantee effectiveness. A newspaper notice in 1818 informed the public that the trustees were placing the school "on a more permanent and respectable footing." It still admitted only boys, who could receive instruction in reading, writing, arithmetic, "other English studies," Latin and Greek.[48] A decade later, when Stephen was ready to enter, the Brandon Academy reorganized itself again. Now it was open to boys and girls. We can glean its curriculum from the exercises that Stephen recorded in his copybook: verse, grammar, arithmetic, and penmanship. Significantly, there is no evidence of any classical language. In comparison to what was offered at a female academy in New Hampshire, the Brandon Academy provided Douglas with an intellectually constricted curriculum.[49] Vermont reformers were aware of the limitations of grammar

1988); Melvin Yazawa, *From Colonies to Commonwealth: Familial Ideology and the Beginnings of the American Republic* (Baltimore, 1985); Linda K. Kerber, *Women of the Republic: Intellect and Ideology in Revolutionary America* (Chapel Hill, NC, 1980).

[43] *Vermont Telegraph*, Oct. 29, 1829.

[44] A decade earlier the Brandon Academy targeted only the sons of gentlemen. *Rutland Herald*, June 17, 1818. On the emergence of academies in the rural North, see J. M. Opal, "Exciting Emulation: Academies and the Transformation of the Rural North, 1780s–1820s," *Journal of American History*, 91:2 (Sept. 2004), 445–470.

[45] Stephen A. Douglas Copybook, Special Collections, Abraham Lincoln Presidential Library, 5C415, folder 1.

[46] During the decade, female academies made progress toward "a nationally uniform curriculum," according to Mary Kelley, "Female Academies and Seminaries and Print Culture," in *An Extensive Republic*, ed. Gross and Kelley, 337.

[47] Vermont Session Laws, 1806, 111–113.

[48] *Rutland Herald*, June 17, 1818.

[49] An exceptionally comprehensive range of studies was available at the Adams Female Academy of Derry, New Hampshire, where Mary Lyon, the eventual founder of Mount Holyoke College, was assistant principal. It included reading, grammar, arithmetic, algebra, geometry, geography, U.S. history, history of England, natural philosophy, astronomy, rhetoric, botany, chemistry, natural theology and moral philosophy, biblical studies, Latin, French, and Italian. It scheduled three thirteen-week terms a year and invited parents to visit and listen to recitations "at all times." EAN, *New-Hampshire Patriot* (Concord), Mar. 16, 1829; www.mtholyoke.edu/offices/library/arch/col/msrg/mancol/mso503r.htm.

schools and academies generally; they wanted to adopt the high school model "becoming so popular in other states" and did so at Castleton Academy, which opened a month before the new Brandon Academy.[50]

Educational theorists considered boys at fourteen or fifteen intellectually ready to replace memorization with understanding.[51] The best academy teachers encouraged students "to take no opinion on mere trust ... push your researches farther than these books will carry you ... [and] cherish a due confidence in your own powers."[52] Instruction at Brandon, however, featured the memorization of epigrams, reflected in Douglas's having to write over and over again such lines as "T'is education forms the common mind" and "Judge ye no person lest you be judged." In addition to formal exercises, Stephen's copybook contains scribbling that is suggestive of his state of mind at sixteen and seventeen. Second in frequency only to his own signature was "Brandon," often immediately after his name. The historian C. Vann Woodward once wrote that a strong sense of place distinguished Southerners from other Americans, whose geographical mobility rendered them indifferent or superior "to place, to locality, to environment."[53] As his copybook reveals, Stephen Douglas connected strongly with his town in his late adolescence. He experimented with flourished script in writing his name and Brandon as if they were inseparable. This identification with place was present, then, before he ever left Vermont. Unlike Woodward's Southerners, however, Douglas proved able to disconnect himself from one place and reconnect with another.

This awareness of place would show itself in the way he learned about issues. He was not inclined to rely on abstractions and generalizations; he taught himself the particulars about cases as a lawyer and judge, the particulars about electoral districts when he ran for office, the particulars about countries when he considered international questions. When he ran for the presidency

---

Some believed that women's schools were generally superior, as indicated in a story told about a three-year-old boy whose speech was slow to develop, inducing his fearful parents to place him in a woman's school, where he "succeeded beyond expectations." *Rutland Herald*, June 17, 1828. For an overview of recent scholarship on female academies, see Lucia McMahon, "'Of the Utmost Importance to Our Country': Women, Education, and Society, 1780–1820," *Journal of the Early Republic*, 29:3 (Fall 2009), 475–506.

50 *Rutland Herald*, July 15, 1828; Sept., 8, 1829. For a sample of subjects that academies offered in 1829, see EAN, *Farmer's Cabinet* (Amherst, NH), Jan. 3, 1929; *Republican Star*, Jan. 13, 1829 (Easton, MD); EAN, *Vermont Gazette* (Bennington), Jan. 13, 1829; EAN, *Baltimore Patriot*, Feb. 3, 1929; EAN, *American Mercury* (Hartford, CT), Feb. 10, 1829. For an overview of the curricula at academies, see Kim Toller, "Mapping the Landscape of Higher Schooling, 1727–1850," in *Chartered Schools: Two Hundred Years of Independent Academies in the United States, 1727–1925*, ed. Nancy Beadie and Kim Tolley (New York, 2002), 19–43. Douglas's experience at Brandon Academy accorded with Joseph Kett's indictment of academies as generally providing "superficial" instruction. *The Pursuit of Knowledge Under Difficulties: From Self-Improvement to Adult Education in America, 1750–1990* (Stanford, CA, 1994), 92–94.

51 *PortFolio*, 3rd series, vol. 1 (1813), 569, 576.

52 [Asa D. Smith], *Letters to a Young Student in the First Stage of a Liberal Education* (Boston, 1832), 58–61.

53 C. Vann Woodward, *The Burden of Southern History* (New York, 1960), 22–24.

in 1860, he transcended sectional divisions by learning the individual interests of states in which he campaigned. He thought about America as a union of diverse peoples, shaped by the unique circumstances of their respective states and territories.

Douglas may have become a Jackson man during the campaign of 1828, but when he entered Brandon Academy he drew the face of Thomas Jefferson above a bald eagle on the cover of his copybook. The icon's papers had just been published to wide press coverage.[54] Returning to school after his stay in Middlebury, then, did not abate Stephen's engagement with politics or his receptivity to news. One can imagine J. N. Chipman, his teacher at Brandon Academy, admonishing those who had political ambitions to keep at their spelling and grammar exercises, if they wanted to avoid the derision that newspapers heaped on President Jackson. The *Rutland Herald* reprinted an excerpt of a letter attributed to Jackson and complained that a country where common schooling was universal could have a candidate for chief magistrate who was deficient "even in the elements of orthography and grammar."[55] There was an obverse point to be made as well: don't become too refined and speak above your peers. The same newspaper told the story of a schoolteacher who chided a pupil for speaking poorly and ordered him to go to the back of the room and tell another boy, in grammatical prose, that the teacher wanted to see him. The pupil told his fellow student, "There is a common substantive, of the masculine gender, singular number, nominative case, and in the angry mood, that sits perched upon the eminence at the other end of the room, wishes to articulate a few sentences to you in the present tense."[56] Literacy without affectation was the standard that newspapers propagated for schoolboys and politicians when Douglas first immersed himself in studying politics.

In December 1830 Douglas accompanied his newly remarried mother to Clifton Springs, New York, and immediately enrolled in the Canandaigua Academy, a few miles from the Granger home. He was a student there for two years. The school was on the wide main street of a wealthy village that a traveler described as having everything "to make life desirable."[57] One of the most fashionable houses in town belonged to a famous politician, Francis Granger, a distant relative of Gehazi's, who provided Stephen with a letter of recommendation when he went west.

---

[54] *Memoir, Correspondence, and Miscellanies, from the Papers of Thomas Jefferson,* ed. Thomas Jefferson Randolph, 4 vols. (Charlottesville, VA, 1829–1830). The increase of citations to Jefferson in EAN newspapers between November 1829 (sixteen) and January 1830 (more than two hundred) indicates the impact of the publication of the papers. For examples of the coverage, see EAN, *Vermont Gazette* (Bennington), Jan. 12, 1830; EAN, *Baltimore Patriot,* Dec. 17, 1829; EAN, *Eastern Argus* (Portland, ME), Jan. 1, 1830; *Portsmouth Journal of Literature and Politics* (Portsmouth, NH), Jan. 2, 1830; EAN, *Pittsfield Sun* (Pittsfield, MA), Jan. 28, 1830. Both Democrats and Whigs would claim to be heirs of Jefferson. David Brown, "Jeffersonian Ideology and the Second Party System," *Historian,* 62:1 (Fall 1999), 17–30.

[55] *Rutland Herald,* Mar. 11, 1828.

[56] *Rutland Herald,* Apr. 1, 1828.

[57] EAN, *New-Hampshire Sentinel* (Keene), June 20, 1833.

Anti-Masonry and Anti-Jacksonianism converged as powerful currents during Douglas's two and a half years at Canandaigua.[58] He went to school on the same street where Anti-Masonry began. The town's Masonic Hall was burned down completely while Douglas was at the academy, a few years after William Morgan had been abducted at the Canandaigua jail, igniting the whole Anti-Mason movement.[59] His failure ever to mention the burning of the hall or the Morgan affair may have been due simply to his own sympathies. Just as he remained a stalwart Jacksonian, he also favored Masonry and was accepted as a member of the Springfield, Illinois, lodge in 1840.[60]

That his support for Jackson did not diminish during his late adolescence at Canandaigua testifies further to the lasting hold his experience at fifteen in Vermont had on him. Not only did the crisis become the centerpiece of the various narratives of his youth, but it fixed his political identification for good. His experience at fifteen also established his lifelong intellectual approach to knowledge: he read to advance an argument or solve a problem; he did not read for self-enrichment or self-awareness. In his autobiography he mentioned no literary works from which he drew insight about his personal development. Just as he began his political education at fifteen by studying "political works" in order to support Jackson's cause in Parker's shop, he read almost exclusively materials that could be applied to his various external pursuits as a lawyer, debater, party organizer, judge, legislator, and presidential candidate. He had neither the inclination nor the time to read for its own sake. This suggests that while his time at Canandaigua Academy was influential, it was not as transformative intellectually as his stay at Parker's workshop in Middlebury had been.

Stephen arrived when the academy was experiencing unprecedented growth under Henry Howe, a Middlebury College graduate, who became principal in

---

58 On Anti-Jackson strength in Canandaigua, see EAN, *Portsmouth Journal of Literature and Politics* (Portsmouth, NH), June 14, 1834. See also J. H. Mather and L. P. Brockett, *A Geographical History of the State of New York: Embracing Its History, Government, Physical Features, Climate* ... (Utica, NY, 1848), 92. On the links between Anti-Masonry and Anti-Jacksonianism, see Daniel W. Howe, *What Hath God Wrought: The Transformation of America, 1815–1848* (New York, 2007), 267–270; Sean Wilentz, *The Rise of American Democracy: Jefferson to Lincoln* (New York, 2005), 272–279; Donald J. Ratcliffe, "Antimasonry and Partisanship in Greater New England, 1826–1836," *Journal of the Early Republic* (Summer 1995), 199–239.

59 EAN, *Vermont Gazette* (Bennington), Feb. 14, 1832. Two months later the legislature authorized the town to form a hook and ladder company. New York Session Laws, 55th sess. (1832), 186.

60 *Letters of SAD*, 81. Aside from political considerations, it is hard to imagine Douglas being comfortable with the evangelical impulse running through early Anti-Masonry. The "lukewarm religious devotion" of Masons would have been more congenial to him. Wilentz, *Rise of American Democracy*, 274. On the evangelical association with Anti-Masonry, see Ronald P. Formisano, *For the People: American Populist Movements from the Revolution to the 1850s* (Chapel Hill, NC, 2008), 102–103. The Masons were, of course, a fraternal order, which appealed to Douglas. Steven S. Bullock, *Revolutionary Brotherhood: Freemasonry and the Transformation of the American Social Order, 1730–1840* (Chapel Hill, NC, 1996). On his acceptance by the Springfield lodge, see George F. Milton, *The Eve of the Conflict: Stephen A. Douglas and the Needless War* (New York, 1834; reprinted 1969), 23n.

1828 and recruited nationally, expanding the enrollment from 85 to 212 in four years. The exposure to students from other parts of the country may have contributed to Stephen's interest in going west.[61] The curriculum was more varied and the instruction more effective than what had been available at Brandon, for he studied "the Greek and Latin languages, mathematics, rhetoric, logic, &c., and made considerable improvement."[62] Douglas may have received some training in teaching, afforded to the older boys, because he would have his own students a year after leaving. Douglas later expressed indebtedness to Howe's instruction and advice.[63]

In January 1833, after two years at Canandaigua Academy, Stephen joined the Hubbell brothers' law firm, where for six months he devoted five days to legal and one day to classical studies, in preparation, he wrote, for meeting New York's statutory requirement of seven years in both areas for passing the bar.[64] In fact, under the state constitution, the Supreme Court, not the legislature, promulgated rules for admission to the bar. Since 1797 it required seven years of legal training as clerk to an attorney, toward which a maximum of four years of classical studies after the age of fourteen could count.[65]

Douglas could have claimed two years of classical studies at Canandaigua Academy. On the basis of his copybook, his year at the Brandon Academy should not have qualified because there had not been any classical instruction there. Even if he could have counted it, he would still have had four years of legal training ahead of him, which could be fulfilled through an apprenticeship or attendance at a law school. By combining legal and classical studies at the Hubbell law firm, he no doubt aimed at meeting the requirement in less time. Then, if he aspired to become a counselor, that is, a trial litigator, he would have to spend three additional years as an attorney in New York's graded system.[66]

After six months with the Hubbell firm, Douglas claimed that he was still four years away from admission to the bar. He must not have counted fully his year at the Brandon Academy. He wrote that his mother could not afford to support him through a "regular course of law studies."[67] The cost at a proprietary law school would have ranged between $200 and $350 per year plus

---

[61] *Academician*, Mar. 1916, 14, 30; Pearson, [ed.], *Catalogue of Graduates of Middlebury College*, 48; Albert H. Porter, *Recollections of Canandaigua from 1812 to 1816: Revived in 1876* (1876). On the founding and early funding of Canandaigua Academy, see Nancy Beadie, *Education and the Creation of Capital in the Early American Republic* (New York, 2010), 123–131.

[62] "Autobiographical Sketch," *Letters of SAD*, 58–59.

[63] Stephen A. Douglas (Jacksonville, IL) to Henry Howe, Jan. 14, 1836, *Letters of SAD*, 32–34.

[64] "Autobiographical Sketch," *Letters of SAD*, 59.

[65] The hold of classical studies on American educational policy lasted until the Civil War. Daniel W. Howe, "Classical Education in America," *Wilson Quarterly*, 35:2 (Spring 2011), 31–36.

[66] Frank S. Smith, "Admission to the Bar in New York," *Yale Law Journal*, 16 (1896–1897), 514–522; Alfred Z. Reed, *Training for the Public Profession of the Law* (New York, 1976, reprint of 1921 ed.), 80–83.

[67] "Autobiographical Sketch," *Letters of SAD*, 59.

travel expenses.[68] If he had remained in New York, therefore, he would have had to clerk at a law firm for four more years.[69]

Douglas was unhappy with the prospect of a prolonged period of preparation. Besides, New York was out of step with the movement elsewhere to eliminate guildlike apprenticeships. Where in 1800 fourteen of nineteen jurisdictions imposed a definite period of legal apprenticeship, by 1820 eleven of twenty-four states "prescribed no specific course of study for prospective lawyers."[70] Moreover, New York's graded system, rooted in the English legal hierarchy, was obsolescent, for American lawyers generally were becoming, in Daniel Boorstin's inimitable phrasing, "versatiles" rather than specialists.[71]

Douglas must have known that it would be easier to become a full-fledged legal practitioner in the "great west," although he said he decided in June 1833 to head there "without having any particular destination in view."[72] He may not have known in advance which state he would choose, but he was certain about his profession. He would settle where he could become a lawyer the fastest and where he would not have to compete with the credentials of his legal mentor in Canandaigua, Walter Hubbell, who graduated from Union College.[73]

Douglas learned mainly by himself, pursuing knowledge that was usable. He usually studied in accord with a task. And he was usually restless about the application of his learning. His intellect suited his temperament. Impatient, he had the quickness of mind to assimilate enough information to achieve his goals in less time than others required. This convergence of intelligence and temper conditioned him to be decisive. He did not agonize over his decision to leave home. He did not regret decisions because of a lack of information. Normally he did his homework quickly but adequately and reached informed conclusions. His emergence as a leader in legislative halls and at political meetings would owe much to this swift, versed intelligence. His family remonstrated against his departure in 1833 but could not dissuade him. They relented and even furnished him with $300, "the last of my patrimony."

---

[68] Craig E. Klafter, "The Influence of Vocational Law Schools on the Origin of American Legal Thought, 1779–1829," *American Journal of Legal History*, 37 (1993), 324.

[69] An example of someone with a similar background who stayed in New York and became a lawyer is John Young, who moved with his family from Vermont to Conesus, where he attended the common school and studied classics at home. Not wanting to burden his family, he supported himself by teaching while struggling through a seven-year clerkship before gaining admission to the bar in 1829 at age twenty-seven. He became governor of the state and died at forty-nine. Lucius B. Proctor, *The Bench and Bar of New York* (New York, 1870), 153–173.

[70] Maxwell H. Bloomfield, "Law: The Development of a Profession," in Nathan O. Hatch, ed., *The Professions in American History* (Notre Dame, IN, 1988), 35; Reed, *Training for the Public*, 86; Robert Stevens, *Law School: Legal Education in America from the 1850s to the 1980s* (Chapel Hill, NC, 1983), 7.

[71] Daniel J. Boorstin, *The Americans: The National Experience* (New York, 1965), 33–42.

[72] "Autobiographical Sketch," *Letters of SAD*, 59.

[73] Walter Hubbell, *History of the Hubbell Family, Containing a Genealogical Record* (New York, 1881), 126, 322.

In fact, he received an additional amount from his uncle Beriah a year later, after he settled in Illinois.[74]

Armed with letters of introduction from Canandaigua attorneys, Douglas arrived in Cleveland and immediately met Sherlock Andrews, a "distinguished lawyer" who offered him his office and library in which to undertake one year of legal study that would qualify him for practice in Ohio. Andrews had also graduated from Union College, after which he served a stint as an assistant professor of chemistry at Yale and pursued a year of study at the New Haven Law School, thereby meeting the Ohio requirement.[75] Douglas claimed that he took up Andrews's offer, began his studies "with increased spirit and zeal," and resolved to become a lawyer in Ohio. A life-threatening bout with "bilious fever" in Cleveland, however, derailed his plan.[76] Upon his recovery he decided to leave the state.

He proceeded to St. Louis, where he introduced himself to two prominent attorneys, neither of whom offered him a place to study law: Edward Bates, a former federal district attorney and congressman whose education was obscure, and Josiah Spaulding, a graduate of Yale who had tutored at Columbia while studying for the bar.[77] One has to wonder whether the visible educational credentials of Andrews in Cleveland and Spaulding in St. Louis were intimidating to Douglas, who had attended only academies. If college graduates headed distinguished firms in Cleveland and St. Louis, as in Canandaigua, how far could Douglas advance as a lawyer in these places? He did not admit to these considerations in his 1838 journal, but by then his autodidactic legal education had proved itself in Illinois.

He did hint at his concerns in a December 1833 letter to his brother-in-law Julius when he exclaimed that he now was a "*Western* man."[78] It was in part an acknowledgment of insufficient schooling. The West, Tocqueville observed, was a place where "the demand for the means of education" was "faster than it can be supplied."[79] Humor played on the stereotype about western ignorance. "'I thought the *wise* men came from the east,' said a western man to a Yankee. 'Well,' said the Yankee, 'and the further you go *west* the more you'll think so – I rather guess.'"[80] Political controversies fueled the prejudice, as when a pro-Jackson newspaper in Maine wrote that Henry Clay "made himself popular with the ignorant and narrow minded portion of [the] Western population."[81]

[74] See Chapter 3.
[75] George I. Reed and Charles T. Greve, *Bench and Bar of Ohio: A Compendium of History and Biography*, 2 vols. (Chicago, 1897), 2: 99–101.
[76] See Chapter 3.
[77] W. V. N Bay, *Reminiscences of the Bench and Bar of Missouri* (St. Louis, 1878), 104 (Spalding), 126 (Bates).
[78] Stephen A. Douglas to Julius Granger, Dec. 15, 1833, *Letters of SAD*, 3.
[79] EAN, *Connecticut Courant* (Hartford), Mar. 1, 1831; Alexis De Tocqueville, *Democracy in America*, ed. Phillips Bradley, 2 vols. (New York, 1945), 1: 316.
[80] EAN, *Connecticut Courant* (Hartford), Sept. 25, 1832; EAN, *New-Hampshire Sentinel* (Keene), Oct. 4, 1832.
[81] EAN, *Eastern Argus* (Portland, ME), Oct. 23, 1832.

Clay and Jackson were the most famous "Western men," and both became law-yers without going to college or law school. Indeed, both were known for their lack of schooling. At the time Douglas wrote his letter to Julius, the American folk hero David Crockett publicized himself as "a *plain, blunt Western man*, relying on honesty and the woods, not on learning and the law, for a living."[82] At twenty, Douglas identified himself as a "Western man" when he found a place where his limited schooling was not likely to handicap him.

He traveled from St. Louis to Jacksonville, Illinois, where he met an attor-ney, Murray McConnel, who advised him that obtaining a law "license was a matter of no consequence, that I could practice before a justice of the peace without one, and could get one at any time I desired to do so." McConnel probably was charting the path he had taken himself.[83] He furnished Douglas with a few law books he would most need and recommended that he open up an office about seventy-five miles north, in Pekin, a small town about ten miles south of Peoria. McConnel thought that with a post office established there only a year earlier, Pekin was ripe for an ambitious practitioner without credentials. Douglas wanted to take the shortest route to a law practice and intended to follow McConnel's advice. The unavailability of a steamboat to Pekin before the following spring forestalled him, forcing him to earn a living during the winter by teaching at Winchester, a stopgap he chose only because he "was too proud to beg." Indeed, he was so embarrassed by having to teach that when he wrote Julius from Winchester in December he did not state what he was doing there. He said only that he was living cheaply, doing "business enough" to meet his expenses and pursue his legal studies until spring, when he planned to "accompany the Circuit Court."[84]

In his attitude toward his makeshift occupation, he was similar to teach-ers about whom Vermont reformers had complained and who taught him at Brandon. Yet only two weeks into his teaching gig, he could tell Julius that although he had not yet selected a permanent residence, Illinois was a wonder-ful place and he was now a "Western man." Douglas was so pleased because he found he was smart enough to satisfy both students and their parents while he concentrated on learning enough law to prepare for his own practice. Part of his preparation was gaining acceptance at the Winchester "Justices Court" on Saturdays as a lawyer, "a sad commentary, perhaps," writes Robert Johannsen, "on the state of the legal profession on this central Illinois frontier."[85]

Douglas's path to becoming a lawyer had implications for how he approached legal issues. "The chief weakness of law-office education," accord-ing to two scholars, was "its failure to teach law as a coherent system – or, as

---

[82] EAN, *Baltimore Patriot*, Jan. 1, 1834.

[83] McConnel's education is not revealed in accounts of him. John M. Palmer, ed., *The Bench and Bar of Illinois: Historical and Reminiscent*, 2 vols. (Chicago, 1899), 2: 1102; Evert A. Duyckinck and George L. Duyckinck, *Cyclopedia of American Literature: Embracing Personal and Critical Notices of Authors*, 2 vols. (New York, 1856), 2: 719.

[84] Stephen A. Douglas to Julius N. Granger, Dec. 15, 1833, *Letters of SAD*, 2.

[85] Johannsen, *SAD*, 20; Wheeler, *History of Congress*, 1: 65.

contemporaries liked to say, as a science."[86] Instead of instructing apprentices in general principles of criminal, civil, or constitutional law, mentoring attorneys would show them how to fill out and file forms or how to look up laws, or would encourage them to learn by imitation and osmosis. It was a haphazard method that had one principal consequence: it taught the importance of mastering local ways.[87] Following the circuit court was another form of apprenticeship, as it enabled Douglas to study firsthand how local lawyers and judges litigated and how local citizens viewed attorneys.

Douglas also had time that winter, he remembered, to read both congressional debates reported in newspapers and a number of political books. By the winter of 1833–1834, before he turned twenty-one, Douglas's self-instruction about American politics and constitutionalism, which had begun in Middlebury when he was fifteen, resulted in his having read "with great care and interest" the debates at the Philadelphia Convention; Jonathan Elliot's volumes on the ratification debates in the states; *The Federalist*; John Adams's three volumes, *A Defence of the Constitutions of Government of the United States of America*; Thomas Jefferson's papers; and *The Legislative and Documentary History of the Bank of the United States* (1832), especially the opinions of Randolph, Hamilton, and Jefferson on the bank.[88] What is revelatory about this reading list is that it wholly comprised primary sources. Before he was old enough to vote, Douglas had immersed himself in all of the available printed records surrounding the ratification of the Constitution and the constitutionality of the national bank, the great issue of Jackson's second term.

The value of learning for Douglas came from its usage, and he had an opportunity to display his erudition on American constitutionalism at the lyceum that was organized at Winchester that winter.[89] One evening a prominent Jacksonville attorney criticized Jackson's assault on the national bank. Douglas defended the president well enough to gain "some little reputation as a public speaker." If he could hold his own against "a lawyer of some distinction from Jacksonville," he did not have to settle for Pekin.[90] His course of self-instruction and forensic skill would enable him to compete with Illinois lawyers in the seat of Morgan County. When he completed his term at the Winchester school on March 1, he determined to return to Jacksonville and start his practice. He was especially fortunate to avoid Pekin, where the following summer cholera took nine lives.[91]

---

[86] Hugh C. Magill and R. Kent Newmyer, "Legal Education and Legal Thought, 1790–1920," in *The Cambridge History of Law in America*, vol. 2: *The Long Nineteenth-Century (1789–1920)*, ed. Michael Grossberg and Christopher Tomlins (New York, 2008), 39.

[87] Ibid.; Alfred S. Konefsky, "The Legal Profession: From the Revolution to the Civil War," in ibid., 79.

[88] *Letters of SAD*, 62.

[89] Johannsen, *SAD*, 20.

[90] *Letters of SAD*, 63.

[91] EAN, *Salem Gazette* (Salem, MA), Aug. 5, 1834.

Upon moving to Jacksonville, he immediately applied to be examined for a lawyer's license by a forty-four-year-old justice on the Illinois Supreme Court, Samuel Lockwood, whose background may have predisposed him in favor of Douglas. Lockwood's father had died when he was ten; his mother remarried, leaving him in Waterford, New York, with an uncle, a lawyer with whom he studied until he obtained his license and opened his own office at the age of twenty-one some 250 miles west in Batavia, New York.[92] A college-educated examiner or one who had struggled more with the seven-year rule in New York might not have been as lenient. Although Lockwood thought Douglas was not as prepared as he should have been, and the Illinois Supreme Court's rule required examination by two judges, he licensed him.[93] Douglas would misinform Henry Wheeler that "judges of the Supreme Court" had examined him.[94] Lockwood's advice that the new lawyer should study more diligently in the future was unnecessary. Douglas usually learned enough to achieve his goal. The looseness of the state's bar admission procedures and enforcement vindicated his decision to go west and proved his course of preparation to have been adequate.[95]

[92] William Coffin, *The Life and Times of Hon. Samuel D. Lockwood* (Chicago, 1889), 13–14.
[93] The Supreme Court had only four judges at the time. Sheahan, *Life of Douglas*, 10.
[94] Wheeler, *History of Congress*, 1: 65.
[95] Thomas Goebel, "Professionalization and State Building: The State and the Professions in Illinois, 1870–1920," *Social Science History*, 18:2 (1994), 309–337; Robert Sprecher, "Admission to Practice in Illinois," *Illinois Law Review*, 46 (1952), 811–850; Johannsen, *SAD*, 21–22.

3

Family Influences, Stress, and Bonds

> All of us were very much disappointed when we found you could not visit us grandma probably felt worse than the others.
>
> Adelaide Granger to Stephen Douglas (1856)[1]

The influence of family on individual maturation is limited. Even the most highly informed and involved parents recognize that they can control only so much of their children's trajectory. Environment (e.g., peers, schools, media, churches) and genes count as well. Biological factors are beyond the range of biography. We can reconstruct only familial and environmental conditions, but in postulating connections between these influences and Douglas's development we should be as cautious as parents must be in predicting the future of their offspring.

The two women in Stephen's family of origin were always allied in regard to him. His mother, Sarah "Sally" Douglass, was the formative influence in his upbringing. Her namesake daughter reinforced her authority. Stephen appears never to have had an independent relationship with his sister. Closely bound to her mother, who married her father-in-law within the same year of her wedding, daughter Sarah either spoke for Sally or communicated to Stephen through her husband, Julius Granger. Birth order researchers have long found that oldest children often assume parental roles with younger siblings, repeating maternal (or paternal) prescriptions.[2] In later years, Sarah was Sally's surrogate with Stephen, which only reaffirmed his mother's continuing importance to him.

---

[1] Adelaide Granger, Manchester Centre, NY, to Stephen A. Douglas, May 24, 1856. SAD Papers, series II, 41:5.

[2] The thesis that the oldest child mimics the role of the mother or father with younger siblings originated with Alfred Adler and has been a truism of birth order theory and investigations. Heinz L. Ansbacher and Rowena R. Ansbacher, eds., *The Individual Psychology of Alfred Adler: A Systematic Presentation of Selections from His Writings* (New York, 1956), 378; Brian Sutton-Smith and B. G. Rosenberg, *The Sibling* (New York, 1970), 7, 99–100, 146–147; Ezra Stotland, Stanley Sherman, and Kelly G. Shaver, *Empathy and Birth Order: Some Experimental Explorations* (Lincoln, NE, 1971), 50. Two overviews of the literature are Cecile Ernst and Jules

Although no one in his Vermont or New York families had a psychological significance for him comparable to his mother's, the influence of men in the Douglass and Granger families should also be examined for the light it can shed on Stephen's political ambitions and associations. What we can glean about his relationships with his uncle, paternal grandfather, brother-in-law, and stepfather contributes to an understanding of why he gravitated to politics and, perhaps more tellingly, why he bonded with the male political community.

The most visible male figure in Douglas's childhood was Edward Fisk. Henry Wheeler claimed that Fisk "adopted" his niece and nephew, but that reflected the avuncular attitude of a bachelor uncle before he wed and had a "family of his own."[3] When Stephen decided to leave home, his uncle could not legally block him. Only a father was entitled to his son's labor until he reached twenty-one.[4] Stephen, as we have seen, cut his ties to the Fisks when he left Vermont. The most discernible influence that his uncle had was to push him away from farmwork, the focal point of their confrontation. After he left home the first time, Stephen never did farmwork again. While his recollection of his uncle softened by the time he informed Wheeler of his youth, he did not reconnect with his Fisk uncle or cousins.

The man who might have stepped in after his father's death in 1813 was his paternal grandfather, Benajah Douglass, who lived in Brandon until he died the year before Sally, Sarah, and Stephen moved to New York. His role in his grandson's life is elusive, however, because Stephen did not write about him in his autobiography and did not discuss him enough even to have Wheeler identify him by name.[5] Stephen's middle name came from this grandmother, Martha "Patty" Arnold, who married Benajah Douglass before 1782, the year in which their first child, Stephen's father, was born. They lived in Stephentown, New York, near Pittsfield, Massachusetts, before moving in 1795 to Brandon, where Benajah became a man of note.[6] He was a founder of the Methodist Church, a justice of the peace, and a state legislator for five terms, the obvious role model

---

Angst, *Birth Order: Its Influence on Personality* (New York, 1983), and Frank Sulloway, *Born to Rebel: Birth Order, Family Dynamics, and Creative Lives* (New York, 1996). Sulloway takes a more positive view of the field than Ernst and Angst, whom he critiques (71–75). Annette Atkins, *We Grew Up Together: Brothers and Sisters in Nineteenth-Century America* (Urbana, IL, 2001), focuses on birth order in examining ten families from 1850 to 1920.

[3] Henry G. Wheeler, *History of Congress – Biographical and Political: Comprising Memoirs of Members of the Congress of the United States, Drawn from Authentic Sources* (New York, 1848), 60.

[4] As Daniel S. Smith has observed, the common law recognized patriarchal authority only in dyadic relationships, such as between master and servant, parents and children, guardians and wards. There was, however, no recognition of the uncle–nephew coupling. "The Meanings of Family and Household: Change and Continuity in the Mirror of the American Census," *Population and Development Review*, 18:3 (Sept. 1992), 431. On patriarchal control of children's labor until they were twenty-one, see Holly Brewer, *By Birth or Consent: Children, Law, and the Anglo-American Revolution in Authority* (Chapel Hill, NC, 2005), 262–263.

[5] "Autobiographical Sketch," *Letters of SAD*, 57; Wheeler, *History of Congress*, 60.

[6] Stephentown genealogy at www.lib.uchicago.edu/e/spcl/douglas.html.

for his grandson's earliest ambitions, although Stephen never acknowledged him as such.[7] Patty died in April 1818, and Benajah remarried the following January.[8] His second marriage lasted until his death at the age of sixty-eight in 1829.[9] He was sufficiently involved with his grandson to arrange for him to live with his stepson, Nahum Parker, in Middlebury in 1828, an example of familial support that Stephen preferred to forget in reconstructing his youth. Stephen may also have been disappointed with the legacy he received from his grandfather, whose estate was inventoried in December 1829 at $2,643. Benajah's widow, however, declared that the estate was "insolvent," therefore forcing the probate court to set up a commission for examining the claims of creditors.[10] The commission's notice was printed in bold type on the front page of several issues of the Brandon newspaper, no doubt much to the embarrassment of the grandson, who had to face schoolmates daily at the town's academy.[11] Not until he moved to New York did he receive part of his "patrimony," when his uncle, Beriah Douglass, wrote that after paying $100 to cancel debts against the estate, he could afford to send Stephen only $175.[12] Two years later, after Stephen settled in Illinois, his brother-in-law Julius would negotiate a final payment from Beriah on his behalf.[13] Stephen did not write about his grandfather again, although a Vermont kinsman would one day ask him to assure the U.S. Pensions Department that "Widow Harris and Widow Douglass is one and the same."[14]

In 1830, when his mother married Gehazi Granger, the father-in-law of her recently married daughter, Stephen went to live with the two couples in

---

[7] Abby M. Hemenway, ed., *The Vermont Historical Gazetteer*, 5 vols. (Burlington, VT, 1868–1891), 3: 416–417; EAN, *Green Mountain Patriot* (Peacham, VT), Nov. 5, 1800; EAN, *Weekly Wanderer* (Randolph, VT), Oct. 29, 1804; EAN, *Middlebury Mercury* (Middlebury, VT), Apr. 17, 1805; *Rutland Herald*, Dec. 5, 1807, Aug. 1, 1810; EAN, *The Washingtonian*, Nov. 29, 1813; *Brandon Vermont: A History of the Town, 1761–1961* (Brandon, VT, 1962), 17–18.

[8] Martha Douglass's date of death is inscribed on her gravestone in the Brandon cemetery. I am grateful to Blaine Cliver for a photograph of it. For the date of Benajah Douglass's marriage to Sarah Harris, see Brandon Record Book, 13: 51–52.

[9] *Vermont Chronicle* (Bellow Falls), Oct. 9, 1829.

[10] Benajah left no will. Benajah's widow, the sole administrator, was awarded one-third of the realty, charges for taking care of the house, and money she held at the time of her marriage. For the estate inventory, appointment of the commission, and charges, see Rutland District Probate Court Records, vol. 13, Dec. 1829 (Ref. 21318), 488; and Public Records Division, Middlesex, Vermont, Rutland Probate Court, Estate of Benajah Douglass, July 2, 1831, file 832.

[11] *Vermont Telegraph*, Dec. 15, 22, and 29, 1829.

[12] Beriah Douglass to Stephen Douglass, June 10, 1832, Letters Not Published, Robert W. Johannsen Papers, Illinois Historical Survey, University of Illinois, Urbana. Beriah, seven years younger than his oldest brother, Stephen, also became a physician. *Letters of SAD*, 5; Stephentown genealogy at www.lib.uchicago.edu/e/spcl/douglas.html.

[13] Stephen A. Douglas to Julius N. Granger, Mar. 11 and June 13, 1834, *Letters of SAD*, 5 and 7.

[14] Nathaniel Harris to Stephen A. Douglas, Middlebury, Apr. 3, 1857, SAD Papers, series I, 5:6. Sarah Harris Douglass, the widow of Lebbeus Harris (1764–1814), married Benajah Douglass and died in 1850 at the age of seventy-four. Nathaniel was a son from her first marriage and therefore Stephen's step-uncle. www.familysearch.org. I am grateful to Blaine Cliver for photographs of the headstones of Lebbeus Harris and his widow.

the same house in Clifton Springs, a village in the town of Manchester, next to Canandaigua, New York, the county seat.[15] As we have seen, his home in Vermont exemplified the differences between a family and a household, for the head of his family was his mother; the head of the household was his uncle. In New York, a similar structure obtained. His mother retained moral authority over him, while Gehazi legally presided over the household. Under common law, a stepfather did not stand in loco parentis for minor stepchildren unless he voluntarily assumed the responsibilities and obligations.[16] Stephen was seventeen when his mother remarried, and Sally certainly did not cede her place to her new husband. Gehazi Granger had no more authority over Stephen than did Edward Fisk, but it is evident that Stephen had more affection for him than for his uncle.

The new family that his sister and mother established in New York enabled Stephen to forge one of the closest relationships of his life. The bond with his brother-in-law Julius Granger endured until he died. When Stephen left their Clifton Springs home in 1833 to go west, the person to whom he wrote continuously through his settlement in Illinois was Julius. Before he began his journal in 1838, he recorded his progress in some fifteen letters to his brother-in-law. These letters, written after Douglas settled in Illinois, provide a contemporaneous record of his relationship with his New York family. Their existence testifies to the strength of Stephen's feelings for Julius and the family in New York, because the postal rate deterred personal letter writing.[17]

Stephen communicated with his sister and mother indirectly through his correspondence with his brother-in-law. Although female literacy was widespread in New England by the end of the eighteenth century and scholars have concluded that "virtually all women born around 1810 were literate," the evidence indicates that neither Sally nor Sarah could do more than write her name.[18] Not

[15] By not remarrying until she was forty-one, Sarah reduced the likelihood of having more children. On the deliberate strategy of white American mothers to limit fertility, see Susan E. Klepp, *Revolutionary Conceptions: Women, Fertility, and Family Limitation in America, 1760–1820* (Chapel Hill, NC, 2009).

[16] "Parent and Child: Liability of Stepfather. Support of Child. White v. McDowell. 132 Pac. Rep. (Wash.), 734." *Yale Law Journal*, 23:1 (Nov. 1913), 100–101.

[17] Richard R. John, "Expanding the Realm of Communications," in *An Extensive Republic: Print, Culture, and Society in the New Nation, 1790–1840*, ed. Robert A. Gross and Mary Kelley (Chapel Hill, NC, 2010), 215. C. Dallett Hemphill, "Siblings for Keeps in Early America," *Early American Studies: An Interdisciplinary Journal*, 9:1 (Winter 2011), 3–31, notes the role of siblings in maintaining ties. Douglas and his brother-in-law provide an example of the role played by the spouses of siblings.

[18] Joel Perlmann and Dennis Shirley, "When Did New England Women Acquire Literacy?" *William and Mary Quarterly*, 3rd ser., 48:1 (Jan. 1991), 50–67, esp. 52. For the expansion of female instruction and reading after the American Revolution, see also Joel Perlmann, Silvana R. Siddall, and Keith Whitescarver, "Literacy, Schooling, and Teaching Among New England Women, 1730–1820," *History of Education Quarterly*, 37:2 (Summer 1997), 117–139; Lucia McMahon, " 'Of the Utmost Importance to Our Country': Women, Education, and Society, 1780–1820," *Journal of the Early Republic*, 29:3 (Fall 2009), 475–506; Mary Kelley, *Learning to Stand and Speak: Women, Education, and Public Life in America's Republic* (Chapel Hill,

a single letter from Stephen to his mother or sister has been uncovered; conversely, there is none from either Sally or Sarah to him. There is only a telegram that Sarah sent to him in August 1860.[19] Moreover, in a September 1834 letter to his brother-in-law, Stephen said that he did not expect either his mother or sister to write but did think that they could prevail upon either Gehazi or Julius to compose a letter on their behalf.[20] Nevertheless, both Sally and Sarah Granger claimed that they could read and write when the census takers came in 1850 and 1860.[21] And Sarah became postmistress of Clifton Springs after her brother died.[22] It is possible that either or both eventually overcame the deficits to which Stephen's correspondence pointed. It is also possible that either could read and sign her name but remain unable to write a letter. As students of early American literacy note, there was a "crucial difference" between the abilities to read and to write.[23] The cases of Douglas's sister and mother also suggest that there was a crucial difference between the abilities to sign one's name and to compose sentences.[24]

What can we infer about his time with the Grangers in Clifton Springs? He lived there from age seventeen to twenty. In his autobiographical sketch he allocated fewer words to his thirty-two months in Clifton Springs than to the first four months after he left in June 1833. What stood out for him at twenty-five about his late-adolescent stay in New York was his studies, both at the Canandaigua Academy and in a Canandaigua law office, as well as his "straightened pecuniary circumstances" because his mother could not afford the four additional years of education that he needed to practice law in that state. He did not intimate any disappointment with the lack of financial support from his stepfather. And in her 1860 interview his sister insisted, "Ambition, far more than necessity, led him to push on to Illinois."[25]

On June 24, 1833, Douglas headed west "without having any particular place of destination in view." He stayed his first night in Buffalo, spent a few days touring battlegrounds and Niagara Falls, and returned to the city to take a steamboat to Cleveland, where in "a very few days" he became bedridden

NC, 2006); Margaret A. Nash, *Women's Education in the United States, 1780–1840* (New York, 2005); William J. Gilmore, *Reading Becomes a Necessity of Life: Material and Cultural Life in Rural New England, 1780–1835* (Knoxville, TN, 1989); and Linda K. Kerber, *Women of the Republic: Intellect and Ideology in Revolutionary America* (Chapel Hill, NC, 1980).

[19] Sarah Granger to Stephen A. Douglas, Aug. 8, 1860, SAD Papers, series II, box 41, file 11. The telegram is in the hand of the telegraph clerk.

[20] *Letters of SAD*, 9.

[21] United States Census, Seventh Census, 1850, National Archives and Records Administration, Waltham, MA, reel 572, p. 322; Eighth Census, 1860, reel 831, p. 418.

[22] "About the Little Giant," *New York Times*, Oct. 27, 1895.

[23] Perlmann, Siddall, and Whitescarver, "Literacy, Schooling, and Teaching among New England Women," 120.

[24] By 1800 nine of ten adults in New England could write their names on legal documents. Robert A. Gross, "Reading for an Extensive Republic," in *An Extensive Republic*, ed. Gross and Kelley, 524.

[25] "A Visit to the Mother of Stephen A. Douglas," USN, *New York Herald*, July 14, 1860.

with bilious fever. That the illness was harrowing is indicated by his preoccupation with it five years later. The experience affected his feelings about family, friends, and strangers. Although doctors had advised him to prepare for his "final dissolution," he recalled a strange equanimity, when he felt that he "was on the dividing line between this world and the next," with no control over his condition. He "enjoyed more peace and contentment of mind, more perfect freedom from all care and trouble, except occasional bodily pain, and more negative happiness than during any other similar period of my life."[26]

His memory of the event five years later differed from what he had written in letters at the time regarding the progression of his illness, its duration, and the people around him. The extended equipoise that he fixed on in his autobiography was only an intermittent stage in the course of the "inflamitory [*sic*] bilious fever" with which he was diagnosed.[27] His memory muted the suffering that he had acknowledged when writing his brother of his "rheumatism."[28] That he recalled less pain than he had actually experienced may explain why he remained incautious regarding his health. His rheumatism became a chronic condition that produced recurring indispositions and ultimately was diagnosed as the cause of his death.[29] Yet what he remembered most about his original

[26] "Autobiographical Sketch," *Letters of SAD*, 59–60. Contemporaries associated "negative happiness" with calm after an episode of "dreadful excitement" or simply with sleep. EAN, *Salem Gazette* (Salem, MA), Aug. 25, 1835; *The Day* (Danbury, CT), May 19, 1812. *The Young Man's Own Book: A Manual of Politeness, Intellectual Improvement, and Moral Deportment* (Philadelphia, 1833), 304, used it to mean the absence of desire and of pain – a characteristic of savages, not civilized men.

[27] Stephen A. Douglas (Cleveland) to Julius N. Granger, Sept. 20, 1833, *Letters of SAD*, 1. "Bilious fever" was a generic term for several disorders involving fever and liver dysfunction. The following description was generally accepted: "When a continual, remitting, or intermitting fever is accompanied with a frequent or copious evacuation of bile, either by vomit or stool, the fever is denominated bilious." William Buchan, *Domestic Medicine: Or, A Treatise on the Prevention and Cure of Diseases by Regimen and simple Medicines* (London, 1798), 247. For an effort to distinguish it from typhoid fever, see Elisha Bartlett, *The History, Diagnosis, and Treatment of Typhoid and of Typhoid Fever; With an Essay on the Diagnosis of Bilious Remittent and Yellow Fever* (Boston, 1842), 101–102. For the course that bilious fever usually took, see Daniel Drake, *A Systematic Treatise, Historical, Etiological and Practical, on the Principal Diseases of the Interior Valley of North America* (Philadelphia, 1854), 55–56; Joseph P. Logan and W. F. Westmoreland, eds., *Atlanta Medical and Surgical Journal*, 2 (Atlanta, 1857), 96.

[28] "Rheumatism" was an umbrella term that physicians commonly applied to cases involving inflammation of the joints. If Douglas did have rheumatic fever, it may well have weakened his heart and contributed to his recurring indispositions and premature death. Peter C. English finds no reference to heart involvement in patients suffering from rheumatism until the eighteenth century (*Rheumatic Fever in Britain and America: A Biological, Epidemiological, and Medical History* [New Brunswick, NJ, 1999], 19–20. I am grateful to Professor English for clarifying the issue in an email to me. For the pain symptomatic of rheumatic fever, see Edward F. Bland, "Rheumatic Fever: The Way It Was," *Circulation* (Dec. 1987), 76:6, 1190–1195. It is very unlikely that Douglas's physician in 1833 examined him with a stethoscope, which was still reported mainly in European usage. For example, EAN, *Rhode Island American* (Providence, RI), Jan. 5, 1830; EAN, *Republican Star* (Easton, MD), Jan. 19, 1830; EAN, *Richmond Enquirer* (Richmond, VA), Aug. 28, 1835.

[29] On his final illness and death, see Chapter 8.

attack were the moments of rapturous calm that he conflated into one lingering stage.

In 1838 he recollected that he had been laid up for four months before he recovered in October.[30] Yet his contemporaneous letters indicate that the duration of his sickness was half that long. On August 6, only about two months before he said he recovered, he described Cleveland prematurely as "the most healthy place I was ever in – Canandaigua not excepted."[31] He became sick a few days after writing this letter, as he noted in his next one to Julius on September 20.[32] Although he experienced a relapse after his September 20 letter, he was disabled for half as long as he remembered five years later.[33]

The people around him during his sickness and those who were absent affected his memory of the experience. He was not as forlorn as he remembered. He recalled being "among entire strangers. During the whole time I never saw a face I had ever seen before." This memory was an exaggeration that derived from a sense of abandonment by his family. Before his illness, he had informed Julius that he planned to leave Cleveland because it was too expensive but that he would stay "until <u>you and father</u> come out in September and then accompany you through some part of your route." From this letter of August 6, 1833, it is evident that before Douglas left home there had been a discussion of the whole family moving west and of Gehazi and Julius going in advance to identify a location and buy a place. "Whether father sells his farm or not, <u>you must both</u> come out in the fall," he implored Julius, "if for no other purpose than to advise me where to establish myself."[34]

Only a few days after sending this letter, Stephen became ill and was not fully recovered by September 20, when he wrote his next letter to Julius, in which he credited his landlady with tending to him so well during his illness that "Mother herself could not have taken better care or exhibited more kindness towards me." He also told Julius that, while he was sick, friends from Canandaigua visited him "almost every day" – testimony that contradicts his autobiographical claim that he saw only strangers.[35] None of his family, however, showed up. Although he did not directly express disappointment over their failure to visit him, he did not write to Julius again for nearly two months, when he acknowledged that his silence must have stirred "great anxiety" among the family for his well-being.[36]

---

[30] "Autobiographical Sketch," *Letters of SAD*, 59, 60.

[31] Stephen A. Douglas (Cleveland) to Julius N. Granger, Aug. 6, 1833, SAD Papers, Addenda, box 7, file 24. The letter is greatly mutilated and is not printed in *Letters of SAD*.

[32] Stephen A. Douglas (Cleveland) to Julius N. Granger, Sept. 20, 1834, *Letters of SAD*, 1.

[33] In 1836 his memory of the episode was already distorted, for he recalled that it lasted from "a few weeks" after his June arrival "until sometime in October." Stephen A. Douglas (Jacksonville, IL) to Henry Howe, Jan. 14, 1836, *Letters of SAD*, 34.

[34] Stephen A. Douglas (Cleveland) to Julius N. Granger, Aug. 6, 1833, SAD Papers, Addenda, box 7, file 24.

[35] Stephen A. Douglas (Cleveland) to Julius N. Granger, Sept. 20, 1834, *Letters of SAD*, 1.

[36] Stephen A. Douglas (Winchester, IL) to Julius N. Granger, Dec. 15, 1833, *Letters of SAD*, 2–3.

This letter of December 15, 1833, to Julius is revealing. After only six weeks in Illinois, the twenty-year-old wholly identified himself with his new state and region: "I have become a Western man have imbibed Western feelings principles and interests and have selected Illinois as the favorite place of my adoption, without any desire of returning to the land of my fathers except as a visitor to see my friends and the improvements that may be made from time to time in the country." Note that he did not say that he would return to visit his family. In September he had mentioned seeing friends from Canandaigua while he lay sick in Cleveland; now he wrote that he would come back only to see "friends and improvements." Illinois was the state that he adopted for himself, unlike Vermont and New York, places his family had chosen for him. His August letter had expressed the expectation that his father and brother would join him in Cleveland and advise him where to settle. They had disappointed him. Their failure to come and his illness proved transformative. After regaining his strength in October, he "became reckless and adventurous, and determined to leave the place." He was now wholly on his own. He had survived a nearly fatal sickness while ministered to by a kind landlady. Friends and strangers had proved more reliable than family during this trial. He could not count on the people who were emotionally closest to him. Their psychological injury, like the spasms of pain, were repressed but continued to affect him.

His December 1833 letter to Julius made only passing mention of his bout with bilious fever but commented at length on the overall disease environment in Illinois. He sought to dispel the eastern perception that Illinois was unhealthy, although he conceded the vulnerability of newcomers to bilious fever and ague in the western states, which he astutely thought would diminish when soil along the banks of waterways was brought under cultivation.[37] Nevertheless, he did not want his family to think there was a problem with his new country; rather, some health risk was to be expected from a journey involving a "change of climate" and "exposure." He closed with the assurance that, in the six weeks he had been in Illinois, he had "never enjoyed better health."

Not until March 1834, after establishing himself in Jacksonville, did he inform Julius that his illness in Cleveland had been nearly "fatal." He explained that he had not been forthcoming about the seriousness of his condition "to prevent that anxiety which I knew it would occasion in the bosom of my friends." Why "friends," not "family"? Friends had visited him in Cleveland during his sickness; his stepfather and stepbrother had failed to make their promised trip there. If he had told them how ill he had been, he might have ended any prospect of their coming. Accordingly, in March, after more than four months of thriving in his adopted state, he could testify to its health-fulness and fully inform his family of what had afflicted him in Ohio. And he could sting them a bit for leaving him on his own by writing that he had wanted to shield his "friends" from anxiety about his well-being. Nevertheless,

---

[37] On the physical environment conducive to the illnesses, see Gerald N. Grob, *The Deadly Truth, A History of Disease in America* (Cambridge, MA, 2002), 128.

he closed this letter by sending his love "to Mother, Sarah, Father and all the rest of the folks."

Just as he had hoped for a visit from his stepfather and stepbrother when he lay ill in Cleveland, he was "particularly anxious" to have them "all move to Illinois."[38] They disappointed him again. Julius did visit in the fall of 1835, but Douglas worried that his brother-in-law would not convey sufficient enthusiasm to induce their father to move the family. Whatever the reason, they did not join him. Thereafter he reconciled himself to their not coming, for he dropped his implorations. Their failure to join him, despite his pleadings, profoundly affected Douglas. The coolness with his mother and sister, later the chill in his first marriage, and the paucity of intimate friendships in adulthood reflected a man who guarded himself from the risks of emotional dependence and disappointment. Not until his second marriage did he thaw out in a personal relationship, except the one with his brother-in-law, the only member of the family to visit him in Illinois.

His letters to Julius are the fullest coeval accounts we have of Douglas's experiences and emotions from his western journey until his congressional candidacy. These letters suggest that Julius served as his alter ego, enabling Stephen to confide in his stepbrother as much as he would his private journal. He expressed his admiration and concern for Julius in letters to their father. After his stepbrother's visit, Stephen wrote to Gehazi that he discovered in "Julius' mind and in the Speeches he has made ... greater intellectual powers than is common for a man of his age" and that he had "sufficient genius and natural powers" to become one of the "brightest ornaments" of the Democratic Party in New York and "one of the first men of the country."[39] Stephen was twenty-two at that moment and Julius was three years older! Projecting his own intellectual precocity and ambition onto Julius testifies to how much he identified with his brother-in-law. When he did not hear from Julius four months after his visit, Stephen wrote to Gehazi of his "great anxiety for the fate of Julius."[40]

The relationship between the two men was not comparable to the kind of "romantic friendship" that Anthony Rotundo has uncovered among young men during the antebellum period.[41] There was not a whisper of eroticism in any of the letters Douglas wrote to Julius. He greeted Julius variously as "My Dear Sir" (six times), "Dear Brother" (five times), "Dear Sir" (once), and "My Dear Brother" (once). Once he addressed a letter to "J. N. Granger and the rest of our folks." He added "& the rest of the folks" to two other letters. Altogether he wrote at least fifteen letters to Julius between 1833 and 1837.[42]

---

[38]   *Letters of SAD*, 7, 19, 22, 23.

[39]   Ibid., 22.

[40]   Ibid., 35.

[41]   E. Anthony Rotundo, *American Manhood: Transformations in Masculinity from the Revolution to the Modern Era* (New York, 1993). For a more detailed discussion of Douglas and male bonding, see Chapter 4.

[42]   In addition to thirteen in *Letters of SAD*, there are letters of Aug. 6. 1833, SAD Papers, Addenda, 7:4 and Jan. 7, 1835, series II, 41:8.

He urged Julius in 1835 to tell his stepfather, mother, and sister that "they must consider my letters to you as directed to them also."[43] He repeated this assertion in several letters, for Julius must have told Douglas that his sister and mother felt left out of his letters home.[44] Not until 1841, however, did Douglas write a letter indicating that he was addressing each member of the family equally: "Dear Brother, Sister, Father & Mother." In the text of the same letter he averred that he missed "the society of a Mother & Sister, a Father & a Brother, the only persons on earth to whom I feel any peculiar attachments." His valedictory inverted the order of his greeting: "your affectionate brother & son." Reading this letter, which abounded with warmth toward the whole family, none of the Granger household could feel neglected. It would be unfair to Douglas to suggest that his ordering was spontaneous rather than calibrated.

Had he used the same greeting in his earlier letters, he would have allayed the sense that he was slighting "the rest of the folks." If he truly wanted his mother and sister to feel included, all he had to do was to reference each in his greeting, as he did in 1841. That he did not do so in any of his earlier letters, despite knowing it was an issue, underscores his ambivalent emotions toward them. He cared deeply about how his mother viewed him. He made sure she was informed about his achievements in Illinois. But he could not express unalloyed affection to her. And he could not write to Julius in the 1830s without tweaking his mother and sister by omitting them from his greeting. When Julius conveyed her reprimand for his failure to write more frequently because of his preoccupation with politics, Douglas acknowledged his negligence but added that his sister, Sarah, must have found some "fascinating employment" in her own right because "I have not received a single line from her before since I have been in Illinois. I will not criminate however for fear that she may recriminate, and that I should find myself no better off than when I began."[45] There was nearly always an edge even in indirect communication with Sarah.

He wanted to return home a success. After he received the Democratic nomination for Congress in 1837, he exulted in the possibility of visiting his mother on his journey to Washington. His unexpected defeat robbed him of his motive for returning to Clifton Springs. Not until 1843, when he won election to the House of Representatives for the first time, did he have an excuse to go home – fully a decade after he had left. His mother later remembered her disappointment at not seeing him for years, until the "day she saw a man coming, and though he had grown and had some of that tired look in the face which the West imprinted on its young men, the woman knew this was her boy. He held in his hand his certificate of election to the lowest house of the National Congress from the district in which he lived in Illinois."[46]

[43] *Letters of SAD*, 14.
[44] Ibid., 12, 14, 23.
[45] Stephen A. Douglas (Springfield, IL) to Julius N. Granger, Dec. 18, 1837, *Letters of SAD*, 50.
[46] "About the Little Giant," *New York Times*, Oct. 27, 1895; James W. Sheahan, *The Life of Stephen A. Douglas* (New York, 1860), 57.

He had only sporadic contact with Vermont relations in later years. George Douglass, a younger brother of his father, wrote him in 1859 after reading Stephen's essay on popular sovereignty, informed him of George's son's death earlier in the year, congratulated Stephen on the birth of his daughter, and assured him that he did not expect a reply because of his nephew's position "before the country."[47] Seven years earlier Julius informed Stephen that he had received a letter from George and that he was doing well.[48] Stephen served in the Twenty-Ninth Congress with Lemuel Arnold, a Vermont cousin who had long lived in Rhode Island. They did get together during Arnold's one term in Washington: a friend of the New England congressman recalled that the three of them spent a pleasant hour together.[49] Some Vermont relations enhanced their own stature by equipping acquaintances with letters of introduction to the famous senator.[50] Others thought they knew him well enough to seek federal appointments for themselves.[51] He was sufficiently interested in his Vermont bloodline to keep a seven-generation Douglass genealogy prepared for him when he was in the U.S. Senate.[52] Yet the letters sent to him over the years by kin from his Vermont family reflect ties that were no less instrumental than those that existed between him and the thousands of acquaintances and strangers who wrote him over his nearly two decades as a national figure. Douglas retained no intimate relationship with anyone from the Douglass, Arnold, or Fisk families, except for his mother and sister.

Although the correspondence between Douglas and his brother-in-law dwindled, the bond between them did not. Julius and Sarah had two sons, who did not survive infancy.[53] Stephen, no doubt reflecting his brother-in-law's pessimism, assumed in 1835 that "there is no probability of him and Sarah's having any body besides themselves to support."[54] After they did have a daughter in 1837, Stephen developed an affection for his niece, Adelaide, whom he sent books and who became the first female member of the family with whom he corresponded. Whereas he never could prod his mother or sister to have Gehazi or Julius write him on their behalf, Adelaide easily served as spokesperson for "Grandma," who "makes me to say that she is very glad you are not going South this season and are going to remain in Chicago because she feels

[47] George Douglass (Albany, NY) to Stephen A. Douglas, Oct. 15, 1859, SAD Papers, Addenda, 6:24.

[48] Julius N. Granger (Manchester, NY) to Stephen A. Douglas, Feb. 1, 1852, SAD Papers, series II, 41:11.

[49] E. H. Hayward to James Arnold (Providence, RI), Apr. 7, 1891, SAD Papers, series II, 42:6.

[50] Charles S. Douglass (New York, NY) to Stephen A. Douglas, Apr. 8, 1852, SAD Papers, series I, 2:13; B. Davenport (Brandon, VT) to Stephen A. Douglas, Dec. 21, 1857, SAD Papers, series I, 7:20.

[51] George Douglass (Albany, NY) to Stephen A. Douglas, June 8, 1857, SAD Papers, series I, 5:17.

[52] Douglas Genealogy, SAD Papers, Addenda, 1:8.

[53] Douglas S. Granger (Nov. 20, 1831 to Jan. 12, 1833), and Stephen D. Granger (Feb. 24, 1835 to Mar. 8, 1835) at www.familysearch.org.

[54] Stephen A. Douglas to Gehazi Granger, Nov. 9, 1835, *Letters of SAD*, 22.

very uneasy when you are travelling."[55] While his sister had chided Stephen for not writing enough twenty years earlier, her daughter was more artful. She wrote, "We were all delighted to hear from you and as it was something unusual for you to write first I thought I ought to answer immediately." She also conveyed the family's disappointment when they learned he could not visit them – "grandma probably felt worse than the others."[56]

Douglas's visits to the Granger home were not regular, especially for someone who traveled indefatigably when campaigning. The twenty-five thousand miles he logged in 1860 were unprecedented. Yet he appears to have stopped in Clifton Springs only en route to other destinations. In 1843 he did so on his first trip to Congress. His next recorded visit was in May 1851 on his return to Illinois. Biographer Robert Johannsen describes this as "a long overdue visit to his mother," but it is likely that he made similar stops at least occasionally while traveling to and from Washington between congressional sessions after 1843.[57] He brought his second wife to the Grangers on a wedding trip to the Finger Lakes region in late 1856, after disappointing his mother earlier that year by failing to make a promised visit. The couple stayed with his family there for a few days again in 1858, and his final visit occurred in September 1860.[58] The irregularity of his visits to his mother became political fodder during his presidential campaign, when he initially tried to mask the purpose of an electioneering trip by stating that his intention was to see her. The press made a joke of Douglas searching for his mother.[59]

Judging by the surviving correspondence, Douglas's relationship with Julius Granger appears to have ebbed when Douglas began a family of his own, but after he suffered a double tragedy early in 1853, the bond between the two brothers strengthened. Douglas's first wife died after delivering a daughter, who also died a few weeks later. Douglas was left with two sons, aged five and two. A friend described him as "more depressed in feeling than I ever saw him before."[60] He wanted to get away and was able to sail to Europe because his brother-in-law and sister came to Washington to care for his younger son, while his older one was sent to their maternal grandmother in North Carolina.[61] He secured for Julius a presidential appointment as recorder of the General Land Office, a post he held under successive Democratic administrations. The appointment must have been doubly satisfying to Julius because it carried a fixed salary of $2,000 and entitled him to be addressed as "Judge,"

---

55 Adelaide Granger (Manchester, NY) to Stephen A. Douglas, Sept. 18, 1850, SAD Papers, series II, 41:11.

56 Adelaide Granger (Manchester, NY) to Stephen A. Douglas, May 24, 1856, SAD Papers, series II, 41:5.

57 Johannsen, *SAD*, 349–350.

58 Ibid., 542, 620, 794.

59 For the press coverage, see Chapter 7.

60 Johannsen, *SAD*, 382.

61 Ibid., 465.

like his patron.[62] Even after he became a senator, Douglas preferred to be called "Judge" and that is how Julius regularly addressed him. Douglas always relished honorifics. Earlier, when Julius was appointed justice of the peace in New York and became entitled to "Esq." after his name, Douglas admitted that "distinctions and titles seem to be the great objects of our aspirations in this world."[63]

In a letter to President Buchanan in 1857, Douglas averred that he had only one relation holding any office in the federal government and that he had not been responsible, because the appointment had come through the influence of New Yorker William L. Marcy, who had been secretary of state when Granger was first appointed. Marcy died two months before Douglas's letter was written and therefore could not deflect the credit.[64] Julius knew better. He knew that while Douglas's rule precluded any interference in behalf of anyone outside his own state, the senator was understood to be his patron.[65] In return, Granger's sense of obligation and commitment to Douglas were well known. An organizer of the Democratic Convention in 1856 told Douglas he wanted Julius to serve as a delegate because he "is more immediately identified with your personal welfare."[66] Before he went to Washington, Granger kept his brother-in-law abreast of relevant political developments in New York; in the capital he supplied Douglas with intelligence gleaned at the Interior Department.[67]

The relationship between the brothers-in-law appears to have had a rough patch over money. In the fall of 1857 Granger carefully crafted a dunning letter to Douglas, who was in Chicago. He opened it with an innocuous description of a Douglas friend's effort to procure a patent at the Land Office. Then came the reason for the letter: "Judge, I wrote you and telegraphed to you some two weeks since inquiring whether you had ever sent me the second dft. of $500.00. I was apprehensive that you had sent it and it had been lost. --- You have never sent me any answer to either communication – I do not understand the cause of your silence."[68] The debt might have resulted from expenses that the Grangers incurred from housekeeping for Douglas in the capital. Whatever the cause, familial monetary obligations can be corrosive, and the next letters from Julius to Stephen had the earmarks of attempted reconciliation. After the *Evening Star* criticized Douglas's reelection as chair of the Senate Committee on Territories,

[62] Ibid., 382; *U.S. Statutes at Large*, 24th Cong., 2nd sess., ch. 33, p. 164; George P. Sanger, ed., *The American Almanac and Repository of Useful Knowledge for the Year 1859* (Boston, 1859), 99; USN, *Daily National Intelligencer* (Washington, DC), June 5, 1861.

[63] Stephen A. Douglas (Springfield, IL) to Julius G. Granger, Dec. 18, 1837, *Letters of SAD*, 50.

[64] Stephen A. Douglas to James Buchanan, Sept. 4, 1857, *Letters of SAD*, 397–398. For Marcy, see *Biographical Directory of the United States Congress, 1774– Present*, http://bioguide.congress.gov/.

[65] Julius N. Granger (Washington, DC) to Stephen A. Douglas, Mar. 16, 1857, SAD Papers, series II, 41:11.

[66] Johannsen, *SAD*, 515.

[67] Julius N. Granger (Manchester, NY) to Stephen A. Douglas, Mar. 5, 1852, and Julius N. Granger (Washington, DC) to Stephen A. Douglas, May 21, 1857, SAD Papers, series II, 41:11.

[68] Julius N. Granger (Washington, DC) to Stephen A. Douglas, Oct. 24, 1857, SAD Papers, series II, 41:11.

Julius sent him the clipping and offered to "whip the scamp" who seemed "anxious for another caning."[69] Next Julius wrote that he had been mistaken about Lecompton but "you were **right!**"[70] Better to remind Douglas about past differences over issues than money.

While feelings between Douglas and Granger might have been strained at times, they did not allow them to affect their children. Julius's nineteen-year-old daughter, Emma, informed him of her "kind reception" and "pleasant visit at Chicago" with her uncle and his second wife in 1858.[71] Adelaide married a Minnesota man who, Julius proudly reported, was a delegate to that state's convention, which wholly supported Douglas. In the same letter, Julius indicated that his son-in-law had just returned to Clifton Springs, where Addie was "terribly ill" and he feared that "she will never be any better."[72] She died three months later in April 1860 at the age of twenty-three.[73] At the time, Douglas's daughter, Ellen, was six months old and sickly. She died in June.[74] The brothers no doubt shared each other's grief.

Julius addressed Douglas's second wife, Adele, as "Sister."[75] The affection he expressed to her was partially the result of her having relieved him and Sarah of their caretaking responsibilities for "Stevie," Douglas's younger son, which they had assumed three years earlier following his mother's death. Whenever he became ill, the Grangers must have felt enormous apprehension. For example, while Douglas was in Chicago dealing with the political fallout from passage of the Kansas–Nebraska Act, Julius thought that "a few lines from home might be agreeable to you." After noting that his own son, Eugene, had been confined for more than two weeks with dysentery to the point that "we thought we should surely lose him," he then described in detail the illness that afflicted his nephew and the steps that he and Sarah were taking. Stevie had been fine until three or four days before, when he "seemed to be very puny & yellow. His bowels are regular, and Sarah gave him some oil yesterday, and today he is better.... We will watch him very closely and if he does not get better in a day or two, I shall call the doctor." The Grangers did not summon a physician for their own son, who was in bed for more than two weeks. Their anxiety over how they were responding to Stevie's condition was much greater.[76] Caring for someone else's child is necessarily more stressful than caring for one's own.

---

[69] Julius N. Granger (Washington, DC) to Stephen A. Douglas, Dec. 29, 1857, SAD Papers, Addenda, 2:6.

[70] Julius N. Granger (Washington, DC) to Stephen A. Douglas, Nov. 12, 1858, SAD Papers, series II, 41:11; bold script his.

[71] Ibid.

[72] Julius N. Granger (Manchester, NY) to Stephen A. Douglas, Jan. 18, 1860, SAD Papers, series II, 41:11.

[73] Death of Adelaide Granger of Manchester, NY, is given as April 12, 1860 at www.familysearch.com.

[74] Johannsen, *SAD*, 713, 767.

[75] Julius N. Granger to Adele C. Douglas, July 10, 1861, SAD Papers, series II, 41:4.

[76] Julius N. Granger (Washington, DC) to Stephen A. Douglas, Nov. 5, 1854, SAD Papers, series II, 41:11.

Stevie issued from Douglas's first marriage. He was a thirty-year-old fresh-man congressman when a colleague from North Carolina introduced him to an eighteen-year-old cousin, the daughter of a wealthy slave-owning planter, Colonel Robert Martin.[77] In September 1846, following the death of her only sibling, Martha Martin became too ill and distraught to write Stephen, let alone see him; therefore, her father wrote him to say that they could not receive any company, "even the most cherished of our acquaintances."[78] In addressing his daughter's suitor, Col. Martin spelled "Douglass" with a double "s," as Stephen and his family had always done. By the following month Stephen dropped the second "s" and consistently spelled his name "Douglas." No explanation for this is known. His courtship of a North Carolina plantation heiress suggests a possible reason. A year earlier, the autobiography of Frederick Douglass had been published.[79] One can imagine that the congressman heard jokes about a putative kinship with the author of the slave narrative. Not only might such humor embarrass him on the campaign trail in Illinois, but it might bring unwanted associations for the Martin family in North Carolina. A new spell-ing of his patronymic would nip the false identification in the bud. It would also produce an orthographical symmetry with his adopted state, a matter that would have appealed to someone who had written repeatedly his name and hometown together in his copybook.[80] The appeal of places spelled like one's name is a phenomenon that has been documented by social psychologists.[81]

Martha Martin added "Douglas" with one "s" to her name when they mar-ried in April 1847.[82] They named their first child, born in January 1849, after her father, who died six months before Robert Martin Douglas appeared. Their second child, Stephen Arnold Douglas, Jr., was born in November 1850. Both were born at their grandmother's plantation. Martha and their sons spent more time in North Carolina than in Washington or Chicago.[83] While we have to be careful about weighting one document too heavily, the only known letter that Martha wrote to her husband reveals a distressed wife, near the end of the first trimester of her second pregnancy, who did not feel well, was uncer-tain as to what she would do with herself over the coming summer, and found that "the very idea of going to the P.[otomac] house makes me sick.... I cant say when I wish to return to Washington, for I have no preference about it at

[77] Johannsen, *SAD*, 207–209.

[78] Robert Martin (Wentworth, NC) to Stephen A. Douglas, Sept. 26, 1846, SAD Papers, series II, 41:12.

[79] Frederick Douglass, *Narrative of the Life of Frederick Douglass, An American Slave, Written by Himself* (Boston, 1845).

[80] Copybook of Stephen A. Douglas, SAD Papers, SC 415, folder 1, Special Collections, Abraham Lincoln Library.

[81] Brett W. Pelham, Matthew C. Mirenberg, and John T. Jones, "Why Susie Sells Seashells by the Seashore: Implicit Egotism and Major Life Decisions," *Journal of Personality and Social Psychology*, 82:4 (2002), 469–487.

[82] "Autobiographical Notes" [Sept.–Oct., 1859], *Letters of SAD*, 473.

[83] Robert practiced law and became a judge in North Carolina, where he lived until his death in 1917. His brother died in 1908. See "Biographical Note," SAD Papers.

all ... & if you should not find it preferably convenient to come here, for me it will not be of the least consequence for I can remain here with my mother until next winter, or even longer. And should it be convenient for you to come for me I am ready to go at any time." Here was a dutiful wife, willing to come to Washington where her husband worked if he wanted to come and fetch her; otherwise, she was content to remain with her mother in North Carolina.

Her dour mood carried to her postscript, wherein she requested Douglas, should he come, to bring a summer hat, "large enough for a child eighteen months old with a very large head. If you get one for an ordinary sized head it will be too small." Young Robert M. Douglas obviously inherited one of his father's most conspicuous features, but Martha lacked the wit or inclination to joke about or even acknowledge the resemblance.[84]

On May 8, 1850, the day on which his wife wrote the letter, Senator Douglas was considering a committee report dealing with the most vexing question of the day, how to deal with slavery in territory acquired as a result of the Mexican War.[85] As chair of the upper chamber's standing Committee on Territories, Douglas was at the center of an issue that preoccupied Congress (and the country) from the opening of the Thirty-First Congress in December 1849 until it adjourned the following September, after passage of the Compromise of 1850. His role in that complex legislation made Douglas famous nationally. His involvement with the issue is examined in Chapter 6. Here what needs to be stressed is his wife's epistolary obliviousness to her husband's political career. Her only allusion to Washington was her abhorrence of their house and her indifference to when she would return or when he would fetch her.

At this time Douglas's priority clearly was political, not familial. After Congress adjourned, he traveled to Chicago to shore up his base in the aftermath of the controversial compromise. His wife's inheritance of a Mississippi plantation fueled charges that he was proslavery.[86] He did not arrive in North Carolina until November, when his wife gave birth to their second son. It is doubtful that he remembered to bring a hat for Robert. It is almost certain that he returned to Washington alone for the start of the second session of Congress in December.[87]

His second marriage was more fulfilling. He had no history of relating easily to women near his age.[88] His sister was only two years older than he, but she aligned herself with their mother and his relationship with her always had a potential sting. Among his peers at Brandon Academy, a boy, not a girl, aroused his romantic feelings.[89] Martha was twelve years younger than he, and their marriage had its strains. At twenty-one, Adele Cutts was twenty-two years

[84] Martha Douglas to Stephen A. Douglas, May 8, 1850, SAD Papers, series II, 41:7.

[85] Johannsen, *SAD*, 285.

[86] See Chapter 9.

[87] For Douglas's travels in the fall of 1850, see Johannsen, *SAD*, 298–303.

[88] His reported romance with Mary Todd, only five years younger than he, is noted but not confirmed by Catherine Clinton, *Mrs. Lincoln: A Life* (New York, 2009), 48–49.

[89] See Chapter 1.

younger than Douglas when they married in late 1856.[90] She was only one year older than his beloved niece Adelaide.[91] Reflecting her mother's background and influence, Adele went to a Catholic academy in Washington, where her father, James Madison Cutts, worked for the Treasury Department. His mother was Dolly Madison's sister, which meant that the former first lady and president, for whom he was named, were Adele's great-aunt and great-uncle.[92]

Before they married, Stephen alternated between the roles of patriarchal mentor, devoted fiancé, and jealous lover in his correspondence with Adele. While he was in the Midwest campaigning for the Democrats and she was with her parents in Washington, he urged her to follow his itinerary with a map and complimented her for keeping an atlas at her elbow when reading American history. He was certain that he would be proud of her proficiency when he returned. He advised her also not to neglect her cookbook: "A perfect Wife must know everything pertaining to her duties in that circle wherein she reigns supreme."[93] When he received letters from her that were caring or affectionate, he admitted how much he yearned for "the Battle" to be over so that he could "rush to the presence of the one I love and lay all my trophies at your feet."[94] She teased him about a suitor but he replied in kind. He claimed to be "interested and amused" by her "charming description" of a male visitor. "You may have no fear that I will get jealous of him for I will manage to pay you off for all such flirtations by my attentions and devotions to the bright eyed girls of the Prairies."[95] Indeed, he let her know that he was not too old to catch the eyes of other young women. He apologized for arousing her jealousy regarding "prairie girls," but assured her that she was wrong to believe that "grown middle aged men may show their gallantry to young ladies with entire impunity and propriety."[96] Later he reported dancing two sets at a ball in Naples, Illinois, but followed this hint of a dalliance with an account of how he met an old friend who asked him to name the couple's newborn daughter, now called "Addie Douglas Greathouse."[97] He could keep her on edge without alienating her.

Adele's religiosity made her a curious choice for Douglas, who, according to his sister, followed his mother in never belonging to a church and, according to friends at the time of the wedding, had no religious preferences, although he had donated land to a Baptist college in Chicago.[98] Adele worried that her

---

[90] Johannsen, *SAD*, 541; USN, *Daily National Intelligencer* (Washington, DC), Nov. 22, 1856.
[91] Adelaide was born Nov. 27, 1836, in Clifton Springs, NY; Adele was born Dec. 27, 1835 in Washington, DC.
[92] Bing G. Spitler, *Hero of the Republic: The Biography of Triple Medal of Honor Winner, James Madison Cutts, Jr.* (Shippensburg, PA, 2001), 4–6.
[93] Stephen A. Douglas to Adele Cutts, Sept. 10, 1856, SAD Papers, Additional Papers, 4:29.
[94] Stephen A. Douglas to Adele Cutts, Sept. 8, 1856, SAD Papers, Additional Papers, 4:29.
[95] Stephen A. Douglas to Adele Cutts, Sept. 21, 1856, SAD Papers, Additional Papers, 4:29.
[96] Stephen A. Douglas to Adele Cutts, Oct. 10, 1856, SAD Papers, Additional Papers, 4:29.
[97] Stephen A. Douglas to Adele Cutts, Oct. 14, 1856, SAD Papers, Additional Papers, 4:29.
[98] "About the Little Giant," *New York Times*, Oct. 27, 1895; "Marriage of Senator Douglas," EAN, *Pittsfield Sun* (Pittsfield, MA), Nov. 27, 1856.

church affiliation would injure him politically, but he professed not to be concerned: "I hold that religion is a matter between each person and his God and that no one else has a right to interfere with them. If the people don't like your religious faith I cannot help it ... [and] leave the consequences to take care of themselves."[99] A Catholic priest solemnized their wedding, and four years later Adele wore a large cross when she sat for a Mathew Brady photograph during the presidential campaign, when she was described as "an earnest, practical Roman Catholic."[100] Douglas certainly knew that his wife's religion would be hurled against him when he ran for president.[101]

Educated, intelligent, elegant, and attractive, she was credited with improving his appearance and softening his rough-hewn manners. Like her great-aunt, Dolly Madison, she turned her home into the social center of the capital, as she hosted afternoon receptions and evening dinners.[102] Her charismatic husband did not suffer when she took center stage. When the Washington correspondent of an Ohio newspaper called upon Douglas for an interview, he found the senator franking copies of a speech to hundreds of people across the country. His wife was addressing envelopes but enthralled the reporter by carrying on a conversation at the same time. "She is truly a very beautiful lady in form and figure, with a countenance expressive not only of intellect and energy, but affection and pure womanly sympathies. She has evidently the mind to investigate and comprehend questions of politics, for some of her remarks exhibited considerable feeling concerning the position of Kansas affairs."[103]

Adele's mother, "the ever young Mrs. Cutts," remained close to her married daughter, even sitting next to her and Stephen at a ball they gave. As a hostess, Adele was observed to possess "no ordinary political abilities, as might be expected of one who was before marriage the belle of this metropolis." While Stephen "appeared to know every one of the thousand" who attended, his wife "had something pleasant to say to almost everyone presented."[104] Since the early days of Washington, balls, soirees, dinners, and receptions had been means by which ambitious wives had been able to strengthen the positions of their husbands, and Adele Douglas, unlike her predecessor, who loathed their home in the capital, provided a showplace that enhanced his stock in the political community. She was much more than a showpiece herself. She was recognized for her political acumen. At their "Lake View House" in Chicago, "she exerted a marked personal influence over the gentlemen congregated there, who as usual, were quite willing to be led by a young, beautiful and brilliant

---

99 Stephen A. Douglas to Adele Cutts, Nov. 2, 1856, SAD Papers, Additional Papers, 4:29.
100 www.npg.si.edu/exh/brady/carte/mrsdoug.htm; EAN, *Farmer's Cabinet* (Amherst, NH), Aug. 1, 1860.
101 See, e.g., "Is Douglas a Catholic?" USN, *Scioto Gazette* (Chillicothe, OH), Aug. 7, 1860.
102 For Dolly Madison as Washington wife, see Catherine Allgor, *Parlor Politics: In Which the Ladies of Washington Help Build a City and a Government* (Charlottesville, VA, 2000), 48–101. See also citations in the Introduction, this volume, note 29.
103 EAN, *Farmer's Cabinet* (Amherst, NH), Jan. 13, 1858.
104 "Mrs. Judge Douglas' Party," EAN, *Farmer's Cabinet* (Amherst, NH), Feb. 16, 1859.

woman.... [S]he is thoroughly initiated into chicanery of political life, and
knows how to touch with a sure and delicate hand its most intricate wires."[105]
After talking to Adele at a dinner in 1860, a Yale-educated lawyer and politician traveling through South Carolina wrote her a long analysis of Stephen's
prospects for gaining the Democratic nomination in Charleston and asked her
to read the letter to her husband.[106]

Her success in Chicago was testimony to her determination, for she did not
like the city at first. "I am trying to like this place but it is very difficult." She
confided to her mother how much she missed "the interesting & very refined
people" of Washington and "how terribly ugly & dirty" she found Chicago. She
did not want to compromise her husband, however, by letting her impression
of his home city become known, and she urged her mother to burn her letters.
She was dutiful, but independent. On her own she went to hear a well-known
abolitionist lecture, apparently unconcerned that the senator's wife would be
seen in the audience.[107]

Stephen adored his wife and wanted her to share his affection for Chicago.
Ironically, where his first wife loathed Washington, Adele preferred it. When
she remained in the capital and he returned to his home city, he relished
reporting that she "would be surprised at the improved condition & appearance of the streets as well as the buildings."[108] When his father-in-law first
visited him in Chicago, Stephen rushed to inform Adele that her father was
pleased with what he had seen to that point and that his view from the
train had taken in Michigan Avenue and Lake Street, which showed "to great
advantage."[109]

Unlike Martha, Adele was Stephen's political partner, hosting events in
Washington that were advantageous to him, representing him with party
leaders in Chicago when he was on the hustings, and accompanying him on
campaigns. And, unlike Lincoln, who fretted about his wife's extravagance,
Douglas enjoyed Adele's elegant ways. When he took her to New York City,
they stayed at the most luxurious hotels, the St. Nicholas and the Fifth Avenue.
They returned to favorite merchants and stores. A dealer who missed the couple at the St. Nicholas expressed disappointment at not being able "to talk
over domestic matters with the judge," but took the liberty of sending Mrs.
Douglas a wine list he offered to fill.[110] Vendors wrote her because she decided
on purchases. She shopped on her own. A glass dealer on Broadway noted her

[105] "The Court Ladies of Washington," EAN, *Farmer's Cabinet* (Amherst, NH), Feb. 23, 1859.
[106] Edwards Pierrepont to Adele Douglas, Feb. 7, 1860, SAD Papers, Additional Papers, 4:28.
I am indebted to Christine Colburn for identifying Pierrepont. For a biographical sketch of
Pierrepont, see http://drs.library.yale.edu:8083/saxon/SaxonServlet?style.
[107] Adele Cutts Douglas to Her Mother, June 24, 1857, *Letters of SAD*, 384–385.
[108] Stephen A. Douglas to Adele Douglas, June 8, 1859, SAD Papers, Additional Papers, 4:31.
[109] Stephen A. Douglas to Adele Douglas, Sept. 11, 1859, SAD Papers, Additional Papers, 4:31.
[110] Isaac Moses to Mrs. Stephen A. Douglas, Dec. 2, 1857, SAD Papers, series II, 41:5. On the St.
Nicholas, see www.nypl.org/research/chss/spe/art/print/exhibits/movingup/labeviii.htm.

interest in a crystal epergne when she "last" visited his store; therefore, he sent her a drawing of it with a price of $500 per pair or $250 each.[111]

How much Douglas shared with Adele about his finances is unclear from his letters, which refer to his property sales and expectations only in a general way.[112] This may reflect the low priority he gave to his business affairs. As systematic and tireless as he was in his mastery of legislative issues, party organization, and campaigning, he placed his finances on the back burner to be attended to after more important political matters were addressed. The only topic more important to him than politics was Adele's welfare.

When Adele was recovering from a miscarriage, Douglas excused himself from engagements in order to be with her.[113] His solicitude toward her was touching. While at the capitol, he dispatched a note stating she was "right in not going today in the rain." He could not leave the Senate at the moment, but as soon as he could he would call on her. "I will make it all right. God bless you my dearest."[114] His postnuptial letters to her had none of the teasing that accompanied his premarital correspondence. He freely expressed his dependence on and yearning for his wife whenever they were apart. He gave her schedules of his tours with locations where he could receive her letters.[115] During his campaign for reelection to the Senate in 1858, he obtained three letters from her at Alton. "They are to me more precious than jewels. They breathe the true devotion of a true wife. My darling you cannot know, you cannot conceive how much joy they imparted."[116] The only time he would reproach her it would be for not writing, but he would do so in the most disarming fashion. During his debates with Lincoln he wrote, "If you knew how anxious I am to hear from you and how sad I am without you I think you would write oftener."[117] Above all, he wanted her to be happy and cheerful and despaired when she was ill or sad or when he did not know how she was. While suffering from a "slight billious [sic] attack" at a hotel in New York City, he received a packet of mail from her but none that she wrote. This disappointed him because he wanted assurance that she was "well and happy."[118] One time, however, he wondered if she "were as lonely and disconsolate as sleepless and nervous without me as I was in consequence of your absence." This was his sentiment after friends in Quincy, Illinois, provided him at midnight with a "charming serenade" that he could not enjoy without her.[119] It is remarkable how much she was on his

[111] C. C. Leigh to Mrs. Stephen A. Douglas, Apr. 8, 1858, SAD Papers, series II, 41: 4.
[112] Stephen A. Douglas to Adele Douglas, June 8 and July 1, 1859, SAD Papers, Additional Papers, 4:31.
[113] *Letters of SAD*, 411–412.
[114] Stephen A. Douglas to Mrs. Stephen A. Douglas, n.d., SAD Papers, series II, 41:9.
[115] See two schedules in SAD Papers, Additional Papers, 4:31.
[116] Stephen A. Douglas to Adele Douglas, Aug. 8, 1858 SAD Papers, Additional Papers, 4:30.
[117] Stephen A. Douglas to Adele Douglas, Oct. 11, 1858, SAD Papers, Additional Papers, 4:30.
[118] Stephen A. Douglas to Adele Douglas, Apr. 29, 1859, SAD Papers, Additional Papers, 4:30.
[119] Stephen A. Douglas to Adele Douglas, Sept. 6, 1857, SAD Papers, Additional Papers, 4:31.

mind when she was not with him, even before they wed. Once while he was preparing to address a crowd of ten thousand in Pittsfield, Illinois, he sat in the courthouse "writing a hasty scrawl" to Adele while listening to a gubernatorial candidate speak. As the man finished, Douglas closed his letter, indicating he had to go into the public square to give his own talk.[120]

With his marriage to Adele, Douglas acquired a father-in-law who lived near enough to oversee his affairs when he was away from the capital. James Madison Cutts drafted and signed letters under his own name in behalf of Douglas; others he wrote as if from the famous man, but without his signature.[121] Cutts also hired clerks to assist with Douglas's correspondence, and he took care of accounts for him.[122] His handling of such matters was particularly valuable during the campaigns of 1858 and 1860, when Douglas had to leave Washington for extended stretches. It was the least Cutts could do for his son-in-law. A longtime clerk in the Treasury Department, Cutts received a promotion from President Buchanan a year after his daughter's marriage, when a widely publicized contretemps ensued because Douglas was accused of sponsoring a relative at the expense of someone from his own state, the normal venue from which patronage beneficiaries were supposed to come. Both the senator and the president strenuously denied that the promotion resulted from Douglas's intervention. In fact, Buchanan appears to have appointed Cutts in order to embarrass Douglas.[123] In 1861 Douglas brought his wife and both her parents to the inaugural ball honoring President Lincoln.[124]

In addition to in-laws whom he liked, Douglas's second marriage brought him a new brother-in-law, J. M. Cutts, Jr., Adele's smart, self-assured younger sibling who was attending Brown.[125] No doubt at Douglas's urging, nineteen-year-old Cutts traveled to Chicago after the wedding in order to explore possibilities for connecting with a legal firm. "Almost any of the lawyers here would be glad to have me," he assured his famous brother-in-law, who must have smiled when he read that. The youth's letter brimmed with a precocious intelligence. He saw the advantages of Douglas's home city, for it had "business enough, crime enough, want enough, wealth enough – to employ five hundred lawyers – & abundant opportunity for fifty great ones." That opportunity was heightened by the quality of the lawyers he saw, for they lacked eminence, talent, and honor. He found that instead of aiding their fellow citizens by securing justice and punishing crime, they viewed their profession "simply as a means of procuring money." Worse, he had not met a single man whose idea of the

[120] Stephen A. Douglas to Adele Cutts, Oct. 14, 1856, SAD Papers, Additional Papers, 4:28.
[121] *Letters of SAD*, 420–422.
[122] Stephen A. Douglas to James M. Cutts, June 22, 1858, *Letters of SAD*, 422; Stephen A. Douglas to James M. Cutts, June 30, 1860, *Letters of SAD*, 496.
[123] *Letters of SAD*, 557–558; George F. Milton, *The Eve of the Conflict: Stephen A. Douglas and the Needless War* (New York, 1834; reprinted 1969), 272.
[124] USN, *New York Herald*, Mar. 10, 1861. See also Chapter 8.
[125] Cutts was born October 20, 1837. On his birth and career at Brown, see Spitler, *Hero of the Republic*, 9.

profession corresponded to his own. "Not one single man whose thoughts I should care to know, or to whom I would tell my own. And this friendly association & sympathy between man & man is the only want I have, the only one which Chicago has not supplied."[126] He was so in need of a "friend and associate," however, that a month later he proposed a "joint plan" with a young man from New England whereby "we are to have a room together" and asked his brother-in-law to aid his new partner.[127]

While Cutts did not find in Chicago a man with whom he could exchange ideas, he openly admired Douglas, whom he studied closely: "I watched the greatness of your mind & followed your thoughts – whenever I knew them." He wanted Douglas "to have reason to be proud of me." Douglas, in turn, advised and encouraged him, expressing confidence that he had a "brilliant future."[128] Cutts became disillusioned with Chicago and entered Harvard Law School. From there he sent Douglas a list of the lectures he attended and wrote that he was "reconsidering" a return to Chicago "to live and labor" near his sister and brother-in-law."[129] He returned to Washington during the summer of 1859, when he spent an hour every evening asking Douglas questions on a variety of subjects and taking notes on his answers. Although he claimed that the conversations were not intended for publication, he turned them into a book in 1866.[130]

Cutts was an affectionate uncle to the Douglas boys, whom he assured would be able to beat him at least "twice out of six times" at chess if they practiced while he was at law school.[131] Douglas was not disingenuous when he claimed that a reason for traveling to New England in 1860 was to attend his brother-in-law's graduation from Harvard. He was genuinely fond of Cutts and knew how much his attendance would mean to him. Cutts began his law practice in St. Louis, but after the Civil War broke out he returned to Washington with a complimentary letter of introduction to President Lincoln from Douglas.[132] During the war, Cutts fought valiantly in the Union cause; afterward he represented his nephews in a claim for losses inflicted by federal troops on their Mississippi plantation.[133]

---

[126] J. M. Cutts, Jr., to Stephen A. Douglas, Jan. 19, 1857, SAD Papers, Addenda, 2:17.

[127] J. M. Cutts, Jr., to Stephen A. Douglas, Feb. 12, 1857, SAD Papers, Addenda, 4:5.

[128] J. M. Cutts, Jr., to Stephen A. Douglas (Providence, RI), Feb. 7, 1858, SAD Papers, series II, 41:2.

[129] J. M. Cutts, Jr. to Stephen A. Douglas (Cambridge. MA), Nov. 30, 1858, SAD Papers, series II, 41:2.

[130] J. Madison Cutts, *A Brief Treatise upon Constitutional and Party Questions, and the History of Political Parties, As I Received It Orally from the Late Senator Stephen A. Douglas of Illinois* (New York, 1866), 5–6.

[131] J. M. Cutts, Jr., to Robert Douglas (Cambridge, MA), Nov. 21, 1859, SAD Papers, series II, 41:2.

[132] Johannsen, *SAD*, 778; Stephen A. Douglas to Abraham Lincoln, Apr. 29, 1861, *Letters of SAD*, 511.

[133] Spitler, *Hero of the Republic*; see also Chapter 9.

Douglas must have seen aspects of his younger self in Cutts. The nineteen-year-old's inability to find a man in Chicago to whom he could be "intimately connected" was reminiscent of Douglas's not making "personal friends" when he settled in Illinois at the age of twenty more than three decades earlier. Cutts, however, blamed his failure on the character of the citizens of western states, who "nearly all at some period of their life emigrated, left their families & their homes – & educated themselves to feel that all things depended upon their individual selves & lived to make every feeling, thought, & act but in the gratification & advancement of self."[134] Douglas, in contrast, had thrived in the company of the young men he met in this western state. While his closest relationship had been with his brother-in-law Julius, whom he had left in New York and whom he had wanted to join him, along with their family, in Illinois, as we will see in the next chapter he almost immediately found a substitute for one-on-one intimacy in the political crowd. Unlike Cutts, Douglas immediately connected with the young men of the West, from whom he drew his own sense of identity.

Young Cutts's hero worship added to Douglas's gains from his second marriage. The beautiful Adele was a loving companion, protective of his health and reputation. He adored her. She reared his sons, bringing them into her faith with his approval. They thought of her as "Mother," her mother as "grand Mother," and young Cutts as "uncle Madison," who together took the boys on outings when Stephen was away.[135] Adele was his political partner, hosting and charming his friends and traveling with him on his arduous presidential campaign. Indeed, without her, he might not have undertaken or endured that pathbreaking ordeal. Compounding the tragedy of his premature death in 1861 was the belated personal happiness that came with his second marriage. His marriage to Martha had lacked this closeness. Her burial in North Carolina was symptomatic of where her heart belonged.[136] His first marriage re-created the tension he had had with his sister and mother. Martha could not compete with his attachment to his political friends. The Illinois political community gave him what he had not received at home in Vermont or New York. By the time he met Martha, his immersion in politics was so deep that only a willing collaborator could become a genuine companion. Martha was not prepared for that role, but Adele would be.

[134] J. M. Cutts, Jr., to Stephen A. Douglas, Jan. 19, 1857, SAD Papers, Addenda, 2:17.
[135] Stephen A. Douglas, Jr., to Stephen A. Douglas, May 8, 1861, SAD Papers, Addenda, 3:11.
[136] See photo of her gravestone in North Carolina at Stephentown genealogy at www.lib.uchicago.edu/e/spcl/douglas.html.

4

Democratic Prodigy in Illinois

> By the inequality of civil and political rights that exists in certain parts of the Union, and the great equality that exists in others, we see the necessity of referring the true character of the institutions to those of the states, without a just understanding of which, it is impossible to obtain any general and accurate ideas of the real polity of the country.
>
> James Fenimore Cooper (1838)[1]

In March 1834 Stephen Douglas passed his bar examination, obtained his license, opened his own law office, and gave a speech that instantly catapulted him to prominence as a Jacksonian partisan in Morgan County. He had scored as a speaker the previous winter in Winchester. Now, on March 29 at the Jacksonville courthouse, his one-hour defense of the president's war on the national bank gained him notoriety from the anti-Jackson press. Before his twenty-first birthday, Douglas was already a man to be reckoned with in the law and politics in Illinois. Within months he became a prodigy of the new Democratic Party of Illinois – a party of young men.

Wanting financially and uncertain about his career and permanent home when he arrived in Illinois only a few months earlier, Douglas could hardly believe what he had achieved, "being less than twenty-one years of age."[2] Opening his law office at twenty remained a source of self-esteem. He noted it in his 1838 journal and brought it to the attention of biographers.[3] What would have taken ten years to attain in the graded legal system of New York he had now accomplished "as an attorney and counsellor at law and Soliciter in chancery under the most favorable auspices."[4]

He was surprised by his own success. Until his string of triumphs in March 1834, he had not been certain even about remaining in Illinois. He delayed

---

[1] J. Fenimore Cooper, *The American Democrat* (New York, 1931; reprint of 1838 ed.), 39.
[2] "Autobiographical Sketch," *Letters of SAD*, 63; Johannsen, SAD, 25.
[3] Ibid.; James W. Sheahan, *The Life of Stephen A. Douglas* (New York, 1860), 16.
[4] Stephen A. Douglas (Jacksonville, IL) to Julius N. Granger, Mar. 11, 1834, *Letters of SAD*, 4.

responding to a January letter from his brother-in-law until he could point to his achievement.[5] Once he tasted success and notoriety, he relished writing letters to Julius.[6] In July he congratulated himself for "having been so fortunate as to have located in the Paradise of the world." He confided to Julius, "I am succeeding here far beyond my expectations, and the prospect before me is fair and flattering."[7]

Fair and flattering, indeed! Until late September 1838 he experienced one political victory after another. In August 1834 three of four candidates he campaigned for won election to the state assembly. During the following winter, he divided his time between his law office in Jacksonville and the capitol in Vandalia, where he and one of the winners collaborated on a bill to transfer the power of appointing state attorneys from the governor to the legislature. Not only did he see the bill enacted, in February 1835 a joint session of the legislature selected him as one of the state's attorneys. He completed two circuits of his eight-county judicial district but did not finish his term. Instead in August 1836 he stood for election to the state legislature and emerged the leading vote getter in Morgan County. Again he did not fulfill his term. After one session in the Illinois legislature (December 1836 to March 1837), he resigned his seat to accept President Van Buren's appointment as register of the Federal Land Office in Springfield.[8] Eight months later one of the first party conventions organized to select a candidate for Congress met in Peoria and nominated Douglas. Whig politicians and editors already recognized him as a major figure in the formation and effectiveness of the Democratic Party in Illinois.[9]

Douglas thought he was about to go to Washington as a congressman when he sat down to write his autobiography on September 1, 1838. The age-conscious twenty-five-year-old felt a need to record and shape a narrative around his meteoric rise. At age twenty, he had been destitute and unsure of his career when he reached Illinois in the fall of 1833. So desperate had his circumstances

---

[5] Stephen A. Douglas (Jacksonville, IL) to Julius N. Granger, Mar. 11, 1834, *Letters of SAD*, 4–5.

[6] The publication of the lives and letters of various founding fathers in the early 1830s might have reinforced the value of letter writing for him. The letters of Gouverneur Morris, George Washington, and John Jay appeared during 1832–1834. William M. Decker, *Epistolary Practices: Letter Writing in America before Telecommunications* (Chapel Hill, NC, 1998), 28. The founders were remembered in book form, and at twenty-five Douglas could not help from imagining himself in their literary company. On the legacy of the founders and the importance of biography, see Richard D. Brown, "The Revolution's Legacy for the History of the Book," in *An Extensive Republic: Print, Culture, and Society in the New Nation, 1790–1840*, ed. Robert A. Gross and Mary Kelley (Chapel Hill, NC, 2010), 58–74, and Scott E. Casper, "Biography," *Extensive Republic*, ed. Gross and Kelley, 458–464. On ambition for young men of Douglas's generation, see George B. Forgie's provocative *Patricide in the House Divided: A Psychological Interpretation of Lincoln and His Age* (New York, 1979), esp. 55–87.

[7] Stephen A. Douglas (Jacksonville, IL) to Julius N. Granger, July 13, 1834, *Letters of SAD*, 8.

[8] There were ten federal land offices in Illinois at that time. Thomas Donaldson, *The Public Domain: Its History, with Statistics* (Washington, DC, 1881), 174.

[9] "Autobiographical Sketch," Sept. 1, 1838, *Letters of SAD*, 64–67; Johannsen, *SAD*, 28–64; Gerald Leonard, *The Invention of Party Politics: Federalism, Popular Sovereignty and Constitutional Development in Jacksonian Illinois* (Chapel Hill, NC, 2002), 138–140.

been that he had been forced to take up teaching to make ends meet during his first winter there. Yet seemingly overnight he became a notable lawyer, dynamic speaker, effective lobbyist, tireless organizer, and ambitious politician. At twenty-one he was a state's attorney, at twenty-three he was Morgan County's most popular choice for state representative, at twenty-four he received a federal patronage plum from the president, and in the same year he became the Democratic Party's candidate for Congress in the Third District.[10]

What explains his phenomenal ascent? The question should be asked for two interrelated reasons. First, we want to know more about Douglas himself. What were the motives and assets that impelled his early success? Second, his precocious rise should tell us something about the politicians and voters who elevated him. Why were they so receptive to him? It is apparent from the outset of his career in Illinois that he possessed a magnetism that inspired people to embrace him as their leader. Some people acquire a special allure as a result of holding a particular office. Douglas, however, acceded to office because he was already charismatic. The key point about charisma, as historian Thomas Brown suggests, is that it does not exist independently of the leader's time and place; rather, it "is ascribed to the leader by his followers."[11] In this case, analyzing what made Douglas so attractive to Illinois during the 1830s deepens our understanding of the early development of Jacksonian democracy.

Douglas emotionally needed the embrace of the political community. Separated from his family and friends in New York, recently recovered from a serious illness, uncertain about his ability to make it in Illinois, he was revived not by intimate relationships but by political gatherings. He remembered that he did not have time for "personal friends," only for "political friends" whose "solicitation" or votes he credited with pushing him ahead.[12] He became a political prodigy in Illinois because of his political friends and "the people" there. He bathed in the adoration of the crowd, which gave him what he did not get from private relationships. He consistently attributed his drive to the people around him. Whether he stood to speak or ran for office, he claimed that he was responding to their entreaties. His connection to voters was affect-laden. A contemporary remembered how Douglas "gave the crowd the color of his own mood as he interpreted their thoughts and directed their sensibilities. His first-hand knowledge of the people, and his power to speak to them in their own language" made him one of the most effective stump speakers the

---

[10] Douglas's age consciousness is at odds with Howard Chudacoff's finding that age blending was the norm before 1850 in the family, the larger community, and cultural values. *How Old Are You? Age Consciousness in American Culture* (Princeton, NJ, 1989). In contrast, Yonatan Eyal, *The Young America Movement and the Transformation of the Democratic Party, 1828–1861* (New York, 2007), 7, suggests that Douglas's cohort of "New Democrats" was "age sensitive" and had a "generational consciousness." They identified with the Young America movement, which had its heyday from 1844 to 1854.

[11] Thomas Brown, "From Old Hickory to Sly Fox: The Routinization of Charisma in the Early Democratic Party," *Journal of the Early Republic*, 11:3 (Fall 1991), 340.

[12] *Letters of SAD*, 63, 65.

observer had ever heard.[13] In saying that he was complying with the demands of others, Douglas was not simply dissembling about his personal ambition; he was also revealing the close the bonds that he had forged with the Illinois political fraternity during his first years there.

Much of his rise has been explained as having been a result of calculation. He is often depicted as an opportunist. Douglas was indeed shrewd. Taking the time at twenty-five to fashion a compelling life narrative itself was evidence of his strategic thinking. But he was also an authentic democrat whose connection to partyists and the electorate was based on feelings that normally buttressed but could transcend instrumental and policy considerations.[14] He undertook the writing of his autobiography in order both to preserve his story and to connect it with the electorate. Those two ends were not inconsistent for someone whose very identity was now so intimately tied to the people he needed.

Why did "political friends" flock to him? In the new democratic society, charisma had two seemingly opposite qualities. On the one hand, the leader had to appear to be similar to a broad portion of the electorate. He had to share their values, goals, and tastes, even dreams. In a self-consciously egalitarian era, he had to show himself to be as ordinary as they were. On the other hand, to lead them he had to be better than they were. He was one of them, but even more so. He could make them feel good about who they were. He could enable them to fulfill who they wanted to be. He could show the way. This is why his life story had to reverberate with them. It had to relate to their experiences so as to validate their disappointments and longings and, through identification, enable them to participate in his resolution of conflicts they knew so well.[15]

There were three components of the common ground between Douglas and the Illinois electorate of the 1830s: their struggle for manhood, their acceptance of bachelorhood, and their feelings about gender. The three issues differentiated the period from previous times. The new democratic ideology called on government to reflect and represent the people more faithfully than had been the case in a more elitist past. Yet the partisan arena remained set apart from the rest of society, but in a new way. Where officeholding once had been the business of elite families, changing attitudes toward manhood, marriage, and masculinity enabled single young men to become prominent players in the rise of party politics, which in turn provided an escape from judgmental women and family life.

Manhood had been an issue for the teenage Douglas. Without a father, brought up by a mother who was closely allied to his older sister, and lacking the size and strength that boys prized, Douglas left home and remembered never being as happy as he was in the shop in Middlebury, where he spent his evenings and Sundays debating politics with his fellow apprentices. They knew

---

[13] William H. Milburn, *Ten Years of Preacher-Life: Chapters from an Autobiography* (New York, 1859), 132.

[14] The term "partyist" is the apt invention of Leonard, *Invention of Party Politics*, passim.

[15] On leadership, see Brian Danoff, "Lincoln and Tocqueville on Democratic Leadership and Self-Interest Properly Understood," *Review of Politics*, 67:4 (2005), 687–719.

they would become freemen in that state at twenty-one. By his own account, apprenticeship fired his political passion and lasting alignment.[16] An apprentice might not be independent economically, but at twenty-one he became a full-fledged voter. Whatever he lacked at home or at work, in the Vermont political sphere he would lack nothing.[17] And so too was it in Illinois, where an impecunious Douglas arrived in 1833. If he decided to stay, he knew that after his next birthday he would be a voter, the status of every white man who resided there for six months.[18]

When Douglas wrote his autobiographical sketch, he knew how well the central conflict of his youth connected with young voters. From Vermont to Illinois, rural boys yearned to leave family farms in order to seek more satisfying work in the growing towns of antebellum America. Under the law, they could not strike out on their own without their father's permission, for he was entitled to their labor until they turned twenty-one. Lincoln exemplified this struggle for independence common to boys who grew up on farms. He chafed at having to stay with his father until he reached his majority. Once he left, he did not come back.[19] Many young men, however, were in what Joseph Kett calls a stage of "semidependency," whereby they left but returned home with their sense of autonomy and manhood in limbo.[20] Douglas had experienced this when he left home at fifteen to take up cabinetmaking, only to return and attend school as his mother wanted. At twenty, however, he left for good and by the eve of his twenty-first birthday had established himself as a lawyer and an up-and-coming political figure. He was a thousand miles from home and wholly self-supporting. He even had a law practice without reliance on a senior partner. On April 23, 1834, by his own light, he was fully a man. He was proud of his uncommon achievement. Those of his peers who had traveled to Illinois with their families, not by themselves, could only look up to him.[21]

---

[16] The role of apprenticeship in political socialization that Douglas experienced is usually passed over. See, for example, the otherwise helpful gender study by Ava Baron, "Acquiring Manly Competence: The Demise of Apprenticeship and the Remasculinization of Printer' Work," in *Meaning for Manhood: Construction of Masculinity in Victorian America*, ed. Mark C. Carnes and Clyde Griffen (Chicago, 1990), 152–163.

[17] Mary Beth Sievens, "Divorce, Patriarchal Authority, and Masculine Identity: A Case from Early National Vermont," *Journal of Social History*, 37:3 (2004), 652, finds her subject in 1823 protecting his manhood as a "citizen, producer, and household head" while trying to defend himself against a divorce action by his wife. Although he lost, he could expect the court to be responsive to multiple dimensions of his identity. In Vermont politics, however, he had only one that counted – voter.

[18] Illinois Constitution of 1818, art. II, sect. 27.

[19] For Lincoln's resentment at having to remain with his father until his twenty-first birthday, see Catherine Clinton, "The Family That Made Him, the Family That He Made," in *Our Lincoln: New Perspectives on Lincoln and His World*, ed. Eric Foner (New York, 2008), 253–257; David H. Donald, *Lincoln* (New York, 1995), 32–35. For his lifelong "aversion" to his father, see Michael Burlingame, *Abraham Lincoln: A Life*, 2 vols. (Baltimore, 2007), 1: 10.

[20] Joseph Kett, *Rites of Passage: Adolescence in America 1790 to the Present* (New York, 1977), 14.

[21] On families moving west, see Daniel W. Howe, *What Hath God Wrought: The Transformation of America, 1815–1848* (New York, 2007), 138, and Christopher Clark, *Social Change in*

Douglas's independence was a goal that most young men in their early twenties longed for but did not attain until they were older. Illinois had a higher proportion of young voters than did the country as a whole.[22] Twenty-one-to twenty-five-year-olds comprised the largest five-year cohort in the state's electorate. In other words, from 1834 to 1838, the largest age group of voters consisted of Douglas's peers.[23] Like him, most were unmarried.[24] Unlike him, most were still at home or were semidependent on their families.[25] His long, solitary, perilous, but ultimately successful journey from his family in New York to economic independence in Jacksonville charted a course to manhood they could all admire. Biographer Gerald Capers has described Douglas as a "man's man" because of his camaraderie with voters.[26] Capers's point is valid but the phrase is also apt because Douglas embodied what it meant to become fully a man. He had struggled to separate himself from his family when he was fifteen, again when he was twenty, and now in Illinois he had achieved full autonomy. He had done what many of his "political friends" still longed to do.[27]

Nevertheless, while most of his peers were not as independent as he was, in the Illinois political arena they were all men. Reaching the "age of manhood" did not have equal import across the country. Vermont, New York, and Illinois were states wherein a white male was eligible to participate in state and national elections on the day he turned twenty-one. He did not have to own

America: From the Revolution to the Civil War (Chicago, 2006), 145. On families going west from Vermont, see Eric Barnouw, "The Benson Exodus of 1833: Mormon Converts and the Westward Movement," *Vermont History*, 54:3 (1986), 133–148.

[22] The Illinois Census of 1830 counted 14,706 free white males aged twenty to twenty-nine, 45% of the 32,667 total in all categories of those twenty and older. Nationally, 956,296 free white males were twenty to twenty-nine years of age, or 40% of the 2,356,663 total in all categories of those twenty and older. Based on *Abstract of the Returns of the Fifth Census* (Washington, DC, 1832), 48.

[23] The number of white males declined with each age cohort; conversely every younger year's total was greater than the next older year's. Accordingly, there were more males twenty-one to twenty-five than twenty-six to thirty. Free persons of color are not included for 1830 because census takers did not record how many were twenty to twenty-nine. In Illinois there were only 547 free black males older than ten years of age, constituting 1% of the total free male population ten or older. Ibid., 59.

[24] The mean age at marriage for men in the 1830s, according to one local study, was twenty-seven. Nancy Osterud and John Fulton, "Family Limitation and Age at Marriage: Fertility and Decline in Sturbridge, Massachusetts 1730–1850," *Population Studies*, 30:3 (1976), 485, table. It had never been below twenty-five or twenty-six. Michael R. Haines, "Long-Term Marriage Patterns in the United States from Colonial Times to the Present," *History of the Family*, 1:1 (1996), 17. See also Clark, *Social Change in America*, 143.

[25] The mean age of leaving home for men at midcentury in the Northeast was over twenty-six. Richard H. Steckel, "The Age at Leaving Home in the United States," *Social Science History*, 20:4 (1996), 507–532, esp. fig. 515.

[26] Gerald M. Capers, *Stephen A. Douglas: Defender of the Union* (Boston, 1959), 14.

[27] Anya Jabour writes that in the Jacksonian era middle-class male teenagers "experienced a turbulent adolescence" because, unlike an earlier generation, they could not simply follow in their fathers' footsteps. "Masculinity and Adolescence in Antebellum America: Robert Wirt at West Point, 1820–1821," *Journal of Family History*, 23:4 (1998), 394.

any property or pay taxes to be accepted as a voter.[28] The presumption was that a twenty-one-year-old possessed the reasoning ability of a man and therefore should be entitled to give his consent to those who would govern.[29]

Financial independence, having one's own household, having a career, being married – all were traditional markers of adulthood that still counted in families but were peripheral in party politics, where the right to vote signified one's manhood.[30] The status that a twenty-one-year-old man had in states with the most democratic franchise should not be understated. By dint of his age alone, every white adult male in these states had cachet. Newspapers regularly solicited his attendance at party meetings, public rallies, and elections.[31] He was asked to write "letters of instruction" to state legislators.[32] He was expected to consider a revision of his state constitution.[33] Circulars implored him to end taxes on property owned by churches and schools.[34] He was told that he had the right to examine financial records kept by public officers.[35] July Fourth

[28] Drawn from Alexander Keyssar, *The Right to Vote: The Contested History of Democracy in the United States* (New York, 2000), table A.2; and Stanley L. Engerman and Kenneth L. Sokoloff, "The Evolution of Suffrage Institutions in the New World," *Journal of Economic History*, 65:4 (2005), 896, table. New York removed property and taxpaying requirements for whites in 1826, four years before Douglas moved there, but retained them for a "man of color." Municipalities in some of these states, however, restricted the vote in local elections to property owners or taxpayers (29–30). Whereas all thirteen of the original states retained a property or tax qualification in 1789, Vermont entered the Union two years later with universal manhood suffrage.

[29] Holly Brewer notes that age requirements for voting were introduced in colonies before they were established in England. She argues that reason became crucial to the American concept of manhood during the late eighteenth century, as age trumped rank. *By Birth or Consent: Children, Law, and the Anglo-American Revolution in Authority* (Chapel Hill, NC, 2005), 41, 122–123, 342.

[30] Joseph Kett finds that during their twenties young men in the rural North were usually in a transitional stage between dependency and independence wherein "no consensus existed as to the moment when a boy became a man." *Rites of Passage*, 31. John Demos characterizes youth in the early 1800s as a stage that was "increasingly disjunctive and problematic" because of new choices available to young men. *Past, Present and Personal: The Family and the Life Course in American History* (New York, 1986), 99. Harvey J. Graff, *Conflicting Paths: Growing Up in America* (Cambridge, MA., 1995), 59–74, identifies several paths that male youth took to manhood during the late eighteenth and early nineteenth centuries. Exploring the coming-of-age experience of Federalists around the time Douglas was born, Albrecht Koschnik finds that in addition to independence and a career, their ideal of manhood included defending one's personal honor, national honor, and social distinctions. "Young Federalism, Masculinity, and Partisanship during the War of 1812," in *Beyond the Founders: New Approaches to the Political History of the Early American Republic*, ed. Jeffrey L. Pasley, Andrew W. Robertson, and David Walstreicher (Chapel Hill, NC, 2004), 159–179, esp. 161.

[31] EAN, *Rhode-Island Republican* (Newport), Jan. 8, 1834; EAN, *Baltimore Patriot*, Jan. 14, 1834.

[32] USN, *Vermont Watchman* (Montpelier), Jan. 31, 1826; EAN, *Richmond Enquirer* (Richmond, VA), Nov. 28, 1834.

[33] EAN, *New-Hampshire Patriot* (Concord), Jan. 6, 1834.

[34] USN, *Vermont Watchman* (Montpelier), Jan. 31, 1826.

[35] USN, *New-York Spectator*, Aug. 1, 1828, col. D.

toasts recognized freemen as "defenders of the Union."³⁶ Editorials praised the freeman who did his duty on Election Day by "giving his vote, his talents and services to perpetuate the institutions of his country, and secure a just and liberal administration of the laws."³⁷ Governors hailed the "great body of enlightened freemen" as the bulwark of the country's freedom.³⁸ State and federal candidates courted them regularly, retiring politicians thanked them in print for their former support, and newspaper editors continuously tried to influence their electoral behavior. Although a bill to exempt them from arrest "on freemen's meeting day" did not pass the Vermont legislature, the proposal reflected the status occupied by men old enough to vote.³⁹ As Rosemarie Zagarri concludes, the expansion of the right to vote meant that "suffrage had become an explicitly male prerogative."⁴⁰

In New England, where Douglas grew up, the term "freeman" reinforced the link between freedom, manhood, and politics. Its usage communicated that to be a freeman was to participate in the political life of the community. Partisans called on freemen to "come manfully up to the support" of a ticket.⁴¹ Attending "freemen's meetings," rallies, and elections was an expression of manhood; conversely, not coming out politically was unmanly.⁴²

While the Northern Democratic Party by midcentury has been described as "geriatric" in its control and composition, in the 1830s Douglas and his political friends in Illinois were still young men in their early twenties.⁴³ The typical young man had a bifurcated identity. Fully a man in the political arena, in his parents' household he could be reminded of how far he was from adulthood. Working under his father's authority, residing with sisters for whom marriage and childbearing were thresholds to womanhood, and wondering what he would do for a living, he found that his sense of being young was necessarily stronger than his sense of being a man. Douglas knew directly how hard it was for parents to accept the adulthood of their sons. In response to his mother's inquiry about how well he was doing in his "profession," after he was made state's attorney with a salary and fees that he expected to reach $500 to $600 a year, he wrote with tongue in cheek that he was doing as well "as could be expected of a Boy of twenty-one."⁴⁴ If his mother was pleased for him, she did

---

³⁶ USN, *Vermont Watchman and State Gazette* (Montpelier), July 11, 1826; *Vermont Patriot & State Gazette* (Montpelier), July 25, 1826.

³⁷ USN, *Vermont Watchman and State Gazette* (Montpelier), Aug. 29, 1826; *Illinois Patriot* (Shawnee-Town), July 5, 1826.

³⁸ USN, *Vermont Patriot and State Gazette* (Montpelier), Oct. 17, 1826.

³⁹ USN, *Vermont Watchman and State Gazette* (Montpelier), Oct. 30, 1827.

⁴⁰ Rosemarie Zagarri, *Revolutionary Backlash: Women and Politics in the Early American Republic* (Philadelphia, 2007), 154.

⁴¹ USN, *Vermont Patriot and State Gazette* (Montpelier), Aug. 4, 1834.

⁴² On the link between the rights of citizenship and masculine identity, see Bruce Dorsey, *Reforming Men and Women: Gender in the Antebellum City* (Ithaca, NY, 2002), 219–220.

⁴³ Jean H. Baker, *Affairs of Party: The Political Culture of Northern Democrats in the Mid-Nineteenth Century* (Ithaca, NY, 1983), 22.

⁴⁴ *Letters of SAD*, 12.

not let him know. His sister certainly did not convey either approval or pride. During his first four years in Illinois, he received not "a single line" from her; yet, through her husband, she scolded him for being "so actively engaged in politics" as to neglect his family in New York.[45] His brother-in-law, however, did congratulate him on his success and credited it to his "character abilities and eminence" as an attorney and his "diligence, close application, and ardent desire of knowledge" as a student. Stephen was so appreciative of Julius's compliment that he relished quoting it in an otherwise self-effacing response.[46]

In December 1837, after his nomination to the House of Representatives, Douglas prematurely instructed Julius, "Ask Mother what she should think if the People of Illinois should be so foolish as to send her 'prodigal Son' to Congress, and give him an opportunity to visit her on his way."[47] His mother remained the significant other whose approbation he wanted but did not receive. Instead he got encouragement and praise from his political friends. The more engaged he became with them, the less he wrote his family. Peers now eclipsed his family as the center of his psychic life. They bolstered his self-esteem. Where adolescent youth groups had always been a source of parental suspicion and warnings, in the partisan arena young men were expected to associate with and be influenced by each other.[48]

Douglas had been emotionally closest to males since his youth in Vermont, where he had been infatuated with "Tom" at Brandon Academy. This attachment and his identification with his brother-in-law provided the emotional underpinning for his political friendships in Illinois. Like many young men who were psychologically more at ease in the company of others of their own sex, Douglas felt secure in partisan politics. The importance of gender to his peer group cannot be exaggerated. Party politics offered young men a self-consciously masculine world that excluded women. The Jacksonian era witnessed the expansion of women in the public sphere as moral reformers and antislavery crusaders, as well as passive attendees at meetings – much to the consternation of some men.[49] Those who left their houses to get away from

---

[45] Ibid., 50.

[46] Ibid., 14.

[47] Ibid., 51.

[48] On the distrust of adolescent groups in early New England, see Roger Thompson, "Adolescent Culture in Colonial Massachusetts," *Journal of Family History*, 9:2 (1984), 127–144; N. Ray Hiner, "Adolescence in Eighteenth-Century America," *History of Childhood Quarterly*, 3:2 (1975), 253–280.

[49] Michael Goldberg, "Breaking New Ground: 1800–1848," in *No Small Courage: A History of Women in the United States*, ed. Nancy F. Cott (New York, 2000), esp. 214–242; Alexis De Tocqueville, *Democracy in America*, ed. Phillips Bradley, 2 vols. (New York, 1945), 1: 250. Mary Kelley, *Learning to Stand and Speak: Women, Education, and Public Life* (Chapel Hill, NC, 2006), 6–7, conceptualizes public space without organized politics as "civil society" and traces women's participation in it from the 1790s. She notes their new level of visibility in the 1830s. Rosemarie Zagarri suggests that the election of Andrew Jackson in 1828 marked a watershed in the exclusion of women from politics, as political activity became more formalized and structured with focus on parties and elections. *Revolutionary Backlash*, 1–10, 147–180. Susan Graham,

mothers or wives were not pleased to find women intruding in their public spaces.[50] Political parties were enclaves of male camaraderie.

The lyceum movement, which provided the setting where Douglas made his initial mark as a speaker, illustrates the gender issue among men and sheds light on why politics was appealing as an exclusively male enterprise.[51] Lyceums proliferated seemingly overnight in the late 1820s as informal institutions of adult education.[52]

A national umbrella organization was formed in 1831.[53] Although no gender restrictions appeared in its constitution, every lyceum faced the question,

"'A Warm Politician and Devotedly Attached to the Democratic Party': Catharine Read Williams, Politics, and Literature in Antebellum America," *Journal of the Early Republic*, 30 (Summer 2010), 253–278, describes Williams's partisan role after 1828 as a "female politician" in Rhode Island and political writer, citing her as a "counterexample" to Zagarri (256). The relationship between women petitioning against injustices and their political consciousness during Jackson's administration is explored in Alisse Theodore, "'A Right to Speak on the Subject': The U.S. Women's Antiremoval Petition Campaign, 1829–1831," *Rhetoric & Public Affairs*, 5:4 (2002), 601–624, and Susan Zaeske, *Signatures of Citizenship: Petitioning, Antislavery, and Women's Political Identity* (Chapel Hill, NC, 2003), 29–46, which suggests that generally women were uncomfortable with overt political participation in the 1830s, as illustrated by those who first petitioned against slavery. Jeffrey L. Pasley, "Minnows, Spies, and Aristocrats: The Social Crisis of Congress in the Age of Martin Van Buren," *Journal of the Early Republic*, 27 (Winter 2007), 614, suggests that women's influence grew "albeit largely outside the formal structures of the party system, through reform movements and lobbying." Men also participated in political movements outside Jacksonian parties. See Reeve Huston, "Popular Movements and Party Rule: The New York Anti-Rent Wars and the Jacksonian Political Order," in *Beyond the Founders*, ed. Pasley, Robertson, and Walstreicher, 355–386. See also Mary P. Ryan, *Women in Public: Between Banners and Ballots, 1825–1880* (Baltimore, 1990), 135, which describes the public sphere becoming between 1825 and 1840 "a relatively one dimensional gender picture." For a comparative perspective on gender and politics, see Paul Nolte, "Republicanism, Liberalism, and Market Society: Party Formation and Party Ideology in Germany and the United States, c. 1825–1850," in *Republicanism and Liberalism in America and the German States, 1750–1850*, ed. Jürgen Heideking and James A. Henretta (Cambridge, 2002), 198.

50 Michael Kimmel, *Manhood in America: A Cultural History* (New York, 1996), 59–60, describes the nineteenth-century middle-class household as a "virtual feminine theme park" from which many men sought escape. Stephen M. Frank, *Life with Father: Parenthood and Masculinity in the Nineteenth-Century American North* (Baltimore, 1998), 69, observes that during the first half of the nineteenth century homes became "a less masculine space, the site of more feminine and child-centered activities." Dana D. Nelson sees the family emerge as the affective monopoly of the republican mother while the male citizen was redefined "as a man of, not in, the family: a civic manager." *National Manhood: Capitalist Citizenship and the Imagined Fraternity of White Men* (Durham, NC, 1998), 76.

51 Douglas defended President Jackson during the winter of 1833–1834 at the Winchester Lyceum. "Autobiographical Sketch," *Letters of SAD*, 62.

52 There were more than an estimated three thousand lyceums in the eastern United States by 1834. Leah G. Stambler, "The Lyceum Movement in American Education, 1826–1845," *Paedagogica Historica*, 21:1 (1981), 177.

53 For the American Lyceum Society constitution, see Henry Barnard, ed., *The American Journal of Education*, n.s., 14 (Hartford, CT, 1864), 535–543. For newspaper coverage of its founding, see USN, *New-York Spectator* (New York) May 13, 1831; *National Daily Intelligencer* (Washington, DC), May 14, 1831.

"Should ladies be admitted?" Why not? An answer came from a lyceum on Cape Cod, where some members admitted that "their want of confidence would not permit them to speak with sufficient freedom and distinctness in the presence of ladies." The organizer, who deemed the exclusion a mistake, urged the admission of women with the assurance that "if they are ladies, they will not, either here or elsewhere, make any unhandsome remarks upon the performances."[54] What a revealing statement! Men could speak freely without embarrassment in front of each other, but worried that women would be censorious either in front of them or behind their backs. Here was fallout from the post-revolutionary emphasis on the role of mothers as moral guardians of republican citizens: young men in the Jacksonian era yearned to isolate themselves from female judgment. Women were in fact invited to attend meetings at some lyceums, but they were not encouraged to participate as equals.[55] Their customary role, as Angela Ray finds, was to provide "appreciative spectatorship at the performance of men."[56] The primary focus of the "Young Men's Lyceum," as Thomas Schwartz found in the second Springfield, Illinois organization bearing that name in the 1830s, was "training a new generation of men with oratorical and analytical skills necessary for leadership."[57] Women could watch and admire, not criticize.

Douglas's closest age peers in the 1830s were mainly single. When he announced his candidacy for Congress, he was only twenty-four. Whig opponents disparaged his youth, never mentioning his marital status. He responded that if he were elected he would be age-eligible by the time Congress met. He did not have to give assurances that he would wed. Nuptiality rates for the early nineteenth century are not well documented, but it is certain that most of the younger voters were unmarried.[58] "From Boston to San Francisco," writes Howard Chudacoff, "it was common for 40 to 50 per cent of men in the age range of twenty-five to thirty-five to be single and for close to one third of adult men of all ages to be unmarried."[59] Delaying marriage, then, was not a liability

---

54 EAN, "Ladies at Lyceums," *Norwich Courier* (Norwich, CT), June 6, 1831.

55 The reasons for the backlash against women in politics, as John Brooke writes, "are complex," but insufficient attention has been paid to family dynamics, an area to which a biographical study particularly points. "Spheres, Sites, Subjectivity, History: Reframing Antebellum American Society," *Journal of the Early Republic*, 28:1 (Spring 2008), 69.

56 Angela G. Ray, "What Hath She Wrought? Woman's Rights and the Nineteenth-Century Lyceum," *Rhetoric & Public Affairs*, 9:2 (2006), 183–214, quote on 189.

57 Thomas F. Schwartz, "The Springfield Lyceums and Lincoln's 1838 Speech," *Illinois Historical Journal*, 83 (1990), 48.

58 Nancy Osterud and John Fulton, "Family Limitation and Age at Marriage: Fertility and Decline in Sturbridge, Massachusetts, 1730–1850," *Population Studies*, 30:3 (1976), 485, table. A delayed age at marriage was the defining characteristic of the Western European marriage pattern for centuries. See the seminal essay by John Hajnal: "European Marriage Patterns in Perspective," in *Population in History: Essays in Historical Demography*, ed. D. V. Glass and D.E.C. Eversley (London, 1965), 101–143.

59 Howard Chudacoff, *The Age of the Bachelor: Creating an American Subculture* (Princeton, NJ, 1999), 29.

to a politically ambitious man. On the contrary, it strengthened his connection to new voters. Stephen Douglas and Abraham Lincoln did not marry until their thirties, well after each had established his political career in Jacksonian Illinois.

Bachelorhood had always been pervasive but never normative in American society. The colonists deemed single men incomplete developmentally and socially suspect, thereby justifying special taxes and obligations on them.[60] Although the egalitarian legacy of the Revolution swept away discriminatory laws and brought greater acceptance of bachelors, they continued to receive widespread criticism in the last quarter of the eighteenth century, while married men who headed their own families remained the paragon citizens of the early Republic.[61]

A man's marital status may have been critical to his sense of identity and a "foundation for republican political virtue" around 1800, but the convergence of manhood suffrage and democratic ideology elevated the credibility of single young men as responsible citizens by the Jacksonian era.[62] Newspapers reported new assertiveness and pride on the part of unmarried men regarding bachelorhood as a permanent status rather than a stage en route to marriage. The formation of bachelor clubs, bachelor toasts and processions at July Fourth celebrations, and lyceum discussions on the merits of the single life – all testified to the new respectability of bachelorhood as a lifestyle choice.[63] Notwithstanding its hyperbole, a newspaper claim in 1834 reflected a measure of cultural change: "Truly we are in the midst of a Revolution – Rise, Bachelors, rise!"[64]

The rise of bachelorhood was concomitant with the rise of political democracy. The single young men who attended party-sponsored meetings, voted, or ran for office were fully adults in the world of electoral politics. An unmarried

---

[60] On the negative view of bachelorhood in early America, see Anne S. Lombard, *Making Manhood: Growing Up Male in Colonial New England* (Cambridge, MA, 2003); Mark E. Kann, *A Republic of Men: The American Founders, Gendered Language, and Patriarchal Politics* (New York, 1998); Thomas A. Foster, *Sex and the Eighteenth-Century Man: Massachusetts and the History of Sexuality in America* (Boston, 2006).

[61] John G. McCurdy, *Citizen Bachelors: Manhood and the Creation of the United States* (Ithaca, NY, 2009), challenges scholarly claims that colonists considered bachelors to be less than men, although he presents evidence that male singles had an uncertain standing everywhere. Nevertheless, he concludes that the bachelor "was not the antithesis of early American manhood, but a variation on it" (7). Hendrik Hartog, *Man & Wife in America: A History* (Cambridge, MA, 2000), 100, asserts the continuing political significance of marriage for men after 1800.

[62] The quote is from Hartog, *Man & Wife in America*, 101, which stresses the continuing importance of marriage to men after 1800. McCurdy, *Citizen Bachelors*, 183, finds that "single men's reputation reached a nadir" in the last quarter of the eighteenth century. Frank, *Life with Father*, 88–89, notes the long pedigree of anti-bachelor moralists, the rise of concern during the 1830s, and the increasing respectability of singleness.

[63] EAN, *New-Bedford Mercury* (New Bedford, MA), Apr. 20, 1827; EAN, *Pittsfield Sun* (Pittsfield, MA), July 17, 1834; EAN, *Portsmouth Journal of Literature and Politics* (Portsmouth, NH), July 19, 1834; EAN, *Boston Commercial Gazette*, Dec. 16, 1826; EAN, *Republican Star* (Easton, MD), Apr. 24, 1827; EAN, *Pittsfield Sun*, Aug. 19, 1830; EAN, *Portsmouth Journal of Literature and Politics*, May 5, 1832.

[64] EAN, *Pittsfield Sun* (Pittsfield, MA), Feb. 6, 1834.

leader like Douglas confirmed their place in society. Politics, moreover, offered all men, single and married, an outlet from female-dominated households. Historian Jan Lewis has suggested that the first generation of American political leaders distrusted power and established the notion that government service was emotionally unsatisfying. Men like Jefferson, she writes, "learned not to rest their identities completely on the public's approval. Instead they would look to family and friends for the love and affirmation that public life could not guarantee."[65] By the 1830s, however, while the family might offer some men a "haven in a heartless world," for others party politics became a refuge from hearth and home.[66]

The family could be a source of multiple pressures for sons and fathers. Historians have explored men's dominion over women but have not examined the ways in which young men might have experienced female power in the family.[67] A mother surely did not require control over property or the law to exert substantial influence over her sons. Sally Douglas's source of power over Stephen was not based on her material holdings. In the family hierarchy a mother may have been legally entitled "to no power, only reverence and respect," but if she was worth her salt she needed neither a court nor property to hold sway over her son. Maternal psychological influence was a force by itself, but strengthened by the ideology of republican motherhood it became especially powerful in post-revolutionary society.[68]

By the Jacksonian era, however, the establishment of bachelorhood as a culturally legitimate option accompanied a new theme in the popular press – the desire to escape from women. Stories warned young men against being ensnared

---

[65] Jan Lewis, " 'Those Scenes for Which Alone My Heart Was Made': Affection and Politics in the Age of Jefferson and Hamilton," in *An Emotional History of the United States*, ed. Peter N. Stearns and Jan Lewis (New York, 1998), 55.

[66] Christopher Lasch, *Haven in a Heartless World: The Family Besieged* (New York, 1977).

[67] Toby Ditz asks, "How can we do histories of men and masculinity without occluding men's power over women?" Toby L. Ditz, "The New Men's History and the Peculiar Absence of Gendered Power: Some Remedies from Early American Gender History," *Gender and History*, 16:1 (2004), 9. By the same token, we might ask, how can we do histories of men and masculinity without assessing women's power over young men?

[68] Recent scholarship has illuminated women in the early national public sphere and in their social relationships. Illustrative are Zagarri, *Revolutionary Backlash*; Mary Kelley, *Learning to Stand and Speak: Women, Education, and Public Life* (Chapel Hill, NC, 2006); Martha T. Blovelt, *The Work of the Heart: Young Women and Emotion, 1780–1830* (Charlottesville, VA, 2007); Lucia McMahon, " 'Of the Utmost Importance to Our Country': Women, Education, and Society, 1780–1820," *Journal of the Early Republic*, 29 (Fall 2009), 475–506; and Ivy Schweitzer, *Perfecting Friendship: Politics and Affiliation in Early American Literature* (Chapel Hill, NC, 2006). Mary Beth Sievens, *Stray Wives: Early National Marital Conflict in New England* (New York, 2005), focuses on the relationship between wives and husbands. Except for matters of child support and child custody, her study reveals little conflict between spouses over childrearing. Were early national parents at one on raising their children? Linda Kerber's seminal essay, "The Republican Mother: Women and the Enlightenment – An American Perspective," *American Quarterly*, 28:2 (1976), 187–205, examines motherhood primarily as it affected women and expectations for their children. We need more work on how republican motherhood was internalized by the male generation that came of age in Jacksonian America.

in marriage. Episodes of marital evasion were relayed with humor or glee. A New England weekly advised young men not to relinquish their freedom too soon, for "[t]here is a time for all things, as Jack said when he swallowed the contents of a Tobacco-hogshead."[69] Notice of the respective marriages of William Lloyd Garrison and Prudence Crandall amused a bachelor editor, who was struck that abolitionists would "voluntarily assume the yoke of servitude themselves."[70] When a Vermont bachelor hanged himself by an iron chain hooked to a beam in his barn, an editor thought "he would not have placed himself in a worse noose, had he chosen a wife."[71] The Bachelors' Club of Providence staged a mock trial of a member who confessed to composing verses to a siren for whom he had considered deserting his "fraternity of bachelors."[72] The message of these stories was that young men should avoid rather than seek marriage.

What did party politics offer besides an escape from women? What were the characteristics of this all-male world that appealed to Douglas and his political friends? How did young men behave with each other? What did they find in their association with other young men that they did not find with young women? If young men recoiled from the remarks of women in integrated lyceums, why would they not shrink from the give and take of a political meeting? Indeed, what is stunning about male camaraderie in politics is how it could transcend the rhetorical excesses of partisanship. Candidates who ridiculed each other during an afternoon debate could lie next to each other at night. Was their rhetorical antagonism on the stump merely a performance? Was their public combat a prelude to a night of private eroticism? Or were they able to compartmentalize their relationship by functional and economic necessities? After all, they had to draw verbal swords to compete for office and at the same time reduce campaign expenses by sharing the same bed.

Douglas slept alongside other men. When he and John Stuart, Lincoln's law partner, campaigned against each other for Congress in 1838, a landlord told two occupants of separate beds that they would have to double up to accommodate the candidates. After asking about their politics, Douglas said that he would sleep with the Democrat and Stuart with the Whig. "The arrangement suited all parties."[73] There is little reason to believe that this involved more than a practical accommodation.

Recent scholarship has heightened attention on the sleeping practices of antebellum men, most particularly Lincoln. Men sharing beds has been considered within the context of possible homosexuality.[74] Masturbation, however,

---

[69] EAN, *Independent Inquirer* (Brattleboro, VT), Aug. 2, 1834.

[70] EAN, *Portsmouth Journal of Literature and Politics* (Portsmouth, NH), Oct. 4, 1834.

[71] EAN, *Rhode Island Republican* (Providence), May 21, 1834.

[72] For the cultivation of antimarriage sentiments by "sporting bachelors," see Chudacoff, *Age of Bachelors*, 36. See also EAN, *Providence Patriot* (Providence, RI), Mar. 7, 1829.

[73] John M. Palmer, *Personal Recollections of John M. Palmer: The Story of an Earnest Life* (Cincinnati, 1901), 24.

[74] Richard Godbeer, *The Overflowing of Friendship: Love Between Men and the Creation of the American Republic* (Baltimore, 2009), 35, writes, "It was not unusual for eighteen-century

was a much greater concern to contemporary men than sodomy. The most popular advice guides of the 1830s warned young men about the dangers of "self-pollution" without ever mentioning same-sex activity. They attributed various illnesses to the practice.[75] If Douglas read Sylvester Graham's manual, he might have worried that the "rheumatic and inflammatory complaints" which he experienced on his solitary journey to Illinois had been caused by autoeroticism.[76] What historian G. J. Barker-Benfield has described as the "masturbation phobia" of the 1830s might have motivated some young men to sleep next to others in order to prevent themselves from indulging in acts of "self-abuse."[77] Nevertheless, as Rodney Hessinger observes, young men often learned the practice from friends, most notoriously at boarding schools.[78]

We do know that young men did form "romantic friendships" with other young men that lasted until they married and that love in these relationships often found linguistic, not physical, expression. Scholars have unearthed such friendships among prominent antebellum political figures, the most controversial being the case of Abraham Lincoln.[79] What we do not know is the extent to which any of these relationships were sexual.[80]

Americans to share a bed for practical reasons, so that sleeping with someone did not necessarily imply an intimacy of some sort in the way it does today."

[75] Sylvester Graham's *A Lecture to Young Men, On Chastity*, 4th ed. (Boston, 1838); John Todd, *The Student's Manual*, 4th ed. (Northampton, MA, 1835).

[76] Graham, *Lecture to Young Men*, 112.

[77] G. J. Barker-Benfield, *The Horrors of the Half Known Life: Males Attitudes Toward Women and Sexuality in Nineteenth-Century America*, 2nd ed. (New York, 2000); he focuses on Todd's *Student's Manual*, which went through seven editions in two years (128). See also Rodney Hessinger, *Seduced, Abandoned, and Reborn: Visions of Youth in Middle-Class America, 1780–1850* (Philadelphia, 2005), 150–151, 160–165. He suggests that "the male chastity ideal" became strong in Jacksonian America "in reaction to, and in competition with, an emerging rake culture" (151). Douglas was never considered a rake.

[78] Hessinger, *Seduced, Abandoned, and Reborn*, 158.

[79] For the example of Daniel Webster, see E. Anthony Rotundo, *American Manhood: Transformations in Masculinity from the Revolution to the Modern Era* (New York, 1993), 77–80, 87–91. Rotondo's work has been seminal in focusing scholarly attention on male friendships. Doris K. Goodwin, *Team of Rivals: The Political Genius of Abraham Lincoln* (New York, 2005), 33, 115–118, describes an intimate friendship of William Seward as a young man and one between Salmon Chase and Edwin Stanton as older men. Lasting, affectionate friendships were common among Southern lawyers who traveled the circuit with each other. Anya Jabour, "Male Friendship and Masculinity in the Early National South: William Wirt and His Friends," *Journal of the Early Republic*, 20:1 (2000), 83–111.

Lincoln's sexuality has drawn the most scholarly attention. For a stimulating psychohistorical examination of his friendship with Joshua Speed, see Charles B. Strozier, *Lincoln's Quest for Union: Public and Private Meanings* (New York, 1982), 41–49. Charles Shively, ed., *Drum Beats: Walt Whitman's Civil War Boy Lovers* (San Francisco, 1989), was the first to characterize the relationship as homosexual and influenced the better-known C. A. Tripp, *The Intimate World of Abraham Lincoln*, ed. Lewis Gannett (New York, 2005). Michael Burlingame pens "A Respectful Dissent," in the afterward of that book (225–245) but dismisses the thesis less respectfully in his *Abraham Lincoln*, 1: 805–806.

[80] After quoting very loving language between male friends in the eighteenth century, Richard Godbeer concludes, "Whether such feelings ever translated into erotic attraction or expressed

Two aspects of Douglas's relationship to men do require some exploration of his sexuality. First were his unrequited feelings for a boy at Brandon Academy.[81] Tom disappeared from his life when he left for New York. There is no evidence that Stephen developed a romantic friendship with anyone at Canandaigua Academy. Friends from there visited him when he was ill in Cleveland, but he seems not to have written letters to any.[82] His most intimate friend was his brother-in-law Julius, and there is no eroticism in any of Stephen's letters to him. Their relationship was unambiguously fraternal.

Second was his physicality. The youth who wrote of his love for Tom became the lawyer and politician who sat on the laps of men. Observers were struck by this practice. Hezekiah Wead recalled that in the courtroom Douglas "would go round among the listeners & spectators, sit upon their knees and chat and laugh & joke with them."[83] Gustave Koerner, a lawyer and politician himself, remembered that Douglas "was full of blandishment" with people he was trying to persuade. "He would sit on their laps, and clap them on their backs." The result was "magnetism" that was "almost irresistible."[84] Another attorney recollected that Judge Douglas left the bench to have a smoke with the lawyers, "often sitting on their laps."[85] His youthful appearance and diminutive size worked to his advantage. When he first ran for Congress in 1838, an observer thought he looked "to be a youth of sixteen."[86]

Was there a link between his love for Tom and his physicality with groups? Did he sit on men's laps to flirt with them? Did it have an erotic connotation? Did he do it to make fun of his diminutive size? One observer suggested that Douglas could sit on men's laps because he was "five feet nothing, or thereabouts and probably weighing about 100 pounds."[87] Why was this not considered unmanly? Why would other men find this act appealing? Contemporaries like Wead and Koerner did take notice of it, believed it contributed to Douglas's effectiveness, but did not invest it with a sexual meaning.

themselves in the form of sexual relations is for the most part impossible to tell." *Overflowing of Friendship*, 56. David S. Reynolds, " 'Affection shall solve every one of the problems of freedom': Calamus Love and the Antebellum Political Crisis," *Huntington Library Quarterly*, 73:4 (2010), 629–642, finds same-sex affection and physicality common and unselfconscious before the Civil War. On the question of sexuality in intimate same-sex relations in the antebellum era, see also Jabour, "Masculinity and Adolescence in Antebellum America."

[81] Copybook of Stephen A. Douglas, SAD Papers, SC 415, folder 1, Special Collections, Abraham Lincoln Library. See Chapter 1, this volume.

[82] Stephen A. Douglas (Cleveland) to Julius N. Granger, Sept. 20, 1834, *Letters of SAD*, 1.

[83] Thomas F. Schwartz, " 'Illinois & Her Politicians': The Observations of Hezekiah Morse Wead, Delegate to the 1847 Illinois Constitutional Convention," *Journal of Illinois History*, 3 (Spring 2000), 47.

[84] Thomas J. McCormack, ed., *Memoirs of Gustave Koerner, 1809–1896*, 2 vols. (Cedar Rapids, IA, 1909), 1: 449.

[85] Quoted by Johannsen, *SAD*, 111.

[86] Jeriah Bonham, *Fifty Years' Recollections* (Peoria, IL, 1883), 188.

[87] Robert Taft, "The Appearance and Personality of Stephen A. Douglas," *Kansas Historical Quarterly*, 21 (Spring 1954), 11.

Douglas's fraternizing style can be placed within the context of the egalitarian ethos of his times. To sit on men's laps was an act less of homoerotic titillation than of homosocial bonding. It signified that the "Little Giant" did not think himself so high and mighty that he could not repose on a man's knees. It figuratively brought him down to the level of his peers. In remembering Douglas's stepping down to smoke with and sit on the laps of lawyers, an attorney called him "the most *democratic* judge I ever knew."[88] Similarly, when he lay down in bed next to another man, he evened the field between them.[89] Lying down closed the social gap between men. The man who shunned sharing a bed with another risked being shunned himself for pretentiousness. Even a dandy would arouse less concern by lying next to another man than he would by acting as if he were superior to other men.[90] Deviance from egalitarianism was a worse sin than sexual divergence or gender blurring.[91]

To call a politician a dandy was to slur him. In contrast to the standard bearer of his party in 1836 and 1840, Douglas was the anti-dandy.[92] He would have been the last person to put on airs. He made sure he dressed like the people. The pro-Jackson newspaper in Vandalia criticized the "vanity of young men" for "loving fine clothes and new fashions." It urged them to "be comely, plain, decent, cleanly, not covetous, nor costly" in their apparel.[93] Douglas fit their bill, for his most prominent fashion statement was unkemptness. His clothes, however, belied his taste for the good things of life. And he was always alert to opportunities for making money. He wanted to afford good wine, cigars, books, furnishings, hotels, travel, and charity. But he did not set himself apart from the people he courted. His physicality and attire symbolized his identification with them. On the campaign trail he accepted the hospitality of a family

---

[88] Quoted in Johannsen, *SAD*, 111.

[89] Douglas wrote, "I live with my constituents, eat with my constituents, drink with them, pray with them laugh, hunt, dance, and work with them; I eat their corn dodger and fried bacon, and sleep two in a bed with them." Quoted in David H. Fischer, *Liberty and Freedom* (New York, 2005), 305.

[90] See "A Dandy in the Backwoods," USN, *Raleigh Register, and North Carolina Gazette*, Aug. 16, 1836. It tells of an innkeeper taming a dandy who, after refusing to sleep in a room with other men, balked at lying in a single room on a bed with "dirty" sheets. Brandishing a horsewhip, the innkeeper forced the dandy to disrobe and lie down on the bed for the night. In the morning the proprietor refused to take money from the dandy and sent him off. The lesson was clear: the foppish young man received a comeuppance for thinking he was better than other men.

[91] Michael D. Pierson, *Free Hearts and Free Homes: Gender and American Antislavery Politics* (Chapel Hill, NC, 2003), 99–109, argues that after 1848 the Democratic Party would respond to the movement for women's rights by stressing male egalitarianism and a firm adherence to domestic patriarchalism.

[92] A biography first published in 1835 described the vice president as "what the English call a dandy. When he enters the senate-chamber in the morning, he struts and swaggers like a crow in the gutter. He is laced up in corsets, such as women in a town wear, and, if possible, tighter than the best of them. It would be difficult to say, from his personal appearance, whether he was man or woman, but for his large *red* and *gray* whiskers." David Crockett, *The Life of Martin Van Buren* (Philadelphia, 1845), 80–81.

[93] *Illinois Advocate and State Register*, Nov. 12, 1834.

that lived in a "fourteen-feet square log cabin" and pleased his hosts with his expressed appreciation.[94]

Not only did sitting on other men's laps signal Douglas's equality with them, it said a good deal about his understanding of manhood. Unlike Lincoln and the Whigs' "Long Nine," who towered over their peers in the state legislature, Douglas lacked the size and strength that immediately conveyed manliness. Within the schoolyards and playing fields of boys, competitiveness and athleticism counted most.[95] The "puny" (his sister's description) Douglas had been at a disadvantage. In his twenties, however, in the courtroom and the playing fields of party politics, a different form of masculinity was respected, even honored. Sitting on men's laps indicated his dependence on them, his merging of his identity with theirs. The act recognized the hegemony of the group and his individual subordination to it. Conversely, his collective acceptance by other men reinforced his sense of manhood. Lap sitting was unusual but not untoward, as it certainly would have become later. It solidified his bond with men in public spaces. It was part of his public performance. There is no evidence that he sat on a man's lap in private.

A later generation of candidates would never have performed this act because of its homoerotic implications, and an earlier generation would not have done it because it would have called into question the independence that republicanism prized and it was blatantly feminine.[96] In the 1790s, for example, Federalists had condemned the style of their Francophile opponents in gender-laden terms, particularly frowning on their fraternal physicality as effeminate.[97] Although physical expressions of affection between male friends were not uncommon in the early Republic, they were displayed largely in private. While they did not necessarily bear an implication of eroticism or threat to masculinity, in public the handshake replaced the more expressive hug and kiss as the typical male-to-male greeting.[98] Politicians were urged to "shake

---

[94] Bonham, *Fifty Years' Recollections*, 188–189.

[95] For a contemporary's account of schoolboy culture in New Hampshire from 1804 to 1818, see Warren Burton, *The District School as It Was* [1833] (New York, 1969; reprint), 104–108. For a succinct, excellent description of rural boyhood culture, see Steven Mintz, *A History of American Childhood* (Cambridge, MA, 2004), 83. See also Brian J. Connolly, "Domestic Intercourse: Incest, Family and Sexuality in the United States," Ph.D. diss. (State University of New Jersey, 2007), 11.

[96] In the evolution of manhood, John Stauffer considers the Civil War to have been a pivotal phase that emphasized muscularity, ruggedness, and a martial spirit. "Embattled Manhood and New England Writers, 1860–1870," in *Battle Scars: Gender and Sexuality in the American Civil War*, ed. Catherine Clinton and Nina Silber (New York, 2006), 120–139.

[97] David Waldstreicher, "Federalism, the Styles of Politics and the Politics of Style," in *Federalists Reconsidered*, ed. Doron Ben-Atar and Barbara B. Oberg (Charlottesville, VA, 1998), 115–116.

[98] Godbeer, *Overflowing of Friendship*, 6–7 and passim. He suggests that the handshake became a substitute for the embrace and kiss in mid-eighteenth-century England possibly because of concerns of sodomy (7). An American woman at the turn of the century claimed that "a friend may shake hands in any company ... but a lover must press it silently, seriously, and alone." EAN, "From the Port Folio," *Providence Journal* (Providence, RI), Sept. 30, 1801.

hands by wholesale" the week before a Connecticut election in 1792.[99] Sitting on men's laps did not take the place of the handshake, but it was acceptable in the self-consciously democratic 1830s and 1840s. It was an act of seduction and dependence by which Douglas signified playfully that he would use his whole being to carry out the will of his constituents. He did not need instructions to embody their desires.[100]

If his physical style was distinctive, his oral style was more typical of men at the time. From his first speech in Jacksonville, as James Huston observes, "Douglas was never afraid to use sarcasm and scorn to embarrass an opponent."[101] A flair for invective was "a particularly masculine style," according to Kenneth Cmiel, who overstates his point by suggesting that Douglas was among antebellum politicians "who built their careers around bitter personal harangues."[102] Nevertheless, his gift for insult especially suited the divisive atmosphere in Jacksonville in the 1830s.[103] His combative rhetoric was manly on the partisan stump and neutralized any doubts that might have been raised by his expressions of egalitarian familiarity with other men.

The new political parties were very much fraternal organizations, urging their members to "rally around our political brethren" when the opposition attacked.[104] They would "appeal to our fellow freemen" in other counties to support their candidate.[105] There was less and less room for the individual maverick. Men had to be accountable to their peers. No one pushed this principle harder than Douglas, whose first office as state's attorney had resulted from an effort to punish the incumbent for having failed to support legislative candidates who had supported him.[106] Loyalty to the party was one of the first principles of the new politics.[107] The party was an all-male organization, with young men in the majority. Democrats did not seek female support until long after Whigs brought women into their campaigns.[108] Douglas was wholly comfortable in the Democratic fraternity of the 1830s and 1840s.

Douglas became a political prodigy in Illinois because his personal story boldly echoed the aspirations and tensions that newly enfranchised young men felt. He instantly connected with them because he could so naturally and

---

99 EAN, *American Mercury* (Hartford, CT), Sept. 17, 1792.

100 On the rise of instructions in the 1830s, see Yonatan Eyal, *The Young America Movement and the Transformation of the Democratic Party, 1828–1861* (New York, 2007), 54–55.

101 James Huston, *Stephen A. Douglas and the Dilemmas of Democratic Equality* (Lanham, MD, 2007), 9.

102 Kenneth Cmiel, *Democratic Eloquence: The Fight over Popular Speech in Nineteenth-Century America* (New York, 1990), 63.

103 Dan H. Doyle describes pluralistic Jacksonville as the "unpeacable kingdom." *The Social Order of a Frontier Community: Jacksonville, Illinois 1825–70* (Urbana, IL, 1978), 39–61.

104 EAN, *New-Hampshire Patriot* (Concord), Nov. 24, 1834.

105 USN, *Vermont Watchman and Gazette* (Montpelier), Jan. 30, 1827.

106 "Autobiographical Sketch," Sept.1, 1838, *Letters of SAD*, 64; Johannsen, *SAD*, 28–30.

107 Leonard, *Invention of Party Politics*, 11, 176.

108 Elizabeth R. Varon, *We Mean to Be Counted: White Women and Politics in Antebellum Virginia* (Chapel Hill, NC, 1998), 71–102.

completely identify with them. His charisma in his early twenties was based on his fraternal relationship to the electorate. He was not a father figure like the founders; rather, he was like a big brother. He understood them and they admired him, cheered him, and lifted him. His credibility as a spokesman for the new democracy was instantaneously apparent. He did not have to prove himself by working his way slowly up the political ladder. He had become an apprentice when he wanted to prepare himself for a career as a cabinetmaker in Vermont, but he needed no comparable tutelage to become a political leader or lawyer in Illinois. He required no mentoring to speak either on the hustings or in court. As both a lawyer and a politician he had authenticity. He was a man's man who was at one with the voters and jurors he sought to persuade. His persona, in short, was what made his message so effective.

Would Douglas have been charismatic if he had been anti-Jackson? It is tempting to suggest that his personal story and style were so powerful that he would have been as successful as a Whig, a formidable rival to Lincoln in his own party. Yet whereas one could imagine Lincoln as a Democrat before slavery became a deep, partisan divide, the fit between Douglas's life story and the principles of the Democratic Party appears inexorably tight. Douglas the Democrat is more self-evident than Lincoln the Whig.[109]

---

[109] Lincoln's embrace of the Whig Party remains problematic, for there is no scholarly consensus. Sean Wilentz writes that his rise "as a Republican leader raises questions about the precise character of his Whig loyalties and outlook." "Abraham Lincoln and Jacksonian Democracy," in *Our Lincoln: New Perspectives on Lincoln and His World*, ed. Eric Foner (New York, 2008), 62–79, quote on 63. Wilentz places him among the more democratically oriented New School Whigs but finds no compelling reason for his joining the party. Douglas L. Wilson, *Honor's Voice: The Transformation of Abraham Lincoln* (New York, 1998), 142–167, esp. 153, examines his entry into the Illinois legislature in 1834 as a Whig while dismissing the significance of party loyalty in local issues at the time. Michael Burlingame, *Abraham Lincoln*, 1: 36–37, suggests that "in all likelihood" his attachment to the National Republicans who formed the Whig Party derived from his dislike of "agrarianism and negative government." Burlingame speculates that Lincoln might have rejected the Democratic Party because it was his father's. In an impressive psychological study, Joshua W. Shenk explains Lincoln's attraction to the Whigs mainly by the party's commitment to reason and his need to control his emotions. Shenk summarizes the party's program but does not connect it to Lincoln's personality, other than to suggest it "signaled his interest." *Lincoln's Melancholy: How Depression Challenged a President and Fueled His Greatness* (Boston, 2005), 74, 97–98. Allen C. Guelzo believes that "there could not have been much doubt with whom Lincoln would find his friends." He concludes that the Whig ideology of liberation from agriculture, social mobility, and free labor perfectly suited him. *Abraham Lincoln: Redeemer President* (Grand Rapids, MI, 1999), 63. Michael F. Holt believes that Lincoln was deeply committed to the Whigs' economic agenda and revered Henry Clay. *The Rise and Fall of the American Whig Party: Jacksonian Politics and the Onset of the Civil War* (New York, 1999), 288. David H. Donald finds that Lincoln "almost worshiped Henry Clay" but that his decision to run as a Whig was due to "political calculation" regarding local issues. *Lincoln* (New York, 1995), 42, 52. Gabor S. Boritt suggests that Lincoln's personal need to overcome his parents' deficits keyed his lifelong commitment to "the American Dream" for everyone and that it could be realized only through Whig economics. "Lincoln and the Economics of the American Dream," in *The Historian's Lincoln: Pseudohistory, Psychohistory, and History*, ed. Gabor S. Boritt (Urbana, IL, 1988), 87–106. J. David Greenstone, *The Lincoln Persuasion: Remaking American Liberalism* (Princeton, NJ, 1993), 32, emphasizes that Lincoln

Douglas's rise in Illinois politics exemplified a pattern of male socialization that accompanied democratization. He displayed an exuberant physicality that betokened his equality with and acceptance of other men. Intimacy between comrades did not necessarily betoken eroticism, which often could be displaced onto absent women through the vehicle of bawdry humor, a Lincoln specialty.[110] Missing from Douglas was the "military masculinity" that Lincoln claimed as a result of his service in the Black Hawk War. The ideal of the citizen-soldier who moved between battlefield and civic life, donning and shedding appropriate masculine identities, was a hallmark of the age of the democratic revolutions in Europe and America.[111] Lincoln embodied this ideal; Douglas did not. Douglas's invocation of the people's right to decide local issues for themselves was an expression of solidarity with men, for only they could vote. His style of political and professional comradeship was different from the "martial manhood" that Amy Greenberg has associated with proponents of manifest destiny, but it was functional in a self-consciously democratic age.[112] Douglas could espouse the militant expansionism of his party while lap sitting with legal and political comrades. The absence of women in law and party politics made it possible for Douglas to be coquettish without forfeiting his masculinity.[113] In an exclusively male terrain one's manliness could be taken for granted. Sitting

"preached" the Whig gospel according to his own "reinterpretation." Kenneth J. Winkle, "The Second Party System in Lincoln's Springfield," *Civil War History*, 44:4 (1998), 267–284, esp. 283, notes that Lincoln "delighted in – and benefitted from – the detailed intricacies" of building a new party organization in the new capital. Perhaps the opportunity to build a new party was what appealed to him most, for he seized that opportunity again two decades later. Joel H. Sibley, "Always a Whig in Politics: The Partisan Life of Abraham Lincoln," *Papers of the Abraham Lincoln Association*, 8 (Jan. 1986), 21–42, esp. 34, argues that Lincoln was a consistently partisan Whig politician but does not try to explain why he so identified with its ethos. In contrast, Matthew Pinsker, "Not Always Such a Whig: Abraham Lincoln's Partisan Realignment in the 1850s," *Journal of the Abraham Lincoln Association*, 29:2 (Summer 2008), 27–46, contends that Lincoln's loyalty to the Whigs attenuated and he embraced realignment in 1854.

110 Peter Lyman, "The Fraternal Bond as a Joking Relationship: A Case Study of the Role of Sexist Jokes in Male Group Bonding," in *Men's Lives*, ed. Michael S. Kimmel and Michael A. Messner, 7th ed. (Boston, 2007), 153–162,

111 Robert A. Nye, "Western Masculinities in War and Peace: Review Essay," *American Historical Review* (Apr. 2007), 417–438; Stefan Dudink and Karen Hagemann, "Masculinity in Politics and War in the Age of the Democratic Revolutions," in *Masculinities in Politics and War: Gendering Modern History*, ed. Stefan Dudink, Karen Hagemann, and John Tosh (Manchester, 2004), 3–21.

112 Amy Greenberg, *Manifest Manhood and the Antebellum American Empire* (New York, 2005), 40–53.

113 For a pioneering treatment of masculinity among antebellum lawyers and judges, see Michael Grossberg, "Institutionalizing Masculinity: The Law as a Masculine Profession," in *Meaning for Manhood: Construction of Masculinity in Victorian America*, ed. Mark C. Carnes and Clyde Griffen (Chicago, 1990), 133–151. He identifies qualities associated with "responsible manhood" by which lawyers and judges were measured – honesty, competitiveness, practicality, impartiality, courage, and nonbookishness. Manly lawyers were expected to wear their learning lightly (138–140).

on men's laps made him the ultimate comrade, signifying his suppression of self to merge with lawyers and party men.[114] Subordinate masculinity was an individual style that recognized the hegemony of the group. Douglas's subordinate style enabled him to win verdicts and elections and thereby demonstrate his own masculinity, for there was nothing more manly than dominating the opposition.[115] Whether his subordinate style was a performance strategy or, as claimed here, an authentic expression of deference to the popular will, it worked, elevating him as the "Little Giant" of Illinois politics.

[114] Peter Lyman, "The Fraternal Bond as a Joking Relationship," 160, suggests that comradeship "is based upon the loss of an individual sense of self to a group identity while friendship is based upon an individual's intellectual and emotional affinity to another individual."

[115] Jennifer Pierce, "Rambo Litigators: Emotional Labor in a Male-Dominated Occupation," in *Men's Lives*, ed. Kimmel and Messner, 225–241; R. W. Connell and James Messerschmidt, "Hegemonic Masculinity: Rethinking the Concept," *Gender & Society*, 19:6 (Dec. 2005), 829–859.

5

Constitutionalism, Part I

Noncitizen Voting, Apportionment, and Internal Improvements

> Congress might ... adopt the Native American creed, with all its narrowness and bigotry and selfishness and injustice; but do what it would, it never could reach the sacred right of suffrage – that was reserved to the states.
>
> Stephen A. Douglas (1845)[1]

Antebellum lawmakers at the state and federal levels needed to know the written constitution applicable to their jurisdiction. This was the great legacy of the founders of the Republic: congressmen were obliged to justify their positions in terms of the Constitution. A biography can illuminate the predisposition that a politician brought to his interpretation of the document. Did he honestly search the meaning of the text, or did he seek only obligatory constitutional wrapping for his position? Conversely, did he tailor his proposal in accord with his understanding of the text? Historians ask whether law or politics motivated a judge's decision.[2] The same question is not asked of politicians, because their political purpose is taken for granted. Their constitutionalism usually is considered mere cover for other interests. Douglas, however, earnestly tried to balance his constitutional values with other political concerns. The Constitution was more than rhetorical packaging for him; it pushed him independently of other pressures. Had he become president, he would have reconstructed the constitutional understanding of territorial rights, either through an amendment or through the sheer force of executive policy.[3] His legislative record over seventeen years in Congress was anchored in his constitutionalism.

---

[1] CG, 29th Cong., 1st sess. (Dec. 30, 1845), 113.

[2] Gerald Leonard, "Law and Politics Reconsidered: A New Constitutional History of Dred Scott," *Law and Social Inquiry*, 34 (Summer 2009), 749.

[3] Keith Whittington, *Political Foundations of Judicial Supremacy: The Presidency, the Supreme Court, and Constitutional Leadership in U.S. History* (Princeton, NJ, 2007), identifies "reconstructive presidents" who ignored the Supreme Court and acted on their own constitutionalism. For citations to legal scholarship that takes seriously the extrajudicial understanding of the Constitution, see Introduction, this volume, note 21.

Douglas's route to Illinois had a formative influence on the direction of his constitutionalism. Although he believed that his politics were set in opposition to an employer's preferences when he was fifteen, the full thrust of his adolescence inclined him toward the federalism of the Democratic Party. Even if his master had favored Jackson instead of Adams in 1828, it remains difficult to imagine him becoming a Whig in the 1830s. That party's tendency toward centralism and elitism put off Douglas, who defended local control and majority rule. His populism was instinctive, rooted in his coming of age in Illinois.

Douglas's journey from adolescence in Vermont to manhood in Illinois made him sensitive to the different ways of each state. His youthful crisis in Brandon remained a lifelong developmental marker for him. He vividly revisited it in his autobiography at twenty-five, shaped it into a narrative for public consumption in his mid-thirties, read his sister's published revision of it when he was forty-seven, and played off it during his campaign stop at Brandon in 1860. His well-publicized insult – that Vermont was a glorious birthplace as long as one left while very young – indicated how ambivalent he always felt about it. When he left his family in New York at twenty, he fled from the tough educational requirements that state imposed for practicing law. In Cleveland he contracted bilious fever, which confined him to bed for several weeks, made him intermittently delirious, and left him at one point unsure whether he was alive or dead. The episode was traumatic, as his recollection of it five years later revealed. Understandably he cited the healthful environment of Illinois as a lure for his family to follow him there. The greater attraction of the state to him, however, was that he could pass the bar on the basis of a few months of self-study and open his own law office. He also could hardly believe the celebrity brought by a speech he gave in Jacksonville. Before his twenty-first birthday, Illinois received him like a full-fledged adult. His appreciation for what his adopted state did for him never diminished.

He, therefore, had good reason to value both local diversity and the breadth of his country. That he was able to travel a thousand miles before finding a place suitable to him was an opportunity that he wanted for all white men, born here or in Europe. He envisioned an expanding, integrated Union based on local self-determination. The more ample the nation, the greater the local diversity, the more choice and chance for success there would be for other emigrants from the East or abroad. This outlook, rooted in his stressful years of adolescence, had psychological resonance for Douglas. His political allegiance and constitutional principles emanated from this period of individual development. His reflexive protectiveness of states and territories against federal power owed much to his deep sense of relief and gratitude at landing in Illinois after tribulations in the East and a nearly fatal illness on his journey west.[4]

---

[4] Jean H. Baker astutely suggests that "the strands of his personal life – his birth in New England, his residence in Illinois and Washington, and his marriages – first to a southern slaveowner's daughter and then to a Roman Catholic – embodied the diversity he wished to retain in the United States." *Affairs of Party: The Political Culture of Northern Democrats in the Mid-Nineteenth-Century* (Ithaca, NY, 1983), 186.

The staying power of his feelings was reflected in the persisting arch of his constitutionalism. From his first run for Congress through his campaign for the presidency in 1860, he leaned toward local autonomy in relationship to Washington. The slogan "popular sovereignty" with which he became linked in the 1850s can be traced in substance to his earlier stand on a variety of issues: alien suffrage, apportionment, internal improvements, and slavery in the territories.

NONCITIZEN VOTING

Douglas's notorious indifference to the bondage of African Americans contrasted with his advocacy of the right of aliens to vote. When he spoke of democracy and of popular sovereignty, he was exclusionary – he meant to empower only people of European descent.[5] He was not, however, a nativist. On the contrary, he included Irish Catholics and German Protestants among immigrants he believed should have the right to vote even before they were naturalized.[6]

Douglas promoted alien suffrage as a Democratic Party organizer in Illinois, as an attorney, as a state Supreme Court judge, and finally as a congressman. When he first ran for Congress in 1838, he claimed Irish descent in courting immigrants who worked the canal. Although he lost, Whigs credited his impressive total to noncitizen foreigners and proceeded to challenge the validity of their vote.[7] The litigation had short-term political implications because Illinois Democrats, like their party nationally, attracted Irish immigrants.[8] The case and Douglas's brief have had a long life, however, in the jurisprudence on alien suffrage.

In May 1839 Horace Houghton brought suit charging Thomas Spragins, an 1838 election judge in Jo Daviess County, with having knowingly counted the vote of an unqualified man in violation of an election law. The man was ineligible, the suit alleged, because he was not a citizen. The crux of the case was the meaning of Article II, Section 27 of the Illinois Constitution of 1818: "In all

---

[5] James L. Huston, *Stephen A. Douglas and the Dilemmas of Democratic Equality* (Lanham, MD, 2007), 32, 90.

[6] Two years before John F. Kennedy became president, Harry Jaffa wrote, "Douglas was the first and perhaps the most popular national leader that Irish-born Americans have ever had." *Crisis of the House Divided: An Interpretation of the Issues in the Lincoln–Douglas Debates* (Chicago, 1982; orig. ed. 1959), 55.

[7] Johannsen, *SAD*, 67–69.

[8] A contemporary claimed that the alien vote was "about 10,000 strong, nine-tenths of which was democratic." Thomas Ford, *A History of Illinois, from Its Commencement as a State in 1818 to 1847* (Chicago, 1854), 215. See also Graham A. Peck, "Politics and Ideology in a Free Society: Illinois from Statehood to Civil War," Ph.D. diss. (Northwestern University, 2001), 164; Kenneth J. Winkle, "The Second Party System in Lincoln's Springfield," *Civil War History*, 44:4 (1998), 267–284, esp. 281; Johannsen, *SAD*, 83–84; Michael F. Holt, *The Rise and Fall of the American Whig Party* (New York, 1999), 117. James J. Connolly, "Immigration and Ethnic Politics," in *A Companion to American Immigration*, ed. Reed Ueta (Malden, MA, 2006), 58–76, offers a valuable overview of the issues and scholarship.

elections, all white male inhabitants above the age of 21 years, having resided in the state six months next preceding the election, shall enjoy the right of an elector." Did the word "inhabitants" include unnaturalized foreigners?

The circuit court ruled in favor of Houghton on grounds that the word "inhabitant" in the Constitution was synonymous with "citizens."[9] Spragins, as expected, appealed to the Illinois Supreme Court, which heard the case in December 1839. Stephen Douglas and the attorney who had befriended him on his arrival in Jacksonville four years earlier, Murray McConnel, were co-counsel for Spragins.[10]

His only modern biographer to discuss this litigation emphasizes Douglas's political stake in the outcome and his cleverness as a lawyer.[11] When the case reached the Supreme Court in June 1840, Douglas, having learned from a conversation with one of the judges that the majority was going to sustain the circuit court decision, gained a continuance until the December term – after the upcoming election.[12] He did so by discovering that the date of Spragins's alleged misconduct was written as August 1839 instead of 1838, thereby rendering the May 1839 suit technically a "fictitious proceeding."[13] The delayed hearing allowed aliens to vote in the 1840 elections, contributing to the Democratic triumph in Illinois, for which Douglas earned much credit.[14] Although the four-member Supreme Court finally ruled in favor of Spragins in January 1841, the three Whig justices did so on narrow grounds without expressing an opinion on the constitutionality of alien suffrage, much to Douglas's disappointment.

The ruling in favor of Spragins was considered at the time to be a response to political pressure. Democrats controlled the new legislature and drafted a bill to reorganize the Illinois Supreme Court, which included an increase in the number of judges from four to nine in order to enable them to secure a majority. The court's decision in Spragins was perceived to be an attempt to placate the Democrats with a favorable decision. Douglas and his partisans, however, were not satisfied by the limited decision, and the bill passed. Although he was not in the legislature, Douglas's prints were all over what some called the

---

[9] Arnold Shankman, "Partisan Conflicts, 1839–1841, and the Illinois Constitution," *Journal of the Illinois State Historical Society*, 63:4 (1970), 353.

[10] The court reporter spelled the appellant's name "Spraggins" in the June hearing and "Spragins" in the December appeal. We can infer that just as the date of the misconduct was incorrectly recorded initially, so too was the spelling of the appellant. Greater care was taken to ensure accuracy in the preparation of materials for the December hearing. "Spragins" normally controls citations to the case. J. Young Scammon, *Reports of Cases Argued and Determined in the Supreme Court of the State of Illinois* (Boston, 1841), 2: 211, 377.

[11] Johannsen, *SAD*, 82–97.

[12] *Letters of SAD*, 95–96; James W. Sheahan, *The Life of Stephen A. Douglas* (New York, 1860), 46.

[13] Scammon, *Reports*, 2: 211. Thomas Ford claimed that the same judge (Theophilus Smith) who had informed Douglas about the disposition of the majority also counseled about the defect in the record that would lead to a continuance. Ford, *History of Illinois*, 220. Ford and Douglas served together on the Supreme Court after it was reorganized in 1841.

[14] Johannsen, *SAD*, 84.

"Douglas bill."[15] When he benefited by being one of the five new members the legislature elected to the Illinois Supreme Court, he was criticized for his political machinations.

What has been overlooked in Douglas's involvement was his contribution to the case law. His brief in *Spragins v. Houghton* typically was well researched. He drew on congressional legislation and debates, the federal Constitution, *The Federalist*, state constitutions, and legal authorities (Blackstone, Story, Kent, and Vattel).[16] Beginning with the Northwest Ordinance, he noted, Congress had permitted alien freeholders to vote in order to encourage emigration to the West. The ordinance of 1787, in fact, imposed a two-year residency requirement on alien freeholders to vote, while "a citizen of one of the states" had to be a resident only at the time of the election. Accordingly, the word "inhabitant" in the ordinance, he said, "included alien as well as citizen inhabitants." As an attorney he selected documents that best made his case. Here the Northwest Ordinance served him well because it clearly conferred the suffrage on territorial "inhabitants" who were not citizens.

He also noted that subsequent acts of Congress "permitted alien inhabitants to vote for, and to be members of the Conventions that formed the Constitutions of Ohio, Indiana, and Illinois." Further, the Illinois Constitution differentiated between voters and the officers whom they elected. It granted the suffrage to every twenty-one-year-old white male inhabitant who had lived there for at least six months, but restricted eligibility to the state legislature and the governorship to citizens of the United States. In sum, the state constitution did not use the terms "inhabitant" and "citizen" as synonyms.[17]

After demonstrating that the Illinois Constitution intended to enfranchise inhabitants who were not citizens of the United States, Douglas proceeded to the fundamental question as to whether a state could grant the suffrage to aliens. Under the federal Constitution, he asserted, "each State has the right to prescribe the qualifications of its own voters." Congressional laws on naturalization had "no reference to the elective franchise" in England or the United States. Just as "immigrant" and "citizen" were separate terms, "naturalization" and "voting" were not interchangeable. The source that appears to have had the greatest influence on him was Story, who laid out the most comprehensive argument for why the Philadelphia Convention left the decision to each state to decide, "upon such a basis, as the majority may deem expedient with reference to the moral, physical, and intellectual condition of the particular state."[18] Story's way of explaining how a variety of "manners, habits, institutions, characters ... and even the climate and products of the soil" could shape

[15] Ibid., 95.
[16] Douglas, like other Democrats, would often cite Emmerich Vattel, the Swiss theorist. Baker, *Affairs of Party*, 150–151.
[17] The brief of Douglass and McConnel is only summarized in Scammon, *Reports*, 2: 379–382.
[18] Joseph Story, *Commentaries on the Constitution of the United States*, 3 vols. (Boston, 1833), 2: ch. 9, §581.

the suffrage reverberated with Douglas, who experientially and intellectually preferred state diversity to national uniformity.

Douglas's brief, then, made three major points. First, Congress, which had exclusive constitutional authority to enact a naturalization rule, had encouraged aliens to vote in federal territory since the Northwest Ordinance.[19] To that end, Congress had distinguished between "inhabitants" and "citizens." Second, states had exclusive constitutional authority to determine their own voting qualifications. They could and did permit alien suffrage. Third, the language in the Illinois Constitution intended to include aliens when it enfranchised "all white male inhabitants above the age of 21 years" who met a residency requirement.

Douglas's argument was reflected in the opinion of Justice Smith, who was the only member of the court to address the constitutional right of aliens to vote. Citing sources that Douglas had specifically referenced, including *Federalist* 52, Story's *Commentaries*, and the Northwest Ordinance, he observed how "misapprehension prevails" regarding the authority of a state to permit a noncitizen to vote. He declared unambiguously, "Each State has the undoubted right to prescribe the qualifications of its own voters. And it is equally clear, that the act of naturalization does not confer on the individual naturalized, the right to exercise the elective franchise."[20]

Douglas faced the issue again during his first term in Congress, when the Democratic majority blunted Whig attempts to tighten naturalization procedures. Suspecting that proposed reforms cloaked a nativist agenda, the Democrats tabled a petition to extend the residency requirement to twenty-one years and shouted down a call to regulate immigrant voting.[21] Whig charges

[19] The Constitution did not make clear that congressional power over naturalization was exclusive. States continued to naturalize under their own laws until 1795, when Congress enacted its sole authority, reaffirmed by the Supreme Court in 1817. James H. Kettner, *The Development of American Citizenship, 1608–1870* (Chapel Hill, NC, 1978), 225, 249–250.

[20] Justice Smith's opinion is in Scammon, *Reports*, 2: 390–414. He was the judge who informed Douglas about the disposition of his colleagues to rule against Spragins in June 1839. Shankman, "Partisan Conflicts," 354. Sheahan, *Life of Douglas*, 45, claimed that *Spragins v. Houghton* was the first case in the country to adjudicate the question regarding the state's authority over suffrage. An earlier alien suffrage case, *Stewart v. Foster* (1809), did not consider the constitutionality of the state's authority over the issue (2 Binn. 110; 1809 Pa. LEXIS 39). *Spragins v. Houghton* is still cited for establishing the rule, before the Civil War, that states controlled their own suffrage qualifications and could enfranchise aliens. Douglas's brief, through the official voice of Justice Smith, therefore, has had a long influence in the American legal community's understanding of noncitizen voting. Bryant Yuan Fu Yang, "Fighting for an Equal Voice: Past and Present Struggle for Noncitizen Enfranchisement," *Asian American Law Journal*, 13 (2006), 59; Virginia Harper-Ho, "Noncitizen Voting Rights: The History, the Law and Current Prospects for Change," *Journal of Law and Inequality*, 18 (2000), 273, 278; Jamin B. Raskin, "Legal Aliens, Local Citizens: The Historical, Constitutional and Theoretical Meanings of Alien Suffrage," *University of Pennsylvania Law Review*, 141 (1993), 1404–1405; Gerald M. Rosberg, "Aliens and Equal Protection: Why Not the Right to Vote?" *Michigan Law Review*, 75:5/6 (1977), 1096–1097, esp. 1096n; CRS, The Annotated Constitution, Article I, Section 8, Clause 4, http://www.law.cornell.edu/anncon/html/art1frag62_user.html.

[21] CG, 28th Cong., 1st sess. (May 31, 1844), 633. The petition was presented by John Quincy Adams, who opposed it but felt obliged to present it. John Quincy Adams Diary 44, 9 July 1843

of election fraud involving aliens, however, could not be permanently ignored. Resolutions from the Massachusetts legislature forced the Twenty-Ninth House to consider the matter. They called for a revision of the naturalization laws to guard the ballot box against "improper influence."[22] A long debate ensued on whether the resolutions should be referred to a select committee or the Committee on the Judiciary. Douglas, newly elected chair of the Committee on Territories, focused on the constitutional issue and showed how well he had mastered it in his preparation for Spragins's appeal five years earlier.

While he thought it was important to prevent corruption at elections, "he believed it equally important that Congress should refrain from the exercise of powers which by the Constitution were reserved to the States." He denied that the suffrage was an inherent right of naturalization. "The privileges of naturalization and of voting were as entirely separate and distinct from each other as were the Federal and State governments." He went beyond his Spragins brief in delineating the rights that accompanied citizenship: to be protected, to sue in time of war, to inherit, hold, and transmit property, and "various other rights." The right to vote was not included.[23]

He reviewed the record of the Philadelphia Convention on the proposals for establishing uniform rules for voting and naturalization. It rejected the former, he said, because the states "were all zealous" for their respective practices. Some restricted voting to citizens; others "threw wide open their doors to the friends of liberty from every clime, even before they were naturalized." Southern members would never dream of "letting their negroes vote side by side with themselves," while Northern delegates were less opposed to Negro suffrage. After a prolonged discussion, the convention found that the Constitution "must split and be shipwrecked on this rock, or that they must come to some compromise." Accordingly, the framers decided that determining voting qualifications should be reserved for each state. Even if Congress had possessed the power to regulate the suffrage, he thought it should be left to "local interests and local circumstances." Sparsely populated agricultural states two thousand miles from the Atlantic would view the question differently from those who lived in seaboard cities. Any rule designed for city dwellers "would not suit Indiana,

---

to 31 December 1844, 342 [electronic edition], *The Diaries of John Quincy Adams: A Digital Collection* (Boston: Massachusetts Historical Society, 2004), http://www.masshist.org/jqadiaries. The congressman shouted down was Joseph R. Ingersoll, whose brother Charles was a Democrat in the same Pennsylvania delegation. CG, 28th Cong., 2nd sess. (Jan. 20, 1845), 150.

22 CG, 29th Cong., 1st sess. (Dec. 17, 1845), 67.

23 Douglas was correct. As Paul Finkelman writes, "Under the antebellum Constitution each state was empowered with the right to decide who was a citizen and who was not. Similarly, each state determined what the qualifications were for voters or office-holders." "Was Dred Scott Correctly Decided? An 'Expert Report' for the Defendant," *Lewis and Clark Law Review*, 12 (Winter 2008), 1235. Lincoln also recognized the authority of states to enfranchise noncitizens. Mark A. Graber, *Dred Scott and the Problem of Constitutional Evil* (New York, 2006), 49. Before the Civil War, Nancy F. Cott observes, "[n]o document stipulated exactly what it meant to be a citizen of the United States." States largely defined it for themselves. "Marriage and Women's Citizenship in the United States, 1830–1934," *American Historical Review*, 103:5 (Dec. 1998), 1444.

Illinois, or Missouri." This showed "how rightly the Convention had judged" when they left suffrage for the states to settle.

As to naturalization, he said that Congress could alter the law to extend the period of probation to twenty-one years, if it pleased. It could "adopt the Native American creed, with all its narrowness and bigotry and selfishness and injustice; but do what it would, it never could reach the sacred right of suffrage – that was reserved to the states."[24] As obnoxious as he might find nativism, he conceded that Congress had the power to decide on naturalization, but it had no say on voting. The states had exclusive authority to determine suffrage qualifications for themselves. In other words, Congress could act amorally but not unconstitutionally.[25]

The House Judiciary Committee, as Douglas advocated, received the resolutions and recommended that no changes be made in the naturalization laws.[26] The next time the issue of naturalization came up was in the context of a territory, not a state. In preparing a bill to organize Oregon, Douglas wrested from his committee the loosest possible residency requirement and considerable latitude for the territorial legislature. It authorized every free white male inhabitant older than twenty-one who was a resident to vote and stand for office at the first election, but afterward the territorial legislature would prescribe the qualifications, provided that the right of suffrage and holding office was limited to American citizens or those who took oaths to become a citizen and to support the U.S. Constitution.[27]

When he brought the bill to the floor of the House, nativists and centralists pounced on it. An American Party congressman from New York was troubled that under the provision every free white man, "whether Jew or Gentile, Englishman or American," would be able to vote. Worse, "there would be nothing to prevent a British alien from walking in and taking his seat in this American territorial legislature."[28] An Ohio Whig was "wholly opposed to surrendering to the Territorial legislature the right of prescribing, permanently, the qualification of voters." That legislature should be a "mere agent of Congress."[29] Douglas argued that "an inhabitant of the territory from the very

---

[24] CG, 29th Cong., 1st sess. (Dec. 30, 1845), 113–114. For newspaper coverage of his speech, see USN, *Daily National Intelligencer*, Dec. 31, 1845; EAN, *New-Hampshire Patriot* (Concord), Jan. 8, 1846. The nativist political party, founded in 1843, changed its name from the American Republican to the Native American Party at a national convention in 1845. Tyler Anbinder, *Nativism and Slavery: The Know Nothings and the Politics of the 1850s* (New York, 1992), 12.

[25] The Supreme Court under Chief Justice Roger Taney similarly took an "amoral" approach to legislative power. Austin Allen, *Origins of the Dred Scott Case: Jacksonian Jurisprudence and the Supreme Court, 1837–1857* (Athens, GA, 2006), 14, 18–19, 25, 217.

[26] CG, 29th Cong., 1st sess. (Feb, 16, 1846), 353.

[27] CG, 29th Cong., 2nd sess. (Dec. 23, 1846), 71. See Bill 571, Section 12.

[28] GC, 29th Cong., 2nd sess. (Jan. 11, 1847), 166–167. On anti-Semitism and American politics at midcentury, see Frederick C. Jaher, *A Scapegoat in the New Wilderness: The Origins and Rise of Anti-Semitism in America* (Cambridge, MA, 1994), 177–196.

[29] GC, 29th Cong., 2nd sess. (Jan. 11, 1847), 167.

beginning ... ought in fairness to be allowed to have a vote."[30] Although he could not block a House amendment that denied the Oregon legislature's control over suffrage qualifications, he managed ultimately to have it overturned and his committee's original terms reinstated.[31]

This debate revealed that even congressional Democrats had become uncomfortable with having aliens vote. In the wake of a new tide of nativism, support for the practice waned.[32] Noncitizen voting struck more and more people as oxymoronic. Douglas's own state was in the process of ending it. The new Illinois Constitution permitted aliens who resided there only at the time of its adoption to vote, but thereafter foreigners would have to become naturalized. Douglas never spoke of aliens as having inalienable rights. His defense of their suffrage was always based on local choice. He did not challenge his state's constitution of 1848. And if a territorial legislature wanted to end alien suffrage, he would support their right to do so.

Douglas's ten-year history with alien suffrage prefigured his approach to slavery. Although he thought that noncitizen immigrants should be able to vote, he fought for them only as long as his state constitution permitted them to do so. Once the local majority decided against the right, the issue ceased to matter to him. Despite his personal abhorrence of nativism, he would have opposed congressional legislation that conferred the franchise on immigrants before they attained citizenship. The crux of the issue for him was never the plight or rights of immigrants but the right of states to determine who could vote. He was as morally neutral on the rights of European immigrants, whom he valued, as he would be on the condition of enslaved African Americans.[33]

---

[30] Ibid.

[31] Ibid., 167, 169.

[32] For the growth of nativism in the 1840s, see Daniel W. Howe, *What Hath God Wrought: The Transformation of America, 1815–1848* (New York, 2007), 822–827; Tyler V. Johnson, "Punishing the Lies on the Rio Grande: Catholic and Immigrant Volunteers in Zachary Taylor's Army and the Fight against Nativism," *Journal of the Early Republic*, 30 (Spring 2010), 63–84; Angela F. Murphy, "Daniel O'Connell and the 'American Eagle' in 1845: Slavery, Diplomacy, Nativism, and the Collapse of America's First Irish Nationalist Movement," *Journal of American Ethnic History*, 26:2 (Jan. 2007), 3–26; Bruce Dorsey, *Reforming Men and Women: Gender in the Antebellum City* (Ithaca, NY, 2002), 195–240; and Dale T. Knobel, *Paddy and the Republic: Ethnicity and Nationality in Antebellum America* (Middletown, CT, 1986). Matthew F. Jacobson, *Whiteness of a Different Color: European Immigrants and the Alchemy of Race* (Cambridge, MA, 1999), 43, suggests that in the 1840s nativism accompanied a shift to a new form of racism that divided white people into "a hierarchically arranged series of distinct 'white races.'" Along these lines, see also Nell I. Painter, "Ralph Waldo Emerson's Saxons," *Journal of American History*, 95:4 (Mar. 2009), 977–985. For an excellent overview of the historiography on American nativism, see Tyler Anbinder, "Nativism and Prejudice Against Immigrants," in *A Companion to American Immigration*, ed. Reed Ueta (Malden, MA, 2006), 177–201. The legislation of the 1840s sought to introduce a new rigor to procedures that had long been lax and that were conducive to fraud. For this administrative analysis, see Ronald Schultz, " 'Allegiance and Land Go Together': Automatic Naturalization and Immigration in Nineteenth-Century America," *American Nineteenth Century History*, 12:2 (2011), 149–176, esp. 159–161.

[33] For positive assessments of Douglas's position on immigration see Jaffa, *Crisis of the House Divided*, 102, and George B. Forgie, *Patricide in a House Divided: A Psychological Interpretation*

APPORTIONMENT

In December 1843 newly elected Illinois Congressman Stephen Douglas was appointed to the House Committee on Elections and Privileges. Although he was not its chair, Douglas wrote and delivered its much-awaited report recommending the seating of four delegations that had been elected at large in violation of the Apportionment Act of 1842, which required states to establish a single electoral district for each of its congressmen.[34] The election of 1840 had brought Whig majorities to both chambers, and they carried the legislation against a nearly unanimous Democratic opposition. The next off-year election, however, resulted in a stunning turnaround, whereby Democrats in the Twenty-Eighth House went from a 7:10 to a 20:10 ratio.[35] The new majority was faced with obeying a law that many thought was unconstitutional or nullifying it by accepting the four at-large delegations. Unlike the struggle for passage of the legislation, which involved both legislative chambers and the president, the question of seating the delegations engaged the House alone.[36]

Article I, Section 5 vested the House with ultimate power over its election returns. As a Democratic member said, "On this subject it [the House] has all the power of a court: its jurisdiction is as complete, and as little to be questioned, as is that of the Supreme Court."[37] The selection of the thirty-year-old freshman, referred to as "Judge Douglass" because of his recent service on the Illinois bench, strengthened the impression that the committee was deliberating like an impartial judicial tribunal.

Both Douglas's report and the minority report, read by Garrett Davis (W-KY), relied on arguments drawn from the apportionment debates of the Twenty-Seventh Congress.[38] Their reports underscored how the two parties traveled the same highway of constitutional construction before going off opposite

---

of Lincoln and His Age (New York, 1979), 163, wherein he contrasts his view to that of the Whig leader, Edward Everett.

[34] The four delegations were those from Georgia, Missouri, Mississippi, and New Hampshire.

[35] Whigs outnumbered Democrats 142 to 98 in the Twenty-Seventh House but held only 72 seats compared with 147 held by Democrats in the Twenty-Eighth. Office of the Clerk, U.S. House of Representatives, clerk.house.gov/histHigh/Congressional_History/index.html. For the election reversal of 1842, see Holt, *Rise and Fall of the American Whig Party*, 151–160.

[36] The Act of 1842 determined both the size of the House and electoral districts. Martin H. Quitt, "Congressional (Partisan) Constitutionalism: The Apportionment Act Debates of 1842 and 1844," *Journal of the Early Republic*, 28:4 (2008), 627–651; David P. Currie, *The Constitution in Congress: Democrats and Whigs, 1829–1861* (Chicago, 2005), 254–268; Charles A. Kromkowski, *Recreating the American Republic: Rules of Apportionment and American Political Development: 1770–1870* (New York, 2002), 333–339; Rosemarie Zagarri, *The Politics of Size: Representation in the United States, 1776–1850* (Ithaca, NY, 1988), 129–131; Johanna N. Shields, "Whigs Reform the 'Bear Garden': Representation and the Apportionment Act of 1842," *Journal of the Early Republic*, 5 (Fall 1985), 355–382; Michele Rosa-Clot, "The Apportionment Act of 1842: 'An Odious Use of Authority,' " *Parliaments, Estates and Representation*, 31:1 (2011), 33–52.

[37] CG, APP, 28th Cong., 1st sess. (Feb. 1844), 125.

[38] House Report No. 60, U.S. Serial Set, 28th Cong., 1st Sess. (Jan. 22, 1844).

ramps to their different destinations. Both sides cited records of the Federal Convention, *The Federalist*, and the state ratifying conventions. Both sides recognized that the American system was a complicated, mixed government of divided powers for which they lacked straightforward descriptive terms, yet each essayed a simplified analysis that reflected where it weighted popular sovereignty – in state legislatures for Democrats, in Congress for Whigs.[39]

The central constitutional question was whether Article I, Section 4 authorized Congress to compel states to establish electoral districts. It states, "The times, places and manner of holding elections for Senators and Representatives shall be prescribed in each state by the legislature thereof; but the Congress may at any time by law make or alter such regulations, except as to the place of choosing Senators."

Douglas laid out the Democrats' view of state–federal relations. The Constitution gave separate powers to the federal and state governments, "making each supreme in its appropriate sphere" and giving each the power to execute its own laws. There were cases "in which the power of legislation is, to some extent, concurrent; or where the laws of the States may be superseded by those of the Union." Neither authority, however, could "direct the legislative discretion of the other, and require enactments to be made in servile obedience to certain prescribed forms." This had been a line of argument in the Twenty-Seventh Congress as well. Where Congress might have a superseding authority, it had to exercise it fully but could not merely mandate the state legislatures to do its bidding. Accordingly, if Congress wanted to establish districts in all states, it must actually form and specify them. Otherwise, the states could ignore the directive, for the power of Congress over the elections was "entirely nugatory and inoperative without the aid of State legislation."

Douglas would remember this argument fourteen years later when Lincoln pressed him to reconcile the Supreme Court's decision in the *Dred Scott* case with his principle of popular sovereignty. Just as Democrats in the apportionment case contended that Congress could not require states to enact laws that would carry out its desire for districts, Douglas would argue that the Court could not compel the territorial legislatures to pass codes that would enforce its desire to protect slave ownership. The two cases were not identical, but the line of reasoning was the same.[40] In 1844 Douglas concluded his report with a resolution invalidating the districting requirement of the Apportionment Act as unconstitutional and calling for the seating of the four delegations.[41]

---

[39] In contrast to the approach here, a recent study of congressional control of voting dates ignores the influence of party ideology; instead it interprets federal policy historically as a nonpartisan accommodation to predominant state practice. Jeffrey M. Stonecash, Jessica E. Boscarino, and Rogan T. Kersh, "Congressional Intrusion to Specify Voting Dates for National Offices," *Publius*, 38:1 (Winter 2008), 137–151.

[40] On the provenance of the Freeport Doctrine see Robert E. May, "Squatter Sovereignty as the Freeport Doctrine: A Note on the Territorial Controversy in the U.S. House of Representatives in the Winter of 1855–1856," *Journal of Southern History*, 53:2 (May 1987), 304–306, esp. 304n.

[41] Report of the Committee of Elections, No. 60, pt. I, 2, 6, 7.

Davis outlined the Whigs' nationalist perspective, denying that federal and state governments were equally supreme in their respective spheres. The power to regulate elections to the House and Senate derives "exclusively from the Federal constitution," which relegated state legislatures below Congress in a single, hierarchically organized political system. "When Congress acts, there are not two distinct and independent systems of legislation; but, by the force of the constitution, it becomes one both of blended jurisdiction and legislation." The subordination of state legislatures to the "untrammeled authority" of Congress made the whole system "simple and harmonious." Article I, Section 4 meant that congressional legislation possessed an "overruling supremacy" regarding elections. Douglas said that a majority of the states during ratification had been unhappy about the language of Article I, Section 4, but none of their proposed amendments was adopted. In fact, the proposed changes gave "a key" to what Section 4 meant: it confided to Congress "the discretion to exercise, or not, either of the powers intrusted [*sic*] to it, at all times." That is why the states had wanted to amend the clause.[42]

Here was the nub of the partisan divergence. Both sides agreed on what the text stated; they disagreed over the interpretative implications of the ratifying conventions. Noting that seven of the thirteen original states had objected to the clause, Douglas wrote, "The constitution was adopted with the understanding (and probably never would have been adopted but for the understanding) that it was never to be exerted except in the few specified cases." Aaron Brown, a Tennessee Democrat, amplified the point in debate: the seven original states that opposed Article I, Section 4 yielded on the assumption that posterity would be guided and instructed by their concerns and would not take advantage of the "trying circumstances" under which they had voted for ratification. Thus Douglas and Brown added to the historical construction of the Constitution the expectation of ratifiers who understood the text to say one thing but who acted on the premise that future generations would honor their reservations. To do otherwise was to betray the faith of the founding generation. This expectation had been fulfilled by congressional acceptance of state election regulations since 1789 and the "universal acquiescence" of the people, who "have sanctioned it at the polls." The expectation of the ratifiers combined with more than a half-century of congressional precedence and popular assent to fortify the Democrats' case for the unconstitutionality of the districting paragraph.[43]

The House voted to seat the delegations from the four states but without approving Douglas's resolution regarding the constitutionality of the districting mandate or a proposal by Aaron Brown to rescind the relevant section of the Apportionment Act.[44] When Douglas said that either the districting provision

---

[42] Ibid., pt. II, 6, 7, 8.

[43] Ibid., pt. I, 5, 10; CG, APP, 28th Cong., 1st sess. (Feb. 9, 1844), 172; Larry D. Kramer, *The People Themselves: Popular Constitutionalism and Judicial Review* (New York, 2004), 78.

[44] *Journal of the House of Representatives*, 28th Cong., 1st sess. (Feb. 13–15, 1844), 372, 377, 395, 396, 1208, Bill 12.

or state laws had to yield, he underestimated the ability of the House to live with a murky compromise: it seated the delegates from the four states that did not comply with the apportionment law but let the legislation stand for its ten-year limit. The act was temporarily nullified but not repealed.

Douglas's response to the Apportionment Act was visceral as well as intellectual. Despite his judicial experience, he did not maintain an even demeanor. He felt impelled to push back against an aggressive central power. Congressman John Quincy Adams described Douglas's emotional state in defending his report: "His face was convulsed, his gesticulation frantic, and he lashed himself into such a heat that if his body had been made of combustible matter it would have burnt out.... And this comes from a man from the judicial bench."[45] Although Douglas's performance was partially deliberate, the affect he brought to the issue could not be wholly controlled. On the Apportionment Act, Douglas's feelings and intellect were in concert. On internal improvements, however, there was disharmony between what he wanted and what he thought possible or proper.

INTERNAL IMPROVEMENTS

Douglas was a champion of manifest destiny and geographic integration. Like the great Whig visionary Henry Clay, Douglas the Democrat would have loved to have had a national government capable of conceptualizing and implementing a comprehensive plan for knitting the West into a continental transportation grid that stretched from the Atlantic to the Pacific and from the Great Lakes to the Gulf of Mexico.[46] Historian Yonatan Eyal sees Douglas as a leader of a younger generation of Democrats, based mainly in the West, who transformed the party in the 1840s, eschewing the agrarianism and "constitutional rigidity" of the Jacksonians and embracing the market economy and internal improvements.[47] Eyal's analysis underscores for us the tension between Douglas's vision of a national infrastructure and his constitutionalism.

Douglas viewed the Constitution as well as congressional politics as obstacles to federally funded public works, as he explained in an August 1852 speech opposing a river and harbor bill. He read from Madison's *Notes on the Debates in the Federal Convention* to document why the Constitution did not authorize Congress to construct canals and internal improvements generally. The power to do so directly or through the medium of a congressionally created corporation was expressly proposed and rejected at the Philadelphia

---

[45] John Quincy Adams diary 44, 233 [electronic edition].

[46] John J. Binder, "The Transportation Revolution and Antebellum Section Disagreement," *Social Science History*, 35:1 (Spring 2011), 19–57, provocatively argues that instead of knitting the sections together as proponents envisioned, the transportation revolution contributed to political divisions in the 1850s by tying the West and East together more closely commercially and demographically while leaving the South less essential.

[47] Yonatan Eyal, *The Young America Movement and the Transformation of the Democratic Party, 1828–1861* (New York, 2007), 44–53, quote on 46.

Convention. Moreover, Douglas's nine years in Washington taught him the futility of trying to gain a sustainable federal program. Only omnibus bills, which gave a little to many but not enough to any, could be passed. The result was a waste of funding.[48]

In light of these impediments to effective federal projects, Douglas proposed that Congress, under the authority of Article I, Section 10, empower the states to assume full responsibility and funding for harbor and river improvements by levying tonnage duties. He reasserted this proposal in a public letter to Governor Joel Matteson of Illinois on January 2, 1854. The main thrust of his open letter was to refine the case for having Congress turn over to the states the authority to raise funds for and manage their own infrastructure requirements. After conceding uncertainty "if the power of Congress to protect navigation has any existence in the Constitution," he suggested that the "existence" and "propriety" of that power were "affirmed in some form and exercised to a greater or less extent by each successive Congress" when it provided "for the erection of light-houses, the planting of buoys, the construction of piers, the removal of snags, the dredging of canals, the inspection of steamboat boilers, the carrying of life boats" and generally for the security and safety of navigation. If Congress consistently exercised a power after 1789, it had "propriety," said Douglas, who thereby reversed the position he had taken on the Senate floor sixteen months earlier.[49]

Why did he change his opinion on the constitutionality of federal internal improvements? It would not enhance his party standing, for, as he acknowledged, "perhaps, a majority of the Democratic party" believed that "a general system of internal improvements by the Federal Government" violated the Constitution. Indeed, this tenet remained the second plank on the Democratic platform from 1840 through 1856, always following and therefore serving as the initial illustration of the party's fundamental doctrine, "[t]hat the federal government is one of limited powers ... and that it is inexpedient and dangerous to exercise doubtful constitutional powers."[50] Douglas's turnabout placed him at odds with a basic position of his party, while it did not advance his argument for shifting the burden to the states.

Equally puzzling was why he opened his letter to Matteson with a discussion of a recently settled legal issue that was irrelevant to his proposal. There long had been a jurisprudential obstacle to the West's receipt of its fair share of funding for waterway projects. Douglas had contributed significantly to the removal of this hurdle during his first term in Congress, when he had

---

[48] CG, APP, 32nd Cong., 1st sess. (Aug. 23, 1852), 1128. For Madison's *Notes*, see Farrand, ed., *Records of the Federal Convention*, 2: 615. For Jackson's view on the constitutionality of internal improvements, see Richard E. Ellis, *The Union at Risk: Jacksonian Democracy, States' Rights and the Nullification Crisis* (New York, 1987), 19–25.

[49] Stephen A. Douglas to Joel A. Matteson, *Letters of SAD*, 273.

[50] Ibid., 275. Party platforms were accessed at John T. Woolley and Gerhard Peters, the American Presidency Project [online], Santa Barbara, CA: University of California (hosted), Gerhard Peters (database), http://www.presidency.ucsb.edu/ws/?pid=29577.

shepherded House passage of a bill that challenged the Supreme Court's tide-water rule restricting federal admiralty jurisdiction to the high seas. His bill expanded federal court jurisdiction to lakes and navigable rivers.[51] In 1852 the Supreme Court reversed itself and upheld the Douglas-sponsored statute. Chief Justice Taney stated that the English common law distinction between fresh- and saltwater was inapplicable to the United States, where the navigability of internal waterways beyond the tidal mark brought them within the constitutional scope of admiralty and maritime jurisdiction.[52] Taney's decision reinforced Douglas's stand against those who argued that congressional responsibility for navigation did not include internal waterways.

Now that both Congress and the Supreme Court had removed the distinction between fresh- and saltwater jurisdiction, why did Douglas reargue his case, especially when the main thrust of his letter was to propose an alternative to federal funding? The most plausible explanation for this extraneous discussion is that he was preoccupied with the question of constitutionalism because of his preparation for the Nebraska bill that he would introduce two days after dating his letter to Governor Matteson. The line of inquiry he had researched was the weight of congressional precedent in establishing the constitutionality of legislation. Both the funding of internal improvements and the prohibition of slavery in the territories had been objects of federal statutes from the beginning of the Republic. Did Congress have the right to prohibit slavery in the territories? Did Congress have the right to undertake river and harbor projects? Neither power was expressly delegated in Article I, Section 8.

What was now clear to Douglas, however, was that the intentions of the framers and ratifiers of 1787 were insufficient to determine the powers of the federal government. The understanding of Congress was another dimension of constitutional propriety. The fact that every successive Congress directed appropriations to the improvement of harbors and rivers and that he himself had urged the inclusion of freshwaters could not be improper. Although legislators had cited the common law to oppose funding freshwater projects, Congress had done so regularly. Moreover, Douglas had sponsored legislation that expanded federal court jurisdiction over internal waterways, an act that the Taney Court reaffirmed.

Foreshadowing recent scholarship that documents or advocates the influence of politics on constitutional meaning, Douglas now claimed that the consistent exercise of a power by Congress affirmed its constitutionality, even where there was evidence that the framers had intended to withhold it.[53]

---

[51] CG, 28th Cong., 2nd sess. (Feb. 25, 1845), 345; *U.S. Statutes at Large*, 5: 726.

[52] *Genesee Chief v. Fitzhugh*, 12 How. (53 U.S.) 443. The decision has been described "as a triumphant marriage of technological development and legal advance, based on a realistic appraisal of adopting one rule of law or another." Harold M. Hyman and William M. Wiecek, *Equal Justice under Law: Constitutional Development, 1835 – 1875* (New York, 1982), 75.

[53] William N. Eskridge, Jr., and John Ferejohn, *A Republic of Statutes: The New American Constitution* (New Haven, CT, 2010), traces judicial deference to certain statutes. Keith Whittington, *Political Foundations of Judicial Supremacy: The Presidency, the Supreme Court,*

This was consonant with the position some Democrats had taken during the Apportionment Act debate ten years earlier, when they claimed that more than a half-century of congressional deference to state control of elections reflected the meaning of the text. This conclusion did not advance Douglas's purpose either with his own internal improvements proposal or with his views on congressional regulation of slavery in the territories. Rather, it reflected his genuine struggle to determine the constitutionality of policies. A historian of internal improvements concludes that constitutional arguments were not a "real constraint" but rather a "legitimating device used by opponents."[54] Certainly politicians invoked the Constitution against proposals they opposed. At the same time, some had sufficient respect for the document to wrestle with its provisions honestly to satisfy themselves as to its intent.

It obscures the balancing act that numerous congressmen experienced to suggest that they mined the Constitution only to rationalize their positions. The lawmaker as advocate had to live with himself as a citizen. As Mark Graber observes, in some cases "constitutional decision-makers make self-conscious decisions to follow the Constitution rather than their policy preferences."[55] In Douglas's case the activist contended with the jurist.[56] His colleagues in

and *Constitutional Leadership in U.S. History* (Princeton, NJ, 2007), and Kramer, *The People Themselves*, show the influence of politics on judicial interpretation. Nevertheless, as Mark Graber demonstrates, most major political questions did not come before the antebellum Supreme Court. "Resolving Political Questions into Judicial Questions: Tocqueville's Thesis Revisited," *Constitutional Commentary*, 21 (Summer 2004), 485–544.

The continuing importance of congressional history to Douglas's constitutionalism was reflected during his last term in the Senate when he supported the purchase of sufficient copies of the *Annals of Congress* (1789–1824) and the *Register of Debates* (1824–1837). CG, 37th Cong., Special Sess., 1520–1521.

[54] Stephen Minicucci, "Internal Improvements and the Union," *Studies in American Political Development*, 18 (Fall 2004), 163n.

[55] Mark A, Graber, "Constitutional Law and American Politics," in *The Oxford Handbook of Law and Politics*, ed. Keith Whittington, R. Daniel Kelemen, and Gregory A. Caldeira (New York, 2008), 316.

[56] He was not alone. Presidents Madison, Monroe, Jackson, and Polk vetoed internal improvement bills. All did so exclusively on constitutional grounds. Their veto messages (including Monroe's attached essay) indicate that constitutionalism was their central concern because they worried about the balance of power shifting toward a consolidating central government. Madison's veto of the Bonus Bill, Mar. 3, 1817, James D. Richardson, ed., *A Compilation of the Messages and Papers of the Presidents, 1789–1897*, 10 vols. (New York, 1901), 1: 584–585; Monroe's veto of a bill to erect tollgates on the Cumberland (National) Road, May 4, 1822, to which he attached an extended essay that he had prepared on the constitutionality of internal improvements, 2: 142–183; Jackson's veto of the Maysville Road, 2: 483–493; and Polk's veto of a harbors and rivers bill, Aug. 3, 1846, 4: 460–466.

Monroe and Jackson recommended a constitutional amendment granting Congress the power to fund internal improvements. Had such an amendment been adopted, we can surmise three results. First, presidents would no longer have vetoed these bills, because constitutionalism was the principal justification for that instrument before the Civil War. Second, without the necessity of a two-thirds override, more improvement bills would have been enacted. Third, a national transportation network still would not have been built, because the antebellum Congress never could come together on a general system of public works.

the House and later the Senate addressed him as "Judge Douglas," as did his own family members. He had served on the Illinois bench for only two years, yet he cherished the title that it brought. In the Matteson letter of 1854 the weight he attached to interpreting the Constitution impartially collided with his proposal to turn internal improvements over to the states. It would have been less problematic for him to restate his party's stand and his own earlier one on the lack of constitutional authority for federal projects. That he did not take the easier route testifies to the earnestness with which he approached the question.

Douglas's research into congressional history in preparation for his Nebraska bill led him to revise his thinking about the propriety of federal internal improvements. If congressional action in the one area had been constitutional despite an absence of explicit textual authority, it had to be proper in the other as well. Neither of these conclusions advanced either of his proposals in January 1854: to leave the slavery decision entirely to the people of the territory and to turn harbor and river projects entirely to the people of the states.

If the federal appropriations were proper, what was now his rationale for having states take over internal water transportation? Recent scholarship demonstrates that Douglas had it right when he explained why the federal government could not be depended upon.[57] His analysis of why congressional politics inhibited a national program of internal improvements was based on his experience in Washington and his research on the history of legislation. Indeed, for all of his skills as an extemporaneous debater, Douglas's persuasiveness in the capitol over the long haul owed much to his preparation. He usually brought an impressive amount of knowledge about the subject.

Illinois voters in the lake districts wanted federal subsidies for the improvement of their harbors and rivers. Douglas had always supported them despite the official opposition of his party.[58] He claimed that he had tried to obtain a river and harbor bill during his entire tenure in Congress but that it had been "a death struggle that taxed the physical strength of members." He said that year after year "at midnight, on the last day of the session," proponents often were defeated, only to launch another effort at the beginning of the next

---

[57] Minicucci, "Internal Improvements"; John J. Wallis, "The National Era," in *Government and the American Economy*, ed. Price V. Fishback et al. (Chicago, 2007), 148–187; John J. Wallis and Barry R. Weingast, "Equilibrium Impotence: Why the States and Not the American National Government Financed Economic Development in the Antebellum Era," Working Paper 11397, National Bureau of Economic Research, Cambridge, MA., June 2005. I am grateful to Professor Wallis for sending me this paper. John L. Larson, *Internal Improvement: National Public Works and the Promise of Popular Government in the Early United States* (Chapel Hill, NC, 2001), comprehensively covers both the failure of federal initiatives and the inadequacy of state-centered programs. His conclusion regarding the lethal influence of logrolling on congressional efforts (183–184) is consistent with Douglas's analysis.

[58] Marc Egnal, *Clash of Extremes: The Economic Origins of the Civil War* (New York, 2009), 113. On the interest of the Great Lakes area in internal improvements see also his "The Beards Were Right: Parties in the North, 1840–1860," *Civil War History*, 47: 1 (2001), esp. 45–50.

session – with the same results.[59] Once every four or five years they would have success, but only by agreeing to an omnibus bill "in which all sorts of works were crowded together, good and bad, wise and foolish, national and local" in order to secure a majority.[60] When they did manage to enact a bill, it would allow for the purchase of dredging machines and other equipment in preparation for projects "without completing the first thing." The next year another struggle would ensue, a follow-up bill would be defeated, and therefore "every farthing in this bill will be wasted."[61] Why? Because once funding stopped, projects would be abandoned, machinery and materials would be auctioned off, "fires and snags" would once again produce shipwrecks and deaths, and a new cycle of starting and stopping improvements would begin again.[62]

For Douglas, history was the best guide by which to make policy. "If we are to judge the system by its results, taking the past as a fair indication of what might reasonably be expected in the future," he urged that it was unwise to continue to do what "has proven a miserable failure." Federal efforts, he added, had been "even worse than a failure" because they had deflected energy and resources from the states, which had a superior record in internal improvements. His example was the growth of railroad lines under state supervision and funding. He claimed in January 1854 that some fourteen thousand miles of track had been completed and that fifteen thousand more were under contract. How much would have been accomplished if railroads had depended on federal appropriations, he asked and answered, as he pointed to the inability of the Washington government to complete a three-hundred-mile national road in a quarter-century. He said he was "not aware that the Federal Government ever completed any work of internal improvement commenced under its auspices."[63]

Accordingly, he proposed having the states assume full responsibility and funding for harbor and river improvements. Again his starting point was what

[59] CG, APP, 32nd Cong., 1st sess. (Aug. 23, 1852), 1130. The bill's sponsor, Jacob Miller (W-NJ), said it was the same bill that had passed the House during the preceding session but had been rejected in the Senate on the last night when it had been too late to have a vote – a delay, he said, that had been the habit in both houses for this kind of measure. CG, 32nd Cong., 1st sess. (Dec. 22, 1851), 130.

[60] Stephen A. Douglas to Joel A. Matteson, *Letters of SAD*, 274.

[61] CG, APP, 32nd Cong., 1st sess. (Aug. 23, 1852), 1130.

[62] Stephen A. Douglas to Joel A. Matteson, Jan. 2, 1854, *Letters of SAD*, 273. Minicucci, "Internal Improvements," 176–181, tries to quantify the logrolling that occurred throughout the period. As Yonatan Eyal writes, Douglas "was willing to champion an expanded federal role in these projects, but Congress let him down." *Young America Movement*, 60.

[63] Stephen A. Douglas to Joel A. Matteson, *Letters of SAD*, Jan. 2, 1854, 275–276. He ignored the role of federal land subsidies in railroad development, especially the Illinois Central, which became the first land-grant railroad in the United States thanks to passage of a bill that Douglas engineered through Congress in 1850. It received 2.5 million acres of federal land and became by 1856 "the longest railroad in the world." John F. Stover, *The Routledge Historical Atlas of the American Railroads* (New York, 1999), 76; Stover, *The History of the Illinois Central Railroad* (New York, 1975), 15; Johannsen, *SAD*, 306–317; Eyal, *Young America Movement*, 47–48, 60.

the Constitution permitted. Article I, Section 10 prohibited a state from levying tonnage duties or entering into an agreement with another state without
the consent of Congress. He proposed that Congress authorize states to levy
tonnage duties solely for improving waterways and to form compacts for
improving rivers that ran between them.[64] Further he favored states having the
discretion to empower their municipalities to levy the duties and make their
own harbors on "the principle that the local authorities at any town are better
capable" than federal engineers of judging which improvements are necessary,
what the costs should be, and how best to achieve them.

Douglas's belief in localism was reinforced by the history of federal failures.
Here he said that he was not depreciating the services, intelligence, or science of
federal engineers; rather, he was pointing to the knowledge of every waterway
that only on-site practitioners would possess. Engineers could not learn in their
science classes at West Point "what effect will be produced in navigable water
by works intended to control or restrain its channel." Only "the pilot, captain,
or owner of a vessel, who, for twenty years" had watched daily the "storms,
currents, and tempests upon these shifting bars and varying channels," he
claimed, could "tell what the effect of the sinking of a buoy, or the construction
of a pier will have upon the channel." He believed such "local knowledge, the
result of long-continued observation," was essential if the money appropriated
was to improve navigability. And he was certain that "local knowledge does
not exist and cannot be found in the Topographical Corps."[65]

When he voted against the Rivers and Harbor Bill of 1852, a bill for
improving rivers and harbors, he unleashed a cascade of criticism on himself.[66]
Nevertheless, in his letter to Matteson he said he would vote against a similar
bill again. Douglas's proposal received widespread attention but insufficient
support in Congress and at home. When he did vote against another rivers and
harbors bill eight months after his Matteson letter, he was criticized again. In
Chicago harbor, flags were lowered to half-mast.[67] The areas most in need of

---

[64] CG, APP, 32nd Cong., 1st sess. (Aug. 23, 1852), 1127.

[65] CG, APP, 32nd Cong., 1st sess. (Aug. 23, 1852), 1127. Distrust of the Topographical Corps
was fueled by a "series of construction fiascos" in the 1830s. Todd A. Shallat, *Structures in the
Stream: Water, Science, and the Rise of the U. S. Army Corps of Engineers* (Austin, TX, 1994),
4–5. The naturally formidable challenge to the corps to improve waterways was complicated
by the ebb and flow of political support and compromised by its chief engineer's financial scan-
dal. Shallat, *Structures*, 140–154, 160–172. The Topographical Corps, comprising primarily
surveyors, was a War Department agency that originated during the War of 1812. From 1831
it remained separate from the older Army Corps of Engineers, founded in 1802, until both
units were merged during the Civil War. Congress formalized their responsibilities for internal
improvements by the General Survey Act of 1824. Forest G. Hill, *Army Engineers, Rails &
Waterways: Army Engineers and Early Transportation* (Norman, OK, 1957), 10–12, 37–95.

[66] Johannsen, *SAD*, 437–438.

[67] For his vote, CG, APP, 33rd Cong., 1st sess. (Aug. 1, 1854), 1210. His participation in the debate
typically displayed his knowledge about the mechanics of particular projects. For example, see
his discussion of past federal attempts to cut through sandbars in the Ohio River (1185). For
the reaction in Illinois, see Johannsen, *SAD*, 438. Illinois had reason to prefer federal support.

river and harbor improvements believed that the policy would place an unequal burden on them while benefiting the "rich states of the Atlantic border."[68] On this issue Douglas proved not to be a prophet in his own section. Some opponents who still admired him preferred to believe that the plan was hatched in the East in order to have the West pay for "the commerce of the merchants of New York and Boston."[69] Besides, by August 1854 the Kansas–Nebraska Act took up so much oxygen that Douglas's scheme for state assumption of internal improvements barely breathed.

In sum, on noncitizen suffrage, apportionment, and internal improvements, from his time as a young attorney in Illinois through his first decade in Washington, Douglas wrestled with the Constitution not simply to justify his policy preferences but to explicate its meaning within the context of the framers' intent, the ratifiers' understanding, and congressional usage. He brought to this task a deeply felt inclination to protect states from the centralizing power. In the case of transportation infrastructure, however, he was willing to set aside his distrust of the federal government but eventually despaired of its inefficiencies and ineptitude and wound up urging Congress to enhance state self-sufficiency. His faith in local self-government vis-à-vis Washington also guided his approach to the territories.

Laurence J. Malone, *Opening the West: Federal Internal Improvement before 1860* (Westport, CT, 1998), 22–24, finds that its region, which included Indiana, Michigan, Ohio, and Wisconsin, received the highest percentage of all federal aid from 1800 to 1860, although it ranked third among nine regions in funding for both rivers and harbors.

[68] USN, *Bangor Daily Whig & Courier* (Bangor, ME), Jan. 7, 1854.
[69] USN, *Daily Cleveland Herald*, Jan. 18, 1854.

6

Constitutionalism, Part II

Slavery in the Territories

> In the absence of any express opinions on the subject with reference to the Territories, the fair inference would be that the same principles that applied to the States applied to the Territories.
>
> Stephen A, Douglas (1860)[1]

Douglas shaped territorial policy as chair of the Committee on Territories, first during his sophomore term in the House of Representatives (December 1845 to March 1847), then for a decade in the Senate (December 1847 to December 1858). He was replaced at the beginning of the second session of the Thirty-Fifth Congress, mainly because of his widely disseminated contention during his Freeport debate with Lincoln that popular sovereignty could trump the *Dred Scott* decision of the Supreme Court and his equally publicized opposition to the proslavery constitution for Kansas that his party's president supported.[2]

That he was chosen chair at the beginning of his second term in the House reflected his standing already as a sectional mediator, an expansionist, a knowledgeable constitutionalist, and a localist.[3] He wanted Congress to be minimally intrusive. Here his intellectual challenge was greater than it was in defending state prerogatives, because the Constitution was straightforward about congressional authority over territories. The framers did not spend much time on the matter, because they did not foresee the expansion that would take place in the nineteenth century. The main concern in the 1780s about western lands was their implication for equality among the original states, and this had been addressed when the oldest ones ceded their claims to the central government under the Confederation.[4] The Constitution simply granted Congress in Article

---

[1] David R. Barbee and Milledge L. Bonham, Jr., eds., "The Montgomery Address of Stephen A. Douglas, *Journal of Southern History*, 5:4 (1939), 531–532.

[2] Johannsen, *SAD*, 685–689; CG, 35th Cong., 2nd sess. (Dec. 13, 1858), 45.

[3] CG, 29th Cong., 1st sess. (Dec. 8, 1845), 25.

[4] On western lands and state equality, see Peter S. Onuf, *The Origins of the Federal Republic: Jurisdictional Controversies in the United States, 1775–1787* (Philadelphia, 1983), 194–198.

IV, Section 3, §2 "power to dispose of and make all needful rules and regulations respecting the territory or other property belonging to the United States."
Congress read this clause to mean that it possessed an absolute power to govern the territories as it chose.

This interpretation struck Douglas as a violation of what the Revolution
was about – equal political rights for people living in colonies or territories. He
did not contest the constitutionality of congressional intervention; rather, he
denied its propriety initially on the basis of the equal footing doctrine, which
he helped exalt as basic law, and later on the broader principle of popular sovereignty, with which he had less success.

He invoked the equal footing doctrine during his first term in Congress,
when he staked out ground as a spokesman for territories' control of their prospective state constitutions. In February 1845 a bill admitting Iowa and Florida
to statehood came to the House floor. The proposed constitution for Florida
prohibited its legislature from emancipating slaves or barring their immigration. A Maine congressman offered an amendment striking the prohibition
from the document. Ad hominem remarks peppered the debate that ensued
between New England and Southern members.[5] Douglas tried to reduce the
forensic temperature by deflecting attention from slavery to constitutionalism.
Here was the first instance in which, according to Michael Sandel's influential formulation, he "bracketed" the hot moral issue of slavery by refocusing
attention on the right procedure that Congress should follow.[6] There were provisions in the Iowa Constitution he found distasteful. Some in the Florida document were "still more objectionable – positively obnoxious so much so, that
he never could sanction and endorse them by any vote of his." But if it were
necessary for every member of the House to endorse every article of a constitution, no new state would ever be admitted. "The great diversity of opinion,
growing out of the variety of climate, soil, productions, pursuits, and customs
would preclude the hope of procuring a general concurrence of sentiment in
favor of every provision of any constitution. Some would require a restricted
suffrage, others universal; some a distinction founded on property, others on
color citizenship, and a great variety of qualifications to be found in the constitutions of the several States. The same difficulty would arise in regard to the
tenure of office, slavery, and many other regulations and institutions peculiar
to each State, and domestic in its character."[7]

In light of these differences, Douglas was confident that the framers of the
Constitution never intended for Congress "to pass on the propriety and expe-
diency of clauses of the constitution of the new states. The people of each
state are to form their own constitution in their own way and in accordance
with their own views; subject to one restriction only; and that was, it should

[5] CG, 28th Cong, 2nd sess. (Feb. 13, 1845), 283.
[6] Michael J. Sandel, *Democracy's Discontent: America in Search of a Public Philosophy* (Cambridge, MA, 1996), 21–23.
[7] CG, 28th Cong., 2nd sess. (Feb. 13, 1845), 284.

be republican in character." The "same obnoxious provisions" in the Florida Constitution could be found in the constitutions of other states. Congress could not reject the application of a territory for statehood "merely on account of its peculiar domestic institutions." To do so would be to treat new states and the original states unequally, "in derogation of the constitution of the United States, and consequently void."[8]

As early as his freshman term in Congress, then, before he was chosen chair of the House Committee on Territories, Douglas outlined his position on slavery there. Although he found the institution "obnoxious" and would not vote for it, the people of the Florida territory should be on equal footing with people in existing states by being able to include slavery in the constitution they would submit with their application for statehood. From 1845 through 1860 Douglas never retreated from this argument, despite the fact that the Constitution did not place the people in territories on equal footing with people in states.

The only ground for Douglas to believe that the Constitution prescribed that new states be admitted on the basis of equal footing with existing ones was congressional precedent. Beginning with its acceptance of the Virginia Cession on March 1, 1784, the national legislature had recognized that new states should enter the Union "with the same rights of sovereignty, freedom, and independence, as the other States."[9] The Northwest Ordinance of July 13, 1787, reworded the principle enduringly: new states were to be admitted "on an equal footing with the original states, in all respects whatever."[10] Six weeks later the Philadelphia Convention debated and rejected a clause in the Constitution whereby "new States shall be admitted on the same terms with the original States." Opponents preferred "leaving the Legislature free" to decide the question for itself.[11] Nevertheless, Congress reenacted the Northwest Ordinance in 1789 and inserted the equal footing phrase routinely in statehood statutes from 1796.[12] This repeated statutory usage gave it canonical standing. By 1845, in Pollard's *Lessee v. Hagan*, the Supreme Court accepted the doctrine "as if it were an inherent attribute of the Federal Union."[13] This

---

[8] Ibid; James L. Huston, *Stephen A. Douglas and the Dilemmas of Democratic Equality* (Lanham, MD, 2007), 65.

[9] Henry S. Commager, ed., *Documents of American History*, 7th ed. (New York, 1963), 120–121.

[10] Ibid., 131.

[11] Max Farrand, ed., *The Records of the Federal Convention of 1787*, 4 vols. (New Haven, CT, 1966), 2: 454–455.

[12] *U.S. Statutes at Large*, 1st Cong., 1st sess., 50–53. Tennessee, June 1, 1796. *U.S. Statutes at Large*, 4th Cong.,1st sess., 492.

[13] CRS, The Annotated Constitution, at www.law.cornell.edu/anncon/html/art4frag13_user. html#fnb260. Pollard's counsel argued that the Constitution explicitly provided that new states "must be admitted into the union on an equal footing with the rest." The Court ruled, "To maintain any other doctrine, is to deny that Alabama has been admitted into the union on an equal footing with the original states, the constitution, laws, and compact, to the contrary notwithstanding" (44 How 212). Justice Joseph Story, who still sat on the Court, had given the entire Northwest Ordinance quasi-constitutional authority in 1833 when he ascribed to it "certain fundamental articles of compact between the original states, and the people and states

opinion was given five days after Douglas cited the principle.[14] Here was a case where congressional constitutionalism influenced the jurisprudential interpretation of the Constitution. Both Congress and the Supreme Court accorded the Northwest Ordinance the standing of what some modern legal scholars would call a "superstatute."[15] Although the equal footing doctrine of the ordinance was specifically rejected at the Philadelphia Convention, it became a foundational principle that is still accepted as if it were in the Constitution.[16] Although Douglas would later try to diminish the standing of the Northwest Ordinance because of its prohibition of slavery, he treated its equal footing doctrine as if it were explicit constitutional text.

Douglas could not play a lone hand, but during his thirteen years as the designated leader on territorial policy in one chamber or the other, he had more cumulative influence than any other individual. His view of federal authority regarding territories gave the settlers great latitude in regulating their affairs: settlers should be subject to executive control in matters affecting international relations; but the local legislature should be able to adopt laws that best suited the people of its territory, although final approval was to rest with Congress. His longevity as chair owed as much to his moderation as to his views. For example, in 1846 he favored a bill establishing a government for the Oregon Territory that left the existing laws in place, "believing them better adapted to the people there than any we could adopt." He was asked if the bill he supported enabled Congress to repeal laws of the Oregon legislature. He responded that territorial laws had to be "reported" to Congress, which could disapprove them.[17] His committee, in fact, reported a bill "disaffirming" all laws in the territory of Wisconsin and Iowa granting franking privileges.[18] He was a pragmatist, not an extremist. Besides, the postal system was the most effective instrument of national integration – a value that was also dear to Douglas, who would not permit local interference with so useful a federal operation.[19]

---

in the territory, which are to remain unalterable, unless by common consent." *Commentaries on the Constitution of the United States*, 3 vols. (Boston, 1833), 3: ch. 31, no. 1312. On the Northwest Ordinance as "ordinary legislation" that could be altered by Congress at any time, see George W. Van Cleve, *A Slaveholders' Union: Slavery, Politics, and the Constitution in the Early American Republic* (Chicago, 2010), 157, and 155–156 on the equal footing clause.

[14] For the date of the decision, February 18, see USN, *Daily National Intelligence*, Feb. 24, 1845.

[15] William N. Eskridge, Jr., and John Ferejohn, *A Republic of Statutes: The New American Constitution* (New Haven, CT, 2010), 16–17, 26–28. Their examples include the U.S. Bank Acts of 1791 and 1816, Sherman Act of 1890, Federal Reserve Act of 1913, Social Security Act of 1935, Civil Rights Act of 1964, Voting Rights Act of 1965, Clean Water Acts of 1972 and 1977, and Pregnancy Discrimination Act of 1978.

[16] Kristina Alexander and Ross W. Gorte, "Federal Land Ownership: Constitutional Authority and the History of Acquisition, Disposal, and Retention," *CRS Report for Congress*, Dec. 3, 2007, incorrectly states, "The equal footing doctrine is based on Article IV, § 3, Clause 1 of the Constitution."

[17] CG, 29th Cong., 1st sess. (Aug. 6, 1846), 1203.

[18] CG, 29th Cong., 1st sess. (May 11, 1846), 789–790.

[19] On the role of the postal system in symbolizing the federal government and knitting the expanding nation together, see Richard R. John, *Spreading the News: The American Postal System from Franklin to Morse* (Cambridge, MA, 1995).

Another example of his pragmatism occurred in June 1850 while he was defending the principle of territorial self-government. His Senate committee recommended without revision a House bill that made appropriations for "the erection of penitentiaries" in the Oregon and Minnesota territories.[20] Two southern Democratic Senators opposed it. Both were concerned with Congress telling a territory how to spend funds. Andrew Butler of South Carolina thought that stipulating the construction of penitentiaries was "anticipating what a State might do for itself." He did not think that Congress had "a right to prescribe as to the mode of punishment, or the public buildings there." Moreover, the whole system of penitentiaries was controversial and had not been adopted in all states.[21] William King of Alabama concurred that "we should not impose upon the people what would not be agreeable to them when they become a State." He too noted the opposition of many states to the penitentiary system.

Douglas shrewdly ignored the issue about which he felt as strongly as anyone in the chamber – the right of the territory to decide internal matters itself. Instead he shifted the focus of the discussion from congressional "prescription" to the pressing need of the territory for aid. He found it "immaterial what you call it, whether a prison, a jail, or a penitentiary." In the absence of such a structure, people charged with murder could not be confined, but instead were watched by military guards at a considerable charge. "In one year, the expense of guarding them, in this way, will be twice what it will cost to build a prison." To return the bill to the House because of some word changes would result in a needless delay. Douglas's overriding goal was to gain passage immediately because the steamer was "about to leave, and the object is to send the money now." The bill passed.[22] His practical concern for getting the funds immediately to the territories overcame scruples he shared over congressional direction of their expenditure.

The slavery question, however, did not lend itself to such moderation, which was a reason that Douglas gave for removing it from congressional deliberations. In August 1846 David Wilmot (D-PA) proposed to exclude slavery from any territory acquired from Mexico. Douglas did not speak on it but consistently voted against the Wilmot Proviso.[23] The acrimony it unleashed in the House disturbed him. He tried to stake out a middle ground on slavery between Northern prohibitionists and Southern expansionists without antagonizing either. In December he submitted a bill to organize the Oregon Territory. His bill extended the Northwest Ordinance as the accepted blueprint for establishing a territorial government and attaining statehood. Its antislavery provision was not a serious consideration for him, because he knew that the institution would not be introduced there and, as he said in

[20] H.R. 148, 31st Cong., 1st sess.
[21] For the "invention of the penitentiary" in Jacksonian America, see David J. Rothman, *The Discovery of the Asylum: Social Order and Disorder in the New Republic* (Boston, 1971), 79–108.
[22] CG, 31st Cong., 1st sess. (June 8, 1850), 1167–1169.
[23] Johannsen, *SAD*, 201.

another context, he did not care what was in a document if it was "a nullity. Nullities had no terror for him."[24]

The fallout from the Wilmot Proviso, however, meant that Oregon could not be insulated from the slavery question. When pressed, Douglas said that the incorporation of the Northwest Ordinance obviated the need for a specific provision excluding slavery because one of its articles did precisely that. Southerners, however, proposed the application of the Missouri Compromise line to the Pacific. That would leave Oregon free, but also would vitiate the Wilmot Proviso by permitting slavery in acquisitions from Mexico south of the 36°30′ line. Douglas said that he would support "the Missouri Compromise, instead of the total prohibition" contemplated by the Wilmot Proviso, although "he deprecated the forcing of this question on the House" while considering Oregon.[25] In fact, he was unable to obtain passage of a territorial bill while he was still in the House.[26] He finally succeeded two years later as chair of the Senate Committee on Territories, when his bill for organizing Oregon was enacted. It also extended the Northwest Ordinance over the territory.[27]

In January 1848, at the time Douglas was introducing his Senate bill to organize the Oregon Territory, newspapers around the country published a letter in which Lewis Cass, the Michigan senator who was positioning himself for the Democratic nomination for president, explained his views on the Wilmot Proviso to A. O. P. Nicholson, a well-known Tennessee figure.[28] Cass believed the public was ready for the slavery question to "be kept out of the national Legislature, and left to the people of the confederacy in their respective local governments."

Cass acknowledged that territories differed from states because some of "their rights are inchoate, and they do not possess the peculiar attributes of sovereignty." The only clause in the Constitution concerning them is Article IV, Section 3, §2, which grants Congress power to dispose of and regulate "the territory and other property belonging to the United States." This authority, argued Cass, was exclusively "for the purpose of making rules and regulations for the disposition and management of property." Accordingly, he inferred that the clause did not delegate to Congress the power to regulate the internal affairs of the people in the territories. Besides, he wrote, the people there "are

---

[24] CG, 28th Cong., 2nd sess. (Feb. 13, 1845), 284.

[25] CG, 29th Cong., 2nd sess. (Jan. 15, 1847), 188.

[26] Ibid.; Johannsen, *SAD*, 202–203.

[27] *U.S. Statutes at Large*, 30th Cong., 1st sess., ch. 177 (Aug. 14, 1848), 329. On the connection between slavery and Oregon statehood, see Barbara Mahoney, "Oregon Democracy: Asahel Bush, Slavery, and the Statehood Debate," *Oregon Historical Quarterly*, 110:2 (Summer 2009), 202–227.

[28] USN, *New York Herald*, Jan. 3, 1848; EAN, *Farmer's Cabinet* (Amherst, NH), Jan. 6, 1848; *New-Hampshire Patriot* (Concord), Jan. 13, 1848; *Weekly Eagle* (Brattleboro, VT), Jan. 14, 1848. The letter of December 24, 1847, is also fully printed in William T. Young, *Sketch of the Life and Public Services of General Lewis Cass* (Detroit, 1852), 320–327. It was customary for antebellum presidential aspirants to address newspaper editors or other influential persons in "platform letters" intended for publication. Jean H. Baker, *James Buchanan* (New York, 2004), 52.

just as capable" as the people of the states to manage their own concerns. Cass did not use the term "popular sovereignty," although later it would be credited to his Nicholson letter.[29]

Douglas did not concur with Cass's interpretation of Article IV. Although he voted against the Wilmot Proviso, he did not deny the constitutionality of a prohibition of slavery in territories; rather, he asserted that the equal footing doctrine gave each territory at the moment that it drafted a constitution for admission to statehood the absolute right to decide the question for itself. This right would be meaningless, however, if Congress could dictate the answer prior to statehood. Nevertheless, instead of the Proviso, he advocated extending the Missouri Compromise beyond the Louisiana Purchase to former Mexican territory because, he said in 1849, it had become so accepted over three decades that "no ruthless hand would ever be reckless enough to disturb [it]."[30] He thought it might preserve sectional peace. In supporting it, however, he compromised his own belief that the people of territories should be free to decide their own domestic affairs – a position he had taken since his first term in Congress.[31] His endorsement of the Missouri Compromise, however, was short-lived. By the following year, he reverted to his traditional stand against congressional dictation.

In March 1850, Douglas gave a much-studied speech prior to reporting bills for California statehood and organizing the territories of New Mexico and Utah.[32] His speech contained two significant themes woven around his

---

[29] Cass's language is not examined in an otherwise helpful discussion of the Nicholson letter in the biography by William C. Klunder: *Lewis Cass and the Politics of Moderation* (Kent, OH, 1996), 177–180. As in the case of Douglas, Cass's position was not new. It drew on his time as governor of the Michigan Territory. William C. Klunder, "The Seeds of Popular Sovereignty: Governor Lewis Cass and Michigan Territory," *Michigan Historical Review*, 17:1 (Spring 1991), 64–81. Christopher Childers, "Interpreting Popular Sovereignty: A Historiographical Essay," *Civil War History*, 57:1 (Mar. 2011), chides historians for narrowly beginning the story in 1847; yet his analysis, nuanced and valuable, focuses on 1847–1860. I agree with his point, however, because Douglas adopted the position long before it received a name in 1847.

The first use by the press of the term "popular sovereignty" following publication of the Nicholson letter was a Philadelphia editorial invoking the principle to condemn Cass's position. USN, *North American and United States Gazette* (Philadelphia), Feb. 12, 1848. The first application of the term to the question of slavery in territories came in a speech by Vice President George Dallas in September 1847, according to Bruce M. Ambacher, "The Pennsylvania Origins of *Popular Sovereignty*," *Pennsylvania Magazine of History and Biography*, 98:3 (July 1974), 339–352.

[30] Quoted in Johannsen, *SAD*, 255, and Huston, *Stephen A. Douglas*, 72.

[31] In contrast to the argument here, Johannsen, *SAD*, 221–222, believes that by 1848 Douglas lacked "any deep conviction regarding territorial government" and that "no clear and consistent pattern in his thinking had emerged." He concludes this while acknowledging that Douglas broke precedent by placing control over slavery and other locally important matters "in the hands of the people who lived in the territory." See also Yonatan Eyal, *The Young America Movement and the Transformation of the Democratic Party, 1828–1861* (New York, 2007), 194–195, and Huston, *Stephen A. Douglas*, 184–194.

[32] CG, APP, 31st Cong., 1st sess. (Mar. 12–13, 1850), 364–374. It is a rich speech from which biographers have mined ore of great variety. Huston, *Stephen A. Douglas*, 77–79; Johannsen,

principal task of responding to John C. Calhoun's charge that federal antislavery legislation reflected Northern aggression by which "the South was deprived of its due share of the territories."[33]

His first theme was that the Constitution took no notice of sectionalism. Calhoun's perspective, Douglas said, was alien to the Constitution, which allocated no share to any section. Federal territories, under the Constitution, "belong to the United State as one people, one nation, and are to be disposed of for the common benefit of all." And each state has an equal right to vote on rules for governing the territory; "but the different sections – North, South, East, and West – have no such right. It is no violation of southern rights to prohibit slavery, nor of northern rights to leave it to the people to decide the question for themselves."

This was a classic example of Douglas's use of constitutionalism to transcend and possibly mitigate sectional discord. The surest means by which each state in every section could protect its interest was to trust the Constitution because it was incognizant of and therefore unbiased toward any region. His reaffirmation of the evenhandedness of the Constitution responded, on the one hand, to Southern ultras like Calhoun who were calling for an amendment that would ensure a balance of slave and free states and, on the other hand, to Northern abolitionists who were condemning the whole document as a "covenant with death" because of its accommodation of slavery.[34] For Douglas the federalist nature of the Constitution, whereby it recognized the nation as a people living only in states, made it the indispensable instrument for negotiating sectional divisions.

His second theme was to explain why federalism was expanding American freedom. His guide, as always, was history, not faith.[35] Like a scholar determined to dispel a myth and advance a thesis, Douglas set out to demonstrate why Congress could not impose its will on the people of territories with regard to slavery. Contrary to what so many believed, he said, federal statutes did not decide the question. The Northwest Ordinance banned slavery in the territory from which five states were created. He acknowledged that all five "are now free," but, he asked, "was it the ordinance that made them free States?" The ordinance, he insisted, "had no practical effect" on the question throughout the region, for "slavery existed there to a greater or less extent." The institution

---

SAD, 277–281; Gerald M. Capers, *Stephen A. Douglas: Defender of the Union* (Boston, 1959), 59; and George F. Milton, *The Eve of the Conflict: Stephen A. Douglas and the Needless War* (New York, 1834; reprinted 1969), 64–65.

[33] CG, 31st Cong., 1st sess. (Mar. 4, 1850), 451–455.

[34] Next to the masthead of William Lloyd Garrison's abolitionist newspaper, *The Liberator*, was the following caption: "The U.S. Constitution is a Covenant with Death, and An Agreement with Hell."

[35] David Zarefsky writes that history mattered to Douglas and Lincoln, "not for antiquarian reasons, but because the successful interpretation of the past would entail a controlling influence on future policy." *Lincoln Douglas and Slavery in the Crucible of Public Debate* (Chicago, 1990, 1993), 164.

"has gradually disappeared under the operation of laws adopted and executed by the people themselves" within their respective states. The gradual elimination of slavery in the states of the old Northwest was the result of local initiatives, not the congressional ordinance.[36] Douglas's best evidence came from his own state, where there were slaves until 1845, when the Illinois Supreme Court belatedly ruled that the ordinance had made the institution illegal.[37] He said, "Illinois became a slaveholding territory under the ordinance, and in utter defiance of its plain and palpable provision."

Evoking the revolutionary era denunciations of parliamentary regulations, Douglas drew from his history of the Northwest Territory "that great truth … that a law passed by the national legislature to operate locally upon a people not represented, will always remain practically a dead letter upon the statute book, if it be in opposition to the wishes and supposed interests of those who are to be affected by it, and at the same time charged with its execution." This was a truth that Americans first learned during the colonial period, when the efficacy of imperial regulation of their internal affairs depended largely on their consent.[38]

Similarly, Douglas believed the Missouri Compromise did not "have any practical effect" on the slavery question. Missouri was admitted as a slave state

---

[36] Although Douglas's claim of federal impotence regarding the slave question in territories ignored the moral force of the Northwest Ordinance, his overall emphasis on the determinative role of local settlers is echoed in recent scholarship. A central theme of John C. Hammond, *Slavery, Freedom, and Expansion in the Early American West* (Charlottesville, VA, 2006), is that the federal government was not strong enough to enforce the Northwest Ordinance ban on slavery, which "became, by default, a local question" (6). On the successful evasion of the slavery ban by Illinois and Indiana, see Paul Finkelman, *Slavery and the Founders: Race and Liberty in the Age of Jefferson* (New York, 1996), 57–79. James Simeone, *Democracy and Slavery in Frontier Illinois: The Bottomland Republic* (De Kalb, IL, 2000), 9, analyzes the push for local control over slavery in the 1820s as accompanying the development of "white folks' democracy." Gerald Leonard writes, "For all its alleged sacredness as a Union-saving compromise, the Missouri Compromise had little operative consequence in the actual territory it purportedly governed." "Law and Politics Reconsidered: A New Constitutional History of Dred Scott," *Law and Social Inquiry*, 34 (Summer 2009), 749. John Reda, "After Statehood: Race and Politics in Illinois and Missouri," Paper read at the 31st Annual Meeting of the Society for Historians of the Early Republic at Springfield, IL, July 2009, discusses how statehood enabled white settlers to "take direct action at the local level to shape the political parameters of race" in Missouri and Illinois. Christopher C. Fennell, "Damaging Detours: Routes, Racism, and New Philadelphia," *Historical Archaeology*, 44:1 (2010), 138–154, notes how Illinois in the 1830s could accommodate both the founding of "the first town in the United States planned, platted, and legally registered by an African American … [and] views towards the rights of slave owners" (138–139).

[37] Paul Finkelman, *An Imperfect Union: Slavery, Federalism, and Comity* (Union, NJ, 2000), 150. The new state constitution of 1848 banned slavery. Illinois Constitution of 1848, Article XIII, §16. On the drafting and ratification of the new constitution, see Janet Cornelius, "Popular Sovereignty and Constitutional Change in the United States and Illinois Constitutions," *Illinois Historical Journal*, 80:4 (1987), 228–247, esp. 234–235.

[38] For the thesis that imperial control of the internal affairs of the colonists depended largely on their voluntary compliance, see John M. Murrin et al., *Liberty, Equality, Power: A History of the American People*, 4th ed. (Belmont, CA, 2005), 168.

and Arkansas was organized as a slave territory. This would have been the case without the compromise because slavery was already well established in both places and "there was no rightful mode of preventing it." Beyond the 36°30′ line, however, Douglas equivocated that "slavery was as effectually excluded ... by the laws of nature, of climate, and production, before, as it is now, by the act of Congress." Nevertheless, he repeated his coda that "it did the South no harm – the North no good," although, he conceded, it benefited all by mollifying sectional tensions.[39]

The prohibition of slavery in the act organizing Oregon was another example for Calhoun of federal exclusion of the South from new territory. Douglas countered that the ban in the 1848 legislation "did nothing more than to reenact and affirm the law which the people themselves had previously adopted" in their own provisional government." The congressional ban was once again a "mere dead letter."

In rebutting Calhoun, Douglas did not want to rub salt in Southern wounds by offering his views on the morality of slavery. To do so would have undercut his primary goal, which was to promote Southern confidence in the evenhandedness of federal policy policymaking. He also wanted to reduce the aggressiveness of Northern antislavery men. He believed that history was on their side and that the Union was better served by statesmen relying on history rather than morality.

At the time of the Declaration of Independence, Douglas observed, all thirteen colonies had slavery. By the time the Constitution was adopted, "there were twelve slaveholding and one free State."[40] Since then, six of those slaveholding states, he noted, had abolished the institution on their own accord. In addition, Vermont and Maine had joined as free states. In fact, "notwithstanding the ordinance of 1787, the Missouri Compromise, and all the kindred measures," every state that has rejected slavery has done so "by virtue of their own choice, and not in obedience to any congressional dictation." He denied that "Congress ever made any country free."

This history "shows that the cause of freedom has steadily and firmly advanced, while slavery has receded in the same ratio." He projected that as many as seventeen new states could be carved from the vast territory between the Mississippi and the Pacific, and all would be free "whether Congress shall

---

[39] Although Robert P. Forbes, *The Missouri Compromise and Its Aftermath* (Chapel Hill, NC, 2007), 271, claims that the compromise "tilted the balance of the Constitution in favor of freedom," he acknowledges that its substantive effect was limited and that its principal influence was symbolic.

[40] Massachusetts alone among the original thirteen states listed no slaves under the census of 1790. Most consequential in the elimination of slavery were three Supreme Court decisions in 1783 under the state constitution. Emily Blanck, "Seventy-Eighty Three: The Turning Point in the Law of Slavery and Freedom in Massachusetts," *New England Quarterly*, 75:1 (2002), 24–51. Legal abolition, however, did not preclude "the persistence of slave relations within the context of emancipation," suggests Joanne P. Melish, *Disowning Slavery: Gradual Emancipation and "Race" in New England, 1780–1865* (Ithaca, NY, 1998), 77. See also Van Cleve, *Slaveholders' Union*, 66–68.

prohibit slavery or not." While he wanted to assure the Southern states that all of their rights under "the Constitution as it is," that is, without Calhoun's amendment, would be protected, he said they had to face "unpalatable truths" – none of the territories could be "adapted to slave labor."[41]

Two days before Douglas's March speech, William Seward had cited a "higher law than the Constitution" to validate his opposition to the extension of slavery.[42] Douglas had little tolerance for basing policy on Scripture.[43] Next to the Constitution, but below it, the only authority he recognized was the people who sent him to Congress. He reiterated the point in June. Although he had always held that the territories should determine slavery for themselves, if he had ever voted contrary to that principle, "it was done under the influence of the pressure of the authority higher than my own will.... I have faithfully obeyed my instructions, in letter and in spirit, to the fullest extent." He said that while he was free to express his opinions, his vote belonged to the people who sent him.[44] He said that he hoped one day to persuade his constituents that the course he proposed would produce the same result they wanted.[45]

Accompanying Douglas's March 1850 speech were his bills for California statehood and territorial organization. This countered the revered Henry Clay's push for a single omnibus bill that aimed at reconciling all sections. In April the Senate chose a Committee of Thirteen, chaired by Clay, to develop the legislation. Douglas opposed the behind-the-scenes committee and declined to serve on it. Yet when the committee reported an omnibus bill in May, he gave it his "active & unwavering support down to its final defeat."[46] Against Southern wishes, Douglas managed to restore the right of the territories in New Mexico and Utah to decide the slavery question by eliminating a clause that exempted that institution from their legislative powers. As he had predicted, however, a single omnibus could not pass, and at the end of July, after two and a half months of debate, it was killed. Clay, an exhausted septuagenarian, left Washington to his thirty-seven-year-old Democratic ally, who proved his indefatigability, legislative skills, and dedication to sectional accommodation by moving separate bills quickly through Congress. President Fillmore signed five bills that respectively enacted California statehood (September 9), territorial status for New Mexico with a boundary adjustment that added part of Texas in exchange for $10 million (September 9), territorial status for Utah

---

[41] Graham Peck, "Was Stephen A. Douglas Antislavery?" *Journal of the Abraham Lincoln Association*, 26:2 (2005), 1–21, esp. 9–10, makes a case for why Douglas was not genuinely antislavery.

[42] CG, APP, 31st Cong., 1st sess. (Mar. 11, 150), 265.

[43] James L. Huston, "Democracy by Scripture versus Democracy by Process: A Reflection on Stephen A. Douglas and Popular Sovereignty," *Civil War History*, 43:3 (1997), 189–200.

[44] CG, APP, 31st Cong., 1st sess. (June 17, 1850), 911.

[45] CG, APP, 31st Cong., 1st sess. (Mar. 13, 1850), 373.

[46] Stephen A. Douglas to Charles H. Lanphear and George Walker, Aug. 3, 1850, *Letters of SAD*, 192.

(September 9), a new fugitive slave law (September 18), and the abolition of slave trade in the national capital (September 20).[47]

Despite an inflamed controversy over the fugitive slave law, Douglas emerged from the Compromise of 1850 with high marks and visibility for being a major architect of the new sectional agreement.[48] Yet he would also be the principal architect of legislation that shattered the sectional peace. On January 4, 1854, he presented the Nebraska bill accompanied by a report from his Committee on Territories. His triumph four years earlier could not help but shape his thinking about Nebraska. In 1850 he had argued for the irrelevance of the Missouri Compromise by showing that slavery had been rejected north of 36°30′ as a result of local conditions and the decision of settlers, not in response to congressional interdiction. Accordingly, the California statehood statute did not mention slavery, implicitly leaving the decision for the people to decide.[49] The acts organizing New Mexico and Utah expressly left the issue of slavery to be resolved by the people of the territory.[50] His January 1854 report cited conflicting views on what the Constitution permitted Congress to do regarding slavery in territories and recommended neither affirming nor denying the Missouri Compromise, which, it conceded, was a "cardinal article of faith" of both political parties. Instead it recommended following the "principles and spirit" of 1850 by leaving all questions regarding slavery to the decision of people residing in the territory.[51]

The initial bill left the decision about slavery to the residents of Nebraska, "through their appropriate representatives."[52] A month later Douglas added the clause "subject only to the Constitution of the United States."[53] This was

---

[47] A recent study of the legislative battle credits Douglas with "rare insight" for disagreeing with Clay's omnibus strategy. Robert V. Remini, *At the Edge of the Precipice: Henry Clay and the Compromise that Saved the Union* (New York, 2010), 123. Sean Wilentz suggests, "Douglas remembered as Clay seemed to have forgotten, how Clay himself had manufactured the Missouri Compromise thirty years earlier." *The Rise of American Democracy: Jefferson to Lincoln* (New York, 2005), 643. For other useful accounts of the whole struggle, see Holman Hamilton, *Prologue to Conflict: The Crisis and Compromise of 1850* (1964); Johannsen, *SAD*, 262–298; and Merrill D. Peterson, *The Great Triumvirate: Webster, Clay, and Calhoun* (New York, 1987), 449–476. Robert R. Russel, "What Was the Compromise of 1850?" *Journal of Southern History*, 22:3 (Aug. 1956), 292–309, advises students to read the statutes and demonstrates why they should do so.

For the five acts, *U.S. Statutes at Large*, 31st Cong., 1st sess. (1850), 446–458, 462–465, 467–468.

[48] Huston, *Stephen A. Douglas*, 84, credits him with a "spectacular triumph in 1850."

[49] *U.S. Statutes at Large*, 31st Cong., 1st sess. (1850), 452–453.

[50] Ibid., 447, 453.

[51] Senate Report No. 15, U.S. Serial Set, 33rd, 1st (Jan. 4, 1854), 1, 3–4.

[52] Bills and Resolutions, 33rd Cong., 1st sess. (Jan. 4, 1854), S. 22, Section 21, p. 35. Although incorporated officially as part of his Jan. 4 bill, Section 21, providing territorial control of slavery, was added a few days later, either to correct an inadvertent clerical error or as an afterthought. Milton, *Eve of the Conflict*, 110–111; Johannsen, *SAD*, 408. All versions of S. 22 are given at http://memory.loc.gov/cgi.

[53] S. 22 (Feb. 7, 1854), Amendment.

troubling to those who believed that the Constitution prohibited territorial rulings against slavery. In his defense, Douglas asserted that the people of a territory could not override the Constitution whether or not the phrase was included. The bill granted the territorial legislature all of the power that Congress could "give under the Constitution." Even if one struck out the added language, he exclaimed, the territorial legislature would still be subordinate to the Constitution. For Douglas popular sovereignty could not override the Constitution, "that sacred instrument."[54]

The bill that the president signed into law five months later (May 30) stated that the slavery prohibition of 1820 was "inconsistent with the principle of non-intervention" as recognized by the compromise measures of 1850 and therefore was "inoperative and void."[55] This was the language that Douglas had introduced in his amendment of February 7. Douglas watchers have long asked why he acquiesced in this explicit repeal of the Missouri Compromise after initially trying to sidestep it. Some believe that he gave in to pressure from proslavery senators because of ignoble motives – his desire for a Northern railroad that would increase the value of his real estate and/or Southern Democratic support for his presidential nomination. The focus of both his critics and defenders has been on what Roy Nichols once described as the "process of becoming" – how the bill reached its final shape as law.[56] It is not possible to extricate from this complex story, however, what Douglas thought at every point. It is evident that despite his boast, "I passed the Nebraska-Act myself," Douglas was not so puissant, although he did dominate his committee. To gain passage he would have been forced to modify his bill no matter what he believed.[57]

[54] CG, APP, 33rd Cong., 1st sess. (Mar. 2, 1854), 287–288.

[55] *U.S. Statutes at Large*, 33rd Cong., 1st sess. (1854), 277.

[56] Roy F. Nichols, "The Kansas–Nebraska Act: A Century of Historiography," *Mississippi Valley Historical Review*, 43:2 (1956), 196–197. The scholarship on the passage of the act is, as Graham Peck says, "monumental." See his compilation to 1998: "Politics and Ideology in a Free Society: Illinois from Statehood to Civil War," Ph.D. diss. (Northwestern University, 2001), 362n, and his own treatment, 299–377, which views it from the perspective of the Northern Democratic Party. Michael F. Holt, *The Rise and Fall of the American Whig Party: Jacksonian Politics and the Onset of the Civil War* (New York, 1999), 804–835, sees it from the Whigs' perspective. For the impact on the new Republican Party in Illinois, see Mitchell Snay, "Abraham Lincoln, Owen Lovejoy, and the Emergence of the Republican Party in Illinois," *Journal of the Abraham Lincoln Association*, 22:1 (2001), 82–99. Sean Wilentz suggests that the historical argument "has, in its contentiousness, at times mimicked the debate itself." *Rise of American Democracy*, 926. Forbes, *Missouri Compromise*, 276–286, illustrates Wilentz's point in his treatment of Douglas and the act.

[57] He made the boast in a private conversation with his brother-in-law, who published it in a book after Douglas's death. J. Madison Cutts, *A Brief Treatise Upon Constitutional and Party Questions, and the History of Political Parties, As I Received It Orally from the Late Senator Stephen A. Douglas of Illinois* (New York, 1866), 122. David M. Potter suggests that Douglas had to make concessions to his committee, while Robert Johannsen makes a strong case for his dominance. Potter, *The Impending Crisis, 1848–1861*, completed and ed. Don E. Fehrenbacher (New York, 1976), 160n; Johannsen, *SAD*, 407, 415–416. Certainly Southerners pressured him during the proceedings. William W. Freehling, *The Road to Disunion: Secessionists at Bay, 1776–1854* (New York, 1990), 537–538.

Instead of focusing on the bill's process of becoming, if we read Douglas's record backward from January 4, his thinking and motives are clear, for he had expressed his views about the Missouri Compromise unequivocally.[58] In 1850, as we have seen, he had argued that the 1820 legislation had no impact on the advance of slavery, which was determined by the nature of the land, climate, and people of a territory or state, not by Congress. By 1852 he favored its repeal, although he knew that it held a symbolic importance for many Northerners.[59] While he believed that the right of the local majority to decide the issue for themselves was fundamental to American constitutionalism, he also worried about the Union. Organizing Nebraska was crucial for tying the United States together with a Pacific railroad. Perhaps he could finesse the Missouri prohibition with clever language. His January 4 bill contained only an oblique reference to the Missouri Compromise. He naively hoped that he could attain a territorial statute without jeopardizing the sectional political accord that he had helped achieve in 1850.[60]

At no point in his career did Douglas feel more assured of his own standing as a spokesman for America than he did on the eve of the Nebraska bill. We cannot underestimate the affect on him of his five-month journey to countries and city-states in Europe. A month after his first wife's burial in April 1853, Douglas embarked on a grand tour that was intended to be both a consolation for his loss and an education in international relations for the rising national statesman. His purpose, as reported in the press, was to study the different forms of government in Europe and observe the conditions of the people there. He went by himself, accompanied only by letters of introduction to prominent figures everywhere. His fame preceded him.[61] Douglas met leading officials in England, France, Italy, Prussia, Sweden, Denmark, Austria, Greece, Turkey, Russia, Ireland, and Scotland. Included were audiences with Napoleon III and Czar Nicholas I, who received him as an influential representative of the U.S. government.[62] Abroad he stood for and spoke for all Americans. It was a heady experience that could only have enhanced his sense of himself as a man for all

---

[58] Michael A. Morrison, *Slavery and the American West: The Eclipse of Manifest Destiny and the Coming of the Civil War* (Chapel Hill, NC, 1997), 128, suggests the need for this approach.

[59] Huston, *Stephen A. Douglas*, 100.

[60] Graham Peck, "Stephen A. Douglas, and the Northern Democratic Origins of the Kansas–Nebraska Act," *Illinois History Teacher*, 10 (Winter 2003), 2–7, suggests that Douglas wanted to stir a national debate that would revive the Democratic Party in the North and position it to spread its hold on settlers pushing to Nebraska and the West. For a more detailed exposition of this thesis, see his *Politics and Ideology in a Free Society*, 342–358. He also believes that Douglas miscalculated the effects of his plan in almost destroying his party (376).

[61] USN, *Weekly Herald* (New York), May 21, 1853, claimed that Douglas was so well known for championing nationalist insurgents like "the Cuban junta," Louis Kossuth, and Giuseppe Mazzini that he had to bypass Spain and Hungary for fear of being arrested by the authorities. Kossuth, the Hungarian insurgent, toured America a year earlier and thrilled Young America Democrats, including Douglas. Eyal, *Young America Movement*, 107–110. Mazzini, the Italian nationalist, was another hero of Young America (93–101).

[62] Johannsen, *SAD*, 382–386.

sections in Washington, where he would take up the Nebraska bill only two months after his return.

As much as his prior success and recent tour abroad may have inflated his confidence at the outset, he could neither command the legislative process that unfolded in Congress nor gauge the anti-Nebraska whirlwind that gathered outside. Although he claimed that he expected protests, he was surprised by the degree of popular animosity toward him and the turbulence that ensued in Kansas.[63] He also did not foresee the impact on the party system.[64] His miscalculation underscores a truism. No matter how shrewd or even high-minded a politician is, no one can predict the full consequences of policy decisions.

His hope to maneuver around the Missouri settlement foundered in his committee, which he could not wholly control. On January 23, bowing to his colleagues, Douglas reported a revised bill that divided the territory into Kansas and Nebraska and repealed the Missouri Compromise.[65] His acquiescence was as much principled as political because he did not believe in the 1820 settlement. A week later the debate in the Senate began and lasted until that chamber voted on March 3.[66]

Douglas's greatest challenge in the debate was to convince colleagues that the Missouri Compromise was not what it had become both to some of them and to the public in the North: an unbreakable compact between the sections. He denied that "it was anything more than an ordinary act of legislation" and insisted that its repeal was only incidental to the main purpose of the Nebraska bill, which was to empower the people there to decide the matter of slavery for themselves.[67]

He did not challenge the constitutionality of the Missouri Compromise; rather, he said it stood in the way of the "great principle of popular sovereignty," which was the principle on which the colonists separated from Great Britain, the Revolution was fought, and "our republican system was founded." He quoted instructions from a half-dozen states in 1776 that authorized their delegations at the Continental Congress to vote for independence provided that

[63] James A. Rawley, "Stephen Douglas and the Kansas–Nebraska Act," in *The Kansas–Nebraska Act of 1854*, ed. John R. Wunder and Joann M. Ross (Lincoln, NE, 2008), 71. As Mark Graber notes, in the 1850s the number of slaveholders moving west was unlikely to produce a majority anywhere. "Kansas was the only territory where slaveholders even put up a fight." "John Brown, Abraham Lincoln, *Dred Scott*, and the Problem of Constitutional Evil," in *The Dred Scott Case: Historical and Contemporary Perspectives on Race and Law*, ed. David T. Konig, Paul Finkelman, and Christopher A. Bracey (Athens, OH, 2010), 58.

[64] Although the origins of the Republican Party preceded the Kansas–Nebraska Bill, according to William E. Gienapp, *The Origins of the Republican Party, 1852–1854* (New York, 1987), the controversy galvanized the new party as a force in the North. See Wilentz, *Rise of American Democracy*, 677–688.

[65] S. 22 (Jan. 23), Sec. 14 (p. 16) and Sec. 21 (p. 19).

[66] CG, 33rd Cong., 1st sess. (Jan. 30, 1854), 275 (Mar. 3, 1854), 532. Immediately after the vote, Douglas moved to add Kansas to the title of the Nebraska bill. Ibid.

[67] CG, APP, 33rd Cong., 1st sess. (Mar. 3, 1854), 328, 326.

the "internal government and police" of their respective states were respected.[68] "It is apparent that the Declaration of Independence had its origin in the violation of the great fundamental principle which secured to the people of the colonies the right to regulate their own domestic affairs in their own way; and that the Revolution resulted in the triumph of that principle, and the recognition of the right asserted by it."[69] For Douglas, then, the Declaration of Independence expressed the collective right of local majorities to self-government, not individual rights.[70]

The Senate's overwhelming passage (37 to 14) on March 3 testified to Douglas's persuasiveness in debate. His knowledge and logic were powerful weapons. James Huston writes that "he easily pulled from memory countless facts to disembowel the propositions of his opponents."[71] He also took his battle to the other chamber, where he pressed representatives to bring the bill to a consideration and then to support its passage. He could offer no patronage, no committee assignments, no campaign war chest – he had only his personal conviction and standing as levers in the House, where he could not speak from the floor. His relentlessness stirred resentment in the House, but that body finally gave him his bill by a margin of 113 to 100 on May 22. No wonder he told his brother-in-law that "the speeches were nothing."[72] The speeches tell us what he thought, but not what he said in his countless one-on-one exchanges with congressmen.

Outside of the capitol, the language of his bill might have played better had it included the phrase "popular sovereignty" instead of "non-intervention," which he used to counter the "old exploded doctrine of congressional interference, as established in 1820."[73] The use of "non-interference" and "non-intervention" conveyed what Congress could no longer do, namely prohibit slavery in territories. The phrase underlined the centrality of the Missouri ban to the legislation, while "popular sovereignty" would have spoken to the right of the people to govern themselves. Moreover, nonintervention or noninterference was hardly a manifesto to rally supporters. People might oppose a

---

[68] Pauline Maier, *American Scripture: Making the Declaration of Independence* (New York, 1997), 203, states, "Douglas recalled correctly, one state after another had explicitly retained the exclusive right of defining its domestic institutions."

[69] CG, APP, 33rd Cong., 1st sess. (Mar. 3, 1854), 337.

[70] Lincoln would agree that the equality clause in the Declaration of Independence "was of no practical use in effecting our separation from Great Britain," but insisted that it was there "for future use." CWAL, 2: 406. David Armitage, "The Declaration of Independence and International Law," *William and Mary Quarterly*, 3rd ser., 59:1 (Jan. 2002), 44, says that the rights clause was a "minor premise" for independence. As he writes in "The Declaration of Independence in World Context," *OAH Magazine of History*, 18:3 (2004), 62, even the world understood that the primary meaning of the document was to assert "the rights of a group of states to enter the international realm as equals with other such states."

[71] Huston, *Stephen A. Douglas*, 103. See also Potter's appraisal of his debating skills. *Impending Crisis*, 165.

[72] Cutts, *Brief Treatise*, 122; Johannsen, *SAD*, 432–434.

[73] CG, APP, 33rd Cong., 1st sess. (Mar. 3, 1854), 337.

specific action by Congress, but they were not apt to rally behind a motto that Congress would do nothing, especially regarding something as "obnoxious" (Douglas's adjective) as slavery. "Popular sovereignty," in contrast, had a long history as an American value. The phrase had been enshrined since the first era of constitution making.[74] It should have leaped off of Douglas's tongue from the moment he began defending territorial self-government. Never inserted into the Nebraska legislation, the phrase did not seem to be intrinsic to it. Critics of the measure snorted at its invocation as a belated, weak rationalization and conflated it with "squatter sovereignty."[75]

Popular sovereignty was not a theatrical piece of rhetoric for him, but a genuine cause.[76] Deeply convinced of the correctness of the principle, Douglas believed he could persuade every audience that leaving the decision about slavery to territorial settlers was both the right thing to do and the best way to defuse sectional tensions. He was credible about the rightness of the policy, but tragically wrong about its impact. In September and October, as he spoke to voters across Illinois in behalf of his party for the upcoming congressional and state elections, pro- and antislavery forces in Kansas competed for electoral domination with more than words.[77] Illegal voters and threatened violence were already on the scene in the territory.[78] This was not how self-government was supposed to work.

Opposition to the Kansas–Nebraska Act led to the loss of Democratic majorities in the Illinois legislature and Congress in the fall of 1854, hastened the demise of the Whigs, and coalesced various antislavery groups into a new

---

[74] An overlooked but original analysis of popular sovereignty underlying American constitutionalism is R. R. Palmer, *The Age of the Democratic Revolution: A Political History of Europe and America, 1760–1800 – The Challenge* (Princeton, NJ, 1959), 213–235, which describes "the people as constituent power." Seminal on the transfer of power from government to the people in the revolutionary era is Gordon S. Wood, *The Creation of the American Republic, 1776–1787* (Chapel Hill, NC, 1969), 344–389. The importance of state constitution making in the development of democratic thinking through the early nineteenth century is the theme of Christian G. Fritz, *American Sovereigns: The People and America's Constitutional Tradition before the Civil War* (New York, 2008). It does not, however, discuss popular sovereignty in relationship to slavery in the territories. For a historical view of the "fiction" of popular sovereignty, see Edmund S. Morgan, *Inventing the People: The Rise of Popular Sovereignty in England and America* (New York, 1988).

[75] Lincoln took "popular sovereignty" seriously, however, and met it head on. Nicole Etcheson, "'A Living, Creeping Lie': Abraham Lincoln on Popular Sovereignty," *Journal of the Abraham Lincoln Association*, 29:2 (Summer 2008), 1–26. "Squatter sovereignty" referred to the claims of people who squatted on land that did not belong to them, Lincoln pointed out. CWAL, 2: 487.

[76] For a thoughtful assessment of Douglas's commitment that claims it can be traced only to 1850, yet correctly finds links to his position about territories as early as 1845, see Eric T. Dean, Jr., "Stephen A. Douglas and Popular Sovereignty," *Historian*, 57:4 (Summer 1995), 733–748.

[77] On Douglas's campaigning in the fall of 1854, see Johannsen, *SAD*.

[78] A select committee of the House of Representatives concluded in July 1856 that there had been "unlawful interference" with every election in the territory from the beginning and placed the blame on nonresident voters from Missouri. At the first election, for a delegate to Congress, in the fall of 1854 the committee found that election judges received death threats. U.S. Serials, 34th Cong., 1st sess., House Report No. 200, 3–4.

exclusively Northern party by the end of 1855. Douglas had foreseen this dangerous consequence of his legislation the night before President Pierce signed it into law. He told the Senate he had learned that "the old political parties are to be dissolved, and that the northern Whigs, disaffected Democrats, Abolitionists, and Free-Soilers, are to be fused and amalgamated into a sectional party ... and that this new party is to wage war upon slavery wherever it may exist." When one of the leaders of this new party challenged Douglas – "What are you going to do about it?" – he replied that he would call the attention of the country to the purpose of the leaders of the new party who "contemplate civil war, servile insurrection, and disunion."[79]

He continued to believe, however, that if the settlers in Kansas were left to decide the issue on their own, the controversy would fade from the country's concern. In 1855 and early 1856, he focused on strengthening the Democrats as a truly national party that could win the next presidential election. He strove to make certain that the principles embodied in the Kansas–Nebraska Act would be declared in the party platform. He gave speeches in Illinois, Indiana, and Iowa and participated in a Democratic organizational meeting in Kentucky. He received too late an invitation to attend a mass meeting in Georgia, which he said he would have been delighted to attend "in order to demonstrate to the South that Democratic principles were the same everywhere and could be enforced by the same arguments in the Slave holding & non-slaveholding states."[80] Indeed, he would demonstrate this point four years later when he campaigned for the presidency in all sections of the country.

The intellectual challenge for Douglas in defending the repeal of the Missouri Compromise was to find a constitutional anchor for his principle of territorial self-determination. His struggle with the problem is evident at the beginning of the report he submitted on March 12, 1856, for his Senate Committee on Territories. Drawing on President Pierce's message calling for Kansas statehood, he began by quoting clauses in the Constitution that established congressional authority to admit new states into the Union (Article IV, Section 3), the right of Congress to do whatever was necessary and proper to execute that authority (Article I, Section 8), and the broad swatch of unspecified powers that were left to the states (Tenth Amendment). Douglas wanted to base his case for popular sovereignty in territories on their eventual transition into statehood, whereupon they would enter the Union on the basis of equality with existing states, possessing the sovereignty that, in his reading, the Tenth Amendment conferred on each. Under that sovereignty, states had an equal right "to decide all questions of domestic policy for themselves, including African slavery."[81]

So what should his colleagues make of the clause empowering Congress "to dispose of and make all needful rules and regulations respecting the territory or other property belonging to the United States" (Article IV, Section 3)?

---

[79] CG, APP, 33rd Cong., 1st sess. (May 25, 1854), 787.
[80] Stephen A. Douglas to Howell Cobb, Oct. 6, 1855, *Letters of SAD*, 342.
[81] U.S. Serials, 34th Cong., 1st sess., Senate Report No. 34, 1–2.

Douglas argued that this language was "much more appropriate when applied to property than to persons." It should be understood as having to do only with the disposal of public lands, not with governing people on those lands. After all, many public lands existed in states and the federal government claimed no jurisdiction over their internal affairs on account of property it owned there. Further, to have Congress impose a decision regarding slavery on a territory would be to deny it the right to enter the Union as a state on an equal footing with existing states – that is, the ability to determine the question for itself without the premature interference of Congress. For Douglas, then, the Constitution recognized the sovereignty of states over their internal affairs and, therefore, Congress should not deprive the people of new states of their equal rights by interfering in their domestic matters while they prepared for statehood as territories.[82]

Kansas, however, posed a major challenge to the implementation of popular sovereignty because even before the act was passed, antislavery activists from as far away as Massachusetts and proslavery ones as close as neighboring Missouri organized to bring settlers or men who could carry the territory for their respective causes. Their competition became as intense and unbridgeable as the sectional divide in the country as a whole. By March 1856, when Douglas released his report, Kansas had two separate governments: the official federally appointed governor and locally elected legislature in Shawnee and their federally unauthorized free-state counterparts in Topeka. Reflecting President Pierce's position, Douglas's report attributed the schism in Kansas to outside agitators, particularly the New England Emigrant Aid Company, which he blamed for provoking the reaction of Missourians. He acknowledged that the great mass of Northern settlers came for "no other motives than to improve their condition and secure good homes for their families" but were forced to align themselves with one of the hostile factions.[83] That was also true for some Missourians who came.[84]

Douglas's sympathies should have been largely with the free-staters, because they took the promise of popular sovereignty most seriously. In fact, historian Nicole Etcheson believes that what united free-staters in Kansas was not antislavery (they also voted to exclude free blacks from the territory), but a deep commitment to genuine self-government.[85] Douglas was at first critical of the free-state movement because of his loyalty to the administration, whose support he wanted as he planned for the upcoming national convention, and his own investment in statutorily allowing for unprecedented autonomy on the part of the territorial legislature.[86] For him defending the territorial government

---

[82] Ibid., 2–3.
[83] Ibid., 10.
[84] Nicole Etcheson, *Bleeding Kansas: Contested Liberty in the Civil War Era* (Lawrence, KS, 2004), 31.
[85] Ibid., 75.
[86] On his ties to Pierce, see Johannsen, *SAD*, 510. On his pushing autonomy for the territory, see Etcheson, *Bleeding Kansas*, 20.

was part of defending the Kansas–Nebraska Act that authorized it. Moreover, he had visceral disdain for New England antislavery extremists trying to push their agenda on the rest of the country. Not until a congressional investigating committee, which heard testimony in Kansas during the spring of 1856, was completing its 1,188-page report did Douglas recognize the massive fraud on which the territorial government rested and the need for a reliable census of the bona fide inhabitants to be taken before the next election.[87] His belated acceptance of the free-staters' protests reflected his openness to new information, despite his biases.

The division over Kansas exploded into violence both in Washington and in the territory less than two weeks before the Democratic National Convention would meet to nominate its presidential candidate. The "sack of Lawrence" (May 21), the caning of Charles Sumner in the U.S. Senate chamber (May 22), and the "Pottawatomie Massacre" (May 24–25) reduced Pierce's likelihood of renomination and did not enhance Douglas's chances. In Lawrence, a proslavery sheriff and posse razed the Free-State Hotel, burned the free-state governor's home, and destroyed free-state newspaper presses.[88] In Washington the nephew of a South Carolina senator who was verbally attacked (as was Douglas) in a two-day Sumner speech beat the Massachusetts senator into unconsciousness. A Boston newspaper reported the incident as transferring the "reign of terror" from Kansas to the capital.[89] This reference to "terror" in the territory came before the act to which historians frequently apply that loaded term – the murder of five proslavery settlers by the New England emigrant John Brown and his sons.[90]

All of this provided a combustible backdrop to the Democratic Convention that opened at Cincinnati on June 2. After sixteen ballots, Douglas withdrew to enable James Buchanan to obtain the nomination.[91] Buchanan's greatest asset was that he had been out of the country as an ambassador all through the Kansas–Nebraska controversy. In light of the heated national coverage of Kansas in late May, that Douglas came as close as he did to winning the nomination was remarkable. That he succeeded in having the Kansas–Nebraska Act and its principle – "non-interference by Congress with slavery in state or territory" – validated in the party platform was noteworthy.[92]

Douglas's grace in withdrawing, not splitting his party, and paving the way for Buchanan to be the Democratic standard bearer did not ensure lasting

---

[87] U.S. Serials, 34th Cong., 1st sess., House Report No. 200, 6, 9.

[88] "Lawrence Sacked," USN, *Weekly Herald* (New York), May 31, 1856; Etcheson, *Bleeding Kansas*, 101–105.

[89] USN, *Boston Daily Atlas*, May 23, 1856.

[90] On the use of the term "terror," see Beverly Gage, "Terrorism and the American Experience: A State of the Field," *Journal of American History*, 98:1 (June 2011), 73–94, esp. 83–84 regarding its application to John Brown.

[91] The most detailed account of Douglas's interaction (he stayed in Washington) with his supporters in Cincinnati is Johannsen, *SAD*, 516–520.

[92] For the 1856 Democratic Party Platform, see John T. Woolley and Gerhard Peters, The American Presidency Project [online]. Santa Barbara, CA, http://www.presidency.ucsb.edu/ws/.

amity between them. Differences over Kansas ultimately sundered their rela-tionship.[93] By the time Buchanan took office, violence had ended in the territory but healing had not occurred. Free-staters maintained their own government in Topeka and boycotted the officially sanctioned election of a constitutional convention in Lecompton. The boycott undercut the legitimacy of the election, because only about 10 percent of eligible voters, mainly from proslavery areas, participated.[94] Further diminishing the credibility of the Lecompton conven-tion was the free-staters' triumph in the fall 1857 elections to the territorial legislature, confirming their majority in Kansas.[95] This time Douglas aligned himself openly with the free-staters at potentially great political cost. He was up for reelection to the Senate, and Buchanan loyalists were poised to block his nomination. Although he was the ultimate Democrat, he stood against the president and the party in rejecting the proslavery Lecompton constitution in Kansas because it did not represent the true will of the inhabitants of the ter-ritory. He reaffirmed the authenticity of his commitment to genuine local self-government.

Perhaps his best-known utterance is his putative response to Buchanan's warning at a December 1857 meeting, to wit: "No Democrat ever yet dif-fered from an Administration of his own choice without being crushed." Douglas claimed that he said, "Mr. President, I wish you to remember that General Jackson is dead."[96] Antislavery Republicans who had vilified him for the Nebraska bill now had to acknowledge the constancy of his position, and some moved to have him switch to their party.[97] Lincoln, however, managed to secure the Republican senatorial nomination in Illinois, while Douglas over-came the Buchanan resistance to his renomination, and the two candidates proceeded to their debates in the late summer and early fall of 1858.

In the opening speech of their first debate, Douglas laid out his views on three issues that separated him from Lincoln: popular sovereignty, slavery, and race. Popular sovereignty underlay his concept of federalism, "that each and

---

[93] The most comprehensive treatment of his split with Buchanan over Lecompton is Johannsen, *SAD*, 576–610. The origins of their dispute is examined systematically by David E. Meerse, "Origins of the Buchanan–Douglas Feud Reconsidered," *Journal of the Illinois State Historical Society*, 67:2 (1974), 154–174, which concludes that their differences had less to do with patronage than with "ideology and principle."

[94] Etcheson, *Bleeding Kansas*, 146–147.

[95] Ibid., 155.

[96] Douglas enjoyed telling the story of his confrontation with Buchanan when he campaigned for the presidency three years later. See his speeches in Milwaukee in USN, *Newark Advocate* (Newark, OH), Oct. 26, 1860, and Chicago in *Chicago Times and Herald*, Oct. 5, 1860, as printed in the *Daily Illinois State Register*, Oct. 6, 1860.

[97] On Republican wooing see Potter, *Impending Crisis*, 321; Allen C. Guelzo, *Lincoln and Douglas: The Debates That Defined America* (New York, 2008), 24–25; James F. Simon, *Lincoln and Chief Justice Taney: Slavery, Secession, and the President's War Powers* (New York, 2006), 141–142. Historians who admire his stand against Buchanan include Wilentz, *Rise of American Democracy*, 717–718; Jean H. Baker, *James Buchanan* (New York, 2004), 104–106; and Richard H. Sewell, *A House Divided: Sectionalism and Civil War, 1848–1865* (Baltimore, 1988), 65.

crowd, although he was pressed to deny the charge that he believed in equality between the two races and to aver his opposition to their intermarriage.[103]

Although Lincoln certainly knew something about Douglas's involvement with slave labor, he did not bring it up during their debates.[104] Instead he pushed Douglas to reconcile the Supreme Court decision the year before in the *Dred Scott* case with his principle of popular sovereignty. The Court ruled that the Constitution recognized slaves as property, delegated no greater congressional power over property in slaves, and therefore did not warrant a prohibition of slavery north of the 36°30′ line.[105] In effect, the Supreme Court wiped out the history of congressional restraint of slavery in federal territory, including the Missouri Compromise, as unconstitutional. This should have troubled Douglas, who had cited congressional action over internal improvements and nonaction over apportionment as evidence of constitutional meaning or "propriety." He had not gone quite as far as Cass, who argued that a federal ban on slavery violated the intention of Article IV, which restricted congressional power to the land, not the people of a territory. He had said only that it was "not appropriate" for Congress to apply that power to the people. And in rendering the Missouri Compromise "inoperative," he had not considered its constitutionality. The Court's decision, however, provided Douglas with too tempting an escape from the heat he had taken over the repeal. One can sense his relief in June 1857 when he told a large audience at the statehouse in Springfield, "It appears that the only sin involved in the passage of the Kansas–Nebraska Act, consists in the fact that it removed from the statute book an act of Congress, which was unauthorized by the constitution of the United States, and void because passed without constitutional authority."[106] He did not linger on the

---

[103] Ibid., 146, 247. Eric Foner concludes that Lincoln's views on race before he became president fell within the context of Northern society "far short of abolitionist egalitarianism," but also far "from the virulent and gratuitous racism of the Democrats." *The Fiery Trial: Abraham Lincoln and American Slavery* (New York, 2010), 123. Lincoln's attitude toward race is considered from different angles in Brian R. Dirck, ed., *Lincoln Emancipated: Then President and the Politics of Race* (De Kalb, IL, 2007). On his views before 1861, see especially the foreword by Allen Guelzo (vii–xiv) and the essays by Kenneth Winkle (8–28) and James N. Leiker (73–98). For a succinct comparison of the appeal to racism by both Lincoln and Douglas during the debates, see Michael Burlingame, *Abraham Lincoln: A Life*, 2 vols. (Baltimore, 2007), 1: 526. Douglas sometimes appears as a foil to soften Lincoln's racism. Still, there is merit to Lucas E. Morel's claim that Douglas was content to exploit the prejudices of their audience in 1858, while Lincoln tried to elevate their "moral horizon." "Lincoln, Race, and the Spirit of '76," *Perspectives on Political Science*, 39:1 (Jan.–Mar. 2010), 7.

[104] See Chapter 9.

[105] For the text of Taney's opinion, 60 U.S. (HOW) 399–454. For an excellent summary, see Earl M. Maltz, *Slavery and the Supreme Court, 1825–1861* (Lawrence, KS, 2009), 245–249. The sesquicentennial of the *Dred Scott* decision has brought an outpouring of rich scholarship to a topic that Don E. Fehrenbacher, *The Dred Scott Case: Its Significance in American History and Politics* (New York, 1978), has dominated. A critical guide to the new literature is Gerald Leonard, "Law and Politics Reconsidered: A New Constitutional History of Dred Scott," *Law and Social Inquiry*, 34 (Summer 2009), 747–785.

[106] Stephen A. Douglas, *Kansas, Utah, and the Dred Scott Decision: Remarks of the Hon. Stephen A. Douglas Delivered at Springfield, Illinois, June 12, 1857* (Chicago, 1857), 6. James A.

matter of its constitutionality and did not address that question directly in his debates in 1858 with Lincoln, who conceded that Douglas did not argue the correctness of the decision, only the authority of its source.[107]

Although he had not denied the constitutionality of Congress to prohibit slavery and had interpreted consistent congressional exercise of a power to reflect its propriety, late in his famous *Harper's Magazine* essay of 1859 Douglas did state that the Supreme Court was "authorized and compelled" to pronounce the Missouri Compromise void because the Constitution did not delegate to Congress the power to prohibit slavery in the territories. Defending the Court's decision was an afterthought. His essay targeted the "house divided" metaphor that gained Lincoln national traction after he invoked it during his speech accepting the Illinois Republican Party nomination for senator in 1858.[108] It troubled Douglas for two reasons: its scriptural origins and its constitutional implications.

He dismissed Lincoln's pretense that "this language of our Lord and Master, is applicable to the American Union and American constitution."[109] On the one hand, he derided Lincoln's invocation of Scripture; on the other, he could not resist suggesting that the growth and prosperity of the country "divided into free and slave states, as our fathers made it," were evidence that "Divine Providence has smiled upon us."[110] He emphasized, however, that the founding fathers, not God, had to be their guide on the question of slavery. He generally opposed the intrusion of religion in politics. The Constitution, not the Bible, was the highest authority that leaders should cite.[111] And he

Rawley notes that historians have paid attention to the constitutional issue in this speech but have ignored how Douglas played to the racial prejudices of his audience in the state capital. *Race & Politics:"Bleeding Kansas" and the Coming of the Civil War* (Philadelphia, 1969), 194–195.

[107] CWAL, 3: 89. Guelzo, *Lincoln and Douglas*, is a highly readable narrative of the entire senatorial campaign, including the seven debates, with helpful grids showing the major points of each, and an analysis of the election that followed.

[108] For Lincoln's "House Divided" speech, see CWAL, 2: 461. His phrase was still being cited in newspapers a year later. USN, *Daily Evening Bulletin* (San Francisco, CA), Feb. 11, 1859; *Weekly Union and American* (Nashville, TN), Mar. 7, 1859; *Congregationalist* (Boston), Mar. 11, 1859; *Semi-Weekly Mississippian* (Jackson), July 15, 1859; *Daily Morning News* (Savannah, GA), July 22, 1859; *National Daily Intelligencer* (Washington, DC), Sept. 22, 1859. Douglas's essay appeared in *Harper's New Monthly Magazine*, 19 (Sept. 1859), 112, 519–537. It was reprinted in newspapers. USN, *Vermont Patriot* (Montpelier), Oct. 1, 1859; *Daily National Intelligencer* (Washington, DC), Oct. 7, 1859. Harper Brothers also published it as a book, Stephen A. Douglas, *The Dividing Line between Federal and Local Authority: Popular Sovereignty in the Territories* (New York, 1859).

[109] CWAL, 3: 111; L-DD, 94.

[110] CWAL, 3: 178; L-DD, 163.

[111] CWAL, 3: 241; L-DD, 208. Five years earlier he had criticized prominent clergymen who had protested against the Kansas–Nebraska Act not simply as citizens but as "ministers of the Gospel." Stephen A. Douglas to Twenty-five Chicago Clergymen, Apr. 6, 1854, *Letters of SAD*, 300–321; Huston, "Democracy by Scripture"; and Nicole Etcheson, "The Great Principle of Self-Government: Popular Sovereignty and Bleeding Kansas," *Kansas History*, 27 (Spring-Summer 2004), 25–26.

viewed the Constitution much like the men who drafted it did, as a "secular humanist text."[112]

He thought that the major purpose of the Constitution was to delineate the line that divided federal and local government. To nationalize antislavery was to obliterate local self-government, the protection of which was the primary impulse behind the Revolution, the goal underlying the equality clause in the Declaration of Independence, and the central challenge of the framers of 1787.[113] For Douglas, Lincoln's proposition that the United States could not endure half slave and half free was belied by American history since 1776.

Douglas's argument in this essay was not equal to his principles. He genuinely believed that territories should have the right to decide the question of slavery for themselves and that federal intervention deprived territorial inhabitants of the right of self-government. The crux of the issue was the Constitution. It did not extend self-government to territories; rather, it expressly conferred on Congress the power to "make all rules and regulations" for federal territory. And Congress had done so since the Northwest Ordinance, which prohibited slavery in that territory. On three accounts Douglas had taken positions in the past that reinforced the validity of the Northwest Ordinance. First, he had cited it to demonstrate that Congress had intended for all inhabitants, including unnaturalized immigrants, to vote in the territory. Second, he had cherished its equal footing doctrine, which he drew on to argue that each new state should enter on a par with the original states and, therefore, that each territory should be free to adopt a statehood constitution that authorized its own "peculiar" ways regarding "domestic" matters. Third, Douglas had argued during the Apportionment Act debate of 1844 and in his open letter to Governor Matteson ten years later that consistent congressional interpretation of its powers established their propriety. In the former case, Congress had never interfered with state control of federal elections and, therefore, could not

---

[112] John M. Murrin, "Religion and Politics in America from the First Settlements to the Civil War," in *Religion and Politics: From the Colonial Period to the Present*, 2nd ed. ed. Mark A. Noll and Luke E. Harlow (New York, 2007), 34.

[113] Barry A. Shain writes, "Douglas may have been close to getting it substantially right when he held that … in contrast to Lincoln," the equality clause in the Declaration of Independence referred to British subjects in the colonies in relationship to British subjects in England. "Rights Natural and Civil in the Declaration of Independence," in *The Nature of Rights at the American Founding and Beyond*, ed. Barry A. Shain (Charlottesville, VA, 2007), 118. See also citations to David Armitage in note 70, this chapter. James Oakes makes a case for why "Lincoln was never the relentless centralizer that Douglas made him out to be." "Natural Rights, Citizenship Rights, States' Rights, and Black Rights," in *Our Lincoln: New Perspective on Lincoln and His World*, ed. Eric Foner (New York, 2008), 126. Drew R. McCoy believes that "Lincoln correctly understood, as Stephen Douglas … did not, that the political thought of the Revolutionary generation was grounded in the logic of natural right and that natural rights inhered in all members of the human species." "Lincoln and the Founding Fathers: A Reconsideration," *Journal of the Abraham Lincoln Association*, 16:1 (Winter 1995), 4–5. On Lincoln's immediate response to Douglas's *Harper* essay, see Gary Ecelbarger, "Before Cooper Union: Abraham Lincoln's 1859 Cincinnati Speech and Its Impact on His Nomination," *Journal of the Abraham Lincoln Association*, 30:1 (Winter 2009), 1–17.

do so; in the latter, Congress had long enacted a variety of internal improvements; therefore, it could do so. By the same reasoning, how could Douglas deny the propriety of Congress's prohibiting slavery in territories in view of the Northwest Ordinance?

In his 1859 essay, however, he tried to discredit the ordinance by stating that in July 1787 it "was passed by the remnant" of the Confederation Congress sitting in New York "while its most esteemed members" were at the Philadelphia Convention.[114] He ignored the fact that the First Federal Congress repassed the Northwest Ordinance two years later.[115] He did not want to acknowledge the constitutionality of the congressional ban on slavery and ultimately cited Taney's ruling that it was unconstitutional. But he had to find his own way of embedding his principle in the Constitution and could not. The irony was that his best case involved the equal footing principle, which he said could not be meaningful unless people of a territory were free to approve any constitution they wanted preparatory to statehood without federal interference. In other words, his strongest argument for territorial autonomy was based on the equal footing doctrine that derived from the Northwest Ordinance.

Douglas's strained reasoning reflected the great anomaly in antebellum constitutionalism. On the one hand, each state had the right to control its internal affairs; on the other, Congress could impose policies during its territorial stage.[116] For Douglas, the latter power rendered the former right hollow. He

---

[114] Douglas, *Dividing Line*, 31. Some scholars now believe that there was close contact between the two bodies in 1787. Congress may have helped the Philadelphia Convention by fashioning a compromise that banned slavery from the Northwest while implicitly preserving the Southwest for slave owners, who would not have to worry about competition in the Northwest. The convention's adoption (IV.2.3) "almost word for word" of language in the Northwest Ordinance that required the return of fugitive slaves, suggests David Waldstreicher, testifies to collaboration between New York and Philadelphia in 1787. *Slavery's Constitution* (New York, 2009), 87–88. Van Cleve, *Slaveholders' Union*, 154, notes that delegates from Philadelphia traveled to New York in the middle of the convention in order to provide a quorum for the Congress when it voted on the ordinance, which he considers to have been a "planned, coordinated action" intended to resolve the stalemate over slavery in the territories (158). On the origins of the Fugitive Slave Clause, see also Maltz, *Slavery and the Supreme Court*, 83–85.

Douglas, however, would have relished the conclusion of Mark A. Graber, *Dred Scott and the Problem of Constitutional Evil* (New York, 2006), 72: "If the persons responsible for the Constitution intended that Congress have the power to ban slavery in every territory, then this was the best-kept secret in American politics during the late 1780s." His point is that the framers had no thoughts about new territories that might be acquired. For a different perspective, see Don E. Fehrenbacher, *The Slaveholding Republic: An Account of the United States Government's Relations to Slavery* (New York, 2001), 253–294.

For an excellent recent analysis of Douglas's argument in the 1859 essay, see Timothy S. Good, *Lincoln for President: An Underdog's Path to the 1860 Republican Nomination* (Jefferson, NC, 2009), 38–43.

[115] Similarly, in 1819 James Madison " 'forgot' that the First Congress had voted almost unanimously to prohibit slavery in the Northwest Territory," when he opposed such a ban. Graber, *Dred Scott and the Problem of Constitutional Evil*, 70.

[116] For an analysis of territorial status and state equality before the Supreme Court and extrajudicially, see Peter S. Onuf, "New State Equality: The Ambiguous History of a Constitutional Principle," *Publius: The Journal of Fderalism*, 18 (Fall 1988), 53–69.

deeply believed that the right of territories to decide their domestic matters was fundamental to the American Revolution and should have been to American constitutionalism, and he would take his message everywhere when he ran for president.[117]

---

[117] On the basis of Douglas's speeches during the debates over the Compromise of 1850 and his "Dividing Line" essay of 1859, Fehrenbacher, *The Slaveholding Republic*, 268, writes that Douglas "stopped short" of claiming that Congress had no authority over slavery in the territories. "Rather, he urged that Congress *should* be guided by 'the great principle' of local self-government." Fehrenbacher evidently does not place much stock in Douglas's belated agreement with Taney's denial of congressional authority. Neither should we.

7

The 1860 Campaign and the Code Against Campaigning

> Every political creed must be wrong which cannot be avowed in all the States of the Union alike.
>
> Stephen A. Douglas (1860)[1]

Between June 27, when he officially accepted the nomination of his party, and November 6, when the presidential election was held, Stephen Douglas spent 160 days campaigning in more than 150 towns in twenty-three of the thirty-three states. What he did was unprecedented both in scale and in purpose. Although he began by paying lip service to the anomalous but powerful tradition that constrained election contests, Douglas eventually cast aside pretense and conducted the first overtly political campaign by a presidential candidate. Crowd estimates of the time were notoriously inflated or deflated according to the partisan leanings of each newspaper, but it is evident that several hundred thousand people were able to see Douglas in person, more than had ever seen or heard a presidential candidate.

Before 1860, only two presidential nominees, both of the Whig Party, had campaigned for themselves – William Henry Harrison in 1840 and Winfield Scott in 1852. Harrison gave twenty-three speeches over four months, according to an account that credits him with appearing "through the old Northwest."[2] In fact, Harrison confined himself to the one state where he had lived for a quarter-century – Ohio. Although he had earned his fame as a general and governor of the Indiana Territory, he declined an invitation to visit that state before the election because "improper motives would be ascribed to me."[3] Moreover, he explicitly disclaimed any electioneering purpose. He was not soliciting votes, only speaking to clear his name of the "continued torrent

---

[1] USN, *New York Herald*, Aug. 23, 1860.
[2] Robert G. Gunderson, *The Log-Cabin Campaign* (Lexington, KY, 1957), 165, 168. M. J. Heale, *The Presidential Quest: Candidates and Images in American Political Culture, 1787–1852* (New York, 1982), 119, correctly notes that Harrison did not leave Ohio.
[3] USN, *Cleveland Daily Herald*, Aug. 3, 1840.

of calumny" poured on him by the opposition. He expressed what was by then the hoary creed of a presidential candidate, that "the bestowment of the office should be the free act of the People; and I have no wish to bias their judgment unjustly in my favor."[4]

Winfield Scott's decision to campaign was made only when his election prospects became desperate. Yet he undertook a tour that was remarkably vigorous for a sixty-six-year-old man. From September 15 to October 22 Scott traveled to eight of the thirty-one states, appearing in at least sixty-six towns.[5] Throughout his trip, however, he disclaimed any political purpose. Instead he adhered to a contrivance: he was carrying out instructions from the Fillmore administration to determine the suitability of Blue Lick Springs, Kentucky, as the site of a western soldiers' home, established by Congress on August 31.[6] He polished the ruse, saying that "[i]f his official duty had not required it, he should not have taken a journey during the Presidential contest."[7]

Why did Harrison fear that "improper motives" would be attributed to him if he campaigned outside his home state? Why would Scott not have taken a multistate tour unless he had an excuse unrelated to the election? From George Washington to Abraham Lincoln, presidential candidates observed what historian Gil Troy calls the "republican code," what we might now call, after historian Gordon Wood, the monarchical republican tradition. The custom against personal campaigning by presidential candidates dated from George Washington and John Adams, who viewed the United States as if it were a "monarchical republic" – Wood's term, taken from Adams, for the perspective of Federalists in the 1790s. The first president and vice president wanted to invest the supreme leader with sufficient dignity to enhance the stature of the new central government. Washington therefore paid close attention to the "style proper for the Chief Magistrate."[8] And openly pursuing office was not considered proper.

Washington never sought the posts that brought him fame. He had always served at the behest of his country, not at the prompting of personal ambition.[9]

4 See his speech in Fort Greenville. USN, *Daily National Intelligencer* (Washington, DC), Aug. 21, 1840.

5 I have tracked his itinerary through two newspaper databases: *19th Century United States Newspapers* and *New York Times* (ProQuest Historical Newspapers). Scott stopped in Maryland (one town), Pennsylvania (four), Ohio (thirty-one), Kentucky (eight), Indiana (four), New York (fourteen), New Jersey (three), and Delaware (one).

6 Charles W. Elliott, *Winfield Scott: The Soldier and the Man* (New York, 1937), 635.

7 USN, *Daily National Intelligencer* (Washington, DC), Sept. 23, 1852.

8 Gordon Wood, *Empire of Liberty: A History of the Early Republic, 1789–1815* (New York, 2009), 53–94, quotes on 77 and 82. Gil Troy, *See How They Ran: The Changing Role of the Presidential Candidate* (New York, 1991), 7–19.

9 Gary Wills, *Cincinnatus: George Washington and the Enlightenment* (Garden City, NY, 1984), 130; Don Higginbotham, "Introduction: Washington and the Historians," in *George Washington Reconsidered*, ed. Don Higginbotham (Charlottesville, VA, 2001), 3–4. Paul K. Longmore believes that Washington disguised his ambition in order to enhance his image – "by making the offer come to him, rather than promoting himself, he increases his influence and authority." *The Invention of George Washington* (Berkeley, CA, 1988), 32.

He thereby provided the iconic model for the national gentry, who exclaimed a disinterest in the limelight and a yearning for private life.[10] Whether or not they were sincere, Robert Wiebe astutely writes, what counted was "how ritualistically they repeated the same self-abnegating, power-denying sentiments."[11] This became the obligatory public stance of presidential aspirants, no matter how false it was for them to camouflage their striving for the office.

Washington and Adams were not false in private. Both remained aloof from electioneering activities in their behalf.[12] They honored the monarchical republican tradition of staying above the fray. We might expect that Jefferson, a champion of what Wood calls "popular republicanism," would have campaigned directly among the people.[13] Instead he set the double standard that became an acceptable part of the American political tradition to 1860.

Electioneering efforts that Jefferson's supporters undertook in 1800 "surpassed anything seen before in national affairs."[14] Partisan newspapers and pamphleteers informed the people about candidates and mobilized them to attend parades, rallies, picnics, and banquets, all of which were reported to readers who could vote – as well as those who could not. Although the vote that decided the presidential election came in the House of Representatives, the level of participation of the whole population in the 1800 campaign, according to Jeffrey L. Pasley, made that election transformative in the development of a democratic political culture beyond the vision of the framers of 1787.[15]

---

[10] Gordon Wood has examined the disinterested, virtuous republican leader from different angles in various studies. "Interests and Disinterestedness in the Making of the Constitution," in *Beyond Confederation: Origins of the Constitution and American National Identity*, ed. Richard R. Beeman, Stephen Botein, and Edward C. Carter III (Chapel Hill, NC, 1987), 69–109; *The Radicalism of the American Revolution: How a Revolution Transformed a Monarchical Society into a Democratic One Unlike Any That Had Ever Existed* (New York, 1992), 104–109; *Revolutionary Characters: What Made the Founders Different* (New York, 2006), 16–24.

[11] Robert Wiebe, *The Opening of American Society: From the Adoption of the Constitution to the Eve of Disunion* (New York, 1983), 13.

[12] Joseph J. Ellis suggests that Washington turned his natural aloofness into a presidential asset by managing "to levitate above the political landscape." *His Excellency: George Washington* (New York, 2004), 206. See also Marcus Cunliffe, "Election of 1792," in *History of American Presidential Elections, 1789–1968*, ed. Arthur M. Schlesinger, Jr., Fred. L. Israel, and William P. Hansen, 4 vols. (New York, 1971), 1: 23. In 1800 Adams did return to Washington from Quincy on one trip by taking a circuitous route through Pennsylvania and Maryland that the opposition press criticized for its political purpose, an intention that the president disavowed. Noble E. Cunningham, "Election of 1800," in *History of Presidential Elections*, ed. Schlesinger, Israel, and Hansen, 1: 101–134.

[13] Wood, *Empire of Liberty*, 84.

[14] Sean Wilentz, *The Rise of American Democracy: Jefferson to Lincoln* (New York, 2005), 97.

[15] "The Cheese and the Words: Popular Political Culture and Participatory Democracy in the Early American Republic," in *Beyond the Founders: New Approaches to the Political History of the Early American Republic*, ed. Jeffrey L. Pasley, Andrew W. Robertson, and David Waldstreicher (Chapel Hill, NC, 2004), 31–56; Jeffrey L. Pasley, "1800 as a Revolution in Political Culture: Newspapers, Celebrations, Voting, and Democratization in the Early Republic," in *The Revolution of 1800: Democracy, Race, and the New Republic*, ed. James Horn, Jan E. Lewis, and Peter S. Onuf (Charlottesville, VA, 2002), 121–152. On the

Despite the unprecedented appeal to the masses, neither Jefferson nor Adams personally appeared before them. In the spring of 1800 Jefferson mulled over attending a popular reception on his way home from the capital if it could be arranged, but was dissuaded by Governor James Monroe, who noted the impropriety of such an event.[16] Instead Jefferson continued to work assiduously behind the scenes, orchestrating what and where surrogates should write in his behalf and advising how supporters might generally advance the party's cause.[17] After Jefferson it became unexceptional for presidential candidates to abjure personal campaigning while privately imploring and directing surrogates to act in their behalf.

If the election of Jefferson was a revolution that promoted the "relentless democratization" of American life, why did the monarchical republican style of presidential campaigning survive?[18] Five influences enabled the taboo against personal campaigning to endure: (1) Washington's example, (2) federalism, (3) the nonpartisan ideal, (4) the party ticket, and (5) candidate fear. The nonpartisan ideal fragmented after 1828; candidate fear intensified after 1844.

(1) The example of Washington, who personified the Republic for the first three generations of Americans, cannot be underestimated. His refusal to solicit office endured as a powerful model for presidential and even gubernatorial candidates.[19] The code rested on a conceit made plausible by Washington's story: the presidency must be thrust upon a reluctant, virtuous leader; an ambitious man should not openly pursue the office. A measure of Washington's hold is suggested by Andrew Burstein, who found him mentioned usually in the second or third toasts at July Fourth celebrations in 1826.[20] Twenty-five years later, Washington was still toasted and remembered reverently in speeches on Independence Day.[21]

---

democratizing impact of the election of 1800, see also Gary J. Kornblith and John M. Murrin, "The Dilemmas of Ruling Elites in Revolutionary America," in *Ruling America: Wealth and Power in a Democracy*, ed. Steve Fraser and Gary Gerstle (Cambridge, MA, 2005), 56. Bruce Ackerman, *The Failure of the Founding Fathers: Jefferson, Marshall, and the Rise of Presidential Democracy* (Cambridge, 2005), 5, sees Jefferson's election as a "mandate from the People for sweeping transformation" and, therefore, his accession "marks the birth agony of the plebiscitarian presidency."

[16] Joanne B. Freeman, "Corruption and Compromise in the Election of 1800: The Process of Politics on the National Stage," in *Revolution of 1800*, ed. Horn, Lewis, and Onuf, 97.

[17] Cunningham, "Election of 1800," 113–114; Ackerman, *Failure of the Founding Fathers*, 20.

[18] For the quote, see Wood, *Empire of Liberty*, 312.

[19] Heale, *Presidential Quest*, 3.

[20] Andrew Burstein, *America's Jubilee: How in 1826 a Generation Remembered Fifty Years of Independence* (New York, 2001), 251.

[21] See the July Fourth ceremonies in Boston, Charleston, Cleveland, Montpelier, and Paris. USN, *Boston Daily Atlas*, July 7, 1851; USN, *Weekly Raleigh Register and North Carolina Gazette*, July 23, 1851; USN, *Cleveland Herald*, July 7, 1851; USN, *Vermont Watchman and State Journal* (Montpelier), July 10, 1851; USN, *Daily Ohio Statesman* (Columbus), July 28, 1851; USN, *National Daily Intelligencer* (Washington, DC), July 28, 1851.

(2) American democracy evolved within the framework of American federalism. The framers deliberately left the question of democracy to the states. The Constitution prescribed no role for the people in choosing the president. Article II delegated power over presidential elections to two institutions – state legislatures and Congress. State legislatures would appoint electors who, in turn, would vote for the candidate. In case no one received a majority of electoral votes, the House of Representatives would choose the winner, as it did in 1800 and 1824. And the House itself would be chosen by voters whose qualifications were established state by state.[22] There was a convergence between the elimination of economic-based suffrage requirements in states and the shift to the popular election of presidential electors. By 1824 only one-fourth of the state legislatures retained the power to choose presidential electors and only one-eighth still attached a property qualification to voting.[23] None of these populist reforms, however, affected the code against directly wooing the people.

(3) Direct electioneering was at odds with the nonpartisan ideal that held sway at the beginning. Federalist and Republican candidates tried to distance themselves from the "partisan contagion" that fueled their campaigns.[24] A great paradox of the new Republic, as Richard Hofstadter observed, was that the founders had "a keen terror of party spirit and its evil consequences, and yet, almost as soon as their national government was in operation, found it necessary to establish parties."[25] Some gentry coped with this antinomy by publicly denouncing partisanship while privately advancing their partisan interests. Nevertheless, the first six presidents on the whole tried to stand above party.[26]

---

[22] For a straightforward narrative of the discussion of the executive at the Philadelphia Convention, see Forrest McDonald, *The American Presidency: An Intellectual History* (Lawrence, KS, 1994), 160–181. The limited record of the convention regarding the election of the president invites varying scholarly emphases. Richard P. McCormick, *The Presidential Game: The Origins of American Presidential Politics* (New York, 1982), 16–40, believes that the founders expected electors to be popularly chosen. Bruce Ackerman, however, stresses the delegates' Whig tradition that viewed the legislature, not the executive, as the voice of the people. *Failure of the Founding Fathers*, 11. The office stirred little controversy in the state ratifying conventions. Pauline Maier, *Ratification: The People Debate the Constitution, 1787–1788* (New York, 2010), 114, 151, 189–190, 371, 415.

[23] The six state legislatures that chose electors in 1824 were Delaware, Georgia, Louisiana, New York, South Carolina, and Vermont. Robert A. Diamond, ed., *Presidential Elections Since 1789* (Washington, DC: Congressional Quarterly, 1975), 4. The states that still had a property qualification were North Carolina, Rhode Island, and Virginia. Stanley L. Engerman and Kenneth L. Sokoloff, "The Evolution of Suffrage Institutions in the New World," *Journal of Economic History*, 65:4 (Dec. 2005), 898, table.

[24] On the "partisan contagion," see Andrew Robertson, "Voting Rites and Voting Acts: Electioneering Rituals, 1790–1820," in *Beyond the Founders*, ed. Pasley, Robertson, and Waldstreicher, 67.

[25] Richard Hofstadter, *The Idea of a Party System: The Rise of Legitimate Opposition in the United States, 1780–1840* (Berkeley, CA, 1969), viii.

[26] Ralph Ketcham, *Presidents Above Party: The First American Presidency, 1789–1829* (Chapel Hill, NC, 1984), esp. 215ff. on the nonpartisan ideal.

(4) The nonpartisan ideal had little currency once the electorate was urged to support a party ticket. Party organizers wanted ballots cast for whole slates, and voters may have become conditioned to endorsing party tickets rather than selecting individuals, particularly in states where congressional delegations were selected at large.[27] Partyists stressed loyalty to the party, not to particular men. Still, we must wonder why voters did not demand face-to-face wooing by individual suitors for state and federal chief executive. Why did they enable gubernatorial and presidential candidates to stay on the sidelines?[28]

These questions become insistent regarding the impact of the election of 1828, which shattered the nonpartisan ideal and mythified the presidency as

[27] I am grateful to Philip J. Lampi, compiler of the First Democratization Project at the American Antiquarian Society, for an email and a personal conversation suggesting how local, state, and federal voting practices through 1825 generally worked against personal campaigning. An exception was Virginia, where legislative candidates had a long history of directly wooing voters. Charles S. Sydnor, *Gentlemen Freeholders: Political Practices in Washington's Virginia* (Chapel Hill, NC, 1952), ch. 4; John G. Kolp, *Gentlemen and Freeholders: Electoral Politics in Colonial Virginia* (Baltimore, 1998), 14, 19, 22, 24; Daniel P. Jordan, *Political Leadership in Jefferson's Virginia* (Charlottesville, VA, 1983), 109–110. The transition from a "deferential electioneering order" to a democratic partisan one brought "ticket voting" that increased turnouts, as shown by Andrew Robertson, but it reduced the need for individual campaigning. "Voting Rites and Voting Acts: Electioneering Ritual, 1790–1820," in *Beyond the Founders*, ed. Pasley, Robertson, and Waldstreicher, 57–78, 72–73. On the statutory termination of at-large elections to the House of Representatives in 1842, see Martin H. Quitt, "Congressional (Partisan) Constitutionalism: The Apportionment Act Debates of 1842 and 1844," *Journal of the Early Republic* (Winter 2008), 627–651.

[28] Studies of five gubernatorial contests in the 1820s reveal no uniform pattern of campaigning. In the Missouri election of 1820, candidate William Clark, the once famous explorer, refused to campaign. In contrast, Alexander McNair ran a populist campaign that took him, according to a critic, "by day and night from churches to grog shops and from lime kilns to boat yards." McNair won. William E. Foley, "After the Applause: William Clark's Failed 1820 Gubernatorial Campaign," *Gateway Heritage*, 24:2 (2003–2004), 104–111, quote on 110. In 1824 in Kentucky, when favorite son Henry Clay first ran for president, Joseph Desha was the only gubernatorial candidate to tour the state, and he won the election handily. Paul E. Doutrich, "A Pivotal Decision: The 1824 Gubernatorial Campaign in Kentucky," *Filson Club History Quarterly*, 56:1 (1982), 14–29. In Vermont in 1826, there are no reports of gubernatorial campaigning, and there appears to have been little interest in the results. When the election returns were slow to come, a newspaper in the state capital lamented, "[N]obody knows and nobody cares who is Governor." Kenneth A. Degree, "Anticipating Antimasonry: The Vermont Gubernatorial Election of 1826," *Vermont History*, 72 (Winter/Spring 2004), 12–14. In Illinois, however, personal campaigning for the governorship was established early. During the campaign of 1822, two of the three candidates traveled across the state and "fired salvoes of whiskey, gingerbread and stump oratory at each other" because "a strongly contested frontier election was not won in the rocking chair on the front porch." Four years later the two candidates toured the state making speeches. Kurt E. Leichtle, "The Rise of Jacksonian Politics in Illinois," *Illinois Historical Journal*, 82 (Summer 1989), 93–107, quote on 97. In the 1829–1830 Illinois campaign, the two gubernatorial candidates gave speeches, and the "tireless" stump speaker, John Reynolds, canvassed more of the state and won, although that is not the reason the author emphasizes. James Simeone, "The 1830 Contest for Governor and the Politics of Resentment," *Journal of the Illinois State Historical Society*, 102:3/4 (Fall 2009/Winter 2010), 282–287.

the voice of the people.[29] Why would the people's most important spokesperson not be expected to campaign personally to hear what the majority had to say? Andrew Jackson had received a plurality of popular votes in 1824, but the House chose John Quincy Adams. After the inauguration in March 1825, Jackson left Washington to return to Tennessee. It was a "triumphal march" as huge crowds came out to cheer him. He was touched by the "almost universal disappointment over his defeat." The voters had done all that they could to elect him, but they and he felt cheated.[30] What better way to make sure that would not happen again than to reverse the sequence and appeal directly to the people before the election? In fact, Democratic politicians tried to get Jackson to do that during the campaign four years later. Although he received invitations from numerous state committees to make personal appearances, he declined all but one because he did not want to give the impression that he was seeking the office. The only invitation he accepted was that of the Louisiana legislature to attend a January 8 celebration of the Battle of New Orleans. He could justify his appearance there as a patriotic act, not a political one, and he conditioned his acceptance on the assurance that organizers would treat his attendance in that manner.[31]

Why would he have to justify it as nonpolitical? Why did he not undercut the influence of Congress in the selection process by taking his campaign directly to the people? Biographer Robert Remini says that in 1828 Jackson "took command of the first reform movement in American political history ... a crusade to restore popular government."[32] Sean Wilentz writes, "Jackson's victory marked the culmination of more than thirty years of American democratic development."[33] Yet Jackson did not challenge the elitist code against personal campaigning. It is evident that people he claimed to speak for did want to see and hear him. Their demand became so intense that he relented a bit by his reelection campaign of 1832. He thought it would be acceptable if on his return to Washington from the Hermitage in September 1832 he stopped at one or two events, but he was criticized in the press. As the *National Intelligencer* scolded, "We do not recollect before having heard of a President of the United States descending in person into the political arena."[34] Notwithstanding the

---

[29] On Jackson's and his party's belief that he spoke for the people, see Joel H. Silbey, *Martin Van Buren and the Emergence of American Popular Politics* (Lanham, MD, 2002), 97. On Jackson's commitment to carrying out the will of the majority, see Wilentz, *Rise of American Democracy*, 382–390. Jennifer R. Mercieca, "The Irony of the Democratic Style," *Rhetoric and Public Affairs*, 11 (2008), 441–449, quote on 447, provocatively suggests that "Jackson's democratic style flattered and enticed the people into believing they had more actual power than they really did while simultaneously rendering 'democracy' an empty, yet powerful term."

[30] Robert V. Remini, *Andrew Jackson and the Course of American Freedom, 1822–1832* (New York, 1981), 103.

[31] Ibid., 131; Robert V. Remini, *The Election of Andrew Jackson* (New York, 1964), 113–115.

[32] Remini, *Andrew Jackson and the Course of American Freedom*, 99–100.

[33] Wilentz, *Rise of American Democracy*, 309.

[34] Quoted in Remini, *Andrew Jackson and the Course of American Freedom*, 384. Jon Meacham overstates Jackson's stops while returning to Washington as constituting "what amounted to the

minor detour, Jackson believed he honored the code. That he did not challenge it alerts us to how limited "Jacksonian democracy" was.[35]

Neither of the Whig candidates who did embark on limited campaign tours openly challenged the taboo. As we noted, Harrison in 1840 and Scott in 1852 came up with rationales for claiming that their travels did not have a political purpose. Douglas began the same way in 1860. He, too, did not at first want to take on the code. Moreover, the conventional wisdom was that talking and touring could only hurt a candidate.

(5) The great fear was that a candidate would say too much about a political issue that would come back to bite him. This was the lesson Lincoln learned from the experience of Henry Clay, a hero of his. Although a party's official nominee could not violate the ban without verbal legerdemain, someone seeking the nomination could travel with less deceit to test or arouse support for his candidacy. Clay, the likely Whig candidate in 1844, received invitations to speak at political rallies around the country and was urged to undertake a national tour. Although he thought it would be presumptuous to do so before his party chose him, he decided to do some speechmaking in order to make certain of the nomination, which had been denied him in 1840. He justified his tours, in fact, on the ground that he was not a candidate but only a private citizen.[36] He set the record for pre-nomination electioneering with a "series of public meetings" in Kentucky, Ohio, and Indiana, private receptions with party leaders in Louisiana, Mississippi, and Tennessee, and a tour of Georgia, North Carolina, South Carolina, and Virginia. These travels were spaced over two years before his nomination by the Whig convention in May 1844.[37] He also campaigned for the nomination by correspondence, responding to questions mailed to him with letters published in newspapers. One letter, explaining his clear opposition to the annexation of Texas, was written in Raleigh, North Carolina, two weeks before the Whig convention. It did not cost him the nomination but, in the view of a biographer, "ultimately destroyed his presidential bid."[38] The lesson that reverberated for the next sixteen years was the advice that his advisers had unsuccessfully pressed on him:

---

first personal presidential campaign tour." *American Lion: Andrew Jackson in the White House* (New York, 2008), 218. Jackson did go on a tour of the Northeast after the nullification crisis was resolved in 1833 in order to "celebrate the Union by seeing face-to-face those he felt he had just saved." David S. Reynolds, *Waking Giant: American in the Age of Jackson* (New York, 2008), 102.

[35] Troy, *See How They Ran*, 297n, suggests that "resistance to the democratization of the campaign reveals the delayed nature" of Jacksonian democratic change.

[36] Heale, *Presidential Quest*, 121.

[37] Robert V. Remini, *Henry Clay: Statesman for the Union* (New York, 1991), 613–638.

[38] Ibid., 638–639.

stay silent. After securing the nomination, Clay did no more touring, but he did write public letters (the Alabama letters) equivocating on the question of annexation. When he lost, his experience was reified as a warning to future candidates: "Don't talk, don't write."[39]

In 1860 there were four candidates for the presidency: John Bell, Constitutional Union, nominated May 10; Abraham Lincoln, Republican Party, nominated May 18; Stephen Douglas, National Democratic Party, nominated June 23; and John Breckinridge, Southern Democratic Party, nominated June 23.[40] As a Republican newspaper headlined its coverage, the two nominations of June 23 represented "Democracy Blown Up." It described the split at Baltimore as the "self-dismemberment and death" of the Democratic Party.[41]

Douglas had expected to be the first official candidate when the Democrats convened in Charleston, South Carolina, on April 23. Disappointed by his failure to gain the nomination of the Democratic Conventions of 1852 and 1856, he now had to overcome the enmity of the sitting president and titular head of his party; yet he was so effective at organizing that he was the clear favorite at Charleston. His pre-convention activities were co-anchored in New York by August Belmont, his campaign manager since December, and in Washington by his wife, father-in-law, and himself.[42] Belmont's Fifth Avenue home became the headquarters for potential donors and politicos, and the would-be candidate traveled there several times. Douglas's Washington home became a social center under the direction of Adele, beautiful, educated, charming – typecast in the savvy hostess role that political wives (or daughters) had held in the national capital since the days of Martha Washington and Dolly Madison, her great-aunt.[43] Her status as a new mother added to her appeal. Further, her father oversaw correspondence at Douglas's office.

---

[39] Michael F. Holt characterizes Clay's decision to publish his Alabama letters as "among the biggest mistakes of his long political career." *The Rise and Fall of the American Whig Party: Jacksonian Politics and the Onset of the Civil War* (New York, 1999), 180. For his explanation of the Whig loss in 1844, see 194–206. On the Alabama letters, see also David S. Heidler and Jeanne T. Heidler, *Henry Clay: The Essential American* (New York, 2010), 390–391.

[40] M[urat] Halstead, *Caucuses of 1860: A History of the National Political Conventions of the Current Presidential Campaign* (Columbus, OH, 1860), 116, 148–149, 209, 224.

[41] USN, *North American and United States Gazette* (Philadelphia), June 25, 1860.

[42] His friendship with Belmont dated from 1853 when the New York banker equipped Douglas for his trip abroad with letters of introduction to European statesmen and financiers. Irving Katz, *August Belmont: A Political Biography* (New York, 1968), 56n. Belmont broke with Buchanan in December 1859 when the president rebuffed his bid to become minister to Spain (59–61). Frederick C. Jaher, *A Scapegoat in the Wilderness, The Origins and Rise of Anti-Semitism in America* (Cambridge, 1994), 181, writes, "No other antebellum Jew equaled the celebrity of August Belmont."

[43] For citations regarding activities of Dolly Madison and political wives in the early Republic, see Introduction, note 29, this volume. The seminal work is Catherine Allgor, *Parlor Politics: In Which the Ladies of Washington Help Build a City and a Government* (Charlottesville, VA, 2000). For the pre-convention activities of Belmont, the Douglases, and Cutts, see Johannsen, *SAD*, 732–748.

Before Charleston, Douglas had personally visited party leaders in New York and New Jersey to secure their support for him at the convention. He had campaigned in Ohio in 1859, and that state with Illinois buttressed his place among delegations from the Northwest.[44] He did not go south of Washington, DC, where he met mainly with Northern delegates en route to Charleston during the weeks before the convention opened.[45] Unfortunately, he declined an invitation to attend the mid-April installation of a statue of Henry Clay in Richmond, Virginia.[46] Tradition frowned on candidates attending the nominating convention, and there is no evidence that Douglas considered challenging it. In retrospect he should have done what he would do only after his party split apart – personally appeal to the South. Douglas's pre-convention failure to anticipate accurately the Southern ultras' response to his nomination foreshadowed Lincoln's pre-election miscalculations regarding secessionist threats.[47]

At Charleston, Southern "fire-eaters" threatened to withdraw from the convention unless the platform contained a federal slave code for territories. Their ultimatum targeted Douglas, whom they despised for his opposition to the proslavery Lecompton constitution and his Freeport doctrine.[48] After failing to obtain their plank, seven Southern delegations walked out, leaving only 248 of the elected delegates. The rule for the presidential nomination required the winner to receive two-thirds of all 303 delegates elected, some 202 votes.[49] This fateful rule reflected Belmont's mismanagement of Douglas's campaign at Charleston. Over the course of 57 ballots, Douglas repeatedly won a majority of those present, but not enough for victory. On May 3 the convention adjourned to June 18 in Baltimore.[50]

The decision by the regular Democratic Convention not to seat at Baltimore all of the delegates who had bolted at Charleston made Douglas's nomination

[44] Johannsen, *SAD*, 737–739.

[45] Ibid., 745–746.

[46] Stephen A. Douglas to ——, Mar. 31, 1860, RJ, ed., *Letters of SAD*, 487–488.

[47] Damon Wells describes Douglas's understanding of the South before the Convention as a "curious compound of realism and naiveté." *Stephen Douglas: The Last Years, 1857–1861* (Austin, TX, 1971), 206.

[48] Mark A. Graber argues that Southern anger at Douglas in 1860 "stemmed almost entirely" from his position on Lecompton, not from his Freeport response to *Dred Scott*. *Dred Scott and the Problem of Constitutional Evil* (New York, 2006). 41. On Southern Democrats' alienation from Douglas, see also William W. Freehling, *The Road to Disunion: Secessionists Triumphant, 1854–1861* (New York, 2007), 272–273, which portrays him in unflattering terms.

[49] George M. Milton, *Stephen A. Douglas and the Needless War* (New York, 1969; reprint of 1934 edition), 443.

[50] Allan Nevins, *The Emergence of Lincoln*, 2 vols. (New York, 1950), 2: 268. Although William Freehling concedes that Douglas would have been the nominee had the two-thirds rule not been adopted, he contends that procedures at the Charleston convention did not cause the breakup of the Democratic Party. He believes that the lower South would have divided the party had Douglas been the nominee at Charleston because "90 percent of Southerners considered ... [Douglas] unelectable in the South (and detestable)." *Road to Disunion*, 310. Douglas's reception on his campaign tour through the South, as we will see, suggests, however, that he was not so widely loathed there.

possible but rendered the factional gulf irreparable. Douglas's nomination came on Saturday, June 23 – two months after the Charleston convention had opened. On the same day, the dissidents met elsewhere in Baltimore for a brief session that nominated John Breckinridge and Joseph Lane.[51] Indicative of the Democrats' disarray, on June 26 some ultras traveled to Richmond, where they held another convention that endorsed Breckinridge and Lane.[52]

By the time he secured his party's prize, Douglas had lost valuable time to organize his campaign. Lincoln now had a five-week start on him. With an intact party oriented entirely to the North, Lincoln could more easily rely on surrogates to be effective. Douglas, in contrast, had a smaller group of loyalists because the Democrats were now fractured. Stumping could help compensate for his organizational challenges. Belmont's biographer credits Belmont with having persuaded Douglas to overcome his reluctance to break with the tradition against personal campaigning, but this suggestion gives too much weight to Douglas's expressed reservations.[53] Directly going to the people had been his instinctive inclination since he was twenty. Canvassing provided him a comfort zone that enabled him to cope with the distress caused by his party's breakdown. A consummate legislative insider, he was also a consummate democratic politician: when he invoked the sovereignty of the people, he felt that he truly understood their will. If he had honored the custom against campaigning, it would have been personally anomalous behavior. His three rivals had no difficulty observing the code.

Except for a quick trip to Kentucky, John Bell stayed at home in Nashville for the entire campaign. Although he was accused of being antislavery, he refused to clarify his views, referring inquirers to his record and the Constitutional Unionist platform, which took no position on the matter.[54] Although John Breckinridge's preference was not "to take part in the general political discussions of the day," he reluctantly agreed to speak before supporters in his home state "on a date and at a place of their choosing.[55] He meant a place only in Kentucky!

Several friends advised Lincoln not to repeat Henry Clay's mistaken communicativeness of 1844. The Republican candidate remained silent. He declined to answer correspondence that might become public, and he refused all invitations

[51] Halstead, *Caucuses of 1860*, 217–230; Nevins, *Emergence of Lincoln*, 2: 271–272.
[52] Halstead, *Caucuses of 1860*, 231–232. This was the second convention the "seceders" held in Richmond. A group of them had met there the first time after withdrawing from the Charleston convention.
[53] Katz, *August Belmont*, 79.
[54] Don Green, "Constitutional Unionists: The Party That Tried to Stop Lincoln and Save the Union," *Historian*, 69:2 (Summer 2007), 238; Joseph H. Parks, *John Bell of Tennessee* (Baton Rouge, 1950), 362.
[55] USN, *Milwaukee Daily Sentinel* (Milwaukee, WI), Aug. 31, 1860. Breckinridge was criticized for a few "impromptu" speeches while returning to Lexington, and he vowed not to speak again, for which he also received criticism. He did give one address in Ashland, Kentucky. William C. Davis, *Breckinridge: Statesman, Soldier, Symbol* (Baton Rouge, 1974), 234–237.

to speak, except one – he agreed to speak in his hometown, Springfield. At an outdoor rally the crowd rushed his carriage, removed him on their shoulders, and carried him to the speakers' platform. They also scared him. He feared that they would crush him and said the American people reminded him of a "flock of sheep."[56] Afraid of both the crowd's physicality and the danger of misspeaking, Lincoln claimed that his positions were well known; therefore, no useful purpose would be served by his talking. Politicians who took the threat of secession seriously implored him to reassure the South that he would not interfere with slavery if he were elected. He refused, saying it would be redundant.[57] He was criticized for a joking comment to a reporter that "he would like to go to Kentucky to discuss issues but was afraid of being lynched."[58] Besides, while the South might be mollified by his reassurances, he knew the region was never going to vote for him and he did not want to offend supporters in the North. The less he said about leaving slavery alone, the less he risked losing antislavery voters. For Lincoln, eschewing stump oratory and correspondence, as Gil Troy suggests, "was motivated less by virtue than by hard-nosed political wisdom."[59] It was simply more advantageous for him to honor the monarchical republican code.

The respective positions of Lincoln, Bell, and Breckinridge on slavery in the territories were clear, as laid out in their comparatively uncomplicated party platforms. Bell told those curious about his beliefs to read the Constitutional Union platform, which condemned platforms as divisive and recognized no political principle other than the Constitution, the Union, and enforcement of the laws. Lincoln and Breckinridge took distinctly opposed positions on the question of slavery in federal territories. The Republican platform denied the authority of Congress or any legislature to legalize slavery in any territory, while that of the Southern Democrats stated that neither Congress nor the local legislature could prohibit citizens from holding their property in a territory.[60]

---

[56] Michael Burlingame, *Abraham Lincoln: A Life*, 2 vols. (Baltimore, 2008), 1: 649–651. Lincoln was "uncomfortable" when delegates at the Illinois Republican state convention of 1860 carried him to the platform. Douglas R. Egerton, *Year of Meteors: Stephen Douglas, Abraham Lincoln, and the Election That Brought on the Civil War* (New York, 2010), 128.44r4.

[57] Harold Holzer, *Lincoln, President-Elect: Abraham Lincoln and the Great Secession Winter, 1860–1861* (New York, 2008), 16–17, judges Lincoln as "astute" for not giving "reassurances as pabulum: easy to concoct, easier to swallow." Robert V. Bruce, however, suggests that Lincoln deluded himself into believing that the unthinkable would not occur, even hoping after South Carolina seceded and the Confederation formed that the South would stay in the Union. "The Shadow of a Coming Civil War," in *Lincoln, the War President*, ed. Gabor S. Boritt (New York, 1992), 26–27.

[58] Quoted in Doris K. Goodwin, *Team of Rivals: The Political Genius of Abraham Lincoln* (New York, 2005), 267.

[59] Troy, *See How They Ran*, 66. William L. Miller, *Lincoln's Virtues: An Ethical Biography* (New York, 2002), 375–391, covers his pre-nomination tour of the East but ignores his post-nomination decision to play it safe.

[60] The party platforms of 1860 are conveniently accessed at John T. Woolley and Gerhard Peters, *The American Presidency Project* [online]. Santa Barbara, CA, http://www.presidency.ucsb.edu/ws/.

The platform of the National Democratic Party, however, was ambiguous. On the one hand, it reaffirmed the platform of 1856, which called for congressional noninterference with slavery in territories; on the other hand, it avowed adherence to the Supreme Court on the question, thereby validating the 1857 *Dred Scott* decision that cast a pall over the right of territorial legislatures to deprive slave owners of their property. The main thrust of *Dred Scott* was that it was unconstitutional for Congress to prohibit slavery in territories, but Chief Justice Taney stretched this to mean also that the federal government could not empower a territorial legislature to do so.[61] Whether this dictum had judicial standing added to uncertainties about the decision. How could the Democratic platform balance support for noninterference and the Court's opinion?

At the Charleston convention, Southern ultras described this ambiguity as the "double construction" of the Democratic platform. A journalist who attended the proceedings believed that the Douglas Democrats wanted to be able to go before the people in the North with a "false and fraudulent pretense" that they favored leaving the decision regarding slavery to the territories, while in fact they were "willing to acquiesce in the decision of the Supreme Court, knowing beforehand that the decision would be against them."[62]

However much this might have been a part of the thinking of delegates, Douglas had no intention of deceiving the public or playing one section off against another. He had already addressed the ambiguity in his senatorial contest with Lincoln, most famously at Freeport, where his response became the eponymous doctrine. "It matters not what way the Supreme Court may hereafter decide as to the abstract question whether slavery may or may not go into a territory under the constitution, the people have the lawful means to introduce it or exclude as they please, for the reason that slavery cannot exist a day or an hour anywhere, unless it is supported by local police regulations."[63] Thus Douglas could reconcile his belief that respect for established political institutions was essential for preserving the Union and his equally genuine conviction that local self-government was central to American constitutionalism.

When Douglas decided to undertake a campaign tour cannot be pinpointed, but the decision itself cannot be considered surprising. It is impossible to

---

[61] Don E. Fehrenbacher, *The Dred Scott Case: Its Significance in American Law and Politics* (New York, 1978), 379.

[62] Halstead, *Caucuses of 1860*, 33. Halstead wrote that Southern "ultras" wanted to replace the "double construction" of the platform with "the unequivocal repudiation of the Douglas doctrine of squatter, or popular sovereignty" (32).

[63] *CWAL*, 3: 51; L-DD, 58. Douglas refused to accept Taney's dictum denying the authority of Congress to empower territorial legislatures to prohibit slavery as established law. Fehrenbacher, *Dred Scott Case*, 494, says that Douglas implied in Freeport that the Court had not decided on the right of territories to prohibit slavery, "thereby treating the relevant passage in Taney's opinion as dictum rather than as part of the official decision." Despite his implicit criticism of Douglas, earlier Fehrenbacher states that the passage in question "was *obiter dictum*, pure and simple" (379). On Taney's ruling as dictum, see also Gerald Leonard, "Law and Politics Reconsidered: A New Constitutional History of Dred Scott," *Law and Social Inquiry*, 34 (Summer 2009), 782, esp. 52–54 of the unabridged version of this essay available at his Web site.

imagine him doing what Lincoln did, staying silent and stationary. Douglas made his mark at twenty when supporters carried him on their shoulders after a speech, and he never tired of the experience. He was more than a handshaker. Unlike Lincoln, he relished the physical embrace of the white crowd. He sat on men's laps, rose on their shoulders, and clasped their hands. He did not consider physicality to be undignified.[64] And, of course, he loved to orate.

The campaign itself would test his sincerity. Advisers feared and opponents hoped he would tailor the ambiguity of his party platform to suit particular crowds he addressed. And thanks to the press, the world would know if he trimmed his position to the localities where he spoke. Although he could be an artful advocate, he had a guileless faith in the straightforwardness, clarity, and consistency of his beliefs, despite the inherent tension between them. He did not worry about misspeaking, about contradicting himself and then having to backtrack. His confidence in his own sincerity, knowledge, and logic emboldened him to explain his principles everywhere. Indeed, if he had any self-doubts, if he harbored any reservations about his position, he would have hesitated before undertaking that ordeal. This exceptional self-confidence overcame any fears he might have had about the risk of campaigning – fears that kept other candidates silent and on the sidelines. Michael Kammen writes that the 1860 election "involved, as no other election before it in U.S. history, a national constitutional debate."[65] Douglas would be the only candidate to participate actively in the debate himself.

As soon as he was nominated, Douglas planned to set up his headquarters at the Fifth Avenue Hotel in New York City, where his campaign manager was connected to the financial community.[66] En route from Washington, he said in Philadelphia on June 30 that he had "no political speeches to make during the pending canvas. If my political opinions are not known to the people of the United States, it is not worth while for me to explain them now."[67] Once in New York he made an appearance on the balcony at Tammany Hall only to acknowledge the crowd below. He begrudgingly said he would not talk politics because this was the first time in his life that he was put "in the position to

---

[64] See Chapter 4.

[65] Michael Kammen, *A Machine That Would Go of Itself: The Constitution in American Culture* (New York, 1986), 104.

[66] Johannsen, *SAD*, 779, states that Douglas's selection of Belmont as national party chairman reflected the importance he placed on financing his campaign. It is worth emphasizing, however, that his choice of Belmont preceded his decision to go on a costly national tour. Belmont was in fact unable to raise enough funds, and Douglas was forced to sell land and borrow heavily (781–782); "Biographical Note," Stephen A. Douglas Papers, Special Collections, University of Chicago. His party's split made him a very risky investment. Nevertheless, his lack of outside funding must be considered in assessing the influence that a "bloc" of businessmen might have had on his campaign, as suggested by Thomas Ferguson, *Golden Rule: The Investment Theory of Party Competition and the Logic of Money-Driven Political Systems* (Chicago, 1995), 55–69; and Ferguson, "Beyond Their Means? The Costs of Democracy from Jefferson to Lincoln," *Journal of the Historical Society*, 6:4 (Dec. 2006), 501–512.

[67] USN, *New York Herald*, July 3, 1860.

see a fight without taking a hand in it."[68] In letters of July 4–5 he told friends he planned to remain in New York "to perfect our organization throughout the Union."[69] Within the next few days, however, he let it be known that he and his wife would attend her brother's graduation from Harvard Law School on July 18.[70] This was not a ploy. In light of his closeness to young Cutts, it is most likely that Douglas had planned on going to Cambridge and then decided to broaden his journey into a campaign tour through Connecticut and Massachusetts. Nevertheless, the commencement provided him a nonpolitical rationale for the first leg of his trip.

On Saturday, July 14, Stephen and Adele Douglas took a train from New York to Guildford, Connecticut, where they spent two nights at a resort.[71] On Monday evening in Hartford (July 16) he received a martial escort to the state house, was introduced by the mayor, and blamed the immense crowd of several thousand for his having "been betrayed into making a political speech." He spoke of his pride in having been born in the Green Mountains of Vermont, his pride in the "wide prairies of the West," and his concern for the interests of the whole country. He then differentiated the Democrats' principle of nonintervention from Republican prohibition and Southern secessionists' protection of slavery in the territories.[72] Here he first struck an early theme of his campaign – he would lay out his political position only in response to the demands of the crowds that came. Why "betrayed"? Because he was acknowledging the code he was violating.

From Hartford (July 17) he took a regularly scheduled passenger railcar that stopped for twenty minutes in Springfield, where the lack of advance notice meant that no crowd appeared to greet Douglas.[73] This failure was not the result of any uncertainty on the part of Douglas's team regarding the purpose of his trip. The railroad expected him to speak before an audience at every depot and asked him to talk for no more than ten minutes, a rule he honored.[74] In Framingham a delegation from Boston boarded the train to accompany him to the capital.[75] This set a pattern that was followed generally for the next three and a half months.

His greeting in Boston, the home of abolitionism, could not have been more surprising or gratifying. He arrived in Boston around 5:00 P.M. So intense was

[68] USN, *Daily National Intelligencer* (Washington, DC), July 6, 1860.

[69] Stephen A. Douglas to Nathaniel Paschall and Stephen A. Douglas to Charles H. Lanphier, *Letters of SAD*, 497–498.

[70] ProQuest, *New York Times*, July 12, 1860.

[71] USN, *New York Herald*, Aug. 25, 1860.

[72] ProQuest, *New York Times*, July 18, 1860; USN, *New York Herald*, July 17, 1860.

[73] Robert W. Johannsen, *The Frontier, Union, and Stephen A. Douglas* (Urbana, IL, 1989),169.

[74] USN, *Lowell Daily Citizen and News* (Lowell, MA) July 18, 1860. Running on time was a safety issue for railroads. A horrific collision between trains running between Providence and Worcester in 1853 killed fourteen passengers, and an inquest revealed that the cause was faulty timekeeping rather than excessive speed. Ian R. Bartky, *Selling True Time: Nineteenth-Century Timekeeping in America* (Stanford, CA, 2000), 25–28.

[75] USN, *Daily National Intelligencer* (Washington, DC), July 20, 1860.

the crowd's enthusiasm that dozens of people climbed into the cars through windows before the train fully stopped.[76] The reception committee wisely arranged for Mrs. Douglas to be safely driven to their hotel while he rode there beside the crowd. Before he alighted, he stood in the barouche and thanked the throng for his extraordinary reception. "It seems as though my entire trip through Massachusetts has been one continuous ovation."[77] His rest at the hotel was short, for he shook hands with several hundred people in its main parlor between 8:00 and 9:00 P.M before he went onto a balcony overlooking a "completely packed" Bowdoin Square.[78] He followed three speakers and spoke for only about ten minutes. He invoked Daniel Webster, who had spoken from the same balcony a decade earlier in defense of the compromise that Douglas said embodied the principle of nonintervention, which again he heralded for avoiding the "irrepressible conflict" that the sectional parties were producing.[79]

The evening of July 17 in Boston was the first great moment of Douglas's campaign and one of the best moments of his career. He was a national celebrity. People who could not hear him wanted to get a glimpse of him. Their enthusiasm impressed the various newspapers that covered the scene. The tradition against presidential campaigning certainly did not reflect the desire of the public that craved seeing the famous Democratic candidate. The following day during the procession to the Harvard commencement, on the platform, and during the walk on college grounds to the banquet, according to newspapers in New York and Massachusetts, amid Edward Everett and other local luminaries, Douglas was the star attraction who gathered the most stares and applause.[80] Had the epicenter of antislavery sentiment been cool to him, he might have ceased campaigning. Instead the overwhelmingly favorable, mainly adulatory reception that he received from the crowds as well as dignitaries in Massachusetts, especially those in Boston and Cambridge, encouraged him to continue his tour.

After stops at Springfield (July 20), where thousands showed up and "almost betrayed" him into giving a political speech, and Albany, he and Adele settled in for six days at a resort hotel in Saratoga, New York (July 21–25, 27), where they mixed socializing with politics.[81] While Stephen has received credit for his

[76] Ibid.

[77] USN, *Dover Gazette* (Dover, NH), July 20, 1860.

[78] Ibid; USN, *New York Herald*, July 19, 1860.

[79] USN, *Daily National Intelligencer* (Washington, DC), July 20, 1860.

[80] USN, *New York Herald*, July 21, 1860; ProQuest, *New York Times*, July 20, 1860; *Springfield Republican*, July 21, 1860, quoted by Johannsen, *Frontier, Union, and Douglas*, 170–171.

[81] From its beginnings in the 1820s, Saratoga Springs, like other watering resorts, was a place of "recuperation, restoration, and recreation" according to Cindy S. Aron, *Working at Play: A History of Vacations in the United States* (New York, 1999), 15–23. In Ballston, a competing spa town six miles south, Benajah Douglass, Stephen's paternal grandfather, built the first hotel in 1792. Jon Sterngass, *First Resorts: Pursuing Pleasure at Saratoga Springs, Newport & Coney Island* (Baltimore, 2001), 12.

exhaustive campaigning, Adele's contribution has not been fully appreciated. She boosted his power to make friends on the campaign trail. Although Adele was whisked away occasionally to the security of a hotel room while he spoke to a welcoming crowd, she rejoined him for platform speeches and evening levees. It is doubtful the crowds knew that the only child she had borne died at eight months of age in early June, for newspapers did not report it and Stephen did not mention their loss in public. The campaign tour begun in mid-July had the appeal of taking the couple away from where their infant daughter had died, just as Douglas's voyage to Europe in 1853 had removed him from the scene of his first wife's death. We can assume that Stephen would never have left Adele to grieve alone in Washington and that her approval would have been essential for undertaking the trip. The tour, however, was more than a diversion for her. Interacting with politicians over several days at Saratoga Springs, mingling with reception committees on railroad cars and at hotels, and co-hosting levees were an extension of what she did year round in the capital. In Saratoga, Douglas publicly disclaimed any partisan agenda, but in private he and his team solidified his schedule for further campaigning in the Northeast.[82] His personal highlight was to be a return to his birthplace.

On Saturday, July 28, he and Adele boarded a train that would make three stops in New York and Vermont before they disembarked at Brandon in the late afternoon. Advance men told locals that Douglas was making a pilgrimage to his boyhood home and that he would eschew politics. Surprisingly at both Castleton and Rutland he honored that promise. In Vermont Douglas had a personal errand beneath his political mission. Here was a potential opportunity for him to resolve the conflicted feelings he had about his Vermont youth. He could not be certain about the reception that awaited him because of his well-publicized insult of his native state upon receiving an honorary degree at Middlebury. He had given it national publicity by repeating the insult during his senatorial debates with Lincoln only two years earlier.[83]

Brandon "wore a holiday appearance" as it prepared for his late afternoon arrival. Houses "were decorated with flags and streamers." A band from Vergennes, nearly thirty miles away, supplemented local musicians in a procession that brought Douglas from the depot through most of the main streets, paused before a large gathering at his birthplace, and concluded at a platform in front of the hotel where he and his wife would stay. Douglas spoke for about forty-five minutes. He said that until he stopped at Rutland, he "could not conceive of such a greeting" as he now received in Brandon. Reminded of his famous jibe, he said he had intended it "perhaps in jest." He then set the record straight. "Vermont is a glorious place to be born in – to educate and train children. Here you inculcate virtue, you educate your children, you train them to habits of industry – you *teach them the necessity of labor*. Yet it does a man good to emigrate. This early discipline prepares him for life on a broader

---

[82] Johannsen, *Frontier, Union, and Douglas*, 172.
[83] See Chapter 1.

theater."[84] The jubilant, adoring crowd enabled Douglas to make peace with his birthplace. He now professed his love for Vermont, although he acknowledged, "I love my own Illinois none the less.[85]

On Sunday he visited his father's grave. With the angst from his adolescent crisis abated, he could integrate his youth and political beliefs in a new narrative. His Vermont boyhood now became rhetorically the springboard of his faith in local self-government and popular sovereignty. He no longer had to equivocate or jest about his Vermont background. He could recall it with a new sense of acceptance. In Burlington he spoke of his own parochialism as a boy, when he thought that the valley where he was born was the center of civilization and that beyond the mountains was only barbarism. He then discovered that the variety of opinions in the West was attributable to the "diversity of circumstances which prevails in the different portions of our extended Union." People there came from different states and sections. This meant that the West stood on the middle ground between abolitionists and secessionists; otherwise, they would sunder ties with kin in states they had left. He called the Green Mountain Boys of Ethan Allen "the first Squatter Sovereigns on the continent" – a characterization with which much of the amused crowd agreed.[86]

At the Concord, New Hampshire, statehouse (July 31), speaking more than an hour before an estimated fifteen to twenty thousand people, he connected his story to his principles in a parable that reflected his newfound accord with his own youth:

> I am a native of New England, and I left the land of my birth, the scenes of my childhood, the grave of my father, and went to the extreme Northwest. And yet New England is my native land, and I love her on that account. Illinois is not your native land and you don't love her, therefore, as much as I do, who live there.... I think the New Hampshire boy who moves to the West when he is twenty years of age, is just as capable of self-government as the brother that remains behind. Just cast your eyes round this neighborhood and find an old gentleman who had two sons. The one was an ambitious, restless, energetic, daring boy; the other was an amiable, kind, lazy, good fellow. (Laughter.) Which of these boys do you think went out West? Which stayed at home, and lived with his daddy and mammy? (Laughter.) The bold and ambitious young fellow went and dug up the prairie; or in the wilderness he carved out his own fortune, made his own farm, put up his own fences and perhaps split his own rails. (Laughter and cheers.) He cultivated his own fields, erected a schoolhouse and a church – yes, and made his own cabinet work, too. [The absence of recorded laughter or cheers indicates that his audience

---

[84] *Northern Visitor* (Brandon, VT), Aug. 2, 1860. I am grateful to Martha Reid, Vermont state librarian, and Paul Donovan, law and reference librarian, for scanning and emailing me a copy. Johannsen, *Frontier, Union, and Douglas*, 174, conflates Douglas's admission of his insult and his correction into a single sentence, thereby muting the force of each statement.

[85] *Northern Visitor* (Brandon, VT), Aug. 2, 1860.

[86] New York's claim to the land west of New Hampshire was backed by the Continental Congress but challenged by what Jefferson called the "Vermont doctrine," to wit, that "the people can create their own states." Michael A. Bellesiles, *Revolutionary Outlaws: Ethan Allen and the Struggle for Independence on the Early American Frontier* (Charlottesville, VA, 1993), 158.

missed his personal reference.] By that time I reckon the wild boy had sown his wild oats pretty well, and was fully capable of self-government as the one that stayed here and acted under father's and mother's advice.... Now, are you going to tell me that such people are not capable of self-government merely because they live in a Territory? ("Not we.")[87]

In Manchester (August 1) he dropped any pretense of nonpartisanship. He said there were two sectional parties in the country – the Republican Party, which demanded the prohibition of slavery "wherever the people want it," and the "Southern Secessionist Party," which demanded the federal protection of slavery "where the people don't want it." In contrast, the Democratic Party stood for federal nonintervention, and according to a reporter he gave "the Revolutionary fathers, the framers of the Constitution, the Whigs of 1850 and 1852, and the Americans of a later day, the credit of supporting Popular Sovereignty."[88]

Throughout New England Adele Douglas attracted considerable attention. A story about the wives of presidential candidates appeared as the Douglases crossed into New Hampshire, and some in the crowds there must have been eager to see "one of the queens of Washington society.... If she were running for President, she would unite all suffrages, unless some fanatic went against her on religious grounds; for Mrs. Douglas is an earnest, practical Roman Catholic."[89] The local press could not have been more complimentary, praising her easy but dignified bearing and unostentatious clothing. She won "golden opinions for herself" and was held up as a "beautiful model for all young ladies who aspire to be ladies indeed."[90] Even the Whig newspaper noted that the crowd gave a special three cheers for "The Woman" as the train departed from Concord.[91] A Buffalo newspaper's claim that she had worked as a clerk at the U.S. Treasury in order to support and educate her younger brother is apocryphal, but it testifies to the high regard for her.[92]

En route to a vacation in Newport, Rhode Island, scheduled for August 2–21, a relaxed Adele entertained acquaintances aboard her train with examples of the "comical behavior of some of her admirers" on the tour. When "she thought herself all alone, she discovered men and women peeping through the window blinds." Once some young men "insisted on seeing Mrs. Douglas" and mistook "a fat motherly lady" for her. At a reception for her, she was forced to leave the room "to avoid a crowd of uninvited and unwashed who rushed into her presence."[93]

In Newport Douglas told a welcoming audience that he came, "not as an aspirant for the Presidency," but "for recreation." He needed to rest, for the

---

[87] USN, *New Hampshire Statesman* (Concord, NH), Aug. 4, 1860.

[88] ProQuest, *New York Times*, Aug. 4, 1860.

[89] EAN, *Farmer's Cabinet* (Amherst, NH), Aug. 1, 1860.

[90] *Rutland Weekly Herald* (Rutland, VT), Aug. 2, 1860.

[91] USN, *New Hampshire Statesman* (Concord, NH), Aug. 4, 1860.

[92] The story was reprinted in USN, *New Hampshire Statesman* (Concord, NH), Aug. 18.

[93] USN, *New Hampshire Statesman* (Concord, NH), Aug. 11, 1860.

"fatigues and efforts" of campaigning had left him so weakened that he could not make himself heard by the crowd that had gathered. The mayor promised to do his best to keep politicians away from Douglas during his stay.[94]

Douglas was not going to ignore politics altogether, because his campaign manager, August Belmont, rented for the summer "Mrs. Ritchie's villa" on Bellevue Avenue, down the street from the Atlantic House.[95] The proprietor of the hotel sponsored a grand reception for Adele Douglas by converting its dining room into a ballroom that accommodated six hundred people. The Douglases "entered fully into the amusements of the evening."[96] The Atlantic House competed with its major rival, the Ocean House, in providing entertainment for its guests. It secured a band that performed "a variety of splendid operatic selections every afternoon and evening in the grand ball of the hotel."[97] A second ball, sponsored by the New York Yacht Squadron, was also held at the Atlantic in honor of the couple. The *New York Times* reported it to be the "affair of the season." The Douglases danced next to their friends the Belmonts.[98]

In addition to listening to music and dancing, Douglas regenerated himself on Saturday, August 4, by attending presentations at the American Association for the Advancement of Science, which was in the fourth day of its annual meeting.[99] On the next day members of the association accompanied Adele to a Catholic church, while other members joined Stephen at his hotel.[100]

Newport was supposed to end Douglas's New England tour. He had traveled through Connecticut, Massachusetts, Vermont, New Hampshire, and Rhode Island. By this point Douglas had not scheduled more travel. His trip had originated from his wife's desire to attend her brother's graduation from Harvard Law School. Once he made the commitment to travel to Boston from New York for the commencement, the decision to expand the trip into a whistle-stop campaign through parts of New England followed, perhaps as a test to determine whether a broader, unprecedented national tour would be viable.

If so, the determination to go beyond New England, except for a visit to his family in upstate New York, was not made before Newport. Biographer Robert Johannsen believes that Douglas decided to complete a circuit of the region only when a delegation from Maine came to Newport and persuaded him that

---

[94] ProQuest, *New York Times*, Aug. 7, 1860.

[95] On Belmont's summer rental, see *New York Times*, June 30, 1860. For the Ritchie mansion, "Fairlawn," see James L. Yarnall, *Newport Through Its Architecture: A History of Styles from Postmedieval to Postmodern* (Lebanon, NH, 2005), 60.

[96] USN, *New York Herald*, Aug. 9, 1860. The two grand hotels were opened respectively in 1844 and 1845. Sterngass, *First Resorts*, 46.

[97] USN, *New York Herald*, Aug. 6, 1860.

[98] ProQuest, *Boston Daily Advertiser*, Aug. 16, 1860.

[99] USN, *Boston Daily Advertiser*, Aug. 6, 1860; USN, *New York Herald*, Aug. 6, 1860.

[100] USN, *Boston Daily Advertiser*, Aug. 6, 1860. Republicans in the North were "whispering about whether Stephen Douglas's wife had converted him to the Church of Rome and what influence she might exert over him." Edward L. Ayers, *In the Presence of Mine Enemies: War in the Heart of America, 1859–1863* (New York, 2003), 79.

he had a chance of winning that state. Strengthening Johannsen's case is the fact that Douglas left Adele at the resort as he embarked on a "whirlwind tour of Maine by boat up the Atlantic coast " (August 15–17).[101]

From Newport he sent a telegram to a close confidant indicating that he would return to Chicago in early September.[102] He was off by a month, for he did not yet anticipate the extent of his travels. By the time he and his wife left Newport for good on August 21, however, he and Belmont planned to expand their campaign beyond the Northeast. The reception and coverage Douglas experienced in every part of New England validated their decision to go national. If the people at the nerve center of antislavery could be so excited to see and hear him, why not take himself, his wife, and his message everywhere?

He made his first trip to the South from August 24 to September 7, starting and ending in Baltimore and stopping at some eighteen towns in Maryland, Virginia, and North Carolina. Although he had a personal excuse to go to North Carolina because his sons were beneficiaries of their newly deceased grandmother's estate, this was a campaign tour despite his denial of an "electioneering" purpose.[103] He amply laid out what he stood for: the Union and local self-government. His theme was sounded in an impromptu response in Norfolk (August 25) that would be reprinted time and again. He spoke for two hours before some six thousand at the courthouse. What made news were his answers to questions on a slip of paper handed to him in the middle of his speech. The paper was a cutout from a local newspaper raising two questions, which he read aloud. If Lincoln were elected, would the Southern states be justified in seceding? If they did secede, would he advocate force to "resist" them? He answered simply "no" to the first question but offered a more complex response to the second. He said it was the duty of the president to enforce the law, "as Old Hickory treated the nullifiers of 1832." This part of his answer received wide coverage and provoked anger in parts of the South.[104] Less attention was paid to his invocation of the "right of revolution whenever a grievance becomes too burdensome to be borne." The election of a new president, however, would not be such a grievance and would not warrant rebellion. His actions after he took office would have to be judged. If he then exceeded his constitutional powers, Douglas would "take as much pleasure in hanging him" as his audience had in hanging John Brown.[105]

[101] Johannsen, *Frontier, Union, and Douglas*, 177–178.

[102] Spencer Benham, the telegram recipient, informed the press in Chicago. *Chicago Times and Herald*, Aug. 13, 1860, as reported in the *Daily Illinois State Register*, Aug. 14, 1860. On Benham, *Letters of SAD*, 369n. On September 9 a dispatch from Douglas nailed down his coming to Chicago on October 4. *Chicago Times and Herald*, Sept. 9, 1860, cited in the *Daily Illinois State Register*, Sept. 10, 1860.

[103] Johannsen, *SAD*, 786–789.

[104] Johannsen, *Frontier, Union, and Douglas*, 201. Newspapers continued to refer to his response. Opponents cited the episode as a "trap for Douglas." USN, *Virginia Free Press* (Charlottesville, WV), Oct. 11, 1860.

[105] Brown was hanged in Charlestown, Virginia, on December 2, 1859. Robert E, McGlone, *John Brown's War Against Slavery* (New York, 2009), 326. Douglas gave the same message

His message, then, as he launched his Southern tour was that should Lincoln win the election, secession would not be a justifiable option for Southern states and would have to be forcibly quelled by the president. He urged that the same questions be put to secessionist candidates and that his audience "insist upon such frank and unequivocal answers as I have given."[106] Posing questions in newspapers that readers were urged to cut out and hand to surrogates of candidates was a press stratagem of 1860.[107] Only in the case of Douglas could these questions be presented directly to the candidate. More than a month later, in fact, a North Carolina editor noted that Breckinridge was campaigning in Kentucky but "is mum on those questions which his Norfolk friend required Mr. Douglas to answer, and promised that he too should answer."[108] The Breckinridge friend who had asked the "Norfolk questions" said he also sent them to Breckinridge, who replied only by sending him a copy of a recent speech.[109]

In Raleigh (August 30) Douglas said his position had not changed over time or place:

> I stand now where I stood then. I stand now where I stood when I brought forward the bill to repeal the Missouri restriction and organize the territories of Kansas and Nebraska.... I will tell you what explanation I have made in every Northern state of my motive for passing the Nebraska bill and repealing the Missouri Compromise.... The object was to allow the people to do just as they pleased both sides of 36ª 30. I assert that if the people of a territory want slavery, they have a right to have it, and if they do not want it, no power on earth should force it upon them. I go farther and say that whether the people will want it or not, depends solely upon the climate, the soil, the productions, and self-interest of the people where it exists.... Slavery, therefore, does not depend on the law.... I care not how many laws you have, or how many armies to enforce these laws. Hence I said in my Freeport speech that no matter how the court might decide the abstract question, that practically slavery would not go where the people do not want it ... that has been tortured into a declaration that I would not obey the decision of the Supreme Court of the United States.[110]

Signs of fatigue showed in his mien and voice. In Richmond (August 31) an observer said his appearance was "more like that of a weary, way-worn, backwoods traveler, seeking repose from the toil and dust of the road, than like that

---

everywhere but knew how to appeal to his particular audiences. He did not make the same remark in the North.

[106] For his speech in Norfolk, see USN, *New York Herald*, Aug. 27, 1860; USN, *Daily National Intelligencer* (Washington, DC), Aug. 31, 1860.

[107] USN, *Dover Gazette* (Dover, NH), Aug. 25, 1860.

[108] USN, *Fayetteville Observer* (Fayetteville, NC), Oct. 4, 1860.

[109] USN, *Daily National Intelligencer* (Washington, DC), Oct. 11, 1860. Biographer William C. Davis writes of Breckinridge's "conspicuous failure" to answer the Norfolk questions as "most disappointing." *Breckinridge: Statesman, Soldier, Symbol* (Baton Rouge, LA, 1974), 240.

[110] His Raleigh speech is printed in Emerson D. Fite, *The Presidential Campaign of 1860* (New York, 1911), 276–300, quote on 289–290.

of a distinguished statesman about to receive a splendid ovation."[111] He did not rest after his first Southern canvass but headed directly across Pennsylvania. In Reading (September 8) his fatigue loosened intemperate language. "I wish to God we had a Gen. Jackson at this day, in order that he might grapple with Northern abolitionists and Southern Secessionism, trample them under foot, and bury both in a common grave."[112] Most of his speech, as usual, was directed against Breckinridge. His anger against the Kentucky Democrat for bolting from their party far exceeded any irritation he felt toward Lincoln.[113]

Douglas knew that he had paved the road to the Republican nomination for Lincoln by agreeing to their debates, but he did not resent him because of it. He described Lincoln as a "kind-hearted, good-natured, amiable man" whom he had bested during their quarter-century rivalry. He poked fun at both their claims to manual labor. "I expect he has split about as many rails as I made bureaus and secretaries." Besides, he said, it was a "new doctrine" that a man's boyhood occupation qualified him for the presidency. He admitted to liking Lincoln and noted that they had had "a great deal of fun" when they traveled together contesting elections in Illinois. His opposition to him was based solely on Lincoln's "radical difference of opinion."[114]

Douglas's weariness and irritability were ascribable in part to the absence of his wife, who did not accompany him on the latter part of his swing through the South (August 24 to September 7), Pennsylvania (September 7–10), and New Jersey (September 10).[115] He rejoined Adele at the Fifth Avenue Hotel in New York for one day of repose before the most extensively advertised event of his campaign – the "Grand Political Carnival and Ox-Roast," or "The Douglas Barbecue" – held on September 12 at Jones Wood, a 150-acre state-owned park overlooking the East River between Sixty-Sixth and Seventy-Fifth Streets.[116]

[111] USN, *New York Herald*, Sept. 1, 1860.

[112] ProQuest, *New York Times*, Sept. 10, 1860.

[113] The breach between the vice president and Douglas preceded the Charleston convention and had been open since the beginning of the year. Davis, *Breckenridge*, 212.

[114] ProQuest, *New York Times*, Aug. 4, 1860. Their relationship is examined in Roy Morris, Jr., *The Long Pursuit: Abraham Lincoln's Thirty-Year Struggle with Stephen Douglas for the Heart and Soul of America* (New York, 2008). Lincoln's early resentment of Douglas is evident in his famous Lyceum speech of 1838, when he warned of an unnamed "towering genius" who would destroy what the founders had created. Douglas was making his first run for Congress against John Stuart, Lincoln's law partner. Michael Burlingame makes a persuasive case for the speech as an attack on Douglas. *The Inner World of Abraham Lincoln* (Urbana, IL, 1994), 365–368; Burlingame, *Abraham Lincoln*, 1: 138–142. Before Burlingame, the most influential interpretation of the Lyceum speech was that by Edmund Wilson, *Patriotic Gore: Studies in the Literature of the American Civil War* (New York, 1962), 107–108, which views the ambitious young Lincoln as projecting himself into the "genius" about whom he was warning. His original 1954 essay has been reprinted in Sean Wilentz, ed., *The Best American History Essays on Lincoln* (New York, 2009), 41–62.

[115] Notice in newspaper accounts is the gauge we use generally for determining Adele Douglas's presence or absence on the tour.

[116] On the beginnings of Jones Wood as a public park in the 1850s and its eclipse by Central Park, see Edwin G. Burrows and Mike Wallace, *Gotham: A History of New York City to 1898* (New York, 1999), 790–792.

The advertising exceeded the planning in terms of effectiveness, despite an organizing committee of 245 vice presidents and secretaries under the direction of August Belmont.[117] As Douglas said during his speech, he had been told that Jones Wood could hold all of New York, but he found that "all of Connecticut and New Jersey are also here." Tens of thousands in fact came.[118]

Preparation for the barbecue was enormous but inadequate. A chef and four assistants cooked a 2,200-pound ox, a sheep, a calf, and a hog Tuesday night through Wednesday morning. The meat was sliced and placed on tables with some two thousand loaves of bread, ten barrels of Boston crackers, and five hundred barrels of beer. Barriers manned by policemen set off the dining area until the "free lunch" began.

Alas, many had hoped "the roasting would take place before their eyes" and were displeased to find the cooking already done. And instead of the "orderly and quiet feeding" which organizers had anticipated, there was a "wild scramble for the choice bits," which resulted in hundreds who had waited for hours going hungry rather than competing for the food. The *Times* could not resist jabbing the man for whom the event was arranged: "Popular Sovereignty in its most extended signification was practically exemplified" in the overthrow of barriers and forced retreat of the police.

During the frenetic feeding, Douglas arrived at the grounds in a covered carriage, which the crowd noisily surrounded and followed to a hotel in the park. He stopped to freshen up before moving to the main grandstand with his vice presidential nominee, Herschel Johnson. This was the first time the two appeared on the same platform during the campaign. Johnson asked that the assemblage look into the future under their Constitution "when all these Territories shall be bound in one common Union, and ... our population, instead of being thirty million will be three hundred millions of freemen. Who can contemplate the future without feeling pride that he is an American citizen?"

Douglas condemned secession as treason. He declared that when Washington, Jefferson, Hancock, and Adams seceded from the Old Empire they knew they were exposing themselves to the penalty for treason. He contrasted the founders to the Southerners who claimed they had a right to secede. He conceded

---

[117] We do not know how much money this group contributed individually to finance the event. It would be useful to know how many of the 244 names were from New York's business community and whether they constituted an "investment bloc," as suggested by Ferguson, *Golden Rule*. For a comprehensive analysis of a large antebellum political rally, see Michael D. Pierson, "'Prairies on Fire': The Organization of the 1856 Mass Republican Rally in Beloit, Wisconsin," *Civil War History*, 48:2 (2002), 101–122, which shows both the planning of politicians and the spontaneity of the crowd.

[118] USN, *Frank Leslie's Illustrated Newspaper* (New York), Sept. 22, 1860, placed the crowd at "over fifty thousand." USN, *Fayetteville Observer* (Fayetteville, NC), Sept. 17, 1860, reported that the numbers attending "have been estimated as high as 75,000." The city dailies estimated ten to twenty thousand. ProQuest, *New York Times*, Sept. 13, 1860; USN, *New York Herald*, Sept. 13, 1860.

no such right to them and reasserted his Norfolk position justifying the use of force to suppress them. He declared that the Union is perpetual and that "revolution is never justified until the evils of submitting to the laws are greater than the horrors of civil war and disunion."[119] Moreover, he expressed his disinclination to join a fusion movement with any candidate who did not pledge to support the Union, the Constitution, and enforcement of the laws.[120]

His speech and the event at Jones Wood received widespread coverage, heightening interest in his belated visit to his mother that followed. As early as July 4 the press had reported that Douglas would see his mother in Clifton Springs.[121] A reporter's interview with her a week later revealed that he had not visited her in two years and had not written when he was coming.[122] Douglas's original announcement on Independence Day provided personal cover for some campaigning, but he abandoned that ruse early on. The press, however, did not let it go. The report that his mother did not know when to expect him was transmuted into Douglas's "search" for her at various places. At rallies the opposition might hold up a banner, "Douglas seeks his mother," which was similar to the caption of numerous newspaper stories regarding his campaign appearances.[123] His "mother-hunt" ended with his triumphant arrival in Clifton Springs by carriage from Canandaigua on September 15.[124] He began his speech there by saying he wanted to relieve the anxiety of his Republican friends "by announcing that he had found his mother." He then expressed regret that "Mr. Lincoln did not find it safe to visit his birthplace, or the graves of his parents, for fear of violence."[125]

After two nights with his family, he proceeded with his campaign in upstate New York. Adele may have stayed over with the Grangers for a few more days, because she does not appear in newspaper accounts of his travels until he reached Ohio. It is likely, however, that she joined him for his overnight stay at Niagara Falls, the most famous tourist attraction in the country, on September 19.[126] He had gone there as a youth and would have wanted Adele to see it.

---

[119] Quotes and details about the event and speeches at Jones Wood come from ProQuest, *New York Times*, Sept. 13, 1860, and USN, *New York Herald*, Sept. 13, 1860. On fusion efforts, see Green, "Constitutional Unionists," 231–253; Johannsen, *SAD*, 787–788, 792–793.

[120] A helpful analysis of Douglas's view of the fusion movement is Wells, *Stephen Douglas*, 244–246.

[121] USN, *New York Herald*, July 4, 1860.

[122] Ibid.

[123] USN, *Bangor Daily Whig & Courier* (Bangor, ME), Aug. 17, 1860; USN, *Ripley Bee* (Ripley, OH), Aug. 16, 1860; USN, *Milwaukee Daily Sentinel* (Milwaukee, WI), Aug. 22, 1860; USN, *Daily Cleveland Herald*, Aug. 24, 1860; USN, *Freedom's Champion* (Atkinson, KS), Sept. 1, 1860.

[124] The phrase comes from USN, *Milwaukee Daily Sentinel* (Milwaukee, WI), Sept. 25, 1860.

[125] For coverage of his arrival and stay, see ProQuest, *New York Times*, Sept. 15, 1860; USN, *New York Herald*, Sept. 15, 1860; USN, *Dover Gazette* (Dover, NH), Sept. 29, 1860.

[126] USN, *New York Herald*, Sept. 21, 1860; Aron, *Working at Play*, 130. So popular was Niagara Falls that Lincoln tried to compose a dithyramb on it, suggests David Donald, to position himself as a public lecturer. *Lincoln* (New York, 1995), 164.

After a huge rally in Buffalo (September 20), he traveled to Cleveland, which, as a local paper noted, was once Douglas's residence. He spent a long weekend there (September 21–24), perhaps visiting places and people he had known nearly three decades earlier when he was bedridden with bilious fever. He also met with a Democrat from Iowa with whom he mapped out a trip to that state.[127] He then traveled to one town in Illinois (September 24), seven in Ohio (September 24–27), and four in Indiana (September 24). Sitting in a railroad car in Ohio, Adele overheard two ministers gossiping that Douglas had been so drunk he had to be helped off the train at Tiffin. She confronted them, confirmed that neither had witnessed the alleged behavior, introduced herself as Douglas's wife, and declared their story to be fiction.[128] In Indianapolis the governors of Ohio and Kentucky and the national ticket lured between thirty-five and a hundred thousand. Douglas rode in a barouche "drawn by four white horses" in a procession that "was about one hour in passing a given point." A reported highlight of the parade was "the young ladies car, in the center of which stood a young lady attired as the goddess of liberty."[129] Douglas spoke for seventy-five minutes, but the press claimed that people were more interested in seeing than hearing him. He again referred to Breckinridge "in severe terms" while challenging the local Whig newspaper to pose the same questions to Lincoln that they asked of him.[130]

From Indianapolis Douglas made a foray to the South – a one-night stay in Louisville (September 29). Kentucky was Breckinridge's home state and the place where Lincoln was born but, according to Douglas, was afraid to visit because of possible violence. Douglas basked in the city's jubilation at his arrival. He arrived to cannon fire shortly after noon on Saturday. After being escorted to the Louisville Hotel, he addressed "some thirty thousand" at Preston Woods for an hour and a half. Bonfires, flags, and illuminated buildings continued the Douglas celebration that night.[131]

After four stops in Indiana (September 30 to October 4) he arrived in Chicago, his hometown, on the evening of October 4. Planning for his reception in his home city probably began on September 9, when he fixed the dates of his

---

127 Rita M. Carey, *The First Campaigner: Stephen A. Douglas* (New York, 1964), 23. The book is a study of Douglas's campaign in Iowa.

128 USN, *Frank Leslie's Illustrated Newspaper* (New York), Oct. 20, 1860; USN, *Dover Gazette* (Dover, NH), Oct. 20, 1860.

129 Mary P. Ryan, *Civic Wars: Democracy and Public Life in the American City during the Nineteenth Century* (Berkeley, CA, 1997), 67, finds that, before the 1830s, women in public ceremonies had been present only "in disguise." By the 1840s, however, the growth of political parties brought women into campaigns as both "audience and symbol." Ryan, *Women in Public: Between Banners and Ballots, 1825–1880* (Baltimore, 1990), 136. David Waldstreicher, *In the Midst of Perpetual Fetes: The Making of American Nationalism, 1776–1820* (Chapel Hill, NC, 1997), 233–235, also finds that while women participated earlier in public political celebrations, they did so not as citizens but primarily as symbols.

130 USN, *Daily Cleveland Herald*, Sept. 29, 1860; USN, *New York Herald*, Sept. 29, 1860; USN, *Daily Omaha Nebraskian*, Sept. 29, 1860.

131 ProQuest, *New York Times*, Oct. 1, 1860.

arrival and major speech. A Committee of Arrangements consisted of twenty-one locally prominent people. All railroads to Chicago agreed to half-fares or less. The major event was to be the "grand mass meeting of the Democracy of the North-West" on October 5, when well-known dignitaries from New York, Maryland, Michigan, Minnesota, Wisconsin, Iowa, and Indiana were expected to attend.[132]

Organizers appealed to both civic and partisan pride in order to attract huge crowds. Towns wanted to outdo each other, while Democrats and Republicans tried to outdraw their chief rivals. Democrats had the advantage of being able to headline the appearance of their candidate. In Chicago the Republicans presented earlier in the week a well-known surrogate for Lincoln, Senator William Seward. His enthusiastic reception spurred Democrats to intensify their efforts, and they succeeded in bringing out a crowd of "probably not less than eighty thousand people" for the main event.[133]

Unfortunately, the pageantry of the procession to Union Park for Douglas's speech undercut his message. Behind his carriage was a "large canopied" vehicle drawn by eight white horses. It held "thirty-three ladies, all dressed in white, and intended to personify the thirty-three American states." It was followed by a smaller float containing "six young girls, also clad in white, and intended to represent the six organized territories that have not yet arrived at the adult condition of the states."[134] All thirty-nine women and girls should have been of the same age group presented on floats of equal size, because the essence of Douglas's pitch was that people in territories should have the same right as those in states to decide their internal matters. In emigrating from states to territories, he said, they did not forfeit their intellectual capacity to govern themselves. How far his argument ran counter to the belief that territories were not on the same level with states was indicated by the symbolism of the smaller territorial floats with its younger occupants in a parade planned by Douglas's own supporters.

Douglas saw the relationship between territories and Washington as similar to that between the colonies and London. This was the meaning of American equality, he said in Chicago: "The Declaration of Independence had no reference to negroes when it spoke of all men being created equal. It had reference to the white men – the men of European blood and European descent. It was speaking of the American colonists in respect to their comparative rights with the British subjects in England." If the revolutionaries had intended to include

---

[132] *Daily Illinois State Register*, Oct. 1, 2, 1860.

[133] USN, *Daily Milwaukee News* (Milwaukee, WI), Oct. 7, 1860.

[134] *Chicago Times and Herald*, Oct. 6, 1860, as collated in the *Daily Illinois State Register*, Oct. 8, 1860. See also USN, *Daily Omaha Nebraskian*, Oct. 13, 1860. Michael D. Pierson, *Free Hearts and Free Homes: Gender and American Antislavery Politics* (Chapel Hill, NC, 2003), 144, has identified twenty of thirty-two women and girls on a Republican Party float in Beloit, Wisconsin, in 1856. He found them to be between 14 and 21 years old with an average age of 17.25.

blacks, he continued, then "they were bound as honest men to have emancipated every slave they had that very day."[135]

He then offered his favorite justification for nonintervention – it had led to a majority of free states. What if the slave state majority had imposed slavery on the whole nation at the beginning? Massachusetts would have been expected to reestablish slavery. Instead the matter had been left to the states to decide, and now eighteen of the thirty-three states were free. "Beginning with a small minority, we have become a controlling majority, under the operation of that just and equal principle which allows every body to do as they please, and now wish to reverse that principle and exercise power over the South which we would never have submitted to when we were the minority. Is it fair?"[136]

Douglas left Chicago for a multiple city tour of Iowa (October 8–12). Local preparations for his visit to Dubuque were detailed in the *Dubuque Herald*, which provides us an exceptional view of the planning that was involved for most of his major stops in twenty-three states. He was scheduled to arrive in Dubuque on October 11. The Democratic Executive Committee of Dubuque County met on Monday evening, October 1. It appointed a finance committee of nine, representing the four wards in the city and West Dubuque. This committee decided on a cannon salute upon Douglas's arrival on Thursday and the firing of guns in the evening, as well as the installation of bonfires on the four most prominent bluffs overlooking the city. A reception committee of seventy-six men was appointed to receive Douglas in Anamosa, where he would speak on the evening of the 10th. Thirty-two members were from Dubuque City. The others represented thirty-four towns in nine counties. The Dubuque reception committee attended Douglas's speech in Anamosa, some forty-five miles southwest of Dubuque, and slept three to a bed there in order to accompany him to their city the next morning.

Two members of the Executive Committee were assigned to address local meetings in Dubuque County for more than a week before Douglas's arrival in order to "organize clubs" that would participate in the event.[137] The local newspapers announced that railroad tickets to the Douglas demonstration were good for two days. Organizers had arranged a half-fare with "all the Railroad Companies leading to Dubuque."[138] The announcement invited

---

[135] Douglas's interpretation of the equality clause in the Declaration of Independence had been a feature of his senatorial debates with Lincoln, who viewed the text "as setting a standard for the future." Pauline Maier, *American Scriptures: Making the Declaration of Independence* (New York, 1997), 201–206, quote on 205. Rooted in her knowledge of the context in which the Declaration of Independence was crafted, Maier offers a balanced view of Douglas's and Lincoln's respective perspectives. On Douglas's interpretation, see also Barry A. Shain, "Rights Natural and Civil in the Declaration of Independence," in *The Nature of Rights at the American Founding and Beyond*, ed. Barry A. Shain (Charlottesville, VA, 2007), 118.

[136] For his speech, taken from the *Chicago Times*, see USN, *Daily National Intelligencer* (Washington, DC), Oct. 12, 1860.

[137] *Dubuque Herald*, Oct. 5, 1860.

[138] Ibid.

Democrats and "Friends of the Union and Constitution" to welcome the "People's Champion."[139]

In light of the preparations taken by the Democratic Executive Committee and the breadth of its reception committee, the expectation that fifteen thousand people from outside Dubuque would come from towns up to a hundred miles away had credibility. A concern for organizers was to "make their coming among us pleasant to themselves and of advantage to the Democratic cause." This required badges for each town's delegation, a designation for its place in the procession, and sufficient banners and flags for participants to carry.[140]

Upon Douglas's arrival, after a four-hour train ride from Anamosa in the morning, he was led to his hotel by a procession of "various clubs from home and abroad," which "together with those following on the sidewalks, numbered not less than 10,000 people," according to the local Democratic paper. A Chicago Republican correspondent estimated a crowd of five thousand.[141] The gathering was dismissed and invited to return at 1:30 in the Public Square, where Douglas would speak.[142]

On the day of the demonstration, the Democratic newspaper in Dubuque expressed the racial consciousness of the party. "The white people of the United States at large are inheritors in common with us and with each other of the bequests of our fathers." The editor proceeded to lambaste "that portion of the people," that is, the Republicans, who would deprive their brethren of rights that the "whole people" inherited.[143] When the Dubuque Democrats celebrated Douglas as the "People's Champion," clearly they meant the "White People's Champion."

After Iowa, from October 11 to 23, Douglas returned to Illinois, traveled to Wisconsin, Michigan, Missouri, and crossed his home state in a strenuous stretch of constant movement except on Sundays, when he almost never traveled.

When he decided on his final trip to the South is uncertain. What is clear is that he was in Iowa when he learned of Republican victories on October 9 in Pennsylvania, Ohio, and Indiana. Some advisers urged him to throw in the towel and spare himself the ordeal of continued campaigning.[144] Indeed, he now believed he could not win. Yet he reaffirmed his plans. He told a confidante that Lincoln would be president but that he would do his "best to save the Union from overthrow" by going south.[145] This decision has garnered respect from

---

[139] Ibid.

[140] *Dubuque Herald*, Oct. 9, 1860.

[141] *Dubuque Herald*, Oct. 12, 1860; ProQuest, *Chicago Press and Tribune*, Oct. 15, 1860.

[142] *Dubuque Herald*, Oct. 12, 1860. The speech appears in that issue and is printed in Carey, *First Campaigner*, 86–103.

[143] *Dubuque Herald*, Oct. 11, 1860.

[144] Although predicted, the results and their implications did not become clear for a few days. ProQuest, *New York Times*, Oct. 8–13, 1860.

[145] John W. Forney, *Eulogy upon the Death of the Hon. Stephen A. Douglas: Delivered at the Smithsonian Institute, Washington, July 3, 1861* (Philadelphia, 1861), 11; Henry Wilson,

historians, especially because it involved traveling to the Deep South, where he had reason to fear possible violence. A Northern newspaperman reported that "more than one of the Southern journals invoked the spirit of the mob to put him down."[146] As it turned out, the people's enthusiasm for seeing and hearing him was no less embracing than it had been in the Northeast and West.

On October 23 Douglas crossed into Tennessee, where he squeezed a trip to Huntsville, Alabama, between stops in Memphis (October 23–25) and Nashville (October 26), where Douglas arrived by train at 8:00 A.M.[147] The governor, other prominent Democrats, and an "immense crowd" greeted him at the depot. An open carriage driven by four horses led him through streets thronged with cheering thousands to his hotel. There he spent the morning with local leaders. He was scheduled to speak outside the courthouse at 11:00 A.M. An onlooker who came out of curiosity later claimed that by 11:00 the area around the platform was already mobbed and that Douglas did not appear until nearly noon. He was cheered all the way to the scene. A bass drum announced his approach, and more cheers sounded as he walked onto the platform. He spoke for two hours, but the crowd was so large that "hundreds, nay thousands could not hear him."[148] To offset the excitement that Douglas's scheduled appearance generated, Breckinridge forces had prevailed upon William Yancey, the "fire-eater" who had led the walkout at the Charleston convention, to speak that night.[149] Although a local newspaper that touted the Bell–Everett ticket had hoped that Douglas and Yancey would have a "Kilkenney cat fight" that would extinguish both of them, it conceded that the judge's "speech, as his speeches always are, was a most powerful one."[150]

Douglas alternated remarks of five to ten minutes from his railroad car platform at small towns in Alabama, Tennessee, and Georgia with major speeches of two to three hours in Chattanooga (October 27), Atlanta (October 30), Macon (October 31), Columbus (Nov. 1), Montgomery (Nov. 2), Selma (Nov. 3), and, finally, Mobile (November 5), the day before the election.

Douglas's courage in undertaking this tour generally has been acknowledged. What has not received sufficient notice, however, was the consistency of what he said in the Deep South with what he said everywhere else. Shortly before he appeared in Montgomery, a local paper published a letter from Senator C. C.

History of the Rise and Fall of the Slave Power, 3 vols. (Boston, 1876–1878), 2: 700; Johannsen, *SAD*, 797–798.

[146] Forney, *Eulogy upon the Death of Douglas*, 12.

[147] The *Memphis Appeal* staunchly supported Douglas and warned that the Democratic split would result in the election of Lincoln. Mary E. Cronin, "Fiend, Coward, Monster, or King: Southern Press Views of Abraham Lincoln," *American Journalism*, 26:4 (2009), 38. Cronin finds that most Southern editors wanted any Democrat, not Lincoln (39).

[148] *Nashville Patriot*, Oct. 30, 1860. The onlooker was George Brick.

[149] *Nashville Patriot*, Oct. 24, 1860. Yancey and Douglas had similarly strong positions against nativism, but the slavery question was overriding to the secessionist leader, who "hated" Douglas, according to Eric H. Walther, *William Lowndes Yancey and the Coming of the Civil War* (Chapel Hill, NC, 2006), 253. For Yancey's views on nativism, see 185–186.

[150] *Nashville Patriot*, Oct. 27 and 30, 1860.

Clay of Alabama describing Douglas as a "man of expedients, and can shift his ground or change his hand to suit emergencies." Clay falsely accused Douglas of denying the obligation of Congress to protect slavery in the territories while maintaining its power to prohibit it.[151] In Montgomery, in fact, Douglas was consistent with his message elsewhere in insisting that the people of territories should decide the issue for themselves without federal intrusion.

He did not trim his principles to curry favor with the crowds. He made the same essential points to proslavery Southerners that he had made to antislavery New Englanders. His brilliance as a national campaigner was that he could dress his principles in language and tone that made listeners everywhere feel that he and they were in synch with each other. Alas, the one commonality that he and his audiences everywhere shared was racism; therefore, attacking the idea of "negro equality" bonded him to white crowds in every section regardless of how they felt about slavery.

Nevertheless, threats continued to be made. As his day of arrival in Macon approached, for example, letters railing against his visit could have filled a week's worth of issues of the *Macon Daily Telegraph*, according to its editor.[152] Local newspapers there and elsewhere urged courtesy and civility toward him. In Atlanta there was fear that hecklers would interrupt his speech. A local Breckinridge daily tried to shift the blame for possible disorder from the crowd to the candidate. The newspaper expected that Douglas would be "treated with the respect his distinguished position entitles him to," unless he were "so reckless" as to repeat here what he had said elsewhere. Just what he might say that would justify discourtesy, the newspaper did not specify, leaving the door open to affix responsibility for any disturbance to the speaker himself.[153] Macon organizers took two steps to protect the Douglases. (1) They arranged for the Douglas's train to sneak into the depot an hour before its scheduled arrival time, and thus the couple was able to make a "hasty retreat" to the Lanier House, leaving the disappointed crowd to console itself in the streets "with shouts, gunpowder and fireworks."[154] (2) They made a special effort to attract women to Douglas's main address. Ads promised that "comfortable seats" would be reserved for the ladies, "who are earnestly want[ing] to attend."[155]

Some newspapers stoked a hostile reaction. A Montgomery weekly could not fathom "what can be the object of this insolent braggart in coming to this portion of the country" and disclaimed responsibility "for the consequences of any act by the desperado."[156] During the procession from the depot to the hotel in the Alabama capital, however, before Douglas even had a chance to say anything provocative, eggs and tomatoes targeted him but hit members of his

[151] *Montgomery Weekly Advertiser*, Oct. 31, 1860.
[152] *Macon Daily Telegraph*, Oct. 20, 26, 27, 30, 31, 1860.
[153] *Daily Intelligencer* (Atlanta), Oct. 29, 1860.
[154] *Macon Daily Telegraph*, Oct. 31, 1860.
[155] Ibid.
[156] *Montgomery Weekly Advertiser*, Oct. 24, 1860.

reception committee. That made more news nationally than the speech he gave at noon the next day on the steps of the capitol before eight to ten thousand people.[157] Following this incident, the planners at Selma made a special effort to have women visibly involved. The "ladies of Selma County" had worked behind the scenes in making a banner that was carried during the procession that brought Douglas to the town square and in decorating the platform on which he spoke. They made their presence known by "the waving of parasols, handkerchiefs, and hundreds of neat little flags inscribed 'Douglas and Johnson'" as well as by clapping. After Douglas spoke, a woman handed him a bouquet of flowers, signaling the ladies in the crowd to shower Douglas with bouquets as "emblems of their love." There were no embarrassing moments for the South in Selma or Mobile, where women had been assured of having four to five hundred seats reserved for them near the platform.[158]

The greatest danger to Douglas, as it turned out, came not from the crowds but from modes of transportation. Railroads were notorious for accidents.[159] A Democratic ad for Douglas's visit to Nashville countered opposition-spread misinformation by assuring readers of his scheduled arrival. "Nothing but sickness, or a railroad breakdown, can prevent him."[160] Douglas traveled mainly by train, occasionally by steamboat, and where neither mode was available, by horse and wagon. Unexpectedly the worst mishap occurred aboard a docked ship during the last week of his long campaign.

After his speech, hotel reception, and private dinner in Montgomery, Douglas and his wife boarded a steamer for Selma at 10:00 P.M. He was giving a farewell speech from the second deck when it collapsed. The initial report was that no one was injured, although both he and Adele were immediately brought to the patron's home where they had had dinner. The reception committee that planned to accompany the couple to Selma followed to find out if they would be able to continue. Adele was too impaired to continue but urged Stephen to go on without her. Although he too was hurt, he left her behind and boarded another steamer.[161] In Selma an observer reported that the candidate was "suffering secretly" from his injury.[162] Adele recovered sufficiently to take a steamer to Mobile, where she participated in the last events before the election. Fittingly

[157] *Daily Intelligencer* (Atlanta), Nov. 3, 1860; *Alabama State Sentinel* (Selma), Nov. 7, 1860; ProQuest, *New York Times,* Nov. 9, 1860.

[158] *Alabama State Sentinel* (Selma), Nov. 14, 1860.

[159] See note 74, this chapter.

[160] *Nashville Patriot,* Oct. 20, 1860.

[161] *Alabama State Sentinel* (Selma), Nov. 7, 1860; USN, *New York Herald,* Nov. 4, 1860; ProQuest, *New York Times,* Nov. 9, 1860. The *Sentinel* reported that the Douglases were brought to Col. John J. Seibels's home; the *Herald* had them return to the hotel. Seibels, editor of the *Montgomery Advertiser,* had described Douglas in 1858 as an "unscrupulous demagogue" but now championed his cause against disunion. *Alabama State Sentinel,* Nov. 7, 1860; *New York Times,* Aug. 24, 1865. More than three weeks later, newspapers stated that both Douglas and his wife were "still lame from the steamboat accident at Montgomery." *Huntsville Advertiser* and *Cincinnati Enquirer,* as reported in USN, *Newark Advocate* (Newark, OH), Dec. 7, 1860.

[162] *Alabama State Sentinel* (Selma), Nov. 7, 1860.

her brother came as well. He had stayed with Adele while she recuperated in Montgomery and now joined the brother-in-law, who had begun his campaign by coming to Cutts's law school graduation.

On Election Day Douglas learned by telegram that one prediction in fact had come to pass – Lincoln had won. He had anticipated that outcome for a month. A question he must have shared with Adele was whether the month of personal campaigning after Iowa had been worth it. Both of them had paid a physical price. He had justified his continued tour in order to persuade Southerners to remain in the Union even if the dreaded Republicans gained the presidency. That purpose, in fact, pushed him to a twenty-fourth state as he and Adele headed to a rally in New Orleans that was held two days after the election. There he emphasized again that the Constitution would protect the South from what it feared in a Lincoln presidency.

For historians Douglas's campaign was his finest hour. David Potter writes that Douglas "exceeded himself and showed a sense of public responsibility unmatched by any of the other candidates." His "was not only the first but also one of the greatest of campaigns by a presidential candidate."[163] Yet he did not achieve either of his goals. Lincoln was elected and the South seceded from the Union.

As a candidate often discovers, how well he speaks and how people receive him are not dependable indices of how they will vote. Mobile was one of the few cities in Alabama where Douglas bested Bell and Breckinridge by healthy margins.[164] More typical were the results in Montgomery, where his speech was so persuasive, according to its modern editors, that they wonder "why it did not have more effect upon those who heard it."[165] Breckinridge and Bell each polled many times Douglas's count there. In Alabama as a whole he garnered only 15 percent of the popular vote. His best result in a slave state was in Missouri, where he captured 35.5 percent of the vote. He campaigned there for four days.[166] The Southern state in which he traveled most was Virginia, where he spent nearly two weeks and won 9.7 percent of the popular vote, slightly less than the percentage he received in Arkansas, where he did not travel. He spent only two full days in Kentucky and obtained 17.5 percent of the vote, the same percentage he received in Louisiana, where he did not appear until after the election.

In fact, as Table 7.1 shows, there is little correlation between Douglas's personal campaigning and his performance on Election Day. His worst showing

---

[163] David M. Potter, *The Impending Crisis, 1848–1861*, completed and ed. Don E. Fehrenbacher (New York, 1976), 440–441.

[164] Bell received 1638 votes, Breckenridge 1533, and Douglas 1802. *Alabama State Sentinel* (Selma), Nov. 14, 1860.

[165] David R. Barbee and Milledge L. Bonham, Jr., "The Montgomery Address of Stephen A. Douglas, *Journal of Southern History*, 5:4 (1939), 528.

[166] Douglas's success in Missouri owed much to the support of Austin King, a former governor who worked for his nomination unsuccessfully in Charleston. Freehling, *Road to Disunion*, 299–302, 339.

TABLE 7.1. *Douglas's Campaigning through November 5 and Election Results*

Campaign Dates	No. of Days[a]	Votes	Percentage of Vote	Rank
Mid-Atlantic				
PA: July 1, Sept. 7–10	5	16,765	3.5	3[b]
NY: July 1–14, 20–28, Aug. 21–24, Sept. 10–21	39	312,510	46.3	2[c]
NJ: Aug. 22–23, Sept. 10	3	62,869	51.9	1[c]
Total	47			
New England				
CT: July 14–17, Aug. 21	5	15,431	20.6	2
MA: July 17–20, Aug. 14–15	6	34,370	20.2	2
VT: July 28–31	4	8,649	19.4	2
NH: July 31–Aug. 1	2	25,887	39.3	2
RI: Aug. 1–14, 17–21	20	7,707	38.6	2[c]
ME: Aug. 15–17	3	29,693	29.4	2
Total	40			
West				
OH: Sept. 21–27	7	187,421	42.3	2
IL: Sept. 24–25, Oct. 4–8, 11–19, 22–23	18	160,215	47.2	2
IN: Sept. 27–29, Oct. 1–4	7	115,509	42.4	2
IA: Oct. 8–12, 13	6	55,639	43.2	2
WI: Oct. 12	1	65,021	42.7	2
MI: Oct. 15–16	2	65,057	42.0	2
Total	41			
South				
MO: Oct. 19–22	4	58,801	35.5	1
MD: Aug. 24–25, Sept. 5–7,	5	5,966	6.5	3
VA: Aug. 25–29, Aug. 31–Sept. 5	11	16,198	9.7	3
NC: Aug. 29–31	3	2,737	2.8	3
KY: Sept. 29–Oct. 1	3	25,651	17.5	3
TN: Oct. 23–29		7	11,281	7.7
AL: Oct. 25–26, Nov. 1–5	7	13,618	15.1	3
GA: Oct. 29–Nov. 1	4	11,581	10.9	3
Total	40			
SC		Only state not to have popularly elected presidential electors		
AR	0	5,357	9.9	3
FL	0	223	1.7	3
MS	0	3,282	4.8	3
TX	0	18	0.0	3
LA	0	7,625	17.5	3
DE	0	1,066	6.6	3
MN	0	11,920	34.3	2
OR	0	4,135	28	3
CA	0	37,999	31.7	2

Note: For the towns at which Douglas stopped, see the Appendix. For state-by-state voting, see Robert A. Diamond, ed., *Presidential Elections Since 1789* (Washington, DC: Congressional Quarterly, 1975), 71; W. Dean Burham, *Presidential Ballots, 1836–1892* (Baltimore, 1955), 246–257. For the "Union" name of the fusion ticket and for the fusion ticket in Pennsylvania, see USN, *North American and United States Gazette* (Philadelphia), Nov. 7, 1860. On fusion, see David M. Potter, *The Impending Crisis, 1848–1861*, completed and ed. Don E. Fehrenbacher (New York, 1976), 437; Damon Wells, *Stephen Douglas: The Last Years, 1857–1861* (Austin, TX, 1971), 245.
[a]Each day that he was in a state, no matter how briefly, is counted.
[b]Douglas and Breckinridge were on a fusion ticket.
[c]Douglas, Bell, and Breckinridge were on a fusion ("Union") ticket.

in the Mid-Atlantic was in Pennsylvania, where by himself he garnered only 3.5 percent of the popular vote despite stopping at eight towns in five days, although the fusion ticket of Breckinridge–Douglas won 37.5 percent of the popular vote. Despite his personal opposition to a fusion ticket with the Southern Democratic Party, local Democrats placed one on ballots in several Northern states, as indicated in the table. In New Jersey, where Douglas spent only three days, his fusion ticket won 52 percent of the vote. A similar ticket drew only 46 percent in New York, where he spent the most time, some thirty-nine days. In New England his best showing was in the state where he spent the fewest days, New Hampshire. In the West (the current Midwest) he trailed Lincoln but scored more than 42 percent regardless of the amount of time he traveled in a state.

The lack of connection between Douglas's personal travel and his vote reveals an important facet of antebellum democracy – the widespread acceptance of the president as a leader who did not subject himself to screening by the people. That Douglas's example did not create a concomitant demand for his rivals to do as he did is a measure of the distance between his world and ours and the proximity of his to the world before the American Revolution.[167] The monarchical republican tradition of the federalist founders remained remarkably resilient in the face of Douglas's unprecedented democratic campaign.

---

[167] On the royalist political culture of colonial America, see Brendan McConville, *The King's Three Faces: The Rise and Fall of Royal America, 1688–1776* (Chapel Hill, NC, 2006).

8

In Lincoln's Shadow

Mr. Douglas called on the President this evening and had an interesting conversation on the present condition of the country.

Stephen A. Douglas (1861)[1]

The great lesson of the past is unpredictability. In 1850 no one, including Abraham Lincoln, imagined that he would be elected president ten years later. A lot of people, however, believed that Stephen A. Douglas was likely to land in the White House. Illinois newspapers had trumpeted that destination for him since his mid-twenties. In 1850 Douglas became a national star whose name appeared in nearly every other issue of northeastern newspapers. Lincoln made a splash during his one term in Congress by challenging President Polk's justification for the Mexican War, but only one year after he left Washington, outside Illinois newspapers did not mention him even once.[2] Before 1858 Douglas hardly had need to think about Lincoln at all, while Lincoln could not help reading about the "Little Giant" in whose shadow he had dwelled since the 1830s.[3]

Until 1858 their rivalry was one-sided, with Douglas looming large in Lincoln's mind. In 1854 Douglas's Nebraska bill induced Lincoln to leave retirement and engage in active partisan opposition. In 1858 he won the Republican nomination for the Senate and stalked the Democratic incumbent until Douglas agreed to a series of debates that made Lincoln famous enough to seek the Republican presidential nomination two years later. The results of November 6, 1860, inverted the rivalry. For the first time Lincoln eclipsed Douglas.

---

[1] "Statement," *Letters of SAD*, 509.

[2] Douglas appeared in 46% of 333 issues of seven newspapers in Massachusetts, New Hampshire, New York, and Vermont digitized for 1850 in *Early American Newspapers*, series I. Lincoln appeared not once.

[3] A newly discovered letter of 1847 indicates that Douglas may have borrowed money from Lincoln while they served together in Washington. *The Little Giant: Newsletter of the Stephen A. Douglas Association*, 20:2 (Aug. 2010), 1.

On the surface Douglas was a gracious, patriotic loser who worked tire-lessly for a compromise that would preserve the Union, personally encouraged and pledged loyalty to the president-elect, and, then, after the Southern attack on Fort Sumter, supported the administration even through his final illness. Yet a close examination of his post-election behavior suggests that he experi-enced psychological distress that lasted into the new year. He had always run hard, but early success had reinforced his self-assurance, which in turn had enhanced his effect on courts, legislatures, and crowds. After Lincoln beat him, however, his self-confidence and influence over others diminished in tandem. The futility of his efforts to achieve sectional reconciliation in December and January compounded his sense of loss. Ironically the president-elect's arrival in Washington in late February would boost his spirits, acumen, and visibility, albeit in Lincoln's shadow.

During the last month of the presidential campaign, when Douglas recog-nized the probability of Lincoln's victory, he focused on the need to preserve the Union by explaining why the South should remain wedded to the established constitutional order. Immediately after the election, he continued to articulate the same message, assuring economic leaders in Louisiana that the South had little need to worry about the new president, because existing laws protected their interests.[4] He then pledged to stay silent until he resumed his seat in the Senate chamber. He and Adele arrived in Washington on December 1, and the next day he conferred with Senator John J. Crittenden of Kentucky, prime mover behind the Constitutional Union Party, to develop a strategy at the lame duck session of Congress for defusing the threat of secession.

Douglas had stated time and again, most recently on his cross-country cam-paign tours, that his great heroes were Whig senators, Henry Clay and Daniel Webster, who had been mainly responsible for the Compromise of 1850. His own contribution to that agreement had been the highlight of his congressional career and had catapulted him to the position of a national leader who was known and respected throughout America and Europe. He was not elected president in 1860, but once again he might achieve greatness in the Senate by collaborating with another Kentuckian.

He and Crittenden worked on constitutional amendments that they hoped would be acceptable as a compromise, but before either could present his proposal, seven senators and twenty-three congressmen signed a manifesto on December 13 urging secession and the formation of the Confederacy. On December 17 a convention in Columbia, South Carolina, voted 159 to 0 for secession.[5] On the next day Crittenden offered constitutional amendments that would have extended the Missouri Compromise line between slavery and free-dom to all territories, prohibited Congress from abolishing slavery in any fed-eral territory, imposed conditions for congressional abolition of slavery in the

---

[4] Stephen A. Douglas to Ninety-Six New Orleans Citizens, *Letters of SAD*, 499–503.
[5] A convenient chronology of the secession crisis is E. B. Long with Barbara Long, *The Civil War Day by Day: An Almanac, 1861–1865* (Garden City, NY, 1973), 3–56.

District of Columbia, precluded Congress from interfering with the interstate traffic in slaves, permitted federal compensation for unreturned fugitive slaves, and proscribed future amendments that would amend any of the foregoing ones. On December 20 the Senate selected a Committee of Thirteen, modeled on Henry Clay's committee that forged the Compromise of 1850, with Crittenden the de facto chair.[6] Douglas was one of three Northern Democrats appointed. On the same day South Carolina voted formally for secession. The progression toward dissolution in the South underscored the urgency of deliberations in Washington, increasing the stress on Douglas.

On December 22 the Committee of Thirteen voted down Crittenden's amendments. For a resolution to be adopted, the committee divided its members by party and required a majority of affirmative votes from each. Although Douglas favored territorial self-determination over a federal mandate, he supported the proposed extension of the $36°30'$ line in the interest of a compromise. None of the proposed amendments, however, received the necessary votes. This rejection, suggests one historian, added "velocity" to the secessionists' cause.[7] Two days later Douglas offered two constitutional amendments of his own.[8] The first replaced the Missouri Compromise line, which had received the least votes, with a complicated version of popular sovereignty: a territory should have a minimum of fifty thousand inhabitants before a decision on slavery should be made, that is, before a constitution should be formed. The only facet of his proposal that was transparent was his intention to reach a compromise.

His second amendment began with the barring of "Africans" from exercising the franchise or holding office in any locality. This was in fundamental contradiction to the central principle of his congressional career – the right of local majorities to decide domestic matters, such as who could vote and who could be elected. He had earned high marks as a lawyer and politician in Illinois by defending the right of states to establish their own suffrage qualifications. In Congress he had championed the right of territories to do likewise.[9] Now he was calling for a constitutional limitation on the discretion of the people – the most undemocratic proposition he had ever brought forth. Why?

It is hard to see how this "concession to the race fears of southerners" would have been acceptable to the South.[10] Secessionists were not asking for a national

---

[6] CG, 36th Cong., 2nd sess. (Dec. 20, 1860), 158. The vice president explained that the author of the resolution to create the committee, Lazarus Powell (KY), had to be chair; therefore, it was unavoidable but proper that "the eminent senior Senator from Kentucky should also be a member of that committee." Accordingly, that state had two members on this critical committee.

[7] George F. Milton, *The Eve of the Conflict: Stephen A. Douglas and the Needless War* (New York, 1834; reprinted 1969), 515.

[8] U.S. Serial Set. 36th Cong., 2nd sess. Senate Report No. 288, 5–7, for Crittenden's proposal; 8–11 for Douglas's.

[9] See Chapter 5.

[10] James L. Huston, *Stephen A. Douglas and the Dilemmas of Democratic Equality* (Lanham, MD, 2007), 183.

policy of black exclusion. At the core of their justification was the assertion of states' rights.[11] Douglas followed this proposition with a related one empowering the United States to acquire places in Africa and South America for the colonization, at federal expense, of free blacks that states and Congress chose to remove from their jurisdictions. While the egregious racism was not uncharacteristic of Douglas, the lack of clear calculation and purpose was.[12] He had been in Washington for three weeks ostensibly seeking a strategy for sectional compromise, yet these baffling propositions were the best he could add to Crittenden's. It was nearly a half-year before his final illness, but these provisions at the head of his second amendment suggest that psychological strain had begun to take a toll on his thinking.

He acknowledged his disquiet in a much-hyped speech of January 3, which he began by admitting that nothing he had ever done in public life had caused him as much "regret" as voting for the compromise amendments in committee.[13] As if to escape his waywardness, he moved immediately into familiar terrain by drawing on the lesson of American history, to wit, "that whenever the Federal Government has attempted to decide and control the slavery question in the newly acquired Territories, regardless of the wishes of the inhabitants, alienation of feeling, sectional strife, and discord have ensued." After referencing the tranquil period of "non-interference by Congress" from 1789 to 1820, he noted the eruption of sectional tensions until the Missouri Compromise restored peace and brought a quarter-century of a "happy and united people." He cited his own support in 1848 for the extension of the 36°30′ line through territory acquired from Mexico, blamed its rejection on the North, and credited Henry Clay with having convinced him and others to forgo the old dividing line in the interest of popular sovereignty as a new formula for sectional harmony. He claimed to support both the Missouri Compromise line and popular sovereignty, "each in turn as a means of attaining a desirable end." His repeal of the Missouri Compromise in 1854, he said, merely clarified what the Compromise of 1850 had done: it nullified the older formula.

This was a flagrant example of Douglas revising history to accommodate an immediate political goal. He had displayed a consistently negative position on the Missouri Compromise though his years chairing the respective committees on territories in the House and Senate. He had temporarily agreed to a proposed extension of the 36°30′ line during the Mexican War as a better alternative to the Wilmot Proviso, but he had always preferred Congress to defer to the wishes of settlers rather than impose a solution to the slavery problem. Now he was refashioning himself as a longtime champion of the 1820 settlement who

---

[11] William W. Freehling, *The Road to Disunion: Secessionists Triumphant, 1854–1861* (New York, 2007), 345–351.

[12] Johannsen, *SAD*, 817, is unable "to see what Douglas hoped to achieve by these propositions."

[13] For the whole speech, see CG, APP, 36th Cong., 2nd sess. (Jan. 3, 1861), 35–42. For the hype and a neutral summary of the speech, see Johannsen, *SAD*, 819–821.

had tried unsuccessfully to apply it to the Mexican cession and who in 1854 provided for its repeal only because it had effectively been nullified in 1850. With his long opposition to the Missouri Compromise now scrubbed from his record, he could claim to support Crittenden's revival of it.

Did he truly believe his revision? Not enough even to repudiate charges of inconsistency: "The country has no great interest in my consistency. The preservation of this Union, the integrity of this Republic, is of more importance than party platforms or individual records.... I am prepared to act on this question with reference to the present exigencies of the case, as if I had never given a vote, or uttered a word, or had an opinion upon the subject."

This had to be an exceptionally painful statement for Douglas. In November he had ended a campaign of three and a half months during which he had spoken at more than 150 stops in every section of the country except the Pacific West and had struck the same theme everywhere: the way to remove contention over slavery from Congress was to let the people of the territories decide the issue themselves. He had claimed that, as a matter of practical policy, federal regulations had never freed anyone: neither the Northwest Ordinance nor the Missouri Compromise had overridden settler preferences regarding slavery. His message, however, had been more than a matter of pragmatism. He had anchored it to his understanding of the American Revolution as a defense of local self-government. Everywhere he had condemned congressional interference as a violation of that principle. To ignore his record now, to cast aside opinions he had articulated in Congress, on the stump, and in print for nearly two decades, to reject all of what he had stood for in the desperate hope of reaching a compromise that would slow the secession express was more than a rational personal sacrifice. His willingness to compromise deeply felt principles had a desperate quality, evidence of emotional vulnerability rather than strength of character.

If he was willing to go so far, he plaintively asked, "why cannot you Republicans accede to the reestablishment and extension of the Missouri compromise line?" He promised not to remind them of their opposition to it when he had supported it in 1848 – as if the Republicans' position was based on their feelings about him. He then brought up his own proposed amendments. He claimed that his proposal of a floor of fifty thousand inhabitants for territorial self-determination would prevent either North or South from adding territory solely to increase its political weight in Congress, because a large portion of people from each section would be necessary to reach the required number; therefore, annexation of new territory would take place only for "national considerations." His reasoning here was neither lucid nor compelling. Yet at least he could offer a rationale for his first amendment. For his second amendment, headed by his propositions to deny political rights to African Americans and to federally subsidize the removal of African Americans from the country, he offered no justification, other than the hope that with his inclusion of several of Crittenden's provisions his amendments would constitute a "fair basis of amicable adjustment."

His January 3 speech, which Adele attended, could not have left him feeling very good about himself.[14] The man who had been accused of opportunism in fact took his own ideas seriously. He had held positions with remarkable consistency. Dismissing a record that he had recently campaigned on, rewriting the history that had always been a guide for him, and then urging Republicans to forget the past and do whatever was necessary to dampen the sectional crisis must have been torturous, made all the worse by his lack of persuasiveness. His plea convinced neither opposition legislators nor editors. His hometown Republican newspaper aptly summarized the substance of his speech: "men ought to have no principles which they are unwilling to surrender, when approached with a threat."[15]

The sectional chasm exceeded the reach of congressional conciliators. On January 9 Mississippi followed South Carolina's example, and on February 4 six states met in Montgomery, Alabama, to form their own union. Each announcement of secession stabbed Douglas, who in continuing alliance with Crittenden tried to find common ground in the Senate chamber and behind the scenes. A dinner party that he and Adele hosted on January 24 inspired a moment of mistaken hope regarding Republican willingness to accommodate secessionists. He worked hard reviewing data to advance a scheme for a North and Central American free trade zone, modeled on the German Zollverein, as a counter to a Republican proposed tariff and as a vehicle for integrating seceding states into a commercial union with the rest of the country. Studying in preparation for a legislative proposal was therapeutic for Douglas, whose surviving notes reveal a man who enjoyed compiling data and developing ideas before making a presentation.[16] The proposal itself, however, made little headway.[17]

The last grasp at compromise came with the "Peace Convention" that convened in Washington on February 4, the same day that six seceding states opened their own convention in Montgomery to establish the Confederation. With numerous Northern Republicans instructed by their state governments to hold the line, the task of the Peace Convention may well have been "hopeless," as Robert Johannsen concludes.[18] Douglas, however, was not so much an optimist as a compulsive player who needed to be at the center of action, no matter what the outcome. He welcomed and consulted with arriving delegates and

---

[14] Douglas R. Egerton, *Year of Meteors: Stephen Douglas, Abraham Lincoln, and the Election That Brought on the Civil War* (New York, 2010), 299, finds the speech "disorganized, repetitive, and contradictory." For a positive reading of Douglas's speech, which credits him with having done the best he could in light of his party's "weak position," see Russell McClintock, *Lincoln and the Decision for War: The Northern Response to Secession* (Chapel Hill, NC, 2008), 114–116, quote on 116.

[15] *Chicago Tribune*, Jan. 8, 1861. The paper chided Douglas and the Northern Democrats for betraying their long-standing commitment to not forcing slavery on people who did not want it. It conceded that they had professed the principle for years and appeared to be sincere. Now they seemed to be losing their "manhood and honor." *Chicago Tribune*, Jan. 18–19, 1861.

[16] Abridgement of Dr. Bowring's Report on the Zollverein, SAD Papers, UC, Addenda, 3: 18.

[17] Johannsen, *SAD*, 832–833.

[18] Ibid., 835.

wanted to invite all of them individually to a party that he and Adele would host.[19] Alas, he could not obtain everyone's local address, a problem he noted in his invitation to John Tyler, the presiding officer of the convention. He asked Tyler to mention the social event to delegates "if the opportunity occurs,"[20] no doubt hoping that Tyler would talk up the Douglas party while he chaired the meeting.

On February 11, when Douglas penned his invitation to Tyler, President-Elect Lincoln began his journey from Springfield to Washington. Friends of Douglas were among those on the train, which reached the capital on February 23.[21] Douglas headed the Illinois delegation, which Lincoln received at his hotel suite late that afternoon. Newspapers highlighted their reunion, characterizing it as "peculiarly" or "particularly pleasant."[22] Two days later Adele called on Mary Lincoln and received credit for her "graceful courtesy" in initiating a series of receptions for the next first lady.[23] On the same day the president-elect paid an informal visit to both houses of Congress. Douglas was one of five Democratic Senators to "go up to him, and give him a cordial and friendly shake of the hand."[24] The next evening Douglas and a small group from the Peace Convention met Lincoln at his Willard suite to try to wrest a concession.[25] They failed, but the next day Douglas returned for a less crowded session with Lincoln hours before the Peace Convention adjourned in a last-ditch attempt to induce him to prevail upon Republican delegates to compromise. Another delegate, a former congressman who knew both men, claimed to be present when Douglas entered for a half-hour meeting and brought Lincoln to tears when he pledged that, no matter what disunionists did, he and his friends would aid and support his efforts to "save our Union."[26] Prior to this emotional climax, Douglas had urged Lincoln "to leave our children a country to live in" and to support a national convention that would explore reconciliation.[27] In relaying his exchange with the president on the next day, Douglas "was more agitated and distressed" than a confidant had ever seen him, to the degree that his listener could "not make out what he expected Mr. Lincoln to do."[28]

[19] John M. Palmer, *Personal Recollections of John M. Palmer: The Story of an Earnest Life* (Cincinnati, 1901), 89. For a list of the 132 delegates, see Robert G. Gunderson, *Old Gentlemen's Club: The Washington Peace Conference of 1861* (Madison, WI, 1961), 105–106.

[20] Stephen A. Douglas to John Tyler, Feb. 11, 1861, *Letters of SAD*, 507.

[21] Harold Holzer, *Lincoln President-Elect: Abraham Lincoln and the Great Secession Winter, 1860–1861* (New York, 2008), 276–277; 281; USN, *New York Herald*, Feb. 24, 1861.

[22] USN, *New York Herald*, Feb. 24, 1861; USN, *Daily Telegraph* (Omaha, NE), Feb. 26, 1861.

[23] ProQuest, *New York Times*, Feb. 26, 1861.

[24] ProQuest, *New York Times*, Feb. 27, 1861.

[25] Holzer, *Lincoln President-Elect*, 425; Johannsen, *SAD*, 841–842.

[26] Esther Cushman, "Douglas the Loyal," *Journal of the Illinois State Historical Society*, 23 (Apr. 1930), 168–169.

[27] Holzer, *Lincoln President-Elect*, 425; Johannsen, *SAD*, 842.

[28] Daniel W. Crofts, *A Secession Crisis Enigma: William Henry Hurlbert and "The Diary of a Public Man"* (Baton Rouge, 2010), 241. Crofts identifies the author of the notorious "Diary," an imaginative memoir first published in 1879, but warns historians against using it (19). Through

In sum, either in an intimate setting or in a group, Douglas made certain that he spoke with Lincoln on four of the president-elect's first five days in Washington. And despite a hopeless effort to enlist him in the crusade for compromise, he reportedly won Lincoln's affection by assuring him of his loyalty to the president for the cause of union. Adele Douglas's visit to Mary Lincoln enhanced her husband's standing with the incoming first family.

The inauguration presented Douglas with another opportunity to get close to Lincoln. Historian Harold Holzer believes that Douglas might have been the one Democrat with whom Lincoln previewed his inaugural address.[29] His inference is certainly reasonable, especially in view of the contacts between the two families after the Lincolns arrived in Washington. On March 4, at the special session of the Senate, Douglas joined the presidential party that formed in the Senate chamber before marching onto the inauguration platform. Both houses had officially adjourned on Saturday, March 2.[30] The special session was officially convened on Monday for the oath taking of the new vice president. Before 1934, the special session was necessary to confirm appointments of the new president.[31] On Sunday evening at 7:00, however, the special session met unofficially before packed galleries. While many napped on sofas, Douglas and Crittenden were among those who "kept a rolling fire of debate" on the Peace Convention amendment, a variation on Crittenden's, that was defeated by a vote of four to one at 5:20 A.M.[32]

Despite having actively participated in the all-night session, Douglas was not too tired to position himself where he might take and hold the hat of the president-elect when he rose to give his inaugural address.[33] Douglas then could be

December 1860, from his post with the *New York Times*, Hurlbert had supported Douglas's presidential candidacy. And he worked closely with New York Democrats during the secession winter, but whether he was in Washington for the Peace Convention in late February is uncertain (68–69). He probably received the account second hand. The indispensable book on the convention, Gunderson, *Old Gentlemen's Club,* 148, notes how "highly realistic reconstructions" tempt historians to rely on the "Public Man" but observes that it "has been rejected as a valid source even for details about dress and weather." Johannsen, *SAD,* 962, advises that the memoir be used "where collaborative evidence is available." In this case, the memoirist's description of Douglas's mood and lack of clarity ring true; nevertheless, readers should be aware of doubts about the source.

[29] Holzer, *Lincoln President-Elect,* 438.

[30] CG, 36th Cong., 2nd sess. (Mar. 2, 1861), 1433; *Journal of the Senate,* 36th Cong., 2nd sess. (Mar. 2, 1861), 398.

[31] The twentieth amendment, ratified in 1933, required Congress to begin a session every year on January 3, which meant that it would be in regular session when the new president was inaugurated on January 20.

[32] For the quote and scene in the Senate, see USN, *New York Herald,* Mar. 5, 1861. For the text, see Gunderson, *Old Gentlemen's Convention,* 107–109, and for the Senate debate, 94–95. For the time of the vote, see USN, *Boston Daily Advertiser,* Mar. 5, 1861.

[33] According to the diagram of the Committee of Arrangements, Senators were seated in a semicircle immediately behind the president and president-elect. Arrangements for the inauguration of the president of the United States on the Fourth of March, 1861 ... Committee of arrangements. [Washington, 1861], http://memory.loc.gov/ammem/rbpehtml.

heard signifying his approval by murmuring sotto voce, "Good," "That's so," "No coercion," and "Good again" as the president spoke.[34] Whether or not he actually held Lincoln's hat, on the inauguration platform Douglas was eager to make visible his rapport with the new administration and at the same time make clear that he remained an important player.

Interest in what Lincoln said could not have been greater. Since the inception of the secession crisis in December, the president-elect had made clear his opposition to any compromise that would expand the possibility of slavery in federal territory. He had done so in private, usually in letters marked "confidential" to key allies, although he had known his determination against concession in the face of secession would be reported.[35] His public silence, however, in the midst of continuous, highly publicized compromise efforts, enormously heightened the importance of his inaugural address. What did the new president intend to do about the seven states that had seceded?

Not only was Douglas among the first on the platform to congratulate Lincoln, he immediately responded to two questioners regarding Lincoln's meaning. To the first, he indicated his satisfaction that Lincoln did not intend to use force to retake federal property seized by the South. To the second, he reiterated this explanation but conceded, "The address is susceptible of a double construction."[36] Being treated as someone who could translate the president's intentions did not make Douglas uncomfortable; rather he relished the role.

Afterward Douglas's intimacy with the new president was on public display at the inauguration ball, which he attended with his wife and in-laws. He danced with Mary Lincoln, earning a paragraph of attention in the *New York Herald*, which reported overhearing that Douglas was a "better match" for Mary, probably because they were "nearly the same height and proportions."[37] How Mary reacted to the luminescent Adele Douglas, who stole the limelight according to the *Herald*, is not recorded.[38] More important, for the first time in their relationship the two partisan rivals were becoming a political match, nearly in agreement on the major issue before the country – nearly but not

No coverage the next day of the inauguration included Douglas holding Lincoln's hat, but several newspapers reported the incident in the next two to three weeks. USN, *Daily Cleveland Herald*, Mar. 13, 1861; USN, *Lowell Daily Citizen and News* (Lowell, MA), Mar. 18, 1861; *New York Herald*, Mar. 22, 1861. The authenticity of the incident has been questioned. See Crofts, *Secession Crisis Enigma*, 112.

34 ProQuest, *New York Times*, Mar. 5, 1861. The journalist for the *New York Times* later claimed it was his "good-fortune to stand by Mr. Douglas during the reading of the Inaugural of President Lincoln." Joseph Howard, Jr., "Reminiscences of Stephen A. Douglas," *Atlantic Monthly*, 8 (Aug. 1861), 211–212.

35 Holzer, *Lincoln President-Elect*, 155–159, 223, 241.

36 Ibid.

37 USN, *New York Herald*, Mar. 6, 1861, reported that Douglas escorted her to the ball, but ProQuest, *New York Times*, Mar. 5, 1861, indicated only that they danced a quadrille, which is what Jean H. Baker, *Mary Todd Lincoln: A Biography* (New York, 1987), 179, concludes.

38 Johannsen, *SAD*, 845; USN, *New York Herald*, Mar. 10, 1861.

exactly. Each was ready to use the other: Douglas wanted to be in the president's inner circle; Lincoln wanted the Democratic standard bearer to broaden support against secession.[39]

Douglas took advantage of their mutual need in order to convey the impression that he was more intimate with the president than he actually was. A Massachusetts newspaper had it right: "Mr. Douglas has been so long in the habit of playing the leader in public affairs that he finds it not easy to adapt himself to the altered circumstances which political changes have wrought." The editor applauded him for his "courtesy and magnanimity" in volunteering to hold Lincoln's hat on Inauguration Day but was upset at how Douglas, a Democratic member of the U.S. Senate, appeared to speak for the new Republican president and cabinet.[40]

Douglas's relationship to Lincoln became an issue almost immediately after the inauguration. On March 6 a normal motion to print the inaugural address opened a debate in the special session on its meaning. A new North Carolina senator stated that Lincoln spoke "as though the acts of secession were mere nullities." Further, his aim to retain control of forts and arsenals in those states was tantamount to a policy of war. Douglas was the first to respond. He said his careful reading of the address led him to conclude that "it is a peace-offering rather than a war message." And he proceeded to a lawyer-like exegesis of the text to demonstrate his thesis that Lincoln intended to enforce revenue laws and to regain control of federal property without military coercion. He found "much cause for hope, for encouragement, in this inaugural." At no point did Douglas imply that anything other than the president's words, which everyone could read, influenced his interpretation.[41]

On March 7 Louis Wigfall (D-TX) noted that no Republican had risen to reaffirm Douglas's explanation of the inaugural address. Moreover, as if to deflate the grandiose expectations of colleagues, the Texan cautioned, "It is impossible for the Senator from Illinois, or for any other Senator to rise here, and by giving a commentary – a construction of the inaugural – to restore peace to the country."[42] Only presidential action could restore peace, not the "masterly inactivity" ascribed to the president by Douglas, who had no authority to speak for him. Although he denied any such authority, Douglas confidently stated that peace was the only option for the administration because it did not have sufficient troops to supply Fort Sumter before it ran out of food in "thirty-one days." Did he have secret information? Douglas asserted that he occupied "no such relation" to the president that gave him "any more

[39] On Lincoln's intimacy with Douglas and the possibility that he might be asked to join the cabinet, see Egerton, *Year of Meteors*, 329.

[40] EAN, *Lowell Daily Citizen and News* (Lowell, MA), Mar. 18, 1861.

[41] CG, 37th Cong., Special Session (Mar. 6, 1861), 1436–1438. Thomas Clingman of North Carolina was newly elected (1433).

[42] Ibid., 1439.

knowledge of his purposes and views than every other Senator can derive from reading the inaugural address."[43]

Douglas's performance in late February and early March could not have been more sure-footed in contrast to his performance in January, when he second-guessed himself for sacrificing popular sovereignty on the altar of sectional compromise. Although he gained kudos for his collaboration with Crittenden, his work during the first two months of the Thirty-Sixth Congress had been stumbling, as his oratory lacked eloquence or persuasion. He was not instrumental in organizing the Peace Convention, but he did co-host with Adele some four hundred delegates, wives, and congressmen eight days after it convened.[44] His role at the convention did not become noteworthy, however, until Lincoln arrived in Washington. Douglas's access to the president-elect's suite made him a major player in the last days of the convention. Similarly his interaction with the Lincolns on Inauguration Day raised his stature in the special session of the Senate, which was the first gathering of the Thirty-Seventh Congress. This meant that newly elected senators were introduced to Douglas as the Democrat who was closest to the new president.

In defending the inaugural address as a peace offering and disclaiming any inside information, Douglas shrewdly presented himself as the old friend, not rival, whose discretion the president could trust and whose analytical skills could be utilized. At the same time, he made clear that his support was conditional and limited: as long as the president pursued peace Douglas was with him; however, on matters unrelated to the preservation of the Union he expected to oppose the administration.[45] Thus he displayed himself to be a valuable presidential ally, a potential confidant, yet an independent Democratic leader and still a dexterous debater. Lincoln's receptivity to him was critical to his standing now, empowering Douglas to recover psychologically and politically from the December–January aftereffect of the presidential election.

Why Lincoln gave Douglas such access is a matter of speculation. Certainly it was beneficial to have a major Democratic figure on his side, although there was a risk that he might be elevating someone who could create mischief for

---

[43] Ibid., 1442. McClintock, *Lincoln and the Decision for War*, 212, believes that Secretary of State William Seward leaked the information to Douglas and that both men wanted the president to order the federal garrison at Fort Sumter to withdraw. Ironically on the day after Douglas spoke, the commander of Fort Sumter wrote to a former Massachusetts congressman that the fort's provisions would not last "many weeks longer." "From the Archives: A Letter Written to Robert C. Winthrop from Fort Sumter," *Massachusetts Historical Society Newsletter*, Mar. 7, 2011.

[44] Gunderson, *Old Gentlemen's Convention*, 58.

[45] CG, 37th Cong., Special Session (Mar. 7, 1861), 1442, (Mar. 6, 1861), 1438. Wigfall poked fun at Douglas's disclaimer regarding his influence with the administration. He asked "whether, as he is speaking for the Administration, though not a part of it, and, I suppose, contrary to what Aeneas said, *magna pars fui* – though not a part of it, nor a large part of it, (laughter) – as he seems to be speaking for the Administration.... " Wigfall questioned whether he recommended the withdrawal of troops from the two forts, the removal of the U.S. flag from borders of the Confederate states, and against collecting taxes on "a foreign people" (1442).

him at a crucial moment. Another motive may have been a variation of scha-denfreude – the satisfaction of being the top dog in the presence of a longtime rival. What could signify his triumph more than having Douglas hold his hat during his inauguration ceremony? Or Lincoln might have felt some genuine empathy for Douglas because he knew how hard political disappointment could be. After all, he had withdrawn from politics altogether for five years after leaving Congress in 1849 and failing to obtain a desirable post from the Whig administration. Whatever Lincoln's motivation, his willingness to provide Douglas with a measure of entrée was balm to the man he finally had surpassed. Lincoln enabled Douglas to regain his self-esteem as a Washington player.

Douglas also saw Lincoln after Inauguration Day, but how often is unknown. The Republicans in the Senate did not take the rapprochement between the two men too seriously. They neither confirmed nor denied Douglas's interpretation of the inaugural address as a peace message. When they remained "mute and silent, neither assenting nor dissenting" regarding his interpretation of the president's peaceful intentions, he introduced a resolution to "quiet the apprehensions of the country" by demonstrating that the president did not contemplate war and that he had no means of prosecuting one even if he wanted to do so.[46] It called on the secretary of war to inform the Senate as to (1) the status of all forts and public works in the seven seceding states, (2) whether the federal government had sufficient "power and means" to reinforce them, (3) what plans there were for recapturing any that had been seized, and (4) what military force would be necessary to restored the seceding states to the Union.[47]

The resolution was tabled and Douglas was unable to obtain the information or smoke out a Republican policy commitment.[48] Despite his lack of success, his performance in his last session as a senator was impressive. He had regained his forensic power. He argued on March 26 that, whatever they might say, the Republicans by their votes had abandoned the Wilmot Proviso and the "doctrine of the congressional prohibition of slavery;" instead they had "applied the principle of non-intervention and popular sovereignty to all our territory."[49] He was thinking of three territories Congress organized in February without mentioning slavery.[50] Accordingly, he claimed that the South had gained even more than what the Crittenden amendment would have ensured, protection of slavery below the 36°30′ line.[51] Here was Douglas reestablishing his faith in local self-determination and reaffirming his constitutional philosophy in a bid to bridge the sectional gulf. This was not the Douglas who had embarrassed himself four months earlier.

---

[46] Ibid., 1457.
[47] Ibid., 1452–1453.
[48] Ibid., 1511; Johannsen, *SAD*, 849–851.
[49] CG, 37th Cong., Special Session (Mar. 26, 1861), 1508, 1510.
[50] Colorado, Nebraska, and Nevada. Eric Foner, *The Fiery Trial: Abraham Lincoln and American Slavery* (New York, 2010), 154.
[51] CG, 37th Cong., Special Session, 1509.

On the very last day of the session, he was the Democratic point man in a debate over a Republican senator's call for an investigation of persons on the chamber's payroll who were not performing appropriate services. Douglas replied that this was a typical charge by the new majority party determined to remove abuses it suspected when it was in the minority. He cautioned that a general indictment of Senate employees was unfair and reflected a lack of specific knowledge. Its purpose was to impute a cover-up, which he denied. "I do not hesitate to declare my conviction that there never has been a time in this body, no matter what party was in power, when it would have sanctioned an abuse of that kind, or concealed it a moment after it had been called to his attention."[52] In his last substantial remarks as a senator, then, Douglas defended the honor of the chamber in which he had long been a dominant voice and credited both major parties with an intolerance of wrongdoing.

Douglas was disappointed that Lincoln and his allies in the Senate had not backed up his effort to assure the South of the administration's commitment to peace. At the same time he remained steady in supporting the president in his commitment to preserve the Union by force if necessary. Despite his crusade for reconciliation, he never renounced the comments he had made in Norfolk the previous summer, when he endorsed the example of Jackson's threat of coercion to suppress nullification. Nevertheless, by the end of the special session, as Russell McClintock suggests, Douglas may well have considered the political separation of the North and South to be permanent, for he discussed the possibility of an alternative commercial union.[53] If he did resign himself to the irreparability of secession, he did so only temporarily. When he learned that the president rejected the evacuation of Fort Sumter and decided to provision it, Douglas crossed the Rubicon with Lincoln.[54]

On April 14, when the federal garrison surrendered Fort Sumter after two days of Confederate bombardment, a Massachusetts Republican prevailed upon Douglas to visit the White House in a demonstration of bipartisan unity. Douglas went. His two-hour meeting was reported the next day in stories about the surrender. He ensured coverage with his own press release. Although he remained "unalterably opposed to the administration on all its political issues," Douglas assured Lincoln that "he was prepared to sustain the President in the exercise of all his constitutional functions to preserve the Union, and maintain the government, and defend the Federal Capital." He urged firmness and "prompt action."[55]

He met with Lincoln again later in the week to explain why he was returning to their home state. The Illinois legislature was scheduled to convene a

[52] Ibid., 1524.

[53] McClintock, *Lincoln and the Decision for War*, 238–239. On his discussion of a North American Zollverein, see Johannsen, *SAD*, 852–854.

[54] Johannsen, *SAD*, 859–869.

[55] "Statement," *Letters of SAD*, 509–510; USN, *Boston Daily Advertiser*, Apr. 15, 1861; *North American and United States Gazette* (Philadelphia), Apr. 15, 1861.

special session on April 23, and Douglas said he wanted to attend in order to rally support for the Union cause. He and Adele left Washington together for the last time on April 19. Their train ride west was a mini-version of the campaign tour. In Wheeling, Virginia, Columbus, Ohio, and Indianapolis, Indiana, he called for the defense of the federal government and the "re-establishment of the Union."[56]

The climax came in Springfield, Illinois on April 25. Upon his arrival the legislature adopted a joint resolution inviting him to address an assembly of both houses that evening. He did not need advance preparation, for he had honed his thoughts in speeches en route to his home state. Upon entering Representative Hall, where nearly five hundred Republicans had cheered Lincoln's victory on election night, Douglas now received a frenzied ovation from an equally packed chamber.[57] His post-inaugural relationship with Lincoln had become in fact a rallying cry for unity in the North and a special source of pride in Illinois. As in his best days, he knew what to say.[58]

He appealed to Republicans and Democrats separately. To the former, "whom I have opposed and warred against with an energy you will respect," he pleaded that they not make "partisan capital out of the misfortune of your country." To his Democratic friends, who believed that the elevation of the Republicans to power was "dangerous to the country," he urged that they not be converted from "patriots into traitors to your native land." And he made clear that patriotism would require men "to rally to the tented field, leaving wife, child, father, and mother behind them to rush to the rescue of the President." Indeed, the more unanimous the support and preparation for war, he believed, "the less blood will be shed" and the faster peace would be restored. Despite the tremendous applause this prediction elicited, he was of course wrong.

From a personal perspective, Douglas's speech in Springfield was as important as his remarks in Brandon the previous July, when he made peace with his native Vermont over his emigration as a young man. Since his arrival, Illinois had always made him feel good about himself. Despite the outbreak of a war he had desperately tried to avert, he was at peace with himself. What has been overlooked in the coverage of his speech was his sense of having triumphed on the question of federal regulation of slavery in the territories. He denounced the "alleged cause" of the Southern "war of aggression" against the federal government – that Southern institutions were not safe under it. He declared, "For the first time in the history of this Republic, there is no restriction by act of Congress upon the institution of slavery any where within the limits of the United States." He was too smart to arouse old antagonisms by reminding his audience that this was the case because of his Kansas–Nebraska Act and the *Dred Scott* decision. He might have illustrated his point by repeating what he

---

[56] Johannsen, *SAD*, 863–864; Milton, *Eve of the Conflict*, 564–565.
[57] Holzer, *Lincoln President-Elect*, 32; Johannsen, *SAD*, 865.
[58] The Republican paper in his hometown published the full speech as a tribute after he died. *Chicago Tribune*, June 6, 1861.

had said in Congress, that Minnesota, Oregon, and Kansas had most recently been admitted as free states, not because of congressional prohibitions, but rather because of the choice of territorial inhabitants. Despite Lincoln's election, congressional noninterference and popular sovereignty governed federal territories.

During the presidential campaign, he had assured Southerners that if President Lincoln acted unconstitutionally against Southern institutions, he would move harshly against him. It was the South, however, not the president, that was now acting against the Constitution. And Douglas was with Lincoln. In fact, four days after his speech he wrote the president a brief letter, delivered by James M. Cutts, Jr., that served two classic Douglas purposes. The first was to reintroduce his brother-in-law to the president. Adele's younger brother had become the senator's worshipful protégé whom he sought to advance. The second was to remind Lincoln how important Douglas could still be to him. Emboldened by the response to his statehouse speech, Douglas wrote that he "found the state of feeling" in Illinois unsatisfactory but hoped "in a few days ... for entire unanimity in the support of the government and the Union."[59] The implication was unmistakable: Douglas would bring about the unanimity of his home state. And he believed he had the rhetorical power to achieve it.

Two days after writing the president, Douglas returned to a hero's welcome in Chicago. The magnitude of the reception was comparable to what he had experienced in his home city during the campaign eight months earlier. This time, however, both Republican and Democrats hailed him. The major Republican daily reported that "not less than ten thousand persons" jammed National Hall to give Douglas a "magnificent and patriotic ovation."[60] Douglas reiterated that "now for the first time there is no act of Congress prohibiting slavery anywhere." The secessionist movement was a long-planned conspiracy that used the slavery question and Lincoln's election merely as an excuse for its cause. The result was that war had come and there was no middle position for anyone. The man who had professed moral neutrality regarding slavery when he campaigned for the Senate declared what he always believed about the Union: "There are only two sides to the question. Every man must be for the United States or against it. There can be no neutrals in this war, *only patriots – or traitors.*"[61]

What no one knew was that while he spoke he was beset by the beginnings of his final illness. He planned to return to Washington after a short visit but decided to rest a few days because of what at first he thought was a cold. He would not leave Chicago again. The progression of his affliction through May and early June was similar to that of his nearly fatal bout with "inflamitory [sic] bilious fever" and "rheumatism" at age twenty, when he

---

[59] Stephen A. Douglas to Abraham Lincoln, Apr. 29, 1861, *Letters of SAD*, 511.
[60] *Chicago Tribune*, May 2, 1861. Its coverage of his campaign the preceding year minimized the size of his crowds and their response.
[61] For his full speech, see *Chicago Tribune*, May 2, 1861.

experienced alternating moments of severity and recovery.[62] It is probable that the earlier episode compromised him permanently, ultimately contributing to the acute rheumatism diagnosed as the cause of his death on June 3 at the age of forty-eight.[63] Had his body been transported to Washington for burial next to his deceased infant daughter, as his widow wanted, the president would have attended and undoubtedly would have doffed the hat that his old rival had held for him three months earlier. Adele Douglas, however, relented when fourteen politicians in the state capital wired the mayor of Chicago to prevent the senator's remains from leaving Illinois: because his life had "been so closely identified with the interests of the State," he should not be separated from it in death.[64]

Had Douglas recovered, he would have remained the leading war Democrat in the Senate. He would have supported the landmark Homestead and Pacific Railway Acts of 1862, for he had long championed the provision of free public land to settlers and the construction of a transcontinental railroad that would bring them west. As the slavery question became more central to the Union effort, however, he and Lincoln would have recapitulated their underlying differences. In the spring of 1862 he would have joined most Northern Democrats in opposing the bill that ended slavery in the nation's capital. He would have justified his opposition on the ground that the local government was against emancipation, although there was no provision for inhabitants of the district to vote on the matter.[65] Douglas also would have been concerned for what this expansion of federal power over slavery portended for the future. August Belmont, his former campaign manager, in fact reflected Douglas's view when he urged the president to assure the South that "we are fighting only for the Union," not to transform Southern society by abolitionism.[66] Belmont and other Democratic Party leaders had prepared to run Douglas again in 1864, and Lincoln's policies may well have provoked the "Little Giant" to do so.[67]

Perhaps what would have been the hardest legislation for Douglas to accept was a bill to abolish slavery in all federal territories, which Congress passed in

---

[62] See Chapter 3.

[63] Johannsen, *SAD*, 871.

[64] *Chicago Tribune*, June 4, 1861; Johannsen, *SAD*, 870–874; [Paul Angle], "Death of a Patriot," *Chicago History*, 6:3 (Spring 1961), 77–81. I am grateful to John Hoffman for sending me a copy and informing me of Angle's authorship.

[65] On the partisan breakdown and Lincoln's signing, see Foner, *Fiery Trial*, 198–199. On the position of the mayor and council, see Constance M. Green, *Washington: A History of the Capital, 1800–1950* (Princeton, NJ, 1962), 275–276.

[66] Irving Katz, *August Belmont: A Political Biography* (New York, 1968), 111; Foner, *Fiery Trial*, 210; Jean H. Baker, *Affairs of Party: The Political Culture of Northern Democrats in the Mid-Nineteenth-Century* (Ithaca, NY, 1983), 152–153. Baker claims that "there is no way of knowing what the Little Giant would have said about emancipation and freedom" (196). I believe we can credibly infer it. Gary W. Gallagher, *The Union War* (Cambridge, MA., 2011) argues persuasively that preservation of the Union, not emancipation, was the driving motivation of Northerners during the Civil War.

[67] On the movement to run Douglas again, see Baker, *Affairs of Party*, 281.

June 1862.[68] Although Democrats in both chambers voted against it and newspapers reported it, the measure was passed with comparatively little debate and fanfare. This quietude would not have prevailed had Douglas still been there. As a Boston editorial put it, under normal circumstances the act "would have been noted as one of the great landmarks in our history."[69] For Douglas, this legislation would have marked the end of his long campaign to establish popular sovereignty as the rule for territories; moreover, he would have condemned it for leading to federal emancipation of slavery in Southern states, although he would not have expected that to occur as a result of a presidential edict. The commander in chief who asserted the authority to free slaves in rebel states was far removed from the Lincoln whose hat Douglas held on Inauguration Day. How the two men would have interacted after the Emancipation Proclamation, however, is a matter for the fictional, not the historical, imagination.

Lincoln survived Douglas by only four years, but in that short span he laid lasting claim to the greatness that their contemporaries had heralded for his younger rival since the 1830s. In contrast, Douglas would be remembered for pursuing greatness by appeasing the South and refusing to face up to the immorality of slavery. The long consistency of his commitment to state and territorial self-determination within an indissoluble Union should shield him from the unfair charge of opportunism, but his equally consistent effort to push slavery from the national agenda ran against the current of American history and leaves him consigned to a shadowy place in our collective memory of the antebellum period. His direct involvement with slavery darkens his place even more.

---

[68] *U.S. Statutes at Large*, 37th Cong., 2nd sess. (June 19, 1862), 432.
[69] USN, *Boston Daily Advertiser*, June 23, 1862. On the partisan alignment, see Foner, *Fiery Trial*, 203.

9

Douglas's Mississippi Slaves

> They all live in good framed houses with two rooms in each & a Porch or Veranda on the front & rear of each its whole length, with glass windows and good floors, perfectly dry and far above the water.
>
> Stephen A. Douglas (1859)[1]

After Douglas's namesake younger son reached his majority in November 1871, he and his older brother, Robert, petitioned Congress "for compensation for their private cotton and other property, taken and used by a portion of the army of the United States."[2] Their claim was for damages sustained at their plantation in Washington County, Mississippi, in March 1863, when they were still minors living in the North and "had no communication with the South."[3] Represented by their uncle, James Madison Cutts, Jr., a Medal of Honor veteran of the Union army, they stated that the cotton plantation had been "one of the largest and most productive in the State of Mississippi," and they submitted a claim for $250,000.[4] They noted that they had been the "sole owners of a large number of slaves" and that their father, as their guardian and the executor of their maternal grandfather's estate, had formed a partnership

---

[1] Stephen A. Douglas to Adele Douglas, May 28, 1859, SAD Papers, UC, Additional Papers, 4:31.

[2] Ironically the Union general who led the Seventeenth Illinois Brigade onto the Douglas plantation was Brigadier General T. T. G. Ransom, who was born and raised in Vermont before leaving to establish himself on his own in Chicago. "Gen. W. T. Sherman's Address on the Life and Services of Gen. T. E. Ransom," *National Tribune* (Washington, DC), July 10, 1884.

[3] Articles of Agreement between Stephen A. Douglas and James A. McHatton, May 31, 1859, Record Group 123, Records of the United States Court of Claims, General Jurisdiction Case File No. 9192, 6–7; *Claim of Rob't M. and Stephen A. Douglas of Rockingham County, North Carolina, for their Private Cotton and Other Property Taken, Used, and Appropriated, in March 1863, in Washington County, Mississippi ... (Washington, DC, 1872)*, 7.

[4] *Claim of Rob't M. and Stephen A. Douglas*, 7–8, 57. On Cutts's military service, see Bing G. Spitler, *Hero of the Republic: The Biography of Triple Medal of Honor Winner, James Madison Cutts, Jr.* (Shippensburg, PA, 2001). On his relationship to his brother-in-law and nephews, see Chapter 3.

to which he brought 142 slaves valued at $113,300, 32 mules at $4,000, and 20 horses at $500.[5]

Both Robert and Stephen Douglas were living in North Carolina when they submitted this petition. After their father died, they had remained under the care of their stepmother, Adele, in Washington. She went to the executive mansion to seek the president's advice. She told him that she was being urged to send her sons south to avoid the confiscation of their property there. Lincoln counseled her not to do so and not to mention his expectation that the property of minor children would not be seized. If his involvement with her were known, he thought the secessionists would certainly "do the worst they can against the children."[6] During the winter of 1864–1865 at a dinner party, Adele met an old flame, Adjutant General Robert Williams, who had courted her before she married Stephen. They married in 1866 and began a new family, which eventually moved with Williams, a career officer, from army post to post.[7] The Douglas brothers did not go with the Williams family after it left Washington. Robert and Stephen studied at Georgetown University and relocated to North Carolina to be close to the surviving relatives of their mother, Martha.[8]

The Douglas sons remained faithful to their father's story regarding his relationship to the family's slaves. They stated in their petition that he had acted "in their best interests" as executor of the estate and their guardian. They, not he, had owned slaves. The implication was clear: since they had been minors and since their father had acted only in a fiduciary capacity, none of them could be held responsible for their involvement with the institution. They therefore echoed what Douglas had maintained from the moment that his first wife, Martha, had died.

To assess the validity of the Douglas version we need to review the history of his connection to slaves in Mississippi. Douglas's direct involvement was a legacy of his first marriage in 1847. His father-in-law, Colonel Robert Martin, presented him a deed to Pearl River plantation. Douglas declined the wedding gift. When Martin died a year later, he bequeathed the plantation to his daughter Martha and her issue with a provision that explicitly recognized her husband's unwillingness to own "this kind of property." Instead Martin provided that Douglas would receive one-third of the profits for managing the

---

[5] Articles of Agreement between Douglas and McHatton, 4–5.

[6] "Memorandum: Advice to Mrs. Stephen A. Douglas," CWAL, 5: 32.

[7] "Gen. Robert Williams Dead," *New York Times*, Aug. 26, 1901. According to this story, Williams courted Adele while he was still a cadet at West Point, from which he graduated in 1851, when she would have been only fifteen or sixteen. Williams was thirty-six and Adele thirty when they married. She died in 1899 at the age of sixty-four, and he remained a widower. They had three sons and three daughters. See also Virginia T. Peacock, *Famous American Belles of the Nineteenth-Century* (Philadelphia, 1901), 186–188.

[8] The brothers were both residents of North Carolina when they submitted their petition. *Claim of Rob't M. and Stephen A. Douglas,* 1. Robert stayed and became a state judge, while Stephen moved to Chicago, where he practiced law. Biographical Note, SAD Papers, UC.

plantation, a responsibility that he accepted while ignoring that slave labor would be the source of this income.[9]

From the outset Douglas felt enormous ambivalence about his relationship to the plantation. As Anita Clinton finds, Douglas limited his direct contact with James Strickland, the man who actually managed the property for him as he had for his father-in-law. Strickland would write multiple letters seeking instructions on the same matter – purchasing land or more slaves, answering a lawsuit, or arranging a right of way with a neighbor. Strickland wrote Douglas about the same issues repeatedly, but despite his pleas, Douglas did not visit nor did he respond promptly, if at all.[10] The man who was tireless as a campaigner, party organizer, legislator, stump speaker, and political correspondent was not equally diligent about his oversight of the eponymous Martinsville plantation. His economic interest was subordinate to his political and psychological need to distance himself from the Mississippi holdings. Had he been as dilatory about what mattered most to him, he would not have been where he was on the national stage.

Only on a few occasions over the years did Douglas's adversaries bring up his connection to plantation slavery either in the press or in Congress. While Martha was still alive, he denied his ownership of the slaves and noted that under Mississippi law a married woman held her own separate estate, not subject to her husband's control, disposal, or debts.[11] When she died in 1853, Douglas became executor of her estate and guardian of their minor children. This made his relationship to the slaves closer because now only he was in charge of them, although he continued to present himself as being at an arm's length from the institution.

He admitted that the abolition press and some "stump orators" called him "one of the largest slaveholders in America," but he claimed to treat this charge normally with "silent contempt."[12] He did respond, however, when his personal motive was questioned on the Senate floor regarding his support in 1855 for a bill that would have enabled fugitive slave litigation to be transferred from state to federal courts in order to overcome Northern opposition to enforcement of the law. Benjamin Wade (W-OH) asked why a Northern man volunteered to be the advocate for the South. "Why is it? What is the reason for it? Have the

---

[9] Martin executed separate wills in North Carolina (November 23, 1847) and Mississippi (February 12, 1848). By the first, Douglas was to receive an annual fee of 20%; by the second, 33⅓%. Anita W. Clinton, "Stephen Douglas: His Mississippi Experience," *Journal of Mississippi History*, 50:2 (1988), 59.

[10] Ibid., 62–70.

[11] Stephen A. Douglas to Charles Lanphier, Aug. 3, 1850, *Letters of SAD*, 189–191. On the establishment of separate estates on married women in one slaveholding colony and state, see the pathbreaking study by Marylynn Salmon, "Women and Property in South Carolina: The Evidence from Marriage Settlements, 1730–1830," *William and Mary Quarterly*, 3rd ser., 39:4 (1982), 655–685.

[12] CG, APP, 33rd Cong., 2nd sess. (Feb. 23, 1855), 330.

people of Illinois forgotten that injunction of more than heavenly wisdom, that 'Where a man's treasure is, there will his heart be also.' "[13]

Douglas did not reply immediately. In fact, he retained his speech for revision before releasing it a few days later for publication in the *Congressional Globe*. He claimed, "I am not the owner of a slave and never have been, nor have I ever received, and appropriated to my own use, one dollar earned by slave labor." He proceeded to review the story of his involvement in an egregiously self-serving manner. He had refused the original gift from his father-in-law not because of any sympathy with abolitionism but because, as a lifelong Northerner, he lacked the knowledge or understanding to "provide for the wants, comforts, and happiness of those people." He was now responsible for the happiness of his "motherless children," an obligation that was strengthened by his "venera-tion" for the memory of their "sainted mother." He viewed his management of the bequeathed property in their behalf as a "domestic trust" to be performed with "fidelity and disinterestedness" and considered himself not "purer or bet-ter than his she [his wife], or they, who are, slaveholders." He did not see him-self as a slaveholder, only as a trustee of his young sons. This distinction was critical for him. "God forbid that I should be understood by anyone as being willing to cast from me any responsibility that now does, or ever has attached to any member of my family." He managed the plantation and slaves because of family duties, not for personal gain. He offered this explanation, he said, to demonstrate "the purity of my motives in the performance of a high public trust." He did so "with extreme reluctance," however, because he believed that his "private and domestic affairs ... ought to be permitted to remain private and sacred."[14]

Yet he sent a copy of the speech to a friendly newspaper editor with the advice, "It will be well to publish."[15] Five years later the editor printed this portion of the speech in a campaign biography of Douglas without mention-ing how Douglas had managed the property after Martha died.[16] Nor did the author note that in 1857 Douglas sold the Pearl River land and on behalf of his sons entered a partnership in a cotton plantation near the Mississippi River, where he transferred the slaves.[17]

In their famous debates of 1858, Lincoln did not mention his rival's involve-ment with slave labor, although he certainly was aware of it. A few weeks before the fall election that would determine their senatorial contest, the pro-Lincoln *Chicago Press and Tribune* charged that slaves Douglas "held in Louisiana" were "badly fed, badly clothed, and excessively overworked."[18] The

---

[13] Ibid., 222. The Fugitive Slave Law of 1850 gave jurisdiction to state and territorial courts. *U.S. Statutes at Large*, 31st Cong., 1st sess., 462–465.

[14] CG, APP, 33rd Cong., 2nd sess. (Feb. 23, 1855), 227, 330–331.

[15] Stephen A. Douglas to James W. Sheahan, Mar. 10, 1855, *Letters of SAD*, 335.

[16] James W. Sheahan, *The Life of Stephen A. Douglas* (New York, 1860), 437–439.

[17] Johannsen, *SAD*, 337–338; *Letters of SAD*, 509n.

[18] *Chicago Press and Tribune*, as quoted in USN, *The Liberator* (Boston), Nov. 12, 1858.

story received only a smattering of coverage nationally. A New Orleans newspaper dismissed it as an "election canard" and focused on the reliability of the Republican paper's information, which turned out to be some second-hand remarks reported to the editor by a local medical professor. More attention was given to the identity of and eventual denial by the putative source, Senator John Slidell (D-LA), than to the actual conditions of the slaves.[19] No newspaper had the resources or interest to travel to investigate conditions independently. While some newspapers picked up the story, it is striking that none used it to comment on a possible link between Douglas's policies and his slaves.[20]

Douglas did not like to acknowledge his association with slavery and did so only when he felt he had to clarify his role. During the mini-controversy regarding the *Tribune* article, in a letter to a Washington newspaper he conceded, "[A]s the guardian of my children, I hold myself responsible for the manner in which these slaves are treated." He highlighted Slidell's repudiation of both the charge and his authorship of it.[21] Douglas was so hesitant to discuss his slaves that he failed to point out the mistaken location in the *Tribune* account. The Douglas plantation was in Mississippi, not Louisiana. The lawyer who had won cases on such technicalities did not want to draw more attention than necessary to the slave property he controlled, even to undermine the story's credibility by pointing to the erroneous location. In fact, he had just completed a "southern pilgrimage" in an extended post-campaign trip that included a visit to his plantation, where he must have investigated the conditions of the slaves firsthand. Yet he remained silent about his Mississippi visits in speeches and letters, except in writing to his wife.[22]

Although the charge of slave mistreatment disappeared in the press, on May 1, 1859, a Mississippi merchant informed Mary Martin, the maternal grandmother of Douglas's sons, that the slaves on their plantation were "not half fed or clothed," that many had run away or died over the preceding sixteen months, and "that there is some ten or fifteen more that will die if there is not a change in management in a short time." The correspondent did not know how to convey his letter directly to Douglas but believed "it is verry [*sic*] important"

---

[19] James W. Sheahan, *The Life of Stephen A. Douglas* (New York, 1860), 439–442.

[20] "The Douglas Creed," USN, *Bangor Whig and Daily Courier* (Bangor, ME), Nov. 27, 1859, which said he was "proslavery" but nothing about his being a slave owner. USN, *New York Herald*, Dec. 3, 1858, simply noted that Douglas stopped in St. Louis "on his route to visit his plantation in the South." USN, *Vermont Watchman and State Journal* (Montpelier), Dec. 17, 1858, reported that his friends were worried that he was on his Southern tour to court Southern support openly but offers not a word about his planned visit to his plantation. John Slidell's letter in the *New York Herald*, Dec. 21, 1858, responded to the article that appeared in the *New Orleans Crescent* on Dec. 11.

[21] Stephen A. Douglas to the Editor of the Washington *States*, Jan, 7, 1859, *Letters of SAD*, 433–434.

[22] For his speech in Memphis on Nov. 31, 1858, see USN, *Vermont Patriot* (Montpelier), Dec. 24, 1858; his speech in New Orleans on Dec. 6, USN, *Daily Missouri Republican* (St. Louis), Dec. 18, 1858; *Daily National Intelligencer* (Washington, DC), Dec. 29, 1858. For the description of the trip as "his southern pilgrimage," USN, *New York Herald*, Dec. 6, 1858.

that he should "Get it."[23] Douglas got it. Before the end of the month, he was in Mississippi. He reported to Adele that the slaves were in better condition than those on any other plantation he had visited. He wrote, "They all live in good framed houses with two rooms in each & a Porch or Veranda on the front & rear of each its whole length, with glass windows and good floors, perfectly dry and far above the water."[24] One has to wonder how far his personal inspection went and on what evidence his report to his wife rested. At most he appears to have observed the slaves' quarters, but not their field labor. He gave no indication of having conducted an interview with any slave and he named none.

Nevertheless, three days after writing Adele, Douglas redrafted the partnership agreement that he had entered into in December 1857, which had transferred the slaves from a plantation on the Pearl River to one near the Mississippi. We do not have the original agreement, which Douglas probably tore up. We can surmise that key language in the later one had to do with the care of the slaves. The May 31, 1859, agreement "stipulated that they shall be well fled, well clothed, humanely treated, and kindly and properly cared for according to the laws of the State and the customs and usages of the best regulated plantations under the most kind and humane masters."[25]

The new agreement also stipulated that the overseer or manager of the plantation mail Douglas monthly a daily record of the condition of the slaves, including the names of those born and died, as well as those sick and absent from work with explanations. He also wanted a regular detailed account of the cotton production. His concern here was twofold. First, he wanted to make certain that the assurance he conveyed to his wife regarding the treatment of the slaves would be reinforced. If another accusation of maltreatment were made, at least he could claim that he had contractually obliged his plantation manager to the humane care of the slaves. Second, as he indicated to Adele, he was worried about his finances and wanted a better accounting of the workings of the plantation than evidently he had been receiving.[26] He would write more directly about his personal financial interest in the slave operation only after his run for the presidency when he begged his partner to advance him some money.[27]

In Douglas's mind the fact that he was acting in a fiduciary capacity in behalf of the estate and his underage sons should have insulated him from the accusation that he personally owned or profited from slavery. He made that clear in

[23] J. J. Ligon to Mary Martin, May 1, 1859, in Clinton, "Stephen Douglas," 79–80. Clinton unearthed this important letter at what is now the Abraham Lincoln Presidential Library.

[24] Stephen A. Douglas to Adele Douglas, May 28, 1859, SAD Papers, UC, Additional Papers, 4:31.

[25] Articles of Agreement between Douglas and McHatton, 4–5. For a former domestic slave's painful description of conditions on a Mississippi cotton plantation, see Louis Hughes, *Thirty Years a Slave: From Bondage to Freedom* (Milwaukee, WI, 1897), 19–58.

[26] Stephen A. Douglas to Adele Douglas, May 28, 1859, SAD Papers, UC, Additional Papers, 4:31.

[27] Stephen A. Douglas to James A. McHatton, Apr. 4, 1861, *Letters of SAD*, 508–509.

the way he delineated his role in the Mississippi partnership. The first sentence stated that the agreement was "between Stephen Douglas, in his capacity as executor of the estate of Robert Martin deceased and guardian of his two sons (Robert M. Douglas and Stephen Douglas Jr.) who are the heirs at law of the said estate," and James McHatton. The Douglas interest was consistently referenced as "the party of the first part." This was more than a matter of legalese for him. He wanted to formalize his arm's-length distance from slavery.

Someone with the analytical skills of Abraham Lincoln could have placed Douglas on the defensive regarding his relationship to the Mississippi property. Yet during their debates Lincoln never broached the subject. Why? Did he fear that Douglas would counter with references to the slave-owning household in which Mary Lincoln was raised?[28] Or did he simply respect a taboo on discussing private matters? When Douglas characterized a politician's domestic interests as "private and sacred," he expressed an ethic that antebellum politicians generally observed. Benjamin Wade's insinuation pushed the boundary of congressional etiquette. The private interests and motives of senators were not subject to review.

Private matters are, of course, the stuff of biography. What do we make of Douglas's involvement with slavery? There is enough consistency in his politics and positions for us to understand why he believed that his stake in the institution did not influence his public role. Certainly his stand on territorial autonomy and his determination to remove slavery from national politics preceded his first marriage. He genuinely believed that his family's interest in the plantation did not affect his public stand. He so sacrificed his financial welfare in the pursuit of political goals that it would be difficult to suggest that his financial interests shaped his politics. He wrote plaintively of how he had neglected his "private business" in order to do his political business.[29] Often he would return from weeks or months of campaigning only to realize after the fact how much it had cost him financially.

Human motivation is very complex. Douglas was more self-deluded than duplicitous regarding his involvement with slavery. His politics were well established before he married Martha Martin. After they wed in December 1847, his involvement with slavery increased over time. From the outset he was entitled to a percentage of the net income from the plantation as a managerial fee. After Martha died, when he served as executor of the estate and guardian of his sons, his direct responsibilities for the property expanded. His options were limited. To sell the slaves would have violated the testamentary wishes of Colonel Martin, who wanted his daughter, if she were childless, to send the slaves to Liberia or another African colony, but if she bore children to retain

---

[28] Mary probably was wet-nursed by a slave, according to Jean H. Baker, *Mary Todd Lincoln: A Biography* (New York, 1987), 18. Her father, who died in 1849, opposed the slave trade as a state legislator but defended the institution, despite being called an abolitionist because his business partner was (66, 34).

[29] Stephen A. Douglas to Adele Cutts, Oct. 27, 1856, SAD Papers, UC, Additional Papers, 4:29.

the slaves because "nearly every head of a family among them has expressed a desire to belong to you and your children rather than go to Africa."[30] To emancipate the slaves also was not an option, for several reasons. First, it would have hurt Douglas politically. Just as accepting the slaves as a wedding gift would have been a liability to him in his own state in 1847, emancipating them after he became a national figure would have made him appear an abolitionist and destroyed his credibility with the South. Second, manumission in Mississippi was possible before 1857 but not easily accomplished, as evidenced by the fact that there were fewer than one thousand freedmen in a black population of approximately four hundred thousand by 1860.[31] Indeed, had Martha died childless, it is questionable whether Mississippi authorities would have permitted Douglas to honor his father-in-law's desire for the colonization of his slaves.[32] Third, as the fiduciary for his sons, he had a financial responsibility to preserve their assets. This third point was what he emphasized in depicting his interest.

As a fiduciary for his sons, Douglas was not prudent. The value of the Mississippi property was considerable. The partnership agreement appraised McHatton's contribution of 2,000 acres at $80,000. The Douglas interest was set "in the ratio of one hundred and eighteen to eighty (118 to 80)" (or 60 percent) for the duration of the partnership, which was to terminate upon Robert Douglas's twenty-first birthday. In 2003 the Douglas's share would have been worth about $2.6 million.[33] This does not include the value of the Martinsville land, some 3,000 acres, that Douglas sold in the process of relocating the slaves and livestock to Washington County. According to the testimony of his sons, who became enmeshed in lawsuits in the 1870s, Douglas was not a diligent steward of their financial interests. They claimed that he converted money that should have been preserved for them to his own use.[34] Yet, as noted earlier, in their petition to the U.S. Court of Claims they declared that he had acted in their best interest. He certainly did not intend to cheat his sons, and they knew it. His priority, however, was politics, not finances. A consistent, indefatigable, analytical politician, he was desultory, neglectful, and improvident generally in regard to his finances but most particularly toward his Mississippi property.

---

[30] George F. Milton, *The Eve of the Conflict: Stephen A. Douglas and the Needless War* (New York, 1834; reprinted 1969), 35n.

[31] James T. Currie, "From Slavery to Freedom in Mississippi's Legal System," *Journal of Negro History*, 65:2 (1980), 117; Dernoral Davis, "A Contested Presence: Free Blacks in Antebellum Mississippi, 1820–1860," *Mississippi History Now* (posted Aug. 2000). In 1822 the state legislature enacted a requirement that it approve cases of manumission.

[32] On the obstacles to manumission in the cotton South during the 1850s, see Ira Berlin, *Slaves Without Masters: The Free Negro in the Antebellum South* (New York, 1974), 138–149, esp. 139n re Mississippi laws.

[33] The conversion ratio for 2003 is from John J. McCusker's file, http://qrc.depaul.edu/Excel_Files/prices/McCusker.xls. For details regarding his methodology, see his *How Much Is That in Real Money? A Historical Price Index for Use as a Deflator of Money Values in the Economy of the United States*, 2nd ed. (Worcester, MA, 2001).

[34] Clinton, "Stephen Douglas," 85.

The one time he acted energetically and expeditiously was in March 1859 when he received a credible report that slaves under his watch were seriously abused. He rushed to Mississippi, reported to his wife, and redrafted his partnership agreement to require and ensure the humane treatment of the slaves. Whether he had a genuine concern for their welfare is impossible to determine.

Certainly Douglas's lack of a moral stance on slavery enabled him to participate in it. His belief in local autonomy was fundamental to him long before he met the slave owner's daughter. In insisting that he did not care how local majorities voted on the institution as long as they had the right to do so, he was not being disingenuous or hypocritical. Southerners who accused him of pushing "popular sovereignty" only when it resulted in freedom certainly did not believe that his interest in slaves shaped his politics.[35] Nevertheless, his lack of forthrightness regarding his interest in his Mississippi slaves is problematic and likely to be a cause for continuing criticism of his character.

What made his self-delusion regarding his personal distance from slavery possible was the ethos of antebellum democracy, which protected the private, domestic affairs of politicians. Just as few of the tens of thousands who met Stephen and Adele Douglas during the presidential campaign of 1860 knew that they had lost an eight-month-old daughter only weeks earlier, few knew that he had an active interest in a cotton plantation. Throughout his unprecedented campaign across the country, he never spoke about his slaves, and newspapers generally ignored the topic. Private matters were usually kept private, reinforcing the politician's belief that his public positions were based on principle.

Stephen Douglas's belief that states and territories should determine all of their domestic institutions derived from his development as a youth and young man – not from a later marital economic interest in slavery. What had more influence on his motivation was his precocious success as an attorney and politician in Illinois after fleeing from a prolonged preparation for a legal career in New York and a conflicted youth in Vermont. He knew emotionally that states were not the same, and he balked at the federal government attempting to homogenize the country with regard to slavery. The Democratic Party's commitment to resisting federal encroachments on state powers suited him psychologically, and his psychology reinforced his political thought. He was neither proslavery nor antislavery. Rather his policy on slavery was true to how he felt about respecting and nurturing the diversity of American life as determined by local white majorities. Whether a psychological underpinning for a politician's principles is more palatable than a material one, however, is an appraisal that each reader must make individually.

---

[35] David Zarefsky, "Lincoln and the House Divided: Launching a National Political Career," *Rhetoric & Public Affairs*, 13:3 (2010), 425.

Appendix

Douglas's Campaign Itinerary, 1860: June 23 to November 6

June 23	Washington, DC (June 23–30)
June 30	Washington, DC, to Philadelphia (June 30–July 1)
July 1	Philadelphia to New York City (July 1–14)
July 14	New York City to Guildford, CT (July 14–16)
July 16	Guildford to Hartford (July 16–17)
July 17	Hartford to Springfield, MA, to West Brookfield to Worcester to Framingham to Boston (July 17–20)
July 20	Boston to Springfield to Albany, NY (Sept. 20–21)
July 21	Albany to Saratoga (July 21–25)
July 25	Saratoga to Troy (July 25–27)
July 27	Troy to Saratoga (July 27–28)
July 28	Saratoga to Whitehall to Castleton, VT, to Rutland, to Brandon (July 28–30)
July 30	Brandon to Burlington to Montpelier (July 30–31)
July 31	Montpelier to Northfield to Roxbury to White River Junction to Franklin, NH to Webster Place to Fisherville to Concord (July 31–Aug. 1)
Aug. 1	Concord to Manchester to Nashua to Providence, RI (Aug. 1–2)
Aug. 2	Providence to Rocky Point to Providence to Newport (Aug. 2–14)
Aug. 14	Newport to Boston (Aug. 14–15)
Aug. 15	Boston to Rockland, ME, to Camden to Belfast to Searsport to Hampden to Bangor (Aug. 15–16)
Aug. 16	Bangor to Augusta: round trip to Togus Springs
Aug. 17	Augusta to Brunswick to Portland to Newport, RI (Aug. 17–21)
Aug. 21	Newport to Norwich, CT, to New York City (Aug. 21–22)
Aug. 22	New York City to Newark, NJ (Aug. 22–23)
Aug. 23	Newark To New York City (Aug. 23–24)
Aug. 24	New York City to Baltimore, MD (Aug, 24–25)
Aug. 25	Baltimore to Norfolk, VA (Aug, 25–27)
Aug. 26	Norfolk: round trip to Portsmouth

(continued)

Aug. 27	Norfolk to Hampton to Point Comfort to Norfolk to Suffolk to Petersburg (Aug. 27–29)
Aug. 29	Petersburg to (depot stops) to Raleigh, NC (Aug. 29–31)
Aug. 31	Raleigh to (depot stops) Weldon to Petersburgh, VA to (depot stops) Richmond (Aug. 31–Sept. 1)
Sept. 1	Richmond to Staunton (Sept. 1–2)
Sept. 2	Staunton to Harrisburg to Newmarket to Woodstock to Strasburg to Winchester (Sept. 4–5)
Sept. 5	Winchester to Charlestown to Harpers Ferry to Frederick City, MD (Sept. 5–6)
Sept. 6	Frederick City to Baltimore (Sept. 6–7)
Sept. 7	Baltimore to Harrisburg, PA (Sept. 7–8)
Sept. 8	Harrisburg to Reading to Pottsville (Sept. 8–10)
Sept. 10	Pottsville to Allentown to Easton to Somerville, NJ, to Plainfield to Elizabeth to New York City (Sept. 10–13)
Sept. 13–14	New York City to Elmira to Jefferson to Havana to Penn Yan to Canandaigua (Sept. 14–15)
Sept. 15	Canandaigua to Clifton Springs (Sept. 15–17)
Sept. 17	Clifton Springs to Syracuse (Sept. 17–18)
Sept. 18	Syracuse to Lyons to Rochester (Sept. 8–19)
Sept. 19	Rochester to Albion to Medina to Lockport to Niagara Falls (Sept. 19–20)
Sept. 20	Niagara Falls to Tonawanda to Black Rock to Buffalo (Sept. 20–21)
Sept. 21	Buffalo to Dunkirk to Cleveland, OH (Sept. 21–24)
Sept. 24	Cleveland to Tiffin to Urbana, IL (Sept. 24–25)
Sept. 25	Urbana to Columbus, OH (Sept. 25–26)
Sept. 26	Columbus to Xenia to Dayton to Hamilton to Cincinnati (Sept. 26–27)
Sept. 27	Cincinnati to Lawrenceburg, IN, to Greensburg to Shelbyville to Indianapolis (Sept. 27–29)
Sept. 29	Indianapolis to Louisville, KY (Sept. 29–Oct. 1)
Oct. 1	Louisville to Richmond, IN, to Lafayette (Oct. 1–2)
Oct. 2	Lafayette to Fort Wayne (Oct. 2–3)
Oct. 3	Fort Wayne to La Porte (Oct. 3–4)
Oct. 4	La Porte to Michigan City to Chicago, IL (Oct. 4–8)
Oct. 8	Chicago to Rock Island to Davenport, IA (Oct. 8–9)
Oct. 9	Davenport to Iowa City to Cedar Rapids (Oct. 9–10)
Oct. 10	Cedar Rapids to Marion to Anamosa (Oct. 10–11)
Oct. 11	Anamosa to Dubuque to Dunleith, IL (Oct. 11–12)
Oct. 12	Dunleith to Galena to Freeport to Janesville, WI, to Fond du Lac (Oct. 12–13)
Oct. 13	Fond du Lac to Milwaukee to Kenosha to Chicago, IL (Oct. 13–15)
Oct. 15	Chicago to Detroit, MI (Oct. 15–16)
Oct. 16	Detroit to Kalamazoo to Chicago, IL (Oct. 16–17)
Oct. 17	Chicago to Bloomington, IL, through Shirley and McLean to Atlanta to Lincoln to Broadwell to Elkhart to Williamsville to Springfield (Oct. 17–19)
Oct. 19	Springfield to Alton to St. Louis, MO (Oct. 19–20)

Oct. 20	St. Louis to Jefferson City (Oct. 20–22)
Oct. 22	Jefferson City to Centralia, IL (Oct. 22–23)
Oct. 23	Centralia to Jackson, TN, to Humboldt to Brownsville to Mason to Memphis (Oct. 23–25)
Oct. 25	Memphis to Huntsville, AL (Oct. 25–26)
Oct. 26	Huntsville to Nashville, TN (Oct. 26–27)
Oct. 27	Nashville to Wartrace to Decherd to Stevenson, AL, to Chattanooga, TN (Oct. 27–29)
Oct. 29	Chattanooga to Kingston, GA (Oct. 29–30)
Oct. 30	Kingston to Ackworth to Marietta to Atlanta (Oct. 30–31)
Oct. 31	Atlanta to Macon (Oct. 31–Nov. 1)
Nov. 1	Macon to Columbus to Montgomery, AL (Nov. 1–2)
Nov. 2–3	Montgomery to Selma (Nov. 3)
Nov. 3	Selma to Mobile (Nov. 3–8)
Nov. 6	Election Day in Mobile

every State of this Union is a sovereign power, with the right to do as it pleases upon this question of slavery, and upon all its domestic institutions." This included determining "what shall be done with the free negro," which, he said, was of much more importance to his Illinois audience because the slavery question had already been decided there. He noted that Maine permitted blacks to vote and that New York did the same as long as they could meet a property qualification. Illinois, however, prohibited black voting. Indeed, Douglas did not have to mention what most people knew, that the black laws of their state were harsh, aimed at discouraging free African Americans from coming or staying there.[98] And they worked, because the black proportion of Illinois declined steadily.[99]

Did Douglas believe such laws were justified? Here he and his rival were closer than he would acknowledge. He claimed that Lincoln believed in racial equality, while he asserted that blacks "belonged to an inferior race." He did not contend, however, that racial inferiority justified slavery. "On the contrary, I hold that humanity and christianity [*sic*] both require that the negro shall have and enjoy every right, every privilege, and every immunity consistent with the safety of the society in which he lives." Which rights and privileges were those? He answered that each state and territory must decide for itself. Illinois had decided that a black could not be a citizen and could not vote. "That policy of Illinois is satisfactory to the Democratic party and to me." The discriminatory policy of his home state satisfied him because his racism was unequivocal. "I believe this government was made on the white basis. I believe it was made by white men, for the benefit of white men and their posterity forever, and I am confining citizenship to white men, men of European birth and descent, instead of conferring it upon negroes, Indians and other inferior races."[100]

Douglas would play on the racial prejudice of the crowd to a degree that jars our sensibility. He knew that a black man with a white woman tapped into a primal fear of white men.[101] In Freeport he claimed to have seen on a previous visit a "beautiful young lady" sitting in a carriage while "her mother reclined inside" with the black abolitionist Frederick Douglass "and the owner of the carriage acted as driver."[102] This tale stoked white male anxieties about sexuality and social order. In contrast, Lincoln did not pander to the prejudices of the

---

[98] Elmer Gertz, "The Black Laws of Illinois," *Journal of the Illinois State Historical Society*, 56:3 (1963), 454–473.

[99] Stacy P. McDermott, " 'Black Bill' and the Privileges of Whiteness in Antebellum Illinois," *Journal of Illinois History*, 12:1 (2009), 8.

[100] CWAL, 3: 9–11. For a discussion of the racism of Douglas and Northern Democrats before the Civil War, see Jean H. Baker, *Affairs of Party: The Political Culture of Northern Democrats in the Mid-Nineteenth-Century* (Ithaca, NY, 1983), 177–196. Her analysis of race prejudice in Northern popular culture generally is illuminating, as she illustrates how white performers of minstrel shows from 1840 to 1880 fanned stereotyped images of blacks among white people who barely knew or had never met any (212–258).

[101] The fear of black male sexual aggressiveness dated from the colonial era. Winthrop D. Jordan, *White over Black: American Attitudes towards the Negro* (Chapel Hill, NC, 1968), 151–152.

[102] CWAL, 3: 55–56.

Index